Native Americans Today

Native Americans Today

A Biographical Dictionary

Bruce E. Johansen, Editor

GREENWOOD

AN IMPRINT OF ABC-CLIO, LLC
Santa Barbara, California • Denver, Colorado • Oxford, England

Library of Congress Cataloging-in-Publication Data

Johansen, Bruce E. (Bruce Elliott), 1950–
    Native Americans today : a biographical dictionary / Bruce E. Johansen.
        p. cm.
    Includes bibliographical references and index.
    ISBN 978-0-313-35554-7 (alk. paper) — ISBN 978-0-313-35555-4 (ebook)
1. Indians of North America—Biography.   2. Indians of North America—History.   I. Title.
    E89.J695   2010
    970.004'97—dc22   2010002231

ISBN: 978-0-313-35554-7
EISBN: 978-0-313-35555-4

14   13   12   11   10   1   2   3   4   5

This book is also available on the World Wide Web as an eBook.
Visit www.abc-clio.com for details.

Greenwood
An Imprint of ABC-CLIO, LLC

ABC-CLIO, LLC
130 Cremona Drive, P.O. Box 1911
Santa Barbara, California 93116-1911

This book is printed on acid-free paper ∞

Manufactured in the United States of America

Contents

List of Entries

Preface

Biography is my favorite mode of history. Some of our richest and most compelling history comes from personal stories with which most can empathize. The most personal of history cuts across racial and cultural barriers, and provides examples of human struggle and courage that reams of statistics and barrels of theory cannot match. Biographies are the most intimate of histories. They also serve very well as role models for young people. Native Americans, who are in the midst of a cultural and political revival, provide many such personal examples.

The scope of this collection of 100 biographical profiles begins in the late-19th century and extends to the present day, profiling Native Americans and a few non-Natives who have significantly contributed to survival and revival of peoples who were widely labeled "the vanishing race." They not only failed to vanish, they also often contributed to North America's dominant culture. The subjects range from scholars and writers to activists to attorneys and athletes and those in the arts. These profiles sketch lives of Native Americans mainly from the last three generations. Most lived within the borders of the United States, with a few from Canada.

This work offers a substantial number of profiles at a depth of personal detail not available elsewhere. Many recent figures profiled here have not been included in other biographical dictionaries. Each profile states the individual's importance, provides information on early life, and traces career trajectory and highlights. Numerous quotations from the subjects and the people who knew them give unique insight. At the end of each entry, a further reading section has recommended sources for more research opportunities, as does the selected bibliography.

The 1880s are really the beginning of the "modern" era for Native Americans because after that time, they were subject to immersion in Anglo-American society with no independent options. In 1879 the first boarding school was started, the same year that a federal court in Omaha defined the Ponca Standing Bear as "a person" under U.S. law. The last brushfire of rebellion at Wounded Knee in 1890 occurred the same year that the U.S. government declared the frontier closed.

Since that time, Native Americans have struggled to establish independent identities while enmeshed in another culture. Biography is used as a tool here to play out personal attributes such as courage and persistence that helped many Native Americans survive at a time when the majority society gave them two choices: emulate us, or die. These two choices were arrayed in the advertising slogan under which the boarding schools were built: "Kill the Indian, Save the Man." In other words, kill the culture, remake the human beings who had practiced it.

I have included a few older figures who were active in the 1880s because their lives evoke strikingly modern themes. I am also seeking to give readers a sense for the texture of a multicultural history that too often appears in monotone. The travails of the Poncas detailed in the entry on Standing Bear is an example. Imagine Omaha in 1877, then a frontier town, rising up in defense of a band of Poncas who had been driven from their lands by a mapmaker's mistake. They had marched home from Oklahoma to the Niobrara River (near the Nebraska-South Dakota border) in the midst of a Midwest winter, arriving in Omaha barefoot, their bare feet bleeding in the snow. They had run out of food, then eaten their horses—and their shoes.

The U'ma'ha (Omaha) Indians rose to the Poncas' defense, including the LaFlesche sisters, Susan and Susette. One could have met the LaFlesche sisters yesterday—two career women, one a medical doctor, the other to become a newspaper correspondent. They lived, however, more than a century ago, at a time when women in Euro-American society could not vote and had nearly no other legal rights. Susan was one of the first female physicians of any race, who served both her U'ma'ha people and neighboring non-Indians at a time when epidemics created a crushing demand for her services that nearly killed Susan from exhaustion.

Susette was the first and very probably the only woman to work as a war correspondent after the Wounded Knee massacre in 1890, on behalf of the Omaha *World-Herald.* She married Thomas Tibbles, an editor at the newspaper, which became a major advocate for Standing Bear and his people beginning in the late 1870s. Standing Bear is notable as the first American Indian to whom a U.S. court applied the legal doctrine of *habeas corpus*—that is, the first American Indian to be identified as a fully capable human being before the bar of U.S. law. The case was filed against George Crook, a general in the U.S. Army who was compelled by his superiors to arrest Standing Bear and the group he led. Crook went to court expecting to lose the case, to make the legal point that the Poncas had a right to return home.

Tibbles and Susette LaFlesche later set off with Standing Bear on a national tour to raise political pressure for return of the Poncas' homeland. This is not a standard cowboy-and-Indian tale. The best part is that at a time when the dominant theme in European American society was an end-of-the-trail, vanishing-race dirge, the Indians won. They beat an eviction that never should have taken place. Standing Bear and his people returned home to the Niobrara River along Nebraska's northern border. Omaha is my hometown, and I relish this story.

This story has multicultural overtones that are amazingly contemporary, so much so that Standing Bear ran a close second as a main design element on the Nebraska state quarter, vetoed by Republican Governor Dave Heineman, who had a taste for covered wagons and Chimney Rock (a mountain-challenged state's best excuse for vertical geology) that provided him a few votes in the western part of Nebraska. Standing Bear is a hero in today's Omaha, with a lake and a school named in his honor. The *World-Herald,* now the city's only daily newspaper, recalls its role in the Standing Bear trial with pride.

I hope that these profiles will be enjoyable as well as instructive. Biography is a form of personal storytelling, so these stories should be enjoyed not only for their factual content, but also for the humanity they evoke, as well as people's roles in larger human events.

Bruce E. Johansen
Omaha, Nebraska
January, 2010

Introduction

❦

As Native American survival became revival in more recent times, the same personal attributes that helped cultures endure have contributed to a flowering of talents expressed in a remarkable political, economic, and artistic recovery seen today. While most of the people in this volume are contemporary, people who lived in the late 19th century, such as Standing Bear and the LaFlesche sisters, establish a context for today's revival.

The personal stories in this volume play out against a broader historical background. The modern era of Native American history conveys Native Americans, as a people, from an era of removal and forced assimilation to a period of cultural, legal, and economic revival that continues in our time. These profiles etch personal courage, persistence, and determination into the broader record.

The 19th century was characterized by harsh and often deadly removal of Native peoples from their traditional homelands, as well as their resistance to these policies. The Ponca Standing Bear is an example of a heroic figure who resisted removal, and, allied with non-Indians in Omaha, Nebraska, won a key court ruling that recognized Native peoples as human beings under U.S. law.

While official policy in the early 20th century emphasized the early European American–style education as a means of assimilation, a large number of outstanding figures used the system to develop talents that triumphed over racist policies, taking control of their educations to preserve their cultures. The Red Power Movement of the 1960s and 1970s ushered in legal challenges that used treaty rights to establish means of economic revival, such as fishing rights. Today, the fruits of these efforts have enabled notable Native Americans to address pressing Indian issues that include many forms of economic and artistic development. The larger society at the same time has come to better understand its own hybrid nature and the importance of Native American contributions to everyone's daily lives.

In an age of Native American revival, many of the people profiled here are called activists, but they also have many other talents. "Activist" is another way of saying that their road has not been easy and that they have helped many other people along the way—as befits people engaged in movements to restore cultural, linguistic, legal, and financial vitality.

This revival movement has been propelled by many multitalented people. Vine Deloria, for example, is arguably the most important Native American in the late 20th century. His work stands out in law, philosophy, religion, and history, as well as Native American studies. Deloria was an activist as well as a scholar who enhanced the abilities of many dozens of other talented people. Ernie Benedict and Ray Fadden, both Akwesasne Mohawks, also began reviving Native cultures long before such efforts were broadly popular. Their educational efforts engendered many talented younger people who are active across North America now.

Ben Nighthorse Campbell was a U.S. senator, but his life has been much more complex. Elouise Cobell became known as the woman who asked questions about Native American bank accounts with the U.S. government (and thereby initiated the largest class-action suit in its history), but she also has been an activist in many other ways, mainly establishing Native American people in businesses.

Personal stories play out against broader issues as well as people's own needs, desires, and shortcomings. Clyde Warrior, a Ponca, whose passionate speeches helped propel the modern Indian civil rights movement in the 1960s, also was an activist. He would have accomplished much more—a friend said he was equal parts fire, lightning, and tears—had he not died from liver failure at age 28, a victim of alcoholism that he could not tame. Richard ("Skip") Hayward, the Pequot most singularly responsible for starting Foxwoods, the world's largest casino, started with a driving desire to find a way that the Pequots (once down to a single reservation resident) could survive in the modern world. John Bennett Herrington, the first Native American astronaut, whose people, the Chickasaw, saw him off on the space shuttle with a celebration that was the closest that NASA and the Kennedy Space Center have ever come to a powwow, upon retirement, undertook a bicycle ride across the United States to educate young Native Americans about the value of education for careers in mathematics and the sciences.

Hank Adams, who has been described as the brains behind the American Indian Movement, never became as well known as Dennis Banks, Russell Means, and John Trudell (who also are profiled). The movement that AIM initiated had at its root the need to find ways, usually using treaty terms, to improve people's lives in both financial and cultural dimensions. Later, Rebecca Adamson's First Nations Development Institute midwifed hundreds of Native American business ventures.

Many individual Native people have taken part in the wide-ranging revival in many different and sometimes surprising ways that these biographies share. Angayuqaq Oscar Kawagley, an Alaska Native, interjects his people's points of view into modern sciences. Laura Tohe, Navajo poet, shares some direct thoughts on the ethnocentric nature of European American feminism. James Luna, a Luiseño from southern California, uses performance art to rebut stereotypes. That "Indian artifact" in a museum case may just be the artist himself. The folksinger Buffy Sainte-Marie recalls that J. Edgar Hoover set the Federal Bureau of Investigation on her trail for singing against the Vietnam War. She won; he lost.

Many of the people profiled here have been tempered by travail. Sheila Watt-Cloutier is an Inuit whose eloquence describing victims of toxic pollution and global warming has evoked tears from large meetings of diplomats and scientists around the world. While many people may think of the Arctic as pristine, it is now so toxic that Inuit mothers often cannot breast-feed their infants without poisoning them. Thinning ice caused by rapid climate change has caused many Inuit hunters to lose their lives. When the 2007 Nobel Peace Prize went to Al Gore and the scientists of the Intergovernmental Panel on Climate Change (IPCC), Watt-Cloutier had been nominated for addressing the urgency of climate change in the Arctic. She was worthy.

Joanne Shenandoah, the Oneida folksinger whose enrapturing voice, even as a child, was reflected in her Oneida name, Tekalihwa:khwa; ("She Sings"), spent many years as an executive secretary before fulfilling her life's calling on stage. Wilma Mankiller endured death threats and had her tires slashed at the suggestion that she become the first woman to serve as principal chief of the Oklahoma Cherokees. She survived that as well as a life-threatening traffic accident, and served many years. More than that: she became the Cherokees' best-known living ambassador across the United States and around the world.

Another entry profiles the life of Leonard Peltier, who was convicted of killing two Federal Bureau of Investigation agents on the Pine Ridge Reservation during 1975 in a trial that was so rigged that Amnesty International declared him a political prisoner. Peltier has languished in prison for decades as millions of people around the world signed petitions calling for a new trial. Peltier's imprisonment is one enduring consequence of a virtual state of war at Pine Ridge during the 1970s that left at least 66 people dead, many of them American Indian Movement activists. The FBI investigated very few of these murders. The shootout at the Jumping Bull Ranch during which the two agents were fatally shot was initiated while they searched for a pair of stolen cowboy boots, while scores of murders went without government attention.

Almost 40 years later, the causes of some of the Pine Ridge deaths are still being debated—Anna Mae Aquash, for example, who very probably was shot fatally by AIM colleagues whom the FBI had convinced, through a whispering campaign, that she was working as a government informant. Such a tactic was used to destabilize ethnic liberation movements (the Black Panthers as well as AIM) so often that it had a generic name in FBI jargon, "The snitch jacket."

Activism has been combined with nearly every other walk of life: Phil Lucas, a filmmaker, also worked to correct stereotypes and deal with the plague of alcoholism on reservations; Oren Lyons, a political figure, advocated Native American causes and points of view at the United Nations—asking, for example, why the eagle, the bear, and other animals had no voice in this world forum. Lawyers, such as John EchoHawk, also act as advocates. Even medical doctors, two examples being Carlos Montezuma and Susan LaFlesche, found themselves in activists' roles. Literary figures such as Sherman Alexie find themselves representing Native peoples and cultures to large audiences.

The people profiled here have filled many roles. Their profiles describe not only what they do, but how they think. Among them are artists, such as R.C. Gorman; comedians and commentators, such as Will Rogers; athletes, including Jim Thorpe, Billy Mills, Sonny Sixkiller, and others; entertainers, including Buffy Sainte-Marie, Charlie Hill, Wes Studi, and Floyd Red Crow Westerman; and military officers, such as Clarence "Tink" Tinker.

This collection includes some people who are not Native American by blood for their essential roles in American Indian life. Native American history would have been much different had they been absent. One example is Felix Cohen, author of the *Handbook of American Indian Law.* More than that, however, Cohen was an advocate, activist, and thinker. Judge George H. Boldt shaped natural resource law forever with his ruling allocating Northwest salmon and shellfish. He understood, as few other jurists before or since, that the economic fate of Native American peoples hinges on the fair apportionment of resources. John Collier, who reshaped government policy toward Native Americans as Franklin D. Roosevelt's Indian Commissioner and endured harsh criticism from many Indians, also is included.

While many of the people profiled here have not appeared in such depth before in a reference work, other references go deeper into other specific fields. Readers who are interested in recent writers should consult Jennifer McClinton-Temple and Alan R. Velie's *Encyclopedia of American Indian Literature* (2007). Readers may wish to supplement this work with *I Tell You Now: Autobiographical Essays by Native American Writers,* edited by Brian Swann and Arnold Krupat (1987, reissued in 2005). For religious people and themes, read Troy R. Johnson's *Distinguished Native American Spiritual Practitioners and Healers* (Greenwood, 2002). A general biographical collection with a recent focus is *Notable Native Americans,* edited by Sharon Malinowski (1995). Dean Chavers published a collection of profiles of Native Americans as well: *Modern American Indian Leaders* (2007). Another good specialty collection is Deborah Everett and Elayne Zorn's *Encyclopedia of Native American Artists* (Greenwood, 2009).

Individuals by Field of Endeavor

Activists

Adams, Hank
Anderson, Wallace ("Mad Bear")
Aquash, Anna Mae Pictou
Banks, Dennis
Bellecourt, Vernon
Benedict, Ernest
Churchill, Ward
Costo, Rupert
Crandell, Barbara
Cruz, Joseph de la
Deloria, Vine, Jr.
Deskaheh
Erasmus, Georges
Fadden, John
Fadden, Ray
Frank, Billy, Jr.
Gage, Matilda Joslyn
George-Kanentiio, Douglas
James, Jewell (tse-Sealth, Praying
    Wolf)
LaDuke, Winona
Lyons, Oren
McCloud, Janet (Yet Si Blue)
Means, Russell
Montezuma, Carlos (Wassaja)
Peltier, Leonard
Sohappy, David
Trudell, John
Warrior, Clyde
Watt-Cloutier, Sheila
Whitebear, Bernie

Actors, Filmmakers

Greene, Graham
Littlefeather, Sacheen
Lucas, Phil
Means, Russell
Silverheels, Jay
Studi, Wes
Westerman, Floyd Red Crow

Artists

Fadden, John
Gorman, R. C.
James, Jewell (tse-Sealth, Praying
    Wolf)
Jemison, G. Peter
Luna, James
Momaday, N. Scott
Nampeyo

Athletes

Bender, Charles Albert
Mills, Billy

Reynolds, Allie
Sixkiller, Sonny
Sockalexis, Louis
Thorpe, Jim
YellowHorse, Mose

Authors, Poets, Playwrights

Alexie, Sherman
Bonnin, Gertrude (Zitkala-sa)
Churchill, Ward
Cohen, Felix
Collier, John
Costo, Rupert
Deer Cloud, Susan
Deloria, Vine, Jr.
Eastman, Charles (Ohiyesa)
Erdrich, Louise
Gage, Matilda Joslyn
Highway, Tomson
Hobson, Geary
LaDuke, Winona
Lyons, Oren
Mann, Barbara Alice
McNickle, D'Arcy
Mohawk, John C.
Momaday, N. Scott
Ortiz, Simon J.
Owens, Louis
Parker, Arthur
    (Gawasowaneh)
Tohe, Laura
Welch, James
Womack, Craig S.

Businesspeople

Adamson, Rebecca
Hayward, Richard ("Skip")

Comedians

Hill, Charlie
Rogers, Will

Educators

Benedict, Ernest
Churchill, Ward
Deloria, Vine, Jr.
Fadden, John
Fadden, Ray
Kawagley, Angayuqaq Oscar
Mann, Barbara Alice
Mohawk, John C.

Journalists, Broadcasters

George-Kanentiio, Douglas
Giago, Tim
Kauffman, Hattie
LaFlesche, Susette (Inshta
    Theamba, Bright Eyes)
Montezuma, Carlos
    (Wassaja)
Trahant, Mark N.

Legal Activists, Attorneys

Boldt, Hugo
Cobell, Elouise
EchoHawk, John
West, W. Richard, Jr.

Military Personnel

Hayes, Ira
Herrington, John Bennett
Tinker, Clarence ("Tink")

Musicians

Bell, John Kim
Sainte-Marie, Buffy
Shenandoah, Joanne
    (Tekalihwa:khwa)
Trudell, John
Westerman, Floyd
    Red Crow

Physicians

LaFlesche, Susan
Montezuma, Carlos
   (Wassaja)

Political Leaders

Bruce, Louis R.
Campbell, Ben Nighthorse
Cohen, Felix
Collier, John
Coon Come, Matthew
Cruz, Joseph de la
Curtis, Charles
Deloria, Vine, Jr.
Deskaheh
EchoHawk, Larry
Erasmus, Georges

Frank, Billy, Jr.
Halbritter, Raymond
Hall, Louis (Karoniaktajeh)
LaDuke, Winona
Lyons, Oren
MacDonald, Peter (Hoshkaisith
   Begay)
Mankiller, Wilma
Reifel, Ben
Shenandoah, Leon
Snake, Reuben
Standing Bear (Ponca)
Watt-Cloutier, Sheila
Wilson, Richard

Religious Leaders

Lyons, Oren
Snake, Reuben

Individuals by Nationality

Anishinabe, Ojibwa, Chippewa

Banks, Dennis
Bellecourt, Vernon
Bender, Charles Albert
Erdrich, Louise
LaDuke, Winona
Peltier, Leonard

Apache, Yaqui, Pueblo

Littlefeather, Sacheen

Arapaho

West, W. Richard, Jr.

Assiniboine-Sioux

Adams, Hank

Blackfeet

Cobell, Elouise
Deer Cloud, Susan

Blackfeet, Gros Ventre

Welch, James

Cahuilla

Costo, Rupert

Cayuga

Deskaheh

Cherokee

Adamson, Rebecca
Churchill, Ward (disputed)
Crandell, Barbara
Mankiller, Wilma
Owens, Louis
Reynolds, Allie
Rogers, Will
Sixkiller, Sonny
Studi, Wes
Womack, Craig

Cherokee, Arkansas Quapaw, Chickasaw

Hobson, Geary

Cheyenne, Northern

Campbell, Ben Nighthorse

Cheyenne, Southern

West, W. Richard, Jr.

Chickasaw

Herrington, John Bennett

Choctaw

Lucas, Phil
Owens, Louis

Cree

Highway, Tomson
Sainte-Marie, Buffy

Creek, Mvskoke/Muskogee

Reynolds, Allie
Womack, Craig S.

Dakota (Yankton)

Bonnin, Gertrude (Zitkala-sa)
Bruce, Louis R.

Dene

Erasmus, Georges

Diné (Navajo)

Gorman, R.C.
MacDonald, Peter (Hoshkaisith Begay)
Tohe, Laura

Hopi-Tewa

Nampeyo

Innu/Cree

Coon Come, Matthew

Inuit

Watt-Cloutier, Sheila

Kansa and Osage

Curtis, Charles

Kiowa

Momaday, N. Scott

Lakota, Oglala (Sioux)

Giago, Tim
Means, Russell
Mills, Billy
Wilson, Richard

Luiseño

Luna, James

Lummi

James, Jewell (tse-Sealth, Praying Wolf)

Métis

Deer Cloud, Susan

Métis; Salish and Kootenai

McNickle, D'Arcy

MicMac

Aquash, Anna Mae Pictou

Mohawk

Bell, John Kim
Benedict, Ernest
Bruce, Louis R.
Deer Cloud, Susan

Fadden, John
Fadden, Ray
George-Kanentiio, Douglas
Hall, Louis (Karoniaktajeh)
Silverheels, Jay

Nez Perce

Kauffman, Hattie

Nisqually

Frank, Billy, Jr.

Northern Shoshone and Bannock

Trahant, Mark N.

Oneida

Greene, Graham
Halbritter, Raymond
Hill, Charlie
Shenandoah, Joanne
    (Tekalihwa:khwa)

Onondaga

Lyons, Oren
Shenandoah, Leon

Osage

Tinker, Clarence ("Tink")

Pawnee

EchoHawk, John
EchoHawk, Larry
YellowHorse, Mose

Penobscot

Sockalexis, Louis

Pequot

Hayward, Richard ("Skip")

Pima

Hayes, Ira

Ponca

Standing Bear
Warrior, Clyde

Pueblo, Acoma

Ortiz, Simon J.

Puyallup

McCloud, Janet (Yet Si Blue)

Quinault

Cruz, Joseph de la

Sac and Fox/Potawatomi and Chippewa

Thorpe, Jim

Seneca

Deer Cloud, Susan
Jemison, G. Peter
Mohawk, John C.
Parker, Arthur (Gawasowaneh)

Seneca, Ohio

Mann, Barbara Alice

Sin Aikst, Colville, Lake Indians, Northern Shoshone

Whitebear, Bernie

A

ADAMS, HANK
BORN 1944 FORT PECK ASSINIBOINE-SIOUX
CIVIL RIGHTS ACTIVIST

While activists such as Russell Means and Dennis Banks became very well known during the Native American revival of the 1960s and 1970s, Hank Adams provided much of the movement's intellectual energy, but remained relatively unknown to the general public. Adams was notable for his humility, and his ability to keep a cool head in a volatile situation. "Part of leadership is not the person who holds the office," he said, "but they are the leaders who act through the agency of others" (Trahant, 2006).

Adams was best known as a negotiator who helped end tense standoffs between the American Indian Movement (AIM) and federal authorities during the 1972 occupation of the Bureau of Indian Affairs (BIA) headquarters in Washington, D.C., as well as Wounded Knee, on the Pine Ridge Reservation, South Dakota, the following year.

Early Life

Adams was born in Wolf Point (also known as Poverty Flats) on Montana's Fort Peck Reservation in 1944. Adams's mother married a Quinault, and moved to coastal Washington State, where Hank graduated from Moclips High School in 1961. At that school, he was a starting football and basketball player, editor of the school newspaper and annual, as well as student body president.

He also became involved in fishing-rights protests. Adams played a major role during 1968 in a protest march by more than 1,000 Indians and supporters in the state capital of Olympia. The Indians were fishing under century-old treaties that allowed them to take fish in their "usual and accustomed places." The state refused to recognize the treaties until they were upheld by federal judge George H. Boldt in 1974.

Adams also developed a passion for politics that was expressed in campaign work for John F. Kennedy and his brother Robert. At the same time, Adams played an important but largely unrecognized role publicizing fishing rights in western Washington by inviting notable people, such as actor Marlon Brando and comedian Dick Gregory, to hoist nets alongside Indians on the Nisqually River, and to face arrest by state game and fish officials. Adams became notorious for rousing members of the press corps in the very early hours of the morning to make sure they would be on scene to witness state raids on fishing Indians, especially when Brando put his body on the line. Newspaper reports described "a new kind of Indian warfare in which Hollywood showmanship and Madison Avenue promotion methods are used for defense" (Chrisman, 2006).

In 1964, Adams made news by refusing induction into the U.S. Army (under the draft) until and unless treaty rights were respected by the U.S. government. The government did not see his case, so Adams was forced to serve. Released from the army after the typical two-year draftee enlistment, Adams was more determined than ever to fight for treaty rights. In 1968, he became director of the Survival of American Indians Association, a fishing-rights support group. Adams also worked with the National Congress of American Indians and the National Indian Youth Council.

At the same time, he became involved more directly in fish-ins at Franks Landing, and was arrested several times between 1968 and 1971. At one point, during January 1971, he was shot in the stomach near Tacoma, Washington, along the banks of the Puyallup River.

The Twenty Points

Adams was a primary author of the Twenty Points that formed the intellectual basis of the Trail of Self Determination that crossed the United States in 1972, ending with an occupation of the Bureau of Indian Affairs headquarters building in Washington, D.C., a few days before that year's presidential elections.

Caravans assembled in Seattle, a center of fishing-rights activism, and in San Francisco, the site of the 1969 American Indian occupation of Alcatraz Island, a former federal prison. The two groups merged in Minneapolis, the birthplace of the American Indian Movement (AIM). Here, the group issued the Twenty Points, a document that advocated revival of American Indian sovereignty. Among other things, the Twenty Points demanded repeal of the federal law that had ended treaty making in 1871, restoration of the ability to negotiate and sign treaties, a commission that would review past violations of treaties, new consideration of treaties that had never been ratified by the U.S. Senate, and elimination of all state jurisdiction over American Indian affairs.

The caravan moved on to Washington, D.C. Upon its arrival on November 3, 1972, the protesters learned that there was not enough lodging. The marchers had not planned to take over the Bureau of Indian Affairs headquarters building at the conclusion of the trail. However, the decision was made after the participants learned that the only lodging available to them in Washington, D.C., was a rat-infested church basement.

The protesters decided to stay in the BIA building for several hours until security guards sought to remove them forcibly. At that point, events turned violent. The protesters seized the building for six days as they asserted their demands that Native sovereignty be restored and immunity be granted to all protesters. Files were seized and damage was done to the BIA building (AIM leaders asserted that federal agents had infiltrated the movement and had done most of the damage). On November 8, 1972, federal officials offered immunity and transportation home to the protesters.

Hank Adams, Native American activist. (By Lucinda Rowlands, Indian Country Today, *www.indiancountrytoday.com)*

The offer was accepted and the crisis was resolved for the moment. A few months later, however, many of the same themes were sounded as AIM occupied the hamlet of Wounded Knee, South Dakota.

Honoring Adams

Adams continued to advise Native American peoples as a speaker well after AIM's heyday. Like Billy Frank, Jr., he became part of the Washington State official infrastructure that maintains fishery resources through the Northwest Indian Fisheries Commission. He sometimes lectured at the college level, especially at the University of Washington Law School. He researched controversial University of Colorado scholar Ward Churchill's genealogy to see whether he was in fact Indian. The newspaper *Indian Country Today* honored Adams with its American Indian Visionary Award in 2006. At the National Press Club in Washington, D.C., the award was presented to Adams as attorney Susan Hvalsoe Komori said: "Hank's a genius. He knows things we don't know. He sees things we don't see." "Adams was always the guy under the radar, working on all kinds of things," said Billy Frank, Jr., a Nisqually who chairs the Northwest Indian Fisheries Commission (Trahant, 2006).

"Hank Adams is the activist's activist who engaged the intellectual and practical efforts required to achieve proper recognition of Indian people. Starting in the 1960s and sustaining to the present, Hank Adams is recognized for his qualities of vision, courage, commitment, discipline—and particularly—the quiet modesty and natural humility of his example," *Indian Country Today*'s award citation said (Trahant, 2006).

Writing in *Indian Country Today,* the journalist Les Whitten said that "Hank Adams is one of the bravest and finest men I have ever known. His bravery is not foolhardy or mad, but that of one who totally recognizes the dangers he faces and goes ahead anyway—not once, but year after year. When I say 'finest,' I think of his kindness, intelligence, humor, and his persistence in good causes" (Whitten, 2006).

Further Reading

"Biography: Hank Adams." Answers.com. 2006. http://www.answers.com/topic/hank-adams.

Chrisman, Gabriel. "The Fish-in Protests at Franks Landing." Seattle Civil Rights and Labor History Project. 2006. http://depts.washington.edu/civilr/fish-ins.htm.

Deloria, Vine, Jr. *Behind the Trail of Broken Treaties: An Indian Declaration of Independence.* Austin: University of Texas Press, 1985.

Harjo, Suzan Shown. "Harjo: Why Native Identity Matters: A Cautionary Tale (Ward Churchill Smacked by Indian Columnist)." *Indian Country Today,* February 10, 2008. http://www.indiancountry.com/content.cfm?id=1096410335.

"Indian Country Today: Hank Adams, the Lifelong Activist." Northwest Indian Fisheries Commission. March 1, 2006. http://www.nwifc.org/2006/01/hank-adams-wins-indian-country-todays-american-indian-visionary-award/.

Trahant, Mark. "Honoring an American Indian Visionary." *Seattle Post-Intelligencer,* March 5, 2006. http://www.seattlepi.com/opinion/261658_trahant05.html.

Whitten, Les. Hank Adams: A Brave and Fine Man." *Indian Country Today,* January 11, 2006. http://www.highbeam.com/doc/1P1-118940793.html.

Wilkinson, Charles F. 2005. *Blood Struggle: The Rise of Modern Indian Nations.* New York: W. W. Norton.

Wilkinson, Charles F., and Hank Adams. *Messages from Frank's Landing: A Story of Salmon, Treaties, and the Indian Way.* Seattle: University of Washington Press, 2000.

ADAMSON, REBECCA
BORN 1949 CHEROKEE
BUSINESS DEVELOPER

Rebecca L. Adamson, long-time president of the First Nations Development Institute and founder of First Peoples Worldwide, has played an important role in developing hundreds of Native American businesses. Native American sovereignty and nation-building is impossible, she says, without an independent economic and educational base. Adamson has aimed for decades to build such a base within the context of traditional Native American history, language, and other attributes of culture.

The organizations that Adamson has developed since 1970 raised and distributed several million dollars in aid to Native American individuals and groups in urban and reservation settings to develop sustainable businesses independent of government. According to one evaluation, "Her work established a new field of culturally appropriate, values-driven development which created the first reservation-based micro-enterprise loan fund in the United States; the first tribal investment model; a national movement for reservation land reform; and legislation that established new standards of accountability regarding federal trust responsibility for Native Americans" (Wood, n.d.).

Early Life

Adamson was born during 1949 in Akron, Ohio, of a Cherokee mother and a Swedish American father. As a young woman, she spent summers with her Cherokee maternal grandmother in the Smokey Mountain region of North Carolina, learning history and culture, hitchhiking south from Akron to visit poor relatives in and near Lumberton, North Carolina. These visits taught her how difficult life could be on reservations, an experience that later shaped her life's work. She also displayed "courage, persistence, trust in strangers and willingness to take risks" ("Heroism," n.d.).

Adamson started college at the University of Akron late in the 1960s, but dropped out in 1970 to work with a group that resisted removal of Native American families to boarding schools operated by the U.S. federal government, where they were shorn of their languages and other cultural knowledge.

The same group also advocated Native control of education, a movement that was affirmed, in 1975, by enactment of the Indian Education Self-Determination Act, which allowed Native peoples to legally establish and maintain their own schools. (Several such schools already had been started.) While raising money for Native-controlled schools, Adamson recognized that education meant little without a viable, Native-controlled economic base. Adamson later returned to college and earned an M.S. degree in economic development at the University of Southern New Hampshire in Manchester. She returned to the school to teach indigenous economics at the graduate level.

Adamson's central idea—to build Native American economic infrastructure that would lift people from poverty within the context of culture—was popular among Native American activists, but new in the world of business. As a single mother struggling with uterine cancer, Adamson traveled to New York City with small savings from unemployment compensation, and began knocking on doors. After several denials, the Ford Foundation granted her $25,000 that she used as seed money to begin the First Nations Financial Project, a nonprofit organization with an office in Fredericksburg, Virginia. By 1990, this organization had evolved into the First Nations Development Institute.

Small Grants to Incubate Businesses

In 1985, Adamson and staff of the First Nations Institute formed the Lakota Fund to counteract poverty in and near the Pine Ridge Reservation in South Dakota, in an area that includes some of the poorest counties in the United States. The Lakota Fund was the United States' first micro-enterprise loan fund, an idea that also has been tried in several African and Asian countries. Such funds provide small loans as start-up capital for specific small businesses that are culturally appropriate, with viable markets, for the peoples of a given area. By 1997, the Lakota Fund had initiated more than 300 loans. This program was cited during the 1990s by the Bill Clinton White House as an outstanding example of business initiative that helped improve people's lives in impoverished areas. The First Nations Development Institute ceded control of the Lakota Fund to local people at Pine Ridge.

The idea of using small grants to start independent businesses caught on during the 1990s. By 1997, the First Nations Development Institute had helped initiate 1,500 businesses in 22 U.S. states. Adamson also expanded outside the borders of the United States with First Peoples Worldwide, assisting the Khwe and San people of Botswana (also known as Bushmen), aboriginal groups in Australia, and several first peoples in Canada. Adamson also engaged multinational corporations, among them Alcoa, Texaco, Rio Tinto, Merck, Ford, and Occidental, in an effort to tailor investment strategies and corporate behavior to protect rights of indigenous peoples.

Many of the First Nations Development Institute's programs have been very innovative and adapted to local conditions. For example, Zuni Entrepreneurial Enterprises (ZEE) of New Mexico hired disabled tribal members who recycled materials from tourist litter. The Nez Perce Young Horseman Program of Idaho enabled elders to train young people who wanted to learn training and selective breeding of Appaloosa horses.

Adamson brought infectious energy to Native American entrepreneurship, but also advocated accountability and frugality, how to make a profit and husband capital, declaring that "People who have been victims may have the attitude that it was never their fault, so they don't have to take responsibility. That is insidious. You have to create projects that lock in accountability because the aim is to build personal efficacy, an 'I-can-do-it' attitude" (Wood, n.d.).

Adamson has continued her advocacy of education as well, playing a major role in establishment of a master's in public and private administration (MPPA) scholarship program for indigenous people at the Yale School of Organization and Management. She also helped to initiate a master's in business administration scholarship at the University of Minnesota's Carlson Business School.

Praise

Adamson was a recipient in 2001 of the John W. Gardner Leadership Award, honoring leaders of groups that "build, mobilize, or unify people, institutions, or causes." She also received the Council on Foundations' 1996 Robert W. Scrivner Award "for creative and innovative grant-making." She was named one of seven *Ms.* magazine "Women of the Year" in 1997. She received an honorary Doctor of Humane Letters from Dartmouth University in 2004. She was honored by the National Women's History Project in 2003.

In the 25th anniversary issue of *Ms.,* Adamson summarized her worldview: "The issue of development, more than any other issue, is the battle line between two competing world views—Euro-American values of individualism, domination, exploitation, and separation, versus tribal values of kinship, balance, reciprocity, and interconnectedness" ("Heroism," n.d.).

Further Reading

Cabral, Elena. "Ford Foundation Report: Rebecca Adamson." Ford Foundation. 1997. http://www.fordfound.org/publications/ff_report/view_ff_report_detail.cfm?report_index=106.

"Dartmouth Honorary Degrees 2004: Rebecca L. Adamson." May 5, 2004. http://www.dartmouth.edu/~news/releases/2004/05/04a.html.

"Heroism 1980s: Rebecca Adamson." n.d. http://www.heroism.org/class/1980/adamson.htm.

"Rebecca Adamson, Fredericksburg: Advocate for Indigenous Peoples." Virginia Foundation for Women. 2002. http://www.virginiawomen.org/vfwposter2002_adamson.pdf.

"Rebecca L. Adamson's Online Biography." *Indian Country Today.* n.d. http://www.indiancountry.com/?author=27.

"2003 Women's History Month Honorees: Rebecca Adamson." National Women's History Project. 2003. http://www.nwhp.org/tlp/biographies/adamson/adamson-bio.html.

Wood, Christine B. "Adamson, Rebecca." Learning to Give: Curriculum Division of the League. n.d. http://learningtogive.org/papers/paper175.html.

ALEXIE, SHERMAN
BORN 1966 SPOKANE/COEUR D'ALENE
AUTHOR

Sherman J. Alexie, Jr., a prolific Spokane and Coeur d'Alene author, has a broad range of talents. He has written award-winning poetry, songs, prize-winning short stories, best-selling novels, essays and screenplays, as well as directed and co-produced films and performing as a stand-up comedian. Alexie is known for his sense of humor, as well as his straight talk, or sometimes sharp honesty. According to one source, Alexie "turned to humor because he was different and got beat up a lot" (Pabst, 2002). Alexie "describes himself as an Indian, liberal, progressive pacifist who is bipartisan in his hatred for politicians" (Pabst, 2002).

Notably, all of Alexie's work deals with the day-to-day lives of contemporary Native Americans. In an interview, Alexie said, "I want my literature to concern the daily lives of Indians. I think most Native American literature is so obsessed with nature

Sherman Alexie, acclaimed Native American author. (AP/Wide World Photos)

that I don't think it has any useful purpose" (Fraser, 2001). One of Alexie's goals in writing meaningful, contemporary, Native American literature—as well as his work in films, music, and comedy—is to reach the younger generations of Native Americans. "There's a kid out there, some boy or girl who will be that great writer, and hopefully they'll see what I do and get inspired by that" (Fraser, 2001).

Growing Up "Different" on the Reservation

Son of a Coeur d'Alene father and a Spokane mother, Alexie was born October 7, 1966, and grew up on the Spokane Indian Reservation in Wellpinit, Washington. His father worked at various jobs, such as logging and truck driving, and suffered from alcoholism. His mother worked on the reservation as an addiction and youth counselor while raising Alexie and his five brothers and sisters.

Born hydrocephalic, Alexie was not expected to survive a brain operation when he was six months old. Despite medical setbacks, Alexie learned to read by the age of three and quickly became a voracious reader. However, Alexie's continuing medical problems (such as seizures) and his love of reading made him different from the others on the reservation, who ostracized and often teased him. Alexie eventually chose to leave the reservation school for a better education at the all-white Reardan High School in Reardan, Washington. Despite being the only Native American at Reardan High, Alexie excelled in both academics and basketball. After his graduation in 1985, Alexie attend Gonzaga University in Spokane for two years before transferring to Washington State University in Pullman. He was the first member of his extended family to graduate from college.

A Love for Writing

Alexie originally planned a medical career, but found a love for poetry and writing in a poetry workshop at Washington State University. After graduating with a BA in American Studies, Alexie received a Washington State Arts Commission Poetry Fellowship in 1991 and a National Endowment for the Arts Poetry Fellowship in 1992. His first poetry collection, *The Business of Fancydancing,* was published in 1991. His second poetry collection, *I Would Steal Horses,* was published in 1993 along with his first collection of short stories, *The Lone Ranger and Tonto Fistfight in Heaven,* for which Alexie received a PEN/Hemingway Award for Best First Book of Fiction. Alexie's early work often references the effects of alcohol and addiction, not just because of their presence in his family and community, but also because of his own struggles with alcoholism, which began while he was attending Gonzaga University. As Alexie told an interviewer in 1998, "When I first started writing I was still drinking, so *Lone Ranger and Tonto* and the first book of poems, *The Business of Fancydancing,* are really soaked in alcohol" (West and West, 1998). However, after publication of his first collection of poetry at the age of 23, Alexie quit drinking and maintained sobriety ever since.

He continued to write and publish prolifically, with his first novel, *Reservation Blues,* published in 1995 closely followed by his second novel, *Indian Killer*

(1996). Both novels gained multiple recognitions—*Reservation Blues* won the Before Columbus Foundation's American Book Award and the Murray Morgan Prize, and *Indian Killer* was named one of *People*'s Best of Pages and a *New York Times* Notable Book.

Moving to Multimedia

Alexie once told an interviewer that "songs are accessible poetry. . . . I also want to express myself in poetic ways that will reach a much wider audience. For me, writing songs is a way to reach a different kind of audience" (West and West, 1998). In the mid-1990s, Alexie began collaborating with friend and musician Jim Boyd, a Colville Indian, to write and record an album. *Reservation Blues: The Soundtrack* was released in 1995, and, in 1996, Boyd and Alexie opened for the Indigo Girls at a benefit concert for the Honor the Earth Campaign. In 1997, Alexie ventured into the film industry. He agreed to collaborate with Chris Eyre, a Cheyenne/Arapaho, and became co-producer and scriptwriter of *Smoke Signals*, a film based on a short story from *The Lone Ranger and Tonto Fistfight in Heaven*, titled "This Is What It Means to Say Phoenix, Arizona." *Smoke Signals* won several awards, including the 1998 Sundance Film Festival Audience Award, and Best Screenplay at the 1998 San Diego World Film Festival. In addition, *Smoke Signals* gained Alexie recognition for his attempt to redress the stereotypical images of Native Americans that have been historically present in cinema. In a 1998 interview, Alexie stated, "What is revolutionary or groundbreaking about the film is that the characters in it are Indians, and they're fully realized human beings. They're not just the sidekick, or the buddy, they're the protagonists" (West and West, 1998).

Alexie went on to write and produce *The Business of Fancydancing*, which was produced independently in 2002 and won several awards. He wrote the screenplay for *49?*, which was also produced independently in 2003. However, his experience with *Smoke Signals* had already disillusioned him somewhat with regard to Hollywood. In an essay written in 2000, Alexie described the monotonous process of constantly rewriting a screenplay to please everybody—the directors, producers, actors, agents, and so on. Alexie then stated, "I'm quitting Hollywood. . . . I'm not going to write screenplays for them anymore. I'm still going to make movies, but I'm going to make them in the same way that I write books: all by myself" (Alexie, 2000/2001).

Just an "Indian Poet"

Alexie's work has not been without controversy. He has attempted to honestly portray the life of Native Americans in his writing—which includes alcoholism, addiction, and other dysfunctions of life on the reservations—and, as a result, many Native Americans have criticized and objected to this often-unflattering portrayal of Native American societies. However, Alexie does not let such criticism stop him. In an interview for *Identity Theory*, Alexie stated, "You know, as an artist, it's not my job to fit in; it's not my job to belong. I'm not a social worker; I'm not a therapist. . . . I'm not here to make people feel good" (Capriccioso, 2003).

One of Alexie's goals, however, is to try to connect with and inspire younger Native Americans. His semiautobiographical *The Absolutely True Diary of a Part-Time Indian* (2007) is his first novel specifically written for a young adult audience. According to Alexie, "I hope my success makes more things possible for young Indians" (Capriccioso, 2003).

By 2010, Alexie had published eleven collections of poetry, four novels, three collections of short stories, and written screenplays for three films. He has also contributed songs to several albums and received innumerable awards and recognitions for his writing, film, and musical work. However, despite his success in so many genres, he insists "I'm still just an Indian poet" (Capriccioso, 2003). Alexie's most recent book is *War Dances,* a collection of poetry and short fiction, published in 2009 by Grove Press.

Natalie Russell

Further Reading

Alexie, Sherman. "Introduction: Death in Hollywood." *Ploughshares* 26, no. 4 (Winter 2000/2001): 7–10. http://www.pshares.org/issues/article.cfm?prmArticleID=4953.

Campbell, Duncan. "Voice of the New Tribes." *Guardian,* January 4, 2003. http://books.guardian.co.uk/review/story/0,12084,868123,00.html.

Capriccioso, Robert. "Sherman Alexie: American Indian Filmmaker/Writer Talks with Robert Capriccioso." *Identity Theory,* March 23, 2003. http://www.identitytheory.com/interviews/alexi_interview.html.

FallsApart Productions. "Official Sherman Alexie Biography." 2008. http://www.fallsapart.com/biography.html.

Fraser, Joelle. "An Interview with Sherman Alexie." *The Iowa Review* 30, no. 3 (2001): 59–66. http://www.english.uiuc.edu/maps/poets/a_f/alexie/fraser.htm.

Grassian, Daniel. *Understanding Sherman Alexie*. Columbia: University of South Carolina Press, 2005.

Pabst, Georgia. "Alexie Sends Strong Signals." *Milwaukee Journal-Sentinel,* March 9, 2002. http://www.jsonline.colm/story/index.aspx?id=25632.

West, Dennis, and Loan M. West. "Sending Cinematic Smoke Signals: An Interview with Sherman Alexie." *Cineaste* 23, no. 4 (Fall 1998): 28–33. http://www.lib.berkeley.edu/MRC/alexie.html.

ANDERSON, WALLACE ("MAD BEAR")
1927–1985 TUSCARORA
TREATY-RIGHTS ACTIVIST

Wallace "Mad Bear" Anderson was a noted Native American rights activist during the 1950s, before a general upsurge in Native self-determination efforts a decade later. Anderson later became a spokesman for Native American sovereignty in several international forums. Writer Edmund Wilson recalled Anderson as "a young man in a lumberjack shirt and cap, broad of build, with a round face and lively black eyes" (Wilson, 1960, 67).

Anderson was born in Buffalo, New York, and raised on the Tuscarora reservation near Niagara Falls. The name "Mad Bear" was first used by Anderson's grandmother in reference to his hot-headedness. He adopted the name from her. Anderson served in the U.S. Navy during World War II at Okinawa. He later also served in Korea. Anderson became an activist after his request for a GI Bill loan to build a house on the Tuscarora reservation was rejected.

Mad Bear led protests against Iroquois payment of New York State income taxes as early as 1957. At the height of the protest, several hundred Akwesasne (St. Regis) Mohawks marched to the Massena, New York, State Courthouse, where they burned summonses issued for unpaid taxes.

In 1958, Anderson played a leading role in protests of a 1,383-acre seizure of Tuscarora land by the New York Power Authority for construction of a dam and reservoir. Anderson and other Iroquois deflated workers' tires and blocked surveyors' transits. When the Tuscaroras refused to sell the land, a force of about 100 state troopers and police invaded their reservation. Anderson met the troopers and police with 150 nonviolent demonstrators who blocked their trucks by lying in the road.

During March of 1959, Anderson helped compose a declaration of sovereignty at the Iroquois Six Nations Reserve in Brantford, Ontario, the settlement established by Joseph Brant and his followers after the American Revolution. The declaration prompted an occupation of the reserve's Council House by Royal Canadian Mounted Police. During the same month, Anderson attempted a citizen's arrest of Indian Commissioner Glen L. Emmons in Washington, D.C., on allegations of misconduct in office. Emmons avoided the intended arrest, but later resigned. During July of 1959, Anderson traveled to Cuba with a delegation of Iroquois and other Native Americans to exchange recognitions of sovereignty with Fidel Castro, whose revolutionary army had seized power only months earlier.

During 1967, Anderson formed the North American Indian Unity Caravan, which traveled the United States for six years as the types of activism that he had pioneered spread nationwide; Anderson also gathered opposition to termination legislation from 133 Native American tribes and nations and carried it to Washington, D.C., effectively killing the last attempt to buy out reservations in the United States. In 1969, he helped initiate the takeover of Alcatraz Island.

Anderson died during December, 1985, after a long illness at age 58 on the Tuscarora Reservation in New York State.

Further Reading

Anderson, Wallace (Mad Bear). "The Lost Brother: An Iroquois Prophecy of Serpents." In *The Way: An Anthology of American Indian Literature,* edited by Shirley Hill Witt and Stan Steiner, 243–47. New York: Vintage, 1972.

Wilson, Edmund. *Apologies to the Iroquois.* New York: Farrar, Straus & Cudahy, 1960.

AQUASH, ANNA MAE PICTOU
1945–1976 MICMAC
AMERICAN INDIAN MOVEMENT ACTIVIST

On February 24, 1976, Roger Amiott, a rancher, found the body of Anna Mae Aquash, one of the American Indian Movement's leading activists, near Wanblee, in the northeastern section of the Pine Ridge Indian Reservation. It has been recounted that "On February 24 [1976], at a quarter to three in the afternoon, a rancher on that part of the South Dakota steppe that crumbles into the badlands was looking for a place to run a fence when he turned a bend in a gully and found, curled on its left side, clothed in a maroon jacket and blue jeans, and looking for all the world like someone sleeping in perfect peace, a corpse" (Hendricks, 2006, 3). This discovery initiated a decades-long debate over who had killed her, which shed much light on the tense relationship between AIM and the Federal Bureau of Investigation during the 1970s.

Aquash was 1 of at least 66 people, many of them AIM activists, who were killed for political reasons on the Pine Ridge Reservation during that period. Most of these murders were never investigated by the FBI, which is responsible for fact-finding related to major crimes on most Indian reservations.

Early Life

Aquash was born of MicMac (or Mi'kmaq) heritage March 27, 1945, near Shubenacadie, Nova Scotia. Her family (she had two older sisters and an older brother) spent much of their youth in Pictou Landing, a MicMac reserve. Her father earned a small income creating beadwork, and exercised a traditional influence on his children. He died when Anna Mae was only 11 years of age, however. Her mother had left the family. Anna Mae, whom many people would later say was a brilliant woman, dropped out of Milford High School after the ninth grade. By the early 1960s, Anna Mae was picking potatoes and berries in Maine; later she moved to Boston with Jake Maloney, also a MicMac. She worked at a sewing factory while he opened a karate school. They had two children, then moved back to New Brunswick, and married. Their marriage ended in 1969, after which Anna Mae moved back to Boston, went back to work sewing, and volunteered at the Boston Indian Council. Having heard AIM co-founder Russell Means speak, she was inspired to become active in the organization. She also came to know Nogeeshik Aquash, an Ojibwa artist from Walpole Island in Ontario, Canada, and, with him, took part in AIM's Trail of Broken Treaties in 1972, as well as the occupation of Wounded Knee a few months later. Anna Mae and Nogeeshik married in a traditional Lakota ceremony during the Wounded Knee occupation. For the next three years, Anna Mae became increasingly closely allied with AIM leadership in various activities across the United States.

Controversy Following Death

W. O. Brown, a pathologist who performed autopsies under contract with the Bureau of Indian Affairs, arrived at Pine Ridge a day after discovery of Aquash's body. After examining the body, Brown announced that the woman, who still had not been officially identified, had died of exposure to the brutal South Dakota winter. The FBI decided that the only way to identify the woman was to sever her hands and send them to the FBI's crime laboratories near Washington, D.C. Agents on the scene reasoned that the body was too badly decomposed to take fingerprints at Pine Ridge. Ken Sayres, BIA police chief at Pine Ridge, would say later that no one had been called to the morgue to attempt identification of the body before the hands were severed.

A week after the body was found, Aquash—now missing her hands as well as her identity—was buried at Holy Rosary Catholic Cemetery, Pine Ridge. On March 3, the FBI announced Aquash's identity. Her family was notified of the death March 5. The family refused to believe that she had died of natural causes. At 32 years of age, Aquash had been in good health and knew how to survive cold weather. She did not drink alcohol or smoke tobacco. Her friends remembered that she had smuggled food past federal government roadblocks into Wounded Knee during another brutal South Dakota winter, almost three years to the day before her body was found. A new autopsy was demanded.

In the midst of the controversy, Aquash's body was exhumed. Her family retained an independent pathologist, Gary Peterson, of St. Paul, Minnesota. Peterson reopened the skull and found a .32-caliber bullet, which he said had been fired from a gun placed at the base of Aquash's neck. The bullet was easy to find and Peterson thought it should have been found the first time. Asked about the bullet he had not found, W. O. Brown, the BIA coroner, replied, according to an account in the *Washington Star* May 24, 1976, "A little bullet isn't hard to overlook" (Johansen and Maestas, 1979, 106).

Following identification of Aquash, the Canadian government and the U.S. Commission on Civil Rights demanded an investigation. The U.S. Justice Department announced that it would look into the case, but the investigation languished in bureaucratic limbo. Aquash's friends refused to let her spirit pass away. On March 14, Aquash's body was wrapped in a traditional star quilt, as several women from Oglala Village mourned her passing for two days and two nights.

Twenty-seven years after Aquash's murder, federal agents on April 2, 2003, arrested Arlo Looking Cloud, 49, once a security guard for AIM, and charged him with first-degree murder in the death, a charge that he denied.

On February 6, 2004, Looking Cloud was convicted of the murder. In *The Unquiet Grave* (2006), author Steve Hendricks built a case that members of AIM had assassinated Aquash after the FBI, using disinformation techniques (applying a snitch jacket), raised suspicion within AIM that Aquash was working as a snitch for the FBI.

The principal question remained about whether Looking Cloud acted alone, and, if not, why not. Hendricks asserted that a number of AIM leaders—no one knows precisely who—ordered Aquash shot on suspicion that she was acting as an FBI informant. "Only the FBI could separate the snitches from the snitch-jacketed," Hendricks (2006, 361) wrote. He recalled that the FBI had seeded AIM with informants purposefully to create an atmosphere of paranoia that made such an assassination possible. Thus, Aquash's grave (and a number of others) remain unquiet to this day.

Further Reading

Banks, Dennis, and Richard Erdoes. *Ojibwa Warrior: Dennis Banks and the Rise of the American Indian Movement.* Norman: University of Oklahoma Press, 2004.

Brand, Johanna. *The Life and Death of Anna Mae Aquash.* Toronto: Lorimer, 1978.

Churchill, Ward, and Jim Vander Wall. *Agents of Repression: The FBI's Secret War against the Black Panther Party and the American Indian Movement.* Boston: South End Press, 1990.

Hendricks, Steve. *The Unquiet Grave: The FBI and the Struggle for the Soul of Indian Country.* New York: Thunder's Mouth Press, 2006.

Johansen, Bruce. "Peltier and the Posse." *The Nation,* October 1, 1977, 304–7.

Johansen, Bruce E., and Roberto F. Maestas. *Wasi'chu: The Continuing Indian Wars.* New York: Monthly Review Press, 1979.

Matthiessen, Peter. *In the Spirit of Crazy Horse.* New York: Viking, 1991.

Weir, David, and Lowell Bergman. "The Killing of Anna Mae Aquash." *Rolling Stone,* April 7, 1977: 51–55.

B

Banks, Dennis
Born 1937 Anishinabe (Ojibwa)
Co-founder of the American Indian Movement

Beginning during the late 1960s, Dennis Banks became nationally and internationally notable as a prominent Native American activist, primarily as co-founder of the American Indian Movement (AIM). In that role, he was a leader in the standoff between the Federal Bureau of Investigation (FBI) and the U.S. Army with AIM at Wounded Knee, South Dakota, during 1973.

Early Life

Banks was born April 12, 1937, at Federal Dam on the Leach Lake Ojibway (Anishinabe) Reservation in Minnesota. He was raised with siblings by his grandparents, and learned traditional lifeways from them. At one point, Banks killed a porcupine, and proud of his first kill as a hunter, told his grandparents. Alarmed that he had killed an animal for no good reason, they told him to return to the forest, find the animal's body, and pray over it, then clean and cook it, all the while asking its forgiveness. Banks never forgot this experience.

At the age of five, in 1942, Banks was forced into the Pipestone boarding school when, as he later recalled, "An agent from the Bureau of Indian Affairs—a large-bellied man smelling of cheap cigars and beer—came into our house waving a bunch of papers and yelling 'Where are those kids who will be going?'" (Banks and Erdoes, 2004, 24). Banks, strong-willed from the beginning, deeply resented the coercion of the boarding schools. He ran away, was caught and beaten, then ran away again.

After finishing his education in a public high school, Banks, in 1954, joined the U.S. Air Force and was stationed in Japan. Returning to poverty in Minnesota a few years later, Banks was arrested and convicted for stealing groceries to feed

Dennis Banks, one of the AIM leaders of the Oglala Sioux Indians, sits in the open prairie at Wounded Knee, South Dakota, on March 4, 1973. (AP/Wide World Photos)

a family of 10. He was married at the time to "Jeanette, a beautiful Indian woman," who had brought four children into the relationship. They had four more together. "I had a miserable, minimum-wage job that could not support us," Banks said, "So I stole food to put on our table" (Banks and Erdoes, 2004, 60).

The Birth of AIM

In prison, Banks was determined to educate himself. At the same time, he was impressed by the civil rights struggle. Banks studied the history of U.S. government treaty making with American Indians, the status of treaties in the Constitution's Article VI as "the supreme law of the land." Following his release, Banks was among the original founders of AIM in Minneapolis during 1968, with Russell Means and Vernon and Clyde Bellecourt. The first purpose of AIM was to bring Native Americans together to resist police brutality. With Means, another prominent co-founder of AIM, Banks developed a talent for attracting media attention.

During 1972, Banks was a leading organizer of the Trail of Broken Treaties, which began in San Francisco and Seattle as two converging caravans that arrived in Washington, D.C., a few days before the 1972 national elections. The members of the caravan seized and ransacked the BIA's headquarters.

AIM members and supporters rallied again early in 1973, beginning on February 27 to occupy the village of Wounded Knee, in South Dakota, for 71 days, at a time when, by Banks's account, Indians in South Dakota were treated no better than blacks in apartheid-ruled South Africa. Wounded Knee soon was surrounded by several hundred well-armed federal agents and troops, and became a battle site, with firefights most nights, and several casualties. Two Indian men died from government gunfire during the siege.

Raw Racism at Wounded Knee

Raw racism was evident when the hamlet of Wounded Knee was seized. Means found, at a small museum, a 19th-century ledger of receipts for beef. The cavalry captain in charge had invented names for the Indians who were provided with beef, such as "Shits in His Food, She Comes Nine Times, F—ks His Daughter, and Maggott Dick, to recall a few" (Hendricks, 2006, 63).

During the same period, Banks played a role in gathering hundreds of Indians to protest anti-Native violence, such as the murder of Raymond Yellow Thunder, in Gordon, Nebraska. Author Steve Hendricks, in *The Unquiet Grave,* described Banks and other AIM leaders at Gordon, as about 1,400 AIM supporters (twice the town's population) streamed into the town to protest Yellow Thunder's death. Hendricks captured the sense of dismissal in the voice of a county prosecutor who described the assault that killed Yellow Thunder as "a cruel practical joke . . . by pranksters" (2006, 28), or a one-time Rapid City chief of police who, during the 1970s, suggested lodging drunken Indians in garbage cans.

In his memoir *Ojibwa Warrior* (2004), during the occupation of Wounded Knee in 1973, Banks recalled dealing with the practical problems of a besieged group under fire. One was the acquisition of food after the stocks of the village grocery store ran out. The need for protein was partially solved, after smuggling and rationing ran short, by rustling stray cattle from nearby white ranchers, whom the Indians wryly labeled illegal immigrants on the independent Oglala Lakota Nation.

Joking, they called their prey "slow elk." Banks wrote, "Some of our young warriors who hunted the slow elk were from the city. They didn't quite know how to go about it. Once they led in a cow that none of them knew how to kill or butcher. A white reporter shot and skinned it for them. Another time they came in with an ancient stringy bull whose meat was likely to break our teeth. I put up a poster showing the rear end of a bull with big balls and a cow with an udder. I jokingly wrote underneath: 'This is a bull. This is a cow'" (Banks and Erdoes, 2004, 189).

Following the occupation of Wounded Knee, the Pine Ridge Reservation was plunged into more than two years of near-warfare between AIM and its adversaries in the tribal government, during which at least 66 people, most of them affiliated with AIM, were killed violently. Facing several federal criminal charges, Banks and compatriots slipped out of Wounded Knee near the end of the siege. While many political murders on Pine Ridge went without investigation by the FBI, the government poured its resources into prosecuting AIMsters who had occupied the hamlet. After 562 arrests and 185 federal indictments related to the occupation, the government obtained only 15 convictions. At a rate of 7.7 percent, that conviction rate was one-tenth the average for criminal trials in the Eighth Circuit, in which the cases were tried (Hendricks, 2006, 141). The legal campaign was not meant to obtain convictions as much as it was pursued to dismember AIM by tying activists into legal knots.

Sanctuary in California and Onondaga

Banks evaded prosecution by taking sanctuary for a time in California under orders from Gov. Jerry Brown. California officials refused to extradite him to South Dakota, in part because Attorney General William Janklow, who was given to bombastic overstatement, had pledged to kill AIM members. While in California, Banks earned an associate of arts degree at Davis University, and also served as chancellor of Deganawidah-Quetzalcoatl (D-Q) University, developing educational programs while organizing in 1978 a march from Alcatraz Island to Washington, D.C, called the Longest Walk, protesting legislation in Congress to abrogate treaties.

Later, Banks took shelter on the Onondaga Nation in New York State, where FBI jurisdiction was not accepted by the Haudenosaunee (Iroquois) Confederacy. Banks met with Tadadaho (Speaker) Leon Shenandoah, who placed his request for sanctuary before the confederacy's council. The council debated the issue, and accepted Banks's residency. "You are safe under the wings of the Onondaga Nation," Shenandoah told Banks (Banks and Erdoes, 2004, 332).

Return to South Dakota

Weary of life in exile, and with a change in political leadership in South Dakota, Banks returned there in 1994 to face criminal charges stemming from confrontations in there at a time when at least 66 AIM members and allies had been victims of unsolved murders on and near the Pine Ridge Reservation. Banks served 18 months in prison, then taught traditional Native American lifeways and organized sacred runs around the world. Later, Banks worked at Pine Ridge as a substance-abuse counselor. He also spent considerable time working on legislation to prevent desecration of Indian graves. Banks published the first of two autobiographies, *Sacred Soul,* during 1988. Banks worked as well on unsuccessful efforts to free Leonard Peltier, who was convicted of killing two FBI agents, and he also acted in a few movies and created recordings of traditional music. Returning to his homeland at Federal Dam in 2002, Banks, among other activities, maintained a natural-foods business.

Further Reading

Banks, Dennis, and Richard Erdoes. *Ojibwa Warrior: Dennis Banks and the Rise of the American Indian Movement.* Norman: University of Oklahoma Press, 2004.

Deloria, Vine, Jr. *Behind the Trail of Broken Treaties.* [1974]. Austin: University of Texas Press, 1985.

Hendricks, Steve. *The Unquiet Grave: The FBI and the Struggle for the Soul of Indian Country.* New York: Thunder's Mouth Press, 2006.

BELL, JOHN KIM
BORN 1952 MOHAWK
ORCHESTRA CONDUCTOR

John Kim Bell, composer, conductor, administrator, pianist, and mentor of many other musicians (including country star Shania Twain), was the first Native American to be employed as a professional orchestral conductor. Bell, conductor with the National Ballet of Canada, also has been guest conductor of London's Royal Philharmonic Orchestra. In 1985, he founded the Canadian Native Arts Foundation in Toronto to promote the participation of Native Americans in the arts through scholarships and grants.

Bell was born on the Caughnawaga (now Kahnawake) Reserve, near Montreal, October 8, 1952, to a Mohawk father and a Caucasian mother from the United States. He began playing piano by the age of eight, when his family moved to Columbus, Ohio; he also displayed talent by age 10 on the saxophone and violin.

Bell earned a bachelor's in music at Ohio State University in 1975, studying with George Haddad. During high school, Bell traveled with local singers who were auditioning for roles in a Broadway musical on a national tour. Although he was only 17 years of age at that time, Bell became assistant conductor of the company. The following year, Bell conducted the group's national tour as the youngest professional conductor in North America.

Bell became a conductor for several Broadway musicals during the late 1970s, including the international company of *Chorus Line* (1978–80). While conducting more than 30 American national tours and Broadway musicals, Bell worked with many notable people, including Lauren Bacall, Juliet Prowse, and Vincent Price. He was a conductor/pianist for the *Redd Foxx Show,* the *Sonny Bono Show,* and the Bee Gees. Bell also studied in Siena, Italy, with Franco Ferrara. Bell worked with the Harlem Dance Theatre, the Eglevsky Ballet, and on several opera productions.

During 1980 and 1981, Bell served as apprentice conductor with Andrew Davis and the Toronto Symphony; he debuted as conductor May 5, 1981. During 1984, Anthony Azzopardi produced a documentary biography describing Bell's musical career that was aired by the Canadian Broadcasting Corp. on October 8, 1984 (a video also was distributed by Kultur International). The show described a talented and passionate young man who broke social and racial barriers to fulfill a dream.

Bell inspired many young Native Canadians by aiding their musical talents through the Canadian Native Arts Foundation, which he started in 1985. This organization organized benefit concerts to fund grants, scholarships, and tours for musicians of schools on Canadian Native reserves.

While the foundation became his major avocation, Bell continued his work as a musician. He conducted the National Ballet of Canada's orchestra during 1985, and was a guest conductor for the Royal Philharmonic Orchestra in London during 1987. He took a role in a benefit concert with the Toronto Symphony in 1991. Bell composed scores for the U.S. Public Broadcasting TV series *The Trial of Standing Bear,* and for the Baton Broadcasting TV film *Divided Loyalties.* Bell organized a national tour of *In the Land of Spirits,* for which he functioned as conductor, in 1992. An adaptation of the music was recorded in 2000 by True North Brass (Opening Day Recordings 9320). He also guest-conducted the Calgary Philharmonic Orchestra in 1993.

During the 1990s, the CNAF assumed a new name, the National Aboriginal Achievement Foundation, as its programs expanded. The foundation initiated the Canadian National Aboriginal Achievement Awards in 1994, and produced an annual awards show. At the same time, Bell became active on several Canadian federal boards, including the Canadian Broadcasting Corporation, the Federal Task Force on Professional Training in the Cultural Sector, and Toronto's 2008 Olympic bid. He became a member of the Order of Canada in 1990, and was promoted to Officer in 1997 (John Kim Bell, n.d.).

In 1990 he was awarded an honorary doctorate from Lakehead University, as well as honorary legal degrees (LLD) from Trent University (1992), the University of Alberta (1999), and the University of Toronto (1999).

Further Reading

"Honorary Doctorate, John Kim Bell. Musician and Conductor." Lakehead University Program for the May, 1990 Convocation. http://aboriginalinitiatives.lakeheadu.ca/solution/aboriginalprofiles.php.

John Kim Bell. *The Encyclopedia of Music in Canada.* n.d. http://www.thecanadianencyclopedia.com/index.cfm.

BELLECOURT, VERNON
1931–2007 OJIBWA
POLITICAL ACTIVIST

Vernon Bellecourt, one of the American Indian Movement's founders during the late 1960s and early 1970s, later gained considerable notoriety for his energetic opposition to the use of Native American images as sports mascots. Through the National Coalition on Racism in Sports and Media, Bellecourt organized many protests against the Washington Redskins, Cleveland Indians, Atlanta Braves, and Kansas City Chiefs, among many others, as he asserted that the mascots perpetuated negative stereotypes. He once was arrested for burning the Cleveland Indian, Chief Wahoo, in effigy.

Bellecourt was born with the Ojibwa name *Wa-Bun-Inini* ("Man of Dawn"), October 17, 1931, on the White Earth Reservation, Minnesota, to a father who had been disabled during a German mustard gas attack in World War I. His mother raised at least a dozen children in a house without electric power or running water. Vernon left school after eight years. He was sent to prison at age 19 for robbing a bar. In prison, Bellecourt learned how to cut hair as both a barber and a beautician; he started a business along those lines after his release. Moving to Denver, Vernon and his brother Clyde started an AIM chapter to reclaim Native American heritage.

Bellecourt first gained international recognition during 1972 as a lead organizer of a cross-country AIM caravan, the Trail of Broken Treaties, which embarked in two groups from San Francisco and Seattle, converging before arriving in Washington, D.C., where they occupied the Bureau of Indian Affairs headquarters building a few days before national elections.

Later, Bellecourt garnered considerable additional press coverage by meeting with international political leaders such as Col. Muammar el-Quaddafi of Libya, whom he described as a "very warm, sensitive human being" (Martin, 2007, C-12) and Yasir Arafat, leader of the Palestinian Liberation Organization (PLO). He helped organize conferences on Native American rights sponsored by the United Nations and played a major role in unsuccessful efforts to gain release from prison for Leonard Peltier, who had been convicted of killing two FBI agents on the Pine Ridge Reservation. Bellecourt also met with Venezuelan President Hugo Chavez in 1975 to request discount heating oil for residents of Indian reservations.

After roughly 1990, AIM split into bitterly contemptuous factions. Bellecourt and others maintained what they called a national office of AIM in Minneapolis, but many local-level chapters refused to recognize it. One was Colorado AIM, in which a leading role was played by Ward Churchill, who later was fired from his professorial position in Ethnic Studies by the University of Colorado. By that time, the two men viscerally hated each other.

Bellecourt died October 13, 2007 of pneumonia, in Minneapolis.

Further Reading

Martin, Douglas. "Vernon Bellecourt, Mascot Foe, Dies at 75." *New York Times,* October 17, 2007, C-12.

BENDER, CHARLES ALBERT
1884–1954 ANISHINABE (OJIBWA, CHIPPEWA)
BASEBALL PITCHER

Philadelphia Athletics and Chicago White Sox pitcher Charles Albert Bender, called "Chief" by fellow players, is generally regarded as the best Native American baseball player of his time. Journalist Tom Swift, in his biography of the right-hander Bender, wrote that he resented the bigotry implied by the nickname "Chief." "I do not want my name to be presented to the public as an Indian, but as a pitcher," he said (Excerpt, 2008). At the time, newspaper reporters, baseball fans, and other players didn't hear him.

Instead, wrote Swift, "There was scarcely a time when Bender was written about when his race was not prominently mentioned. Bender didn't win games. He scalped opponents. Bender wasn't a talented pitcher with an impressive repertoire. He pitched in his best Indian way. Bender wasn't a player with guile. He was [Manager Connie] Mack's wily redskin" (Excerpt, 2008). After pitching in the 1905 and 1911 World Series games, reporters ignored Bender's prowess on the mound and called him "a child of the forest," and "a typical representative of his race . . . sufficiently below the white man's standard" (Excerpt, 2008). Cartoonists drew him swinging a tomahawk. Fans yelled war whoops at him from the

Charles Albert Bender of the Philadelphia Athletics baseball team, 1909. (Library of Congress)

bleachers. Bender often cupped his hands and replied to the war whoops: "Foreigners! Foreigners!" Off the field, Bender often was refused food and lodging, even as he became one of the best pitchers of his time.

As he endured taunts, Bender, who has been installed in the Major League Baseball Hall of Fame, developed a unique pitching delivery that included what probably was the game's first slider. He was known for his steely composure, especially in tight games and important contests, such as the World Series.

Bender was born May 5, 1884, in Crow Wing County, Minnesota, as an enrolled member of the Ojibwa. His birthdates are sometimes also given as 1883 or 1885. He was raised on the White Earth (Anishinabe, also known as the Chippewa or Ojibwa) Reservation in Minnesota. Bender developed his talents as a baseball player at the Carlisle Indian School. His debut game was April 20, 1903, the beginning of a 22-year career that ended July 21, 1925, with the Chicago White Sox at the age of 41.

Bender compiled a won-loss record of 212–127, with an earned-run average of 2.46, which ranks among the best in baseball history for a starting pitcher. Bender threw a no-hitter during the 1910 season. He played in five World Series with a 2.44 ERA and six wins. Bender was known for his endurance; in the 1911 World Series, he threw three complete games, a Major League record. Bender struck out 1,711 batters while pitching for four teams: the Athletics (1903–14), the Baltimore Terrapins of the short-lived Federal League (1915), the Philadelphia Phillies (1916–17), and the White Sox (1925).

Mack called Bender his "money pitcher," relying on him to deliver crucial wins. At the same time, Mack also exercised his bigotry by paying Bender half as much as other star pitchers in the Athletics' lineup. In the book *Money Pitcher* (2006), a case is made that Bender intentionally underperformed in the 1914 World Series, his last with the Athletics, in retribution for discrimination against him. The Athletics were favored against the Boston Braves before the series, but lost four consecutive games.

During 1918, Bender took a leave from baseball to work in shipyards during World War I. He then returned to the game as a coach for the Chicago White Sox. Bender worked with Connie Mack as a scout until Mack's half-century of managing the Athletics ended in 1950. Bender was included in the 1981 book, *The 100 Greatest Baseball Players of All Time.* More than 120 American Indians played major-league baseball after Bender opened the doors, at a time when blacks were banned from the game.

Bender became the first American Indian elected to the Baseball Hall of Fame in 1953, a year before he died, May 22, 1954, aged 70.

Further Reading

Excerpt: *Chief Bender's Burden,* by Tom Swift. 2008. http://tom-swift.com/cbb/excerpt/.

Kashatus, William C. *Money Pitcher: Chief Bender and the Tragedy of Indian Assimilation.* University Park: Pennsylvania State University Press, 2006.

Ritter, Lawrence, and Donald Honig. *The 100 Greatest Baseball Players of All Time.* [1981]. New York: Random House, 1988.

Swift, Tom. *Chief Bender's Burden: The Silent Struggle of a Baseball Star.* Lincoln: University of Nebraska Press, 2008.

BENEDICT, ERNEST
BORN 1918 MOHAWK
EDUCATOR, POLITICAL LEADER, AND SPIRITUAL LEADER

Mohawk Ernest Benedict's range of accomplishments is unusual. He has been a central figure in an effort that resulted in recognition of Native elders and spiritual leaders as equals of chaplains in Canadian prisons; he also helped win recognition and provision of Native religious ceremonies in those prisons. He has started Indian youth traditional dance and culture clubs that inspired young people to learn and practice their cultures. Some of these students later worked with the North American Indian Travelling College and utilized their cultural knowledge to benefit others. Benedict was the founder and long-time director of the Onake Corporation ("Birch Bark Canoe" in Mohawk), a corporation that applies for money for the benefit of other unincorporated community-based organizations to canoe the money to them so that they will be able to carry on beneficial community work. At various times in his long life, Benedict has been an athlete—a swimmer, skater, and long-distance runner—as well as a graceful traditional dancer.

As a political figure at Akwesasne, Benedict has served as an elected chief on the St. Regis Band Council, which is recognized by the State of New York, as well as the Mohawk Council of Akwesasne, the elected council recognized by the Canadian federal government. (Akwesasne spans the border, so it has an elective council on each side, as well as a traditional chiefs' council, the Mohawk Nation Council of Chiefs.) He served on the council for close to 20 years, with seven terms of office between 1956 and 1982. He was voted in as a Chief of the Kawehnoke District, which is also known as Cornwall Island; he was elected by the council in his last term of office to serve as the Head Chief, a title now known as Grand Chief. Benedict is a condoled (officially installed) Life Chief (*Rotinonkwiseres*) with the traditional community government at Akwesasne, the Mohawk Nation Council of Chiefs.

Benedict has been a member of the Elder's Council within the Canadian Assembly of First Nations, a national Indian organization in Canada similar in purpose to the National Congress of the American Indian in the United States. Ernie and his father, Charles, both were members of the North American Indian Brotherhood, which was formed after World War II as a precursor of the Assembly of First Nations in Canada.

As a spiritual leader, Benedict was chosen by indigenous peoples of Canada to present Pope John Paul II with an eagle feather September 15, 1984, at an 18th-century mission site in Midland, Ontario. As he presented the eagle feather, Benedict told John Paul:

> We, who are sheltered by the Great Tree of Peace, have placed at the top of the tree, the Eagle who can see far, even into the coming days. His courage is the greatest among living creatures and he travels high above us all. It is therefore fitting that we award you a feather from the wings that have brushed against the heavens, as a symbol of your courage and spiritual achievement. Even as you fearlessly proclaim the heavenly messages we consider that the Master shed his blood for the world. You also have shed your blood. This has been recorded on the feather. We will continue to wait for your words, for you have proved the strength of your devotion to truth. *Ne to niio wennake:* These are my words (Benedict, 2005).

In 1994, Benedict received a National Aboriginal Achievement Award for his work in education, one of 14 aboriginal achievement awards given to First Nations leaders in several categories across Canada by the Canadian Native Arts Foundation. He was an elder for the Indian Claims Commission and testified to the Royal Commission on Aboriginal Peoples.

Family and Early Years

Benedict, a member of the Mohawk Wolf Clan, was born July 14, 1918, at Akwesasne. His mother was Julia Kiohawihtoh Jandrew Benedict and his father was Charles Kiorenhakwente Benedict, both from Akwesasne. Ernie's maternal grandmother, Sarah Kanataiehwas Claus, raised Benedict on occasion, teaching him traditional medicines and other elements of Mohawk traditional culture. Ernie's uncle Ira Benedict was a condoled Mohawk Nation Longhouse Traditional Chief. He died at age 97, as did Benedict's grandfather Louis Skaroniati Benedict (in whose 19th-century home Ernie now lives) and great-grandfather Mitchell Sawennakarati Benedict.

Ernie Benedict's wife, Florence Katsitsienhawi Benedict, is a master basket maker. One of his sons (Lloyd Skaroniati Benedict) served as a chief on the Mohawk Council of Akwesasne for more than 10 years. Lloyd has farmed contaminant-free yellow perch in an aquaculture project at Akwesasne. Another son, Daniel Kiorenhakwente Benedict, has worked as a media specialist and technician for Akwesasne's radio station, and as a computer technologist for the St. Regis Mohawk Tribe Environmental Division. Daughter Rebecca Wenniseriiostha Benedict has been a medical laboratory technician and a traditional artist and works for the St. Regis Mohawk Health Service Dental Clinic. His daughter Salli M. Kawennotakie Benedict works for the Mohawk Council of Akwesasne Aboriginal Rights and Research Office, and has been instrumental in many community revitalization efforts. She also is a traditional and contemporary artist.

Members of the family have shown the same penchant for invention as their father. For example, Lloyd and Salli Benedict and others developed a radio station at Akwesasne in 1984 that has operated more than 20 years. Situated in a building astride the U.S.-Canada border in the middle of Akwesasne, CKON 97.3 FM has provided community news and promoted local Mohawk artists, the Mohawk language and culture. The station is known locally as "Sekon" Radio (a Mohawk greeting) and is licensed by the Mohawk Nation Council of Chiefs.

Ernie Benedict graduated from Massena High School at age 16 in 1936; he actually had graduated in 1935, but was too young for college, so he repeated his senior year on a postgraduate basis. He walked and hitchhiked to school from the reservation, 15 miles one way. Benedict attended Syracuse University as a freshman and then transferred to St. Lawrence University in Canton, New York, graduating in 1940 with a bachelor's degree in sociology, at a time when Native Americans with university degrees were rare. Benedict took an anthropology course from the noted anthropologist William Fenton at St. Lawrence University during Fenton's first teaching job, after his graduation from Dartmouth University; he also occasionally babysat Fenton's young daughter. Fenton was impressed with Benedict because he never used a pencil or a notebook (he couldn't afford them), but paid very close attention in class.

Benedict's advocacy of Iroquois revitalization already had begun in 1941, when he said: "We Six Nations of Indians feel we have potentially a superior social system. . . . If we were only left alone, we could redevelop our society . . . which was old in democracy when Europe knew only Monarchs" (Horn, 2001).

Activist and Journalist

Benedict volunteered for military service in World War II, after objecting to the draft in peacetime on grounds that the United States could not conscript Haudenosaunee (Iroquois) to enlist in its armed forces. Benedict initially served three months in jail for refusing to be drafted because he could not afford even minimal bail. First Lady Eleanor Roosevelt intervened with local Selective Service authorities to allow Benedict's release from jail. He later volunteered for service to avoid further prosecution, and because war had been declared following Japan's attack on Pearl Harbor.

A journalist at times throughout his life, Benedict started Akwesasne's first newspaper, called the *War Whoop,* during the late 1930s. During the 1940s, he initiated the newspaper *Kawehras* ("It Thunders" in Mohawk), which published news in both Mohawk and English. All of these preceded *Akwesasne Notes,* which became a national news journal for Indian Country during the activist 1970s. (Benedict later released *Akwesasne Notes* to the Mohawk Nation Council of

Chiefs where it operated until the 1990s.) It was briefly revived as *Akwesasne Notes Magazine* in 1994 and continued for another two years, edited by Benedict's daughter, Salli Kawennotakie.

Benedict became an active member of the Indian Defense League of America, beginning in the 1940s. During the 1950s, he resisted termination legislation (which proposed to eliminate Native reservations) in the United States. When Canada attempted termination during the late 1960s, he fought that, too. At one congressional hearing, in 1948, Benedict confronted Senator Arthur Watkins, the best-known advocate of termination legislation, after Watkins said that the federal government was tiring of its trust responsibilities to Indians and intended to divest itself of them. "What about solemn treaty commitments?" asked Benedict. "Can an honorable nation, just because it is tired, shrug off its responsibilities regardless of the wishes and conditions of the ward. . . . Perhaps Indians are tired too! Tired of poverty and ignorance and disease. They are weary of neglect and broken promises and fruitless hoping" (Hauptman, 1986, 49–50).

Citing environmental problems that became obvious after it was built, Benedict strongly opposed the construction of the St. Lawrence Seaway through Akwesasne during the 1950s; a half-century later, he continues to consult with the Mohawk governments on Seaway issues. Benedict warned that the Seaway would cause silt build-up in the river; in places, the St. Lawrence has not cleared to this day.

Origins of the North American Indian Travelling College

Benedict started the North American Indian Travelling College (now called the Native North American Travelling College and Ronnatahonni Cultural Center) in 1968 to promote Native cultural revitalization across Canada and the United States.

Benedict began to plan the Travelling College in 1966, after he heard accounts of Indian children running away from residential (boarding) schools. One was 12-year-old Charlie Wenjack, who froze to death on train tracks. Benedict believed that Native children should not be removed from their homes for education, even in remote locations. Instead, Native-controlled education should travel to them with curricula that community people wanted.

The college provided a mobile, accessible source of knowledge about Native American history and culture through curricula, visual aids, books, and artifacts, at a time when Native American studies programs were generally in their infancy. Benedict initially carried books, materials, tapes, magazines, and musical instruments in the back of a Volkswagen van, driving from one reserve (or reservation) to another. Benedict's advocacy of Native-controlled education encouraged numerous Indian Survival Schools at Kahnawake, Akwesasne, and elsewhere. His efforts forged a network of educators and young leaders across Canada.

By 2008, the Travelling College offered a travel troupe of Native American singers, dancers, and speakers who respond to invitations to visit other First Nation Reserves, non-Native organizations, workshops and conferences, prisons, and educational institutions. The college also publishes cultural material and posters opposing use of alcohol and drugs, and educates young Native people as cultural providers.

Benedict has been likened to a living museum of Iroquois culture. One source remarked: "Ernie Benedict from Akwesasne taught me some songs for Alligator Dances which are Iroquoian social dances. They were brought into the Confederacy by the Tuscaroras when they joined in the 18th century. Not too many alligators around Lake Ontario! I love the borrowing . . . it reminds me that our cultures ARE still alive, despite what the textbooks might try to tell you" (Corrigan, 2003).

"Ernest is a treasure to our people," wrote Michael Mitchell, former Grand Chief of the Mohawk Council of Akwesasne, in a letter of support for Benedict's nomination in 1995 for a National Aboriginal Achievement Award. "He is a gifted and caring man who has taken on the responsibility of an elder, for all who seek his wisdom and knowledge. He is an educator, a philosopher, and advisor, and a friend. He is a man of peace and great spirituality. He is a man of wisdom and honour. He is a humble man, who unselfishly imparts his knowledge and wisdom to all who come to his door" (Mitchell, 1994, 2).

Research for this entry was provided by Salli Bendict, Ernie Benedict's daughter.

Further Reading

Benedict, Salli. Personal communication, January 8, 2004.

Benedict, Salli. Personal communication, April 8, 2005.

Corrigan, Chris. *Ohwejagehka: Ha'Degaenage. Daguerreotype.* December 19, 2003. http://www.languagehat.com/archives/001037.php.

Hauptman, Laurence M. *The Iroquois Struggle for Survival: World War II to Red Power.* Syracuse, NY: Syracuse University Press, 1986.

Horn, Greg. "Canada/Kahnawake Relations Agreement Announced." *Eastern Door* 10, no. 12 (October 12, 2001). http://www.easterndoor.com/10-12/10-12-1.htm.

Mitchell, Michael to Manager, Order of Ontario, Personal communication, October 1994.

BOLDT, HUGO
1903–1984
UNITED STATES DISTRICT COURT JUDGE, FISHING RIGHTS

On February 12, 1974, United States District Court Judge George Hugo Boldt ruled that American Indians who had signed treaties in western Washington State during the 1850s were entitled to an opportunity to catch as many as half the salmon returning to off-reservation sites that the treaties had called their "usual and accustomed places" for harvest. The case became an object of major controversy between Indians and commercial and sports fishermen. Judge Boldt's ruling had a profound effect not only on who would be allowed to catch salmon in Puget Sound, but on white-Indian relations generally.

Boldt was born in Chicago, December 28, 1903. He was educated as a lawyer, and served as a colonel in the U.S. Army during World War II. After the war, during 1953, he was appointed as a judge of U.S. District Court for the Western District of Washington. He assumed senior status in 1971.

Boldt put three years into *United States v. Washington*; he used 200 pages to interpret one sentence of the treaty in an opinion that some legal scholars say is the most carefully researched, thoroughly analyzed one ever handed down in an Indian fishing-rights case. The nucleus of Boldt's decision dissected 19th-century dictionaries' definitions of "in common with." Boldt said the word meant "to be shared equally." During the next three years, the Ninth Circuit Court of Appeals upheld Boldt's ruling, and the U.S. Supreme Court twice let it stand by refusing to hear an appeal.

Non-Natives in Washington State reacted immediately, and sometimes violently, to Boldt's ruling. Non-Indians, who had long come to regard the salmon harvest as virtually their own, were suddenly faced with the possible prospect of being forced out of the fishing industry, facing large reductions in their catch. Hostility became so serious that Indians armed their fish camps after enduring attacks on themselves and their equipment. Many whites displayed their reaction to the decision with bumper stickers proclaiming "Can Judge Boldt" on their cars. A widely held view was that the Boldt decision had given an unfair advantage to Indians in the fisheries.

State officials and the fishermen whose interests they represented were furious at Boldt. Rumors circulated about the sanity of the 75-year-old judge. It was said that he had taken bribes of free fish and had an Indian mistress, neither of which was true. Judge Boldt was hung in effigy by angry non-Indian fishermen, who on other occasions formed convoys with their boats and rammed Coast Guard vessels that had been dispatched to enforce the court's orders. At least one Coast Guardsman was shot.

Lost in the fray were a number of small, landless western Washington tribes that were not recognized by the federal government and therefore not entitled to participate in the federally mandated solution. A few such tribes, such as the Upper Skagit and Sauk-Suiattle, were recognized after the Boldt decision. A number of others remained in legal limbo, as nonpersons with no fishing rights under federal law. While the commercial interests raged, the Indians were catching nothing close to the 50 percent allowed by the Boldt ruling; in 1974, they caught between 7 and 8 percent; in 1975, between 11 and 12 percent; in 1976, between 13 and 25 percent; and in 1977, 17 percent, depending on who did the counting, the Indians or the state.

Among state officials during the middle and late 1970s, a backlash to Indian rights formed that would become the nucleus for a nationwide non-Indian campaign to abrogate the treaties. Washington State Attorney General (later U.S. Senator) Slade Gorton called Indians "supercitizens" with "special rights," and proposed that constitutional equilibrium be reestablished not by open state violation of the treaties (Boldt had outlawed that), but by purchasing the Indians' fishing rights. The tribes, which had been listening to offers of money for Indian resources for a century, flatly refused Gorton's offer. To them, the selling of fishing rights would have been tantamount to termination.

Boldt died March 18, 1984.

Further Reading

American Friends Service Committee. *Uncommon Controversy: Fishing Rights of the Muckleshoot, Puyallup, and Nisqually Indians.* Seattle: University of Washington Press, 1970.

Barsh, Russel L. *The Washington Fishing Rights Controversy: An Economic Critique.* Seattle: University of Washington School of Business Administration, 1977.

Brack, Fred. "Fishing Rights: Who Is Entitled to Northwest Salmon?" *Seattle Post-Intelligencer Northwest Magazine,* January 16, 1977, n.p.

Brown, Bruce. *Mountain in the Clouds.* New York: Simon & Schuster, 1982.

Miller, Bruce J. "The Press, the Boldt Decision, and Indian-White Relations." *American Indian Culture & Research Journal* 17, no. 2 (1993): 75–98.

Roderick, Janna. "Indian-White Relations in the Washington Territory: The Question of Treaties and Indian Fishing Rights." *Journal of the West* 16, no. 3 (July 1977): 22–34.

United States v. Washington: 384 F. Supp. 312 (1974).

Wilkinson, Charles F. *Messages from Frank's Landing: A Story of Salmon, Treaties, and the Indian Way.* Seattle: University of Washington Press, 2000.

BONNIN, GERTRUDE (ZITKALA-SA)
1876–1938 YANKTON DAKOTA
WRITER

Gertrude Simmons Bonnin, a Yankton Dakota (Sioux) writer whose Native American name was *Zitkala-sa,* provided a written window on Sioux life at the juncture of the Native American and Anglo-American worlds. Born the year of the Battle of the Little Bighorn, she died on the eve of World War II. Bonnin was one of several prominent literary figures to come out of the boarding schools, whose engines of assimilation produced strident critiques of their methods (and of Anglo-American society generally) by the likes of Luther Standing Bear and Charles Eastman, among others.

Bonnin distrusted most non-Indians, but early sought a formal education against her mother's wishes, eventually attending the Boston Conservatory of Music. One of Bonnin's books, the autobiographical *American Indian Stories* (1921), described her changing perceptions of the Euro-American world and her gradual acceptance of Christianity. She authored *Old Indian Legends* (1901), among other titles.

Bonnin also edited *American Indian Magazine,* a publication of the Society of American Indians. She was among a number of very literate American Indian activists in her time who valued printed media (non-Indian outlets as well as their own) to advocate for change.

Critique of Boarding Schools

Bonnin honed her English skills in boarding schools, then resisted their oppressive curricula. "Many boarding-school students, including Bonnin, used the English language, a primary tool of colonization, to 'talk back' to the system" (Spack, 2002). As surely as the boarding schools' inventors understood that language is the vessel of culture, none of them gave much thought to the ways in which Native Americans would use English to critique the schools into which many of them had been unwillingly enrolled.

Thus, Bonnin and other Native American students took control of English as a means of expression even as they were forced to speak it to the exclusion of their Native tongues. This was not always the kind of assimilation that their Anglo-American teachers had anticipated.

Bonnin and other Native American students in boarding schools often forged new identities, taking a degree of authorial control even as they were victimized by an intense campaign to deny them indigenous language, culture, and identity. There were conflicts between Native American writers and boarding school administrators.

It has been noted that Bonnin "wage[d] a linguistic rebellion against the boarding-school ideology" (Katanski, 2005, 122). Zitkala-sa, who was both a student in and a teacher at boarding schools, criticized their methods in large-circulation magazines, in articles such as "Red Man's Helper" in the June 1900 edition of *The Atlantic Monthly.* This piece, and another in *Harper's* during 1901, acutely embarrassed the boarding school system's founder, William Henry Pratt, who attacked her writings in retaliation. Bonnin's autobiographical essays, including "Impressions of an Indian Childhood," "School Days of an Indian Girl," and "An Indian Teacher among Indians," also enraged Pratt even as he publicized her reputation as an example of how Native American children were being helped by the schools.

As a teacher at Carlisle Industrial School, Bonnin developed a curriculum for boarding school education from a Native American perspective, which was rejected by the school authorities. Bonnin favored a bilingual approach similar to prevailing educational attitudes a century later. Several other Native Americans advocated bilingualism as an alternative at the same time. One example was Sarah Winnemucca, who served as a translator for General Oliver O. Howard (who played a major role in the founding of Howard University). Winnemucca designed an entire bilingual curriculum for Native American boarding school students during the 1880s, and won some congressional support. Many Native parents also opposed monolingualism. The Americanists, however, refused to utilize her program in the boarding schools.

Bonnin's critique of boarding school education questioned the entire web of assumptions that propelled European colonization. The boarding schools were built on 19th-century European American notions of what comprised civilized life, as stated, with some sense of irony, by Booker T. Washington: "No white American ever thinks that any other race is wholly civilized until he wears the white man's clothes, eats the white man's food, speaks the white man's language, and professes the white man's religion" (Spack, 2002, 23). Eastman also inverted these assumptions by saying of his education at Dartmouth College: "It was here that I had most of my savage gentleness and native refinement knocked out of me" (Spack, 2002, 134).

"A Story of Linguistic Ownership"

In the late 19th century, the U.S. government went to great lengths to establish English as the primary language in the country. Thus Bonnin and other Native American writers educated in the boarding schools turned on its head an educational system predicated on the elimination of Native languages and cultures to stamp out tribal identity.

Even as the curricula of the boarding schools assumed termination of Native American sovereignty as well as culture and language (as did the General Allotment Act, enacted at about the same time), Bonnin and other boarding school students exercised a sense of ownership of the words they spoke and wrote, making of English a device by which culture, identity, and sovereignty could be preserved in a bilingual world.

Gertrude Bonnin in Native regalia. (Library of Congress)

Bonnin intensely resented the use of her work by boarding school supporters to support theories of social evolution; at one point, she wrote, "No one can dispute my own impressions and bitterness" (Katanski, 2005, 29). Much of Bonnin's work has been characterized as "images of angry, pain-filled students, whose plight challenged white educators' justifications of the boarding schools" (Katanski, 2005, 166). However, Bonnin recognized the compromises between tradition and non-Native change that so affected her life, as in the first sentence of "Impressions of an Indian Childhood," in which she described living with her mother in a tepee made not of buffalo hides, but canvas.

With Eastman, Bonnin was a founder of the Society of American Indians, an early pan-Indian advocacy organization in the 1920s. She also was known for her talent on the violin. Bonnin investigated the swindling of Indians in Oklahoma by settlers who swarmed into the area after the discovery of oil, and she advised the government's Meriam Commission, which compiled a statistical portrait of massive poverty on Indian reservations, in the late 1920s. Bonnin remained active in Indian affairs until she died in 1938.

Further Reading

Katanski, Amelia V. *Learning to Write "Indian": The Boarding School Experience and American Indian Literature.* Norman: University of Oklahoma Press, 2005.

Spack, Ruth. *America's Second Tongue: American Indian Education and the Ownership of English, 1860–1900.* Lincoln: University of Nebraska Press, 2002.

BRUCE, LOUIS R.
1906–1989 DAKOTA SIOUX AND MOHAWK
BIA COMMISSIONER

Louis Rooks Bruce served as commissioner of the Bureau of Indian Affairs during President Richard M. Nixon's first term, from 1969 to 1973. Bruce's tenure coincided with activist Native American political movements during the late 1960s and 1970s. Bruce was the third person of Native American descent to serve as commissioner of the BIA. The first was the Seneca Ely Parker, appointed after the Civil War by President Ulysses S. Grant. The second was Robert F. Bennett, who led the agency under President Lyndon Johnson, from 1966 to 1969.

Bruce was raised on the Onondaga reservation south of Syracuse in New York State. His father, Louis Bruce, a Mohawk, worked as a dentist, a major-league baseball player, and a Methodist missionary. He was a stern and highly religious person who taught his son to value education. Bruce's mother, Nellie Rooks, was Dakota (Sioux). Bruce attended Cazenovia Seminary, at his father's behest, the only Native American student there, where he excelled in several sports and graduated in 1929. Bruce then worked his way through Syracuse University (as a construction worker, farmhand, waiter, and employee of a saw mill) and became known as a star pole-vaulter. After his graduation from college, Bruce worked as a clothing-store manager, as an official in the Works Progress Administration, and as a dairy farmer. He married Anna Wikoff, a former classmate at the Cazenovia Seminary, in 1930.

In 1935, Bruce went to work in New York State as director for Indians for the National Youth Administration of the Works Progress Administration. The agency, a Great Depression employment program, put Native young people to work teaching Indian culture and history at summer camps.

He was a founder and executive secretary of the National Congress of American Indians. Bruce was an unofficial advisor to New York Governor Thomas Dewey and a friend of First Lady Eleanor Roosevelt. He worked on many New Deal programs during the 1930s to preserve Native American art, dance, music, and other oral traditions. In 1957, Bruce played a major role in organizing the first Native American Youth Conference. In the late 1950s, he chaired the President's Advisory Committee on Indian Affairs during the Eisenhower Administration.

After Bruce was named BIA commissioner by President Nixon in 1969, he set out to Indianize the bureau by appointing a number of Native Americans to influential positions. His aim was to create a true service agency. Bruce served as Commissioner of Indian Affairs from 1969 to 1972; his tenure in that office came to an abrupt end after the BIA building was occupied by Indian activists a week before the 1972 election, and Bruce was fired by President Nixon.

Bruce's policies at the BIA ran up against a considerable amount of opposition from interests that had benefited by keeping Native Americans in a subordinate position. In this respect, his ouster recalled that of the first BIA commissioner of Native American descent, Ely Parker, who had been drummed out of the office almost exactly a century earlier.

After his dismissal as BIA commissioner, Bruce started and directed Native American Consultants Inc., to provide advice to Native American organizations. On May 24, 1989, Bruce died of cancer and heart disease in Arlington, Virginia. He was survived by his wife, as well as three children, a sister, and eight grandchildren.

Further Reading

Ballentine, Betty, and Ian Ballentine. *The Native Americans Today.* Atlanta, GA: Turner Publishing, 1993.

Cook, Joan. "Louis R. Bruce, Ex-Commissioner of Indian Affairs, Is Dead at 83." *New York Times,* May 24, 1989. http://www.nytimes.com/1989/05/24/obituaries/louis-r-bruce-ex-commissioner-of-indian-affairs-is-dead-at-83.html.

C

CAMPBELL, BEN NIGHTHORSE
BORN 1933 NORTHERN CHEYENNE
U.S. SENATOR

Ben Nighthorse Campbell was elected to the U.S. House of Representatives as a Democrat from Colorado in 1986. He was elected to the U.S. Senate in 1992, becoming the only modern-day Native American to serve in that elite body. Campbell served two terms, until 2005, when he retired at the age of 70. At the same time, Campbell was a member of the traditional Council of Forty-Four on his Northern Cheyenne homeland in eastern Montana.

Early Years

Mary Vierra, Campbell's mother, immigrated to the United States from Portugal at age six. She was raised in a Portuguese community near Sacramento, California. She met her husband-to-be, Albert Campbell, a Cheyenne, while she was under treatment for tuberculosis in the same hospital where he was being treated for alcoholism.

Benjamin Nighthorse Campbell was born April 13, 1933, in Auburn, California. His father's alcoholism continued, and the elder Campbell was absent from the family for long periods; Benjamin's mother also continued to suffer from tuberculosis. Without care at home, the young Campbell led an unstable life and often found himself in trouble with police. By the age of 10, Campbell had spent half his life at Sacramento's St. Patrick's Catholic Orphanage. He later attended Placer High School, dropping out in 1951 to enlist in the U.S. Air Force. Campbell then served in the Korean War, before he was discharged in 1953 as an Airman Second Class. He also was awarded the Korean Service Medal and the Air Medal during his term of service.

Sen. Ben Nighthorse Campbell, R-Colo., wearing Cheyenne regalia, walks to the Senate floor on Capitol Hill, September 21, 2004. (AP/Wide World Photos)

Back in the United States, Campbell found himself picking tomatoes for 15 cents a box in California's vegetable fields. While picking, Campbell met a truck driver who helped him obtain a Teamsters card and training for a job similar to his, despite the fact that Campbell ruined his first truck driver's lesson by backing the big rig over a fence.

Campbell studied for a bachelor of arts in physical education and fine arts at California State University (San Jose), after attending San Jose City College for a year to make up for his lack of a high school diploma. Campbell earned his BA from San Jose State in 1958. During his college career, Campbell also became an outstanding competitor in judo (having first taken up the sport in Asia during his Air Force career), winning a U.S. collegiate championship three times. Campbell became the youngest person in the United States to hold a fourth-degree black belt. Later, Campbell won a gold medal in the 1963 Pan American Games. While competing in judo, Campbell broke his nose nine times, separated a shoulder four times, broke seven ribs, as well as all of his fingers and toes.

Campbell then studied at Meiji University (Tokyo) between 1960 and 1964, where he majored in Japanese culture. The same year, Campbell was captain of the U.S. judo team at the 1964 Olympic Games in Tokyo. Campbell also wrote a manual for judo training, *Championship Judo Training Drills* (1974). Between 1964 and 1977, Campbell taught in the San Juan Unified School District, California.

Political Career

During 1983, Campbell became the second Native American to be elected to Colorado's legislature, where he served until his election to the U.S. House of Representatives in 1986. Campbell served in the House from 1987 to 1993, after which he was elected to the U.S. Senate, becoming the first Native American to serve in the Senate in more than 60 years. Campbell was the most prominent Native American politician in Congress since Charles Curtis, who was born in 1860 and died in 1936, a U.S. representative, senator, and vice president with Herbert Hoover.

Campbell was re-elected to the Senate in 1998 and chaired the Committee on Indian Affairs. After Campbell declined to run for re-election to the Senate in 2004, his Senate seat was won by Democrat Ken Salazar in the November 2004 election. Campbell resisted tax increases and tried to raise standards for accountability in federal spending.

While many states require by law that their budgets be balanced, the U.S. federal government has both the power to print money and the legal ability to spend more than it receives in taxes. Spending is often used to satisfy constituents' demands and win votes. Campbell fought that system, but did not make much headway against it.

A Recognized Leader

Campbell became a leader in policy related to public lands and natural resources, sponsoring bills that created Sand Creek Massacre National Historic Site, the Black Canyon of the Gunnison National Park, and the Colorado Ute Settlement Act Amendments of 2000.

In March 1995, Campbell became a Republican. Some in the Democratic Party responded by calling Campbell a turncoat and "Benedict Campbell" (a reference to the famous Revolutionary traitor, Benedict Arnold) and demanding the return of $255,000 in donated funds used by the party to help elect him to the Senate.

Some observers noted that Campbell was switching parties to enhance his political access as the Republicans took over the entire federal government (executive, legislative, and judicial branches), and to improve his ability to advocate American Indian issues in Congress. The unwillingness of the Democrats to support the Balanced Budget Amendment, among other issues, also contributed to Campbell's switch in party loyalty.

Influence

While Campbell has been influential across the United States, he sometimes was criticized for his conservatism. Campbell is conservative enough to have received praise from U.S. President George W. Bush at the opening of the National Museum of the American Indian on the Smithsonian Mall in Washington, D.C., on September 23, 2004: "I'm honored to call Ben Nighthorse Campbell a friend. He is a strong, strong leader. He is a proud Indian and a proud American. He represents the best of public service" ("President Honors . . .", 2004). Campbell was instrumental in initiating the legislation that established the museum, and in committing time and energy toward its passage.

As a senator from Colorado, Campbell also was swept up in emotional condemnation of Ward Churchill, an ethnic studies professor at the University of Colorado (whose partial heritage as a Cherokee has been disputed). Churchill became nationally notable (and an infamous object of ridicule by many conservatives) after his comments in September 2001 on the Internet that compared the employees in the World Trade Center to "Little Eichmanns," as cogs in U.S. imperialism, who deserved their fate. Churchill later was dismissed from his post, having been found guilty of academic misconduct (including inventing historical material and plagiarism) by an internal committee at the University of Colorado. Campbell condemned Churchill in a very emphatic fashion, joining a large number of other important Colorado political figures, and called for his dismissal for political reasons long before an investigation of Churchill's academic misconduct was undertaken. The university itself refused to fire Churchill for his "Little Eichmanns" remark, holding it to be an exercise of his freedom of speech rights.

Campbell, who has been married to the former Linda Price for more than 35 years, is father of two children, Colin Campbell and Shanan Longfellow, and grandfather to Luke and Saylor Longfellow and Lauren Campbell. He has been a rancher and horse trainer in his adopted hometown of Ignacio, Colorado, and has long maintained a jewelry design business.

Further Reading

Chavers, Dean. *Modern American Indian Leaders: Their Lives and Their Works.* 2 vols. Lewiston, NY: Edwin Mellen Press, 2007.

Henry, Christopher, and W. David Baird. *Ben Nighthorse Campbell: Cheyenne Chief and U.S. Senator.* New York: Chelsea House, 1994.

"President Honors the National Museum of the American Indian." George W. Bush White House Archives. September 23, 2004. http://georgewbush-whitehouse.archives.gov/news/releases/2004/09/20040923-2.html.

CHURCHILL, WARD
BORN 1947 CHEROKEE (DISPUTED)
EDUCATOR, AUTHOR, POLITICAL ACTIVIST

Ward Churchill, as professor of Native American Studies at the University of Colorado until 2007, authored many provocative books with titles like *Fantasies of the Master Race* and *A Little Matter of Genocide*. He was no stranger to controversy, but beginning early in 2005, he became the target of a nationwide campaign by right-wing opponents of his stated belief that the victims of the September 11, 2001, attacks on the World Trade Center had acted like "Little Eichmanns," cogs in an imperial machine.

Until that time, Churchill had built a reputation as a prolific, often incendiary, and widely cited author and activist. Churchill said that the university had dragged up years-old accusations to retaliate for his political beliefs, allowing opponents with political motives to cherry-pick his writings for assertions of factual errors and scholarly misconduct. Churchill was relieved of his university post for plagiarism and scholarly misconduct after a lengthy investigation, the first University of Colorado tenured professor to be fired for cause. At the same time, a number of Churchill's opponents accused him of ethnic-identity fraud in claiming Cherokee heritage, but these charges did not play a part in the university's investigation.

A Controversial Life

Ward Churchill, who was named after his grandfather, was born to Jack LeRoy Churchill and Maralyn Lucretia Allen in Urbana, Illinois, in 1947. Churchill's parents divorced before his second birthday. Churchill's high school classmates recalled him as "a friendly teen who liked to debate politics" (Curtin, Pankratz, and Kane, 2005, A-1). He graduated from Elmwood Community High School during 1965, and was drafted a year later to serve a tour of duty in Vietnam as the war there escalated.

Ward Churchill, writer and activist. (AP/ Wide World Photos)

Churchill has variously described his service in Vietnam as editor of an Army newspaper (on an employment application at C.U. in 1980), and as a member of an elite reconnaissance patrol (Curtin, Pankratz, and Kane, 2005, A-1). Churchill has also asserted that he led a patrol in combat in Vietnam.

Service in Vietnam formed Churchill's politics hard left. After discharge, he burned a U.S. flag on the steps of the Peoria County Courthouse. He attended meetings of Students for a Democratic Society and became friends with Mark Clark, a Black Panther leader who later was killed in a shootout with police in Peoria. Churchill became friends with Russell Means about the time of the 1973 siege at Wounded Knee, and wrote some speeches for him.

Churchill, who is 6 foot, 5 inches, and smokes two to four packs of Pall Malls a day, took his first teaching job as an art instructor at Black Hills State College in Spearfish, South Dakota, during 1975 and 1976. Churchill became a lecturer at the University of Colorado in 1978 and was granted tenure in the university's Communications Department in 1991. After that, he transferred to Ethnic Studies.

In 2004, about 240 protesters, including Churchill, were arrested in Denver for blocking Columbus Day parade activities. Churchill had described the parade as a "celebration of genocide that caused millions of Indians' deaths with the advent of European colonization" (Johnson, 2005). Denver has experienced the largest protests of Columbus Day in the world. Churchill and several other leaders of the protest later were acquitted on charges of failure to obey a police order to disperse.

Churchill's "Little Eichmanns" statement first reached the attentive ears of various right-wing media gatekeepers during January 2005, after he had been invited to Hamilton College, with a student body of about 1,750, which is housed in century-and-a-half-old stone buildings near Utica, New York. Churchill had been invited as part of a panel discussion on the limits of free speech titled "Limits of Dissent." Very quickly, the real world intruded on an academic debate over how far an individual could take free speech. The debate was canceled because of the uproar.

On February 3, 2005, C.U.-Boulder Interim Chancellor Phil DiStefano (with Arts and Sciences Dean Todd Gleeson and Law School Dean David Getches) initiated a 30-day review of Churchill's speeches and writings to determine whether he had overstepped the boundaries of academic conduct, and whether his "Little Eichmanns" statement and others might be grounds for dismissal. The University of Colorado Ethnic Studies Department, the chancellor's office, and Churchill himself received about 1,000 e-mails and dozens of phone calls *each day* at the height of the controversy during February 2005, many of which were explicitly racist.

Indianness

The controversy over Churchill quickly spread from his right to engage in unpopular political commentary to other matters, including the nature of his ethnic identity. Questions about Churchill's ethnicity had dogged him for many years. During May 1994, he was granted an "associate membership," or honorary status, with the Keetoowah Cherokee. He would have had to show proof of one-quarter blood quantum to be granted full membership; he said that he has 3/16. In July of that year, the Keetoowah Cherokee stopped issuing associate memberships. Late in May 1994, a revised statement from the United Keetoowah Band of Cherokee Indians asserted, according to a report in the *Rocky Mountain News,* that it had found no legal records to indicate that Churchill is a federally recognized American Indian. The statement also clarified the group's reasoning behind its award to Churchill of an associate membership by the Tahlequah, Oklahoma–based tribe in 1994 (Flynn, 1994).

Official certification of Native American status has long been a debatable credential. Many Native people resent having to prove their ethnicity (like a dog's breed, some complain) at the behest of a government agency created under U.S. law. Some assert that the whole idea of classifying people by degree of blood is an Anglo-American notion born in the 19th century of a desire to divide people racially. Others have blood in Native groups that no longer have organized governments or government recognition.

The university decided not to pursue the identity question on the rationale that declarations of race for affirmative-action purposes are self-identified (as are U.S. Census classifications). If the university had pursued this question regarding Churchill, it would have opened the cases of everyone else who had declared a minority identity on a university employment form.

On September 9, 2005, the University of Colorado, having found that Churchill's comments about the World Trade Center bombings were free speech, initiated a formal inquiry into earlier charges of research misconduct against him, including allegations that he had published work mischaracterizing blood-quantum requirements in the Indian Arts and Crafts Act of 1990 and the General Allotment Act of 1887; that he had repeatedly advanced a theory charging the U.S. Army with an act of genocide against the Mandans in 1837 by intentionally spreading smallpox; that he plagiarized the work of Professor Fay Cohen of Dalhousie University in Nova Scotia, Canada, and that he had plagiarized a defunct Canadian environmental group's pamphlet on a water-diversion project that was never undertaken.

In his defense, Churchill said the allegations were trivial. In an e-mail Natsu Saito, C.U. associate professor of ethnic studies and Churchill's wife, stated that "Out of dozens of accusations . . . ranging from treason to advocacy of violence to personal threats to misrepresenting his identity to plagiarism, all that remain are a handful of questions regarding historical interpretation and the conventions of citation or attribution." "On the whole," argued Churchill in response, "I submit that no scholar with a comparably extensive publication record would have fared better. Certainly, my accusers would not. The real question, then, is not the integrity of my scholarship. Rather, it is whether the University of Colorado is going to subject the writings of all its faculty to a degree of scrutiny similar in 'rigor' to that visited upon mine."

Investigative Report and Subsequent Events

The university assembled a five-member committee of scholars, which investigated the charges for several months, researching historical events and calling witnesses. The committee then released a 125-page report, on May 9, 2006, that found Churchill culpable on six of seven instances of plagiarism, falsification, and violation of academic research norms, and called for suspension or termination of his employment.

Churchill asserted that the committee, acting as prosecutor and judge, had done "exactly what it accuses me of doing: it tailored its report to fit its conclusions" (Churchill, personal communication). Churchill's books contain roughly 12,000 references by his count, and thus he argues that not even "any even marginally prolific scholar's publications could withstand the type of scrutiny to which mine has been subjected." The work under examination was "years, sometimes decades, old," Churchill argued (Churchill, May 20, 2006, 2).

On June 13, casting secret ballots, Colorado University's Standing Committee on Research Misconduct accepted the special committee's report. Six of nine members who cast ballots (two were ex-officio, without voting authority) said he should be fired, saying he "has committed serious, repeated and deliberate research misconduct," including plagiarism and fabrication of material (Burnett, 2006).

The research misconduct committee's 20-page report and recommendations were forwarded to Provost Susan Avery and Arts and Sciences Dean Todd Gleeson, who then sent them to Interim Chancellor Phil DiStefano, who made the final decision to terminate Churchill's employment contract, subject to approval by the C.U. Board of Regents. After DiStefano recommended on July 26 that Churchill be fired, he was entitled to one more review: an appeal to the university's Committee on Privilege and Tenure, which upheld the original findings.

David Lane, Churchill's attorney, retorted that the committees' findings were a pretext for firing on freedom-of-speech grounds. "It's window dressing," Lane said. "They want to make it look legitimate so then they can fire him and say, 'Look, it had nothing to do with free speech'" (Johnson, 2006).

Lane filed a lawsuit based partially on those grounds seeking reinstatement of Churchill at the university. A Denver District Court jury found that Churchill's political views had played a substantial role in the firing, but awarded him only $1 in damages. On July 7, 2009, Judge Larry J. Naves refused to reinstate Churchill at the University of Colorado, saying that the Board of Regents had acted in a judicial capacity when Churchill was dismissed. The board thus was legally protected from the lawsuit, the judge ruled. Lane said he would appeal.

Further Reading

Brennan, Charlie. "Churchill Finds Fans at Calif. Fest; C.U. Professor Gives Keynote Address at Anarchist Book Fair." *Rocky Mountain News,* March 28, 2005, 4-A.

Brennan, Charlie. "Tribe Clarifies Stance on Prof.; Milder Statement Explains Churchill's 'Associate' Label." *Rocky Mountain News,* May 21, 2005, 16-A.

Burnett, Sara. "C.U. Panel: Fire Prof; Churchill Should Be Cut Loose, Say Six of Nine Who Cast Secret Ballots." *Rocky Mountain News,* June 14, 2006. http://www.rocky mountainnews.com/drmn/education/article/0,1299,DRMN_957_4773332,00.html.

Churchill, Ward. "Some People Push Back: On the Justice of Roosting Chickens." 2001. http://www.kersplebedeb.com/mystuff/s11/churchill.html.

Curtin, Dave, Howard Pankratz, and Arthur Kane. "Questions Stoke Ward Churchill's Firebrand Past." *Denver Post,* February 13, 2005, A-1.

Flynn, Johnny P. "Ward Churchill Finds a Home with the Friendly United Keetoowah Band." *Indian Country Today,* December 15, 1994. http://www.highbeam.com/doc/1P1-2302597.html.

Johansen, Bruce E. *Silenced! Academic Freedom, Scientific Inquiry, and the First Amendment under Siege in America.* Westport, CT: Praeger, 2007.

Johnson, Kirk. "University President Resigns at Colorado amid Turmoil." *New York Times,* March 8, 2005. http://www.nytimes.com/2005/03/08/national/08colorado.html.

Johnson, Kirk. "University of Colorado Chancellor Advises Firing Author of Sept. 11 Essay." *New York Times,* June 27, 2006. http://www.nytimes.com/2006/06/27/edu cation/27churchill.html.

Rave, Jodi. "Reporter's Notebook: Controversial C.U. Professor Stretches Truth." *Billings Gazette,* February 6, 2005. http://www.billingsgazette.com/index.php?display= rednews/2005/02/06/build/nation/67-reporters-notebook.inc.

Wesson, Marianne. *Report of the Investigative Committee of the Standing Committee on Research Misconduct at the University of Colorado at Boulder Concerning Allegations of Research Misconduct against Professor Ward Churchill.* May 9, 2006. www.colorado.edu/news/reports/churchill/churchillreport051606.html.

COBELL, ELOUISE
BORN 1946 BLACKFEET
BANKER AND ACTIVIST

While working as an accountant on the Montana Blackfeet reservation during the 1990s, Elouise Cobell began to inquire into the management of bank accounts managed "in trust" by the federal government. She uncovered mismanagement that became the gist for the largest class-action suit ever filed against the U.S. government, with 500,000 plaintiffs. The "trust" accounts ranged in size from 35 cents to $1 million for individuals. Among Native bands and nations, the largest single account was the roughly $400 million set aside for the Sioux settlement of the Black Hills land claim, which has not been paid because the Sioux have not agreed to accept it.

Beginning in 1887, through the General Allotment Act (sometimes known after its primary congressional sponsor, Senator Henry Dawes), American Indians were designated as owners of individual lands, going against communal traditions that were thousands of years old. These lands, like the rest of Indians' lives, were micromanaged by the Bureau of Indian Affairs, part of the Department of the Interior. In theory, like other owners of resources, the Native land owners were supposed to be paid royalties through the Bureau of Indian Affairs and Treasury Department, through accounts called "Individual Indian Monies."

Elouise Cobell near an oil well on the Blackfeet Indian Reservation in Montana, September 1999. (AP/Wide World Photos)

More than a century later, when Cobell filed a lawsuit to allow Indians' access to their money, she had only the slightest inkling of the financial morass she had discovered. First estimates of mismanaged funds ranged from $2 billion to $4 billion—a lot of money, surely, but a pittance compared to the $176 billion that was estimated 10 years later. By 2006, the Individual Indian Monies (IIM) mess had become the stuff of political and legal legend; nine years after the case that became known as *Cobell v. Norton* class action was first filed, it employed more than 100 lawyers on the payrolls of the Interior and Treasury departments.

Cobell rented a modest four-room office in Browning, Montana, and, by 2005, had funded her legal challenge with about $12 million in grant money. In 2002, the Blackfeet awarded Cobell status as a warrior, a rare honor for a woman.

Early Life

Cobell has spent much of her life in and near the reservation town of Browning, Montana, where she was born as one of eight children in a house with no electricity or running water. The major form of entertainment was old-fashioned: oral history—parents telling stories to children, sometimes describing Baker's Massacre, during which U.S. soldiers killed about 200 Blackfeet, a majority of them women and children, following an ambush near the Marias River. As a child, Cobell also sometimes heard stories from her parents and their neighbors about small government checks they received that never seemed to bear any relationship to reality because the transactions had never taken place.

After high school, Cobell graduated from Great Falls Commercial College and then studied for two years at Montana State University. Her education was interrupted when she returned to the reservation to take care of her terminally ill mother. During a sojourn off the reservation in her 20s, Cobell met Alvin, her husband, who is also Blackfeet, in Seattle. He was fishing off the Alaska coast, and she worked as an accountant at a Seattle television station, KIRO.

At the age of 30, Cobell returned to Browning with Alvin, to resume a life on the family ranch. As one of the few Blackfeet with training in accounting, Cobell was offered a job with the reservation government. At the time, Browning had practically no Native-owned businesses; unemployment rose to more than 70 percent in winter (which can last into May), when construction employment ceased.

Cobell found the Blackfeet accounting system "in total chaos" (Kennedy, 2002). Some trust accounts were being charged negative interest. Checks were being posted against accounts without her knowledge, even though she was supposed to be the only valid signatory. Cobell served as treasurer of the Blackfeet from 1970 through 1983, putting Blackfeet accounting on a sound footing, while also working her ranch with her husband.

In 1983, after the government shut down the only bank on the reservation, Cobell got the idea of founding an Indian-owned bank. Told it would never work, she went back to school, became a banker, and, in 1987, opened the Blackfeet National Bank, the first Native-owned bank on a reservation in the United States. Within 15 years, this institution had grown into the Native American Bank, with

23 Native American nations from across the country investing as much as $1 million apiece.

Following its creation, the bank provided loans to Native Americans to help start businesses that otherwise never would have been financed. In a few years, Cobell could point to several businesses in Browning that she had helped to finance, such as the Glacier Restaurant, Browning Video, and the Dollar Store. Cobell's assay into banking by 2005 had helped to provide Browning with more than 200 enterprises, 80 percent of them Indian-owned. Cobell soon was spending much of her time (apart from the many hours devoted to the court case and ranch chores with Alvin) tutoring Blackfeet and other Native peoples in ways to best start their own businesses.

"Wards" Put the BIA on Trial

Before Cobell's challenge, many IIM accountholders had been wary of confronting the system because the BIA could (and sometimes did) declare them incompetent to handle their own money. The U.S. Treasury holds the accounts in trust for the Indians, as wards of the government. "Trust" is also the legal rubric under which the BIA (or other agencies of the Interior Department) first became Indians' bankers. The handlers of Indians in the War Department, Interior Department, and BIA have always had available to them two versions of reality: one is the official ideology of "trust," "guardianship," and so forth, the kindly language of a supposedly benevolent Great White Father, of "the most exacting fiduciary standards," "due care," and "moral obligations of the highest responsibility and trust." In the other reality, the federal agencies that had lost, abused, and otherwise bungled the Indians' funds were empowered, by their interpretation of the law, to decide whether Native individuals were competent to handle their own money.

With broad Native American support, the Department of Interior hired Paul Homan, a former director of Riggs Bank and an expert at cleaning up failing private financial institutions, as Special Trustee for American Indians. Homan, having taken stock of the situation, later quit in disgust, as he described a banker's nightmare. Day by day, piece by piece, the IIM inquiries were producing evidence of what must have been the world's sloppiest banking record-keeping. Even Cobell was amazed at the sorry state of the BIA's banking system, if it could be called that.

Homan soon beheld the world's worst excuse for financial accounting. The BIA had never established an accounts receivable system, so its bankers never knew how much money they were handling at any given time. More than $50 million had not been paid to individual Indians because the BIA had lost track of them, or because they had not left forwarding addresses. Roughly 21,000 accounts listed the names of people who were dead. Large numbers of records were stored in cardboard boxes in leaky warehouses, destroying them.

"Years after our lawsuit was filed," said Cobell, "someone discovered a barn filled with discarded and missing trust records in Anadarko [Oklahoma]. These records were being watched only by the rats in that leaky building. Interior officials testified that when the barn filled up, they just tossed out the oldest records and stacked in newer ones." She continued, "As for the leases of Indian lands that were supposed to be the sources of trust account funds, thousands of those leases were never recorded. So how can the trust records be accurate? They can't" (Cobell, 2005).

"Honestly, I have never seen anything like it in my 30-year career as a banker," Homan told the U.S. Senate Committee on Indian Affairs in June 1996 (Johansen, 1997, 18). About $695 million in Native funds had been sent to the wrong Indian group, tribe, or nation. Some of the funds never were sent at all. Some funds had been posted to the wrong accounts. One property record valued three garden-variety chain saws at $99 million each. During 1996, $17 million in trust fund money simply vanished due to sloppy bookkeeping. Exhumation of the BIA's financial record-keeping came to resemble an archaeological dig. Asbestos had contaminated some of the financial records, and other records had been paved over by a parking lot.

Filing Suit

In 1996, Cobell finally became fed up with government inaction after Attorney General Janet Reno reneged on a promise to look into the money-funds mess. With Cobell, the Native American Rights Fund announced the class-action suit on behalf of the 300,000 (later 500,000) holders of IIM accounts. Attorneys pointed to people such as Bernice Skunk Cap, an elderly Blackfeet, who lost her cabin to fire in 1994. Planning to build a new home, Skunk Cap applied to the BIA for $2,400 from her IIM account, but was told she could have only $1,000 of it. She was forced to move into a nursing home.

The chief judge in the case, Royce C. Lamberth, was a Republican appointee, a Texan with a taste for fancy boots and large cars, who seemed, on the surface, an unlikely candidate for a serious interest in a Native American class-action suit. However, Lamberth possessed a keen knowledge of bureaucratic politics and an ability to read and comprehend vast amounts of information. He also was a serious jurist—so serious that the government soon sought to remove him from the case. Like fishing-rights judge George Hugo Boldt (also a Republican appointee), Lamberth has a sharp sense of justice, regardless of vested interests. He is hard-working and ruthlessly honest.

A native of San Antonio, Lamberth earned his undergraduate and law degrees from the University of Texas. He was drafted out of law school in 1967 and entered the Army Judge Advocate General Corps during the Vietnam War. Lamberth worked in the civil division of the U.S. Attorney's Office in Washington, D.C., until 1987, when he was appointed to the federal bench.

On December 21, 1999, Judge Lamberth, who was overseeing the case in the Washington, D.C. Federal District Court, issued his first (Phase One) opinion (the case is divided into two phases). The 126-page opinion stated that the government had baldly violated its trust responsibilities to Native Americans. He called the

IIM mess the "most egregious misconduct by the federal government" (Johansen, 2004, 26).

In a major victory for the plaintiffs, Judge Lamberth ruled September 29, 2004, that all sales and transfers of Indian-owned land by the Department of the Interior's Bureau of Indian Affairs must include a detailed, court-approved notification of landowners' rights as trust beneficiaries and class members. For the first time in history, individual Indian landowners would be informed of their rights as trust beneficiaries and class members before the sale of their lands.

On June 20, 2005, several prominent Native American leaders, including Cobell, convened in Washington to announce principles for legislation that they said could settle the case. Most significantly, they said they would settle the case for $27.5 billion. The government refused the offer.

By 2008, the case was dragging on, with the Native accountholders having received nothing. The U.S. government showed little inclination to solve the money-funds problem. Instead, the Department of the Interior's small army of attorneys went to federal appeals court and removed Judge Lamberth from the case, arguing that he was biased in favor of the plaintiffs. The appeals court agreed.

Late in 2009, the Obama administration submitted to Congress a plan to pay $1.4 billion to the plaintiffs in Cobell's lawsuit, as well as an additional $2 billion to repurchase land, ending the 13-year-old lawsuit. Under the settlement, most of the plaintiffs would get $1,000, with some who suffered larger losses receiving more. Some of the money will pay attorneys' fees. "This is significantly less than the full accounting to which individual Indians are entitled," Cobell said. "We are compelled to settle now by the sobering realization that our class grows smaller" as older members have died, she said (Fahrenthold, 2009).

Further Reading

Cobell, Elouise. "Indians Not Being Told Truth." *Daily Oklahoman* [Oklahoma City], April 22, 2005, n.p.

"Court Rejects Judge's Plan in Indian Case." Associated Press in *New York Times,* December 11, 2004. http://query.nytimes.com/mem/tnt.html?tntget=2004/12/11/national/11indian.html&tntemail1.

Fahrenthold, David A. "Government to Settle Suit over Indian Land Trusts; $1.4 Billion in Payments to End 13-Year-Old Battle." *Washington Post,* December 9, 2009. http://www.washingtonpost.com/wp-dyn/content/article/2009/12/08/AR2009120802549_pf.html.

Johansen, Bruce E. "The BIA as Banker: 'Trust' Is Hard When Billions Disappear." *Native Americas* 14, no. 1 (Spring 1997): 14–23.

Johansen, Bruce E. "The Trust Fund Mess: Where Has All the Money Gone?" *Native Americas* 21 (Fall/Winter 2004): 26–33.

Kennedy, J. Michael. "Truth and Consequences on the Reservation." *Los Angeles Times Sunday Magazine,* July 7, 2002, 14–20.

Talhelm, Jennifer. "Cowboy Judge in Indian Case Holds Little Back." Associated Press in LEXIS, November 28, 2005.

Whitty, Julia. "Accounting Coup." *Mother Jones,* September/October, 2005. http://www.motherjones.com/news/feature/2005/09/accounting_coup.html.

COHEN, FELIX
1907–1953
LEGAL SCHOLAR, GOVERNMENT OFFICIAL, ACTIVIST

Felix Solomon Cohen was the author of the *Handbook of Federal Indian Law* (1942, revised 1982), a basic reference book in its field for decades. Cohen also served as associate solicitor of the Interior Department, and chaired the department's Board of Appeals. He played an instrumental role in drafting the legal infrastructure of the Indian Claims Commission, founded in 1946. Cohen was especially active in securing for American Indians the right to vote as well as Social Security benefits.

Cohen authored a number of other books, including *Ethical Systems and Legal Ideals* (1933) and *Combating Totalitarian Propaganda: A Legal Appraisal* (1944). Elegant in speech, erudite in writing, and possessing a humane heart, Cohen sailed headlong into the political gauntlet that had once favored allotment and in his time sought termination of Native American nations as collective bodies.

Cohen's brilliant legal mind never lost a view of how the law affected human beings, especially Native Americans. He fought a political tide that had brought allotment and was bringing termination to American Indians, both of which removed large portions of their remaining land base. Cohen died of cancer at a very young age (46) at the height of his legal career, a year before termination legislation was passed by Congress.

Early Life

Cohen was born in New York City, the son of Morris Raphael Cohen, who was a legal philosopher, writer, and professor at City College, New York City. Cohen earned an AB degree (summa cum laude) in 1926 from City College, where he edited a student newspaper, *The Campus.* Cohen earned a PhD from Harvard in 1929 and a law degree from Columbia Law School in 1931.

Cohen became well known in the field of law well beyond cases concerning American Indians. In 1951, Cohen co-authored a textbook in law with his father, *Readings in Jurisprudence and Legal Philosophy.* The book contained the usual descriptions of European legal precedents, from Aristotle to the English Common Law, but also included a chapter titled "Law and Anthropology," which described the legal traditions of Native peoples in North America, including the Sioux and Cheyenne.

Cohen resigned from government service in 1948 to practice American Indian law in the New York City–Washington, D.C., firm of Riegelman, Stasser, Schwartz, and Spiegelberg. Cohen often represented the interests of the Montana Blackfeet, Oglala Sioux, All-Pueblo Council, and San Carlos Apaches. Cohen served as a visiting professor of law at Yale University and City College. He also taught at Rutgers Law School and the New School for Social Research.

Historian

In an article he wrote for *The American Scholar,* Cohen described the Iroquois role in shaping democracy in America. He probably honed his knowledge of these ideas through friendship with Mohawk culture bearer Ray Fadden of Onchiota, New York. For many years during the 1940s, Cohen maintained a cabin at Buck Pond, within walking distance of the Fadden home. John Kahionhes Fadden, Ray's son, recalled watching his father and Cohen walking in the woods and having long conversations.

On one occasion, Cohen compared the Native American influence on immigrants from Europe to the ways in which the Greeks had shaped Roman culture: "When the Roman legions conquered Greece, Roman historians wrote with as little imagination as did the European historians who have written of the white man's conquest of America. What the Roman historians did not see was that captive Greece would take captive conquering Rome [with] Greek science [and] Greek philosophy" (Cohen, 1952, 180).

In 1952, Cohen argued that "It is out of a rich Indian democratic tradition that the distinctive political ideals of American life emerged." These ideals included, said Cohen, "universal suffrage for women as for men, the pattern of states that we call federalism, the habit of treating chiefs as servants of the people instead of their masters, the insistence that the community must respect the diversity of men and the diversity of their dreams." "All these things," Cohen wrote, "were part of the American way of life before Columbus landed" (Cohen, 1952, 179–180).

Cohen wrote that American historians had too often paid attention to military victories and changing land boundaries, while failing to see that in agriculture, government, sport, education, and our views of nature and of other people, the first Americans also had helped shape their battlefield conquerors. American historians have seen America mainly as an imitation of Europe, Cohen asserted. In his view, the real epic of America is the yet unfinished story of what he called "the Americanization of the white man."

In the introduction to *The Legal Conscience,* Eugene V. Rostow wrote of Cohen:

> Felix Cohen died at forty-six, but he had already moved mountains as a public servant, as a practitioner, and as a law teacher and philosophical scholar of law. . . . Both the scholarly and practical aspects of Felix Cohen's work in law represent the same noble thought: the truth is with us . . . and it is something to be done, not said. Man's duty is goodness. And the men of law must forever labor to make the measure of ethics the measure of law. (Cohen, 1960, xv–xvi)

Cohen himself saw law as "a social tool." Cohen wrote that "law must be valued in terms of what it *does* in our social order, in terms of its effects upon human lives. If a given legal rule helps men to lead good lives, it is good; if it helps men to lead bad lives, it is bad" (Cohen, 1960, 30).

Opposition to Termination

Cohen's major political battle was against termination, the last official gasp, before the liberating currents of the 1960s, of an ideology that sought to expunge Native Americans' cultures from America's collective memory. It is significant that the termination bill was passed a year after Cohen's death. He had long fought it as one more attempt by special interests to lay their hands on what remained of Native American land. As with removal as well as allotment, the land-tenure implications of termination were largely ignored by its sponsors. Instead, also like removal and allotment, termination was enacted as a purported favor to the Indians, to propel them into the mainstream.

Passed as House Concurrent Resolution 108 (1953), termination legislation was aimed at dissolving remaining Indian lands and Indian communal relationships. The act was phrased in terms of equality, an attempt to make Indians subject to the same laws and entitled to the same privileges as other citizens of the United States. The Termination Act was designed to end Indians' status as wards of the United States. Between 1954 and 1966, 109 American Indian nations and bands were dissolved under the provisions of this legislation. Roughly 11,400 people lost their status as Indians belonging to Native American governments recognized by the U.S. government; 1.5 million acres of land was removed from trust status. Most of the terminated groups were small bands, but two of them, the Menominees of Wisconsin (with 3,270 members at termination) and the Klamaths of Oregon (with 2,133 members), were substantial-sized communities.

The Menominees of Wisconsin shared ownership of property valued at $34 million when their termination bill was enacted in 1953. By 1961, the federal government was out of Menominee County, and each of the Menominees' former members had become the owner of 100 shares of stock and a negotiable bond valued at $3,000, issued in the name of Menominee Enterprises, Inc. (MEI), a private enterprise that held the former nation's land and businesses. Governmentally, the Menominee Nation had become Menominee County, the smallest (in terms of population) and poorest (in terms of cash income) in Wisconsin.

As a county, Menominee was forced to raise taxes to pay for its share of services, including welfare, health services, utilities, and the like. The only taxable property owner in the county was MEI, which was forced to raise the funds to pay its tax bill by restructuring so that stockholders had to buy their homes, and the property on which they had been built. Most of the Menominees had little money saved except their $3,000 bonds, which were then sold to MEI to make the required residential purchases. Many Menominees also faced private-sector health costs (which earlier had been paid by the federal government), property taxes, and other expenses with no more money than they had before termination. Unemployment in Menominee County rose to levels that most of the United States had known only during the Great Depression.

By 1965, health indicators in Menominee County sounded like a reprint of the Meriam Report, issued in 1928, which described the massive extent of poverty on Indian reservations, almost four decades earlier. Tuberculosis afflicted nearly

35 percent of the population, and infant mortality was three times the national average. Termination, like allotment, was an abject failure at anything other than alienating Indian land. The termination of the Menominees was such an abysmal failure that in 1973 their federal trust relationship was re-established by Congress.

Remembrances

Cohen died of cancer October 19, 1953, at his home in New York City. At his funeral, which was held in Washington, D.C., pallbearers included Felix Frankfurter, an associate justice of the United States Supreme Court; Senator Hubert H. Humphrey; John Collier, former commissioner of Indian Affairs; and Oliver LaFarge, author and president of the Association on American Indian Affairs. Three days after his death, the *New York Times* editorially eulogized Cohen, saying that his death came at a time when the American Indian could least afford to lose a stalwart friend. The editorial mentioned efforts to alienate Indian land through termination legislation, and efforts to allow state jurisdiction over Native American lands, later expressed as Public Law 280.

Rostow evaluated Cohen's career:

> Felix Cohen was a teacher of power and purpose. He talked with his students as equals. He left them with a renewed awareness of the issues in law that spell the difference between life and death. . . . [H]is writings have been a force in the world's literature of legal philosophy and jurisprudence. In my judgment, his has been, and will remain, one of the best-balanced and one of the most creative voices in the literature of what is loosely called American legal realism. (Cohen, 1960, xvi)

Further Reading

Cohen, Felix. "Americanizing the White Man." *The American Scholar* 21, no. 2 (1952): 171–91.

Cohen, Felix. *The Legal Conscience: Selected Papers of Felix S. Cohen.* Edited by Lucy Kramer Cohen. New Haven, CT: Yale University Press, 1960.

COLLIER, JOHN
1884–1968
COMMISSIONER OF INDIAN AFFAIRS

John Collier served as Indian Commissioner (chief executive officer of the Bureau of Indian Affairs) for nearly the entire length of Franklin Roosevelt's presidency, 12 years (1933–1945), more time than any other person. Collier recognized that Native cultures and land bases should be maintained, but believed that they should be subject to the government's rules. The result of this synthesis was the Indian

Reorganization Act (IRA), passed by Congress and signed into law by President Roosevelt during 1934. Mixing liberalism with bureaucratic prerogative, the IRA offered Native people a measure of self-government, but demanded that those governments be created and conducted by its rules.

Through the IRA, Collier's policies initiated a Native resurgence in some degree. Some land was added to the national Native estate, reversing a century-and-a-half-long trend in the United States. While he was reviled frequently by political right-wingers for favoring Native communalism over assimilation, Collier also encountered considerable criticism from many Native American people for ignoring their traditional systems of governance. Even while it was criticized, the IRA stopped the allotment policies that had dismembered much of Native America's collective land base.

Removal of restrictions on Native religious freedom may have been Collier's most lasting accomplishment. It has been noted that, "In his memoirs Collier depicts ceremonial tribal dances as the core of Indian religion. . . . Through the dances are united body and soul, and self with the community, and self and tribe with nature and with God" (Talbot, 2007, 691–92). Upon taking office as commissioner, Collier immediately reversed the old Bureau policy of religious persecution by issuing Circular No. 2970, "Indian Religious Freedom and Indian Culture." He also issued an order curtailing missionary activity on reservations. Yet the issue of Indian religious freedom was excluded from the Indian Reorganization Act.

John Collier, Indian Affairs Commissioner, with Blackfeet leaders. (Library of Congress)

Early Life

Collier was born in Atlanta, Georgia, in 1884. His father, a lawyer and banker, was elected mayor of Atlanta. His mother, who was from New England, instilled in her son a love of literature and nature. Both parents died when Collier was a teenager. As a young man, Collier became interested in Native cultures as he traveled to the southern Appalachian Mountains. Collier began studies at Columbia University during 1902; he also studied at Woods Hole Marine Laboratory in Massachusetts. According to a biographer, Collier encountered a book by the Russian anarchist, Prince Peter Kropotkin, *Mutual Aid,* which provoked his interest in precapitalist societies (Talbot, 2007, 689).

Collier worked as a newspaper reporter following college. In 1907, however, he became a reform social worker; for 12 years Collier aided European immigrants on Manhattan Island. Collier also became civic secretary at the People's Institute, an immigrant-aid organization, where he used his journalistic skills editing its bulletin. The institute sponsored regular forums on relevant social issues for Jewish and Italian immigrants. Collier was a vigorous opponent of the Americanization policy that pressured immigrants to give up their native languages and cultures.

Witnessing debates in socialite Mabel Dodge's salon in New York City, Collier became acquainted with American Indian issues. By 1916, Collier and his family had moved to Los Angeles, California, where he directed the state's adult-education program. He lectured and organized public forums on progressive (left liberal) issues much like those of the People's Institute.

After a visit in 1920, Collier lived for two years at the Taos pueblo in New Mexico, developing an interest in the preservation of Pueblo culture and art. Collier later took a lecturer position at San Francisco State College. During 1923, having developed opposition to the Allotment Act, Collier played a major role in founding the American Indian Defense Association (AIDA), which presaged his later work in the Roosevelt Administration. His belief that allotment was misguided was confirmed by issuance of the Meriam Report in 1928. Harold Ickes, appointed as President Franklin D. Roosevelt's Secretary of the Interior, also had worked in the AIDA, and thus appointed Collier as Indian Commissioner.

The Indian Reorganization Act

The Indian Reorganization Act (IRA), as designed by Collier, was the most fundamental and far-reaching piece of legislation relating to Native Americans passed by Congress during the first half of the 20th century. It eliminated the allotment system (which broke Native American lands into individual holdings) and established governments for some reservations under systems that were partially self-governing. The IRA also established hiring preferences for Native Americans within the Bureau of Indian Affairs. Although it was criticized by some Native American groups, the IRA also was widely acclaimed during the 1930s as a step beyond the repression of the 19th century. For example, Native peoples were allowed by this act to resume their religious ceremonies openly, after a half-century of repression.

Before passage of the IRA, Native tribes and nations had been operated more or less as colonial enclaves by the United States. They were legally held to be subject to Congress and the president, delegated through the Bureau of Indian Affairs. According to legal scholars, "No local laws or assemblies were recognized, and a special police force was established to maintain federal supremacy. Traditional leadership was deposed, prosecuted, and sometimes killed when in conflict with federal Indian policy" (Barsh and Henderson, 1980, 209). Under the IRA, colonialism was relaxed somewhat. Leaders were no longer appointed, but were elected under constitutions that themselves were subject to U.S. government veto. In many cases, even individual ordinances passed by councils were subject to Interior Department review.

The IRA was introduced by Representative Edgar Howard of Nebraska and Senator Burton K. Wheeler of Montana, and became known popularly as the "Wheeler-Howard Act." The initial drafts of the 50-page bill were the work mainly of Collier, whom Roosevelt had appointed Commissioner of Indian Affairs. Before its provisions were modified during debates in the House and Senate, the IRA declared a federal policy that American Indians be encouraged to establish and control their own governments.

Another part of Collier's draft required Indian schools to develop materials relevant to Native American histories and cultures. The third title of the original bill stopped allotment of Indian land and restored title to "surplus" lands still held by the government, as well as the creation of reservations for Native American groups left without land by the usurpation of the previous century. Collier's bill also called for a Court of Indian Affairs. After compromise in the legislative process, many of Collier's ideas were discarded. Even so, the IRA established a new framework for Indian affairs, a hybrid of Collier's ideas and the older paternalistic system.

Native nations and tribes were allowed two years after passage of the IRA to accept or reject its provisions. Within that period, 258 elections were held, with 181 Native groups accepting the terms of the IRA and 77 voting negatively. Some of those that rejected the IRA objected to its requirements that the federal government approve policies on land use, selection of legal counsel, and other matters (including constitutions). While the act said that it upheld Native self-determination, it imposed a federal veto power over most major (and many minor) decisions that each Native government had proposed.

Opposition to the "Indian Raw Deal"

Frank Fools Crow, a Sioux, described the effects of the Indian New Deal: "Being beaten in war was bad enough. Yet being defeated and placed in bondage by programs we could not understand . . . is worse, especially when it is done to one of the most powerful, independent, and proudest of the Indian nations of North America" (Mails, 1990, 146–47). Fools Crow believed that, for the Sioux people, the "years from 1930–1940 rank as the worst ten years I know of." Fools Crow stated that the traditional family structure was crumbling because "Individual independence and . . . irresponsibility was being encouraged among the young people. Bootleggers were after the Indian's money, and were hauling cheap wine and whiskey onto the reservation by the truckload. . . . Even the young women were drinking now, and this assured a future tragedy of the worst possible proportions" (Mails, 1990, 146–47).

California was a major center of opposition to Collier's "Indian New Deal." One of the principal leaders of this opposition was Rupert Costo, a young Cahuilla who had attended college and had the respect of his people. Costo believed that the Indian New Deal was a "great drive to assimilate the American Indian." Costo believed that the IRA was merely a new form of Indian colonization because, in his view, genocide, treaty making and treaty breaking, substandard education, disruption of Indian culture and religion, and the Dawes Allotment Act had failed. Costo knew that partial assimilation already had taken place in Native American societies through the use of "certain technologies and techniques," but he knew that total assimilation, which meant "fading into the general society with a complete loss of" culture and identity, was another thing altogether. Costo called the IRA "The Indian Raw Deal" (Mails, 1990, 146).

By 1940, the IRA had come under enough criticism to prompt congressional hearings to consider its repeal. As of that date, according to an Indian law scholar, 252 Indian nations and bands had voted on the IRA as required by the act, including 99 small bands in California with a total population of less than 25,000. Seventy-seven groups had rejected it. Nationwide, 38,000 Indians voted in favor of IRA governments, while 24,000 voted against. Another 35,000 eligible voters did not take part, most as a silent protest against the IRA.

Some Native Americans asserted that Collier manipulated elections on reservations to favor acceptance of the IRA, imposing an Anglo-American model on peoples who had their own democratic procedures, undercutting the authority of traditional leaders. Collier's promotion of the IRA provoked formation of factions on some reservations that continue to this day.

Following retirement from government service in 1945, Collier published a summary of American Indian history, *Indians of the Americas* (1947). He also taught at City College of New York as a professor of sociology and anthropology until 1955. Collier died at Taos in 1968.

Further Reading

Barsh, Russel, and James Henderson. *The Road: Indian Tribes and Political Liberty.* Berkeley: University of California Press, 1980.

Collier, John. *From Every Zenith.* Denver, CO: Sage Books, 1963.

Kelly, Laurence C. "Indian New Deal." In *Native America in the Twentieth Century: An Encyclopedia,* edited by Mary B. Davis, 218–20. New York: Garland, 1996.

Mails, Thomas E. *Fools Crow.* Lincoln: University of Nebraska Press, 1990.

Philip, Kenneth R. *John Collier's Crusade for Indian Reform: 1920–1954.* Tucson: University of Arizona Press, 1977.

Stefon, Frederick J. "The Indians' Zarathustra: An Investigation into the Philosophical Roots of John Collier's New Deal Educational and Administrative Policies." *The Journal of Ethnic Studies* Part I: 11, no. 5 (Fall 1983): 1–28, Part II: 11.

Talbot, Steve. "Collier, John." In *The Encyclopedia of American Indian History,* edited by Bruce E. Johansen and Barry M. Pritzker, 689–92. Santa Barbara, CA: ABC-CLIO, 2007.

COON COME, MATTHEW
BORN 1956 INNU/CREE
POLITICAL LEADER

Born in a bush tent on his father's trap-line near Mistissini, in northern Quebec, Matthew Coon Come became grand chief of the Crees at a time when they were rallying against ruination of their land by hydropower development in northern Quebec. Later, he played a major role in brokering a compromise. In so doing, Coon Come became one of Canada's best-known indigenous leaders in modern times.

Coon Come's Cree name is *Ne-Ha-Ba-Nus,* "The One Who Wakes Up with the Sun." His parents raised him in a traditional Cree manner. At age 6, however, Coon Come was removed to a residential school. Later Coon Come attended Trent University, where he studied political science, and McGill University, where his studies emphasized law. At the age of 16, he began to attend meetings of community elders as they discussed Phase One of the James Bay Project, a system of dams that was being built to supply eastern Canada and New England with electricity.

Coon Come also played an important role as the United Nations drafted a Universal Declaration of the Right of Indigenous Peoples. During the Meech Lake and Charlottetown Accord discussions in Canada, he contributed to negotiations on constitutional amendments meant to guarantee Aboriginal and treaty rights. While these accords failed, Coon Come's contributions raised standards for future negotiations regarding Canadian indigenous rights.

Coon Come first was elected as grand chief and chairman of the Grand Council of the Crees in Quebec during 1987. He received a National Aboriginal Achievement Award in 1995. In 1998, he received an honorary Doctor of Laws degree from Trent University. Coon Come was elected National Chief of the Canadian Assembly of First Nations between 2000 and 2003. He received the Goldman Prize, which has been called "the Nobel Prize of environmental awards," in 1994.

Coon Come chaired the Cree Housing Corporation, as well as the James Bay Eeyou Corporation, which manages more than $100 million in assets. He also chaired the James Bay Native Development Corporation, and has assisted in starting more than 50 businesses in the Cree communities.

Coon Come married Maryann Matoush in 1976; they have three daughters and two sons.

Cree Indian chief Matthew Coon Come speaks at a news conference in New York City on October 8, 1991, after delivering 50,000 signatures to city hall, calling for cancellation of the Hydro-Quebec power project to deliver electricity to New York City. (AP/Wide World Photos)

James Bay Project

During the 1970s, planners and engineers at Hydro-Quebec planned to make their utility the largest supplier of electricity in the world. The utility planned to harness dozens of rivers flowing into James Bay, reshaping the ecology of an area the size of Iowa for electrical generation. The James Bay area is home to 10,000 Cree and 6,000 Inuit people who were not consulted before construction began on "James Bay I." James Bay hydroelectric development was first interjected into the Crees' lives April 30, 1971, when Quebec Premier Robert Bourassa (after whom part of the complex later was named) announced its inception to the people of the province.

James Bay I involved nine dams, 206 dikes, five major reservoirs, and the diversion of five major rivers over an area roughly the size of Connecticut. Rotting vegetation in the area had released about 184 million tons of carbon dioxide and methane into the atmosphere by 1990, adding to global warming. In the meantime, James Bay I had saddled each of Hydro-Quebec's ratepayers with an average of $3,500 in debt. James Bay I uprooted 2,000 Crees from Chisasibi Island (also known as Fort George Island). "It's painful to look at young people caught between two worlds. I've seen their faces, knowing that their heritage is under water. It was a whole disintegration of the spirit—all that was drowned," said Coon Come ("Canadian Indians," 1990, A-2).

Hunting and fishing are the heart of the Cree and Inuit economies. The Crees have traditionally hunted migratory birds, particularly during the spring, as well as terrestrial mammals such as moose. The Crees fish the rivers in the region and trap fur-bearing mammals such as muskrat and beaver. Traditionally, Inuit also harvest fish and marine mammals such as seals, walrus, and whales. Some communities also depend heavily on caribou.

The Crees and Inuits, who at first were scarcely even recognized as long-time occupants of the land by Hydro-Quebec, soon challenged the construction project in court. They argued that it was a matter of life and death not only for traditional cultures, but also for the peoples themselves. The construction ruined many traditional hunting areas, and replaced them with poisoned earth laced with life-threatening mercury compounds.

The Crees and Inuits of northern Quebec signed a comprehensive claims agreement (formally named the James Bay and Northern Quebec Agreement) with the Canadian federal and Quebec provincial governments in 1975. The Crees entered agreements (in essence, treaties) with the governments of Quebec and Canada, but they found the terms of these treaties being violated by the ecological consequences of hydroelectric construction.

The 1975 agreement provided the Crees $22 million (Canadian) and the right to continue to hunt, fish, and trap in their usual territories. Not even Hydro-Quebec anticipated that its plans would make a significant portion of the territory unsustainable for many of those activities.

The Crees' Homeland Transformed

Coon Come led Crees who found that the James Bay project's first phase had transformed large areas of their homelands. Rivers that once spawned large numbers of fish were reduced to trickles or stopped entirely by the creation of reservoirs behind energy-generating dams. What fish survived were too toxic to eat. Forests were clear-cut and burned, adding greenhouse gases to the atmosphere. More than 10,000 caribou drowned after Hydro-Quebec's rearrangement of the landscape spilled deep water across their migration routes. Hydro-Quebec called the deaths an "act of God" (Biegert, 1995, n.p.). This incident was yet another reminder that while hydroelectricity is often touted as clean energy that does not emit pollution or directly increase the atmosphere's overload of greenhouse gases, it is not environmentally benign.

Mercury contamination occurs when vast areas of land are disrupted. Plant decay associated with the James Bay project's earthmoving caused large amounts of ordinary mercury to become methyl mercury, a bio-accumulative poison. Rotting vegetation accelerated microbial activity that converts elemental mercury in previously submerged glacial rocks to toxic methyl mercury. By 1990, many Crees were carrying in their bodies 20 times the level of methyl mercury considered safe by the World Health Organization. Hydro-Quebec did not anticipate the accelerated release of methyl mercury into the waters of the region, contaminating the entire food chain for the Crees, Inuits, birds, fish, and other animals. This type of mercury poisoning can cause loss of vision, numbness of limbs, uncontrollable shaking, and chronic brain damage. By the late 1980s, the Quebec government's health ministry was telling the Crees not to eat fish from their homeland.

Coon Come told Hydro-Quebec, on behalf of the Crees, that fishing represents more than sustenance. Fishing was not a sport for the Crees. Fishing activities are important in knitting family and community, he maintained. Mercury contamination thus disrupted an entire way of life. Before 1978, concentrations of mercury in 700-millimeter pike was approximately 0.6 microgram per kilogram. After completion of Phase I, the concentrations increased gradually. In 1988, concentrations were 3 milligrams per kilogram, five times the original concentration and six times the maximum permissible concentration for commercial fish (e.g., for human consumption) in Canada (Dumont, 1995).

Coon Come and other Crees arranged to have the toxicity of their bodies tested. By 1984, the concentration of mercury in the hair of Crees at all ages was much higher than in surveys conducted during the 1970s. During 1993 and 1994, the Cree Board of Health completed an assay of mercury levels in the hair of the Crees. This survey revealed a wide variation in exposure levels between different communities: "If the 6 microgram per kilogram (mg/kg) maximum hair concentration recommended by the World Health Organization is used, at least half of the population of several communities is over that limit. In 1984, when Whapmagoostui (the Great Whale Hydro-electric Project) was surveyed, 98 percent of the population surveyed had mercury concentrations above 6 mg/kg" (Dumont, 1995). Mercury levels increased generally with a person's age. Persons recognized as trappers in their communities consistently tested for higher mercury concentrations. It was noted that "during the past ten years, the number of individuals with high mercury concentrations has decreased considerably," due in large part to programs persuading the Crees to avoid eating tainted fish (Dumont, 1995).

Public Forums

Coon Come led the Crees into public forums in New York and Vermont, where a large part of the electricity generated by Hydro-Quebec would be sold, to tell people that they shared complicity in the devastation of northern Quebec. The Crees also urged electricity consumers and utilities to conserve, and to consider other sources of supply. Several non-Indian environmental groups joined with the Grand Council of the Cree against the James Bay projects. In New York and New England, electricity users were urged to conserve energy to eliminate a need for more generating capacity. Coon Come asserted that: "Beavers are the only ones who should be allowed to build dams in our territory" (Biegert, 1995).

The Crees had came to this conclusion as scientists from Quebec's health ministry warned everyone (especially women of childbearing age) not to eat local fish, which were becoming contaminated with methyl mercury. Predatory fish, such as the pike, had been accumulating a great deal of methyl mercury in their bodies since Hydro-Quebec began its ambitious plans to reduce the natural landscape of northern Quebec into a shape and a function suitable for generating electricity. Until then, fish had been a major constituent of the Cree diet for thousands of years.

Said Coon Come: "Nobody asked us or told us, but three or four times from 1670 on, our people and our lands were handed between kings and companies and countries. We found out about all of this when they came to build the dams and when the courts told us that we did not have any rights, that we were squatters on our own land" (Coon Come, 2001).

Coon Come recalled:

> In the early 1970s, I was a young student in Montreal when I read in the newspaper that Hydro-Quebec . . . was going to build a hydroelectric mega-project of the century in our territory, by diverting and damming the rivers and flooding our traditional lands. I looked at a map and saw that my family's trap-line and our community was going to be underwater! I immediately returned home, and as a result of a speech I made from the back of a community hall I was launched on my political career. (Coon Come, 2001)

"Twenty-five years later," Coon Come recalled in the year 2000, "Our people know that the treaty we signed was more broken than honored. Many of the most important promises, such as for economic involvement and development, for protection of the environment and our traditional economy and way of life, and for housing, community development, and infrastructure have been twisted, ignored, or broken" (Coon Come, 2001).

Ten Cree and Inuit activists paddled a 25-foot combination kayak-canoe from Ottawa to New York City during the spring of 1990, crossing the Quebec-Vermont border at the northern end of Lake Champlain, timing their arrival in Central Park to coincide with Earth Day. In mid-April, 1993, Native leaders and their supporters bought a full-page advertisement opposing James Bay II in the *New York Times*. Robert Kennedy, Jr., and Coon Come held a joint press conference, also in New York City, yet another high-profile action that turned more New Yorkers against the project. New York State then yielded to growing consumer protests and canceled a $17 billion export contract with Hydro-Quebec.

On November 18, 1994 (a few months after Hydro-Quebec's president Armand Couture had asserted that electricity would begin to flow from James Bay II in 2003), Quebec Premier Jacques Parizeau said that the project was being shelved "indefinitely." He told the press: "We've not saying never, but that project is on ice for quite a while" ("Quebec Will Shelve," 1994, 7). The decision was made after two governmental review committees said that Hydro-Quebec "would have to go back to the drawing board to correct 'major inadequacies' in its environmental assessment of the project." Hydro-Quebec had been stopped by a blizzard of paper; company officials complained that its environmental-impact study, which ran to 5,000 pages and took 11 years to compile, had cost $190 million ("Quebec Will Shelve," 1994, 7).

Great Whale Redux

The Great Whale (James Bay II) hydroelectric project was revived on a reduced scale during 2001 after having been shelved seven years earlier. The new proposal, brokered by Coon Come and other Cree leaders, involved diversion of the Great Whale River at its headwaters, Lac Bienville, at an estimated cost of $350 million. Under this plan, the river's water would be redirected through 10 kilometers of canals into Hydro-Quebec's La Grande hydroelectric complex, increasing water flow through its turbines to produce power. In 1997, Hydro-Quebec had proposed to divert the Great Whale and, for the first time, sought the Crees' consent and offered them a minority partnership in the project. This proposal was shelved after 92 percent of Whapmagoostui Crees voted against any development projects on the river. The new proposal retained the diversion idea, but proposed that the Crees would own the facility once its debt was paid off.

Coon Come was a key negotiator as Quebec's government and Natives in the James Bay region signed an agreement in principle October 23, 2001, to end a bitter legal dispute over hydroelectric development in the area and make further resource development in northern Quebec possible. Under the agreement, the Crees received a promise of $3.5 billion (Canadian) worth of natural-resources royalties from the province over 50 years as they agreed not to take up legal action against a major power project in the region. "This agreement constitutes, I am sure, the basis of a great peace between Quebec and the Crees," Quebec Premier Bernard Landry said before a signing ceremony with Cree Grand Chief Ted Moses. "This is an historic turning point and a truly profound revolutionary vision for the Cree and aboriginal peoples generally," Moses said (Conférence, 2001).

The project, which had been on hold for several years because of opposition from the Crees, should produce 1,300 megawatts, or about 15 percent, of the power from the entire James Bay area, and create about 8,000 jobs during six years of construction.

The Crees agreed to drop their environmental lawsuits in part because legal fees were costing them $9 million a year, but also because many of the cases were faring badly in the Canadian court system. Courts in Quebec had ruled against the Crees on forestry issues, as well as their opposition to hydroelectric development on the Eastman River. The agreement also was less harmful to Cree hunting and fishing lands than earlier plans; it saved roughly 8,000 square kilometers of land from being flooded, according to Coon Come. "We want jobs," he said after the new agreement was negotiated. "We want a say in where development takes place [and] what happens in our own backyard" (Matteo, 2002).

During late January 2002, Quebec Crees voted in favor of the $3.4-billion deal with the provincial government. Of the 6,500 eligible voters, 69.35 percent, or 3,106, voted in favor of the deal, with 30.65 percent, or 1,373, against.

Further Reading

Biegert, Claus. "A People Called Empty." In *Amazon of the North: James Bay Revisited,* by Rainer Wittenborn and Claus Biegert. Program for Show, Santa Fe Center for Contemporary Arts, August 4 through September 5, 1995, unpaginated.

"Canadian Indians Paddle to New York City to Protest Quebec Power Plant." *Syracuse Post-Standard,* April 5, 1990, A-2.

"Conférence de presse de M. Bernard Landry, premier ministre du Québec, et de M. Ted Moses, grand chef du Grand Conseil des cris. Le mardi 23 octobre 2001." Government of Quebec. October 23, 2001. http://www.assnat.qc.ca/fra/conf-presse/2001/011023BL. HTM.

Coon Come, Matthew. *Remarks of the National Chief Matthew Coon Come: People's Summit of the Americas Environment Forum.* April 18, 2001. http://www.afn.ca/Press%20 Realeses%20%20speeches/april_18.htm.

Dumont, C. *Proceedings of 1995 Canadian Mercury Network Workshop. Mercury and Health: The James Bay Cree.* Cree Board of Health and Social Services. Montreal, 1995. http://www.cciw.ca/eman-temp/reports/publications/mercury95/part4.html.

Dumont, Charles, Manon Girard, François Bellavance, and Francine Noël. "Mercury Levels in the Cree Population of James Bay, Quebec, from 1988 to 1993/94." *Canadian Medical Association Journal* 158 (June 2, 1998): 1439–45. http://www.cma.ca/cmaj/ vol-158/issue-11/1439.htm.

Grinde, Donald A., Jr., and Bruce E. Johansen. *Ecocide of Native America: Environmental Destruction of Indian Lands and Peoples.* Santa Fe, NM: Clear Light, 1995.

LaDuke, Winona. "Tribal Coalition Dams Hydro-Quebec Project." *Indian Country Today,* July 21, 1993, A-3.

Matteo, Enzo di. "Damned Deal: Cree Leaders Call Hydro Pact Signed in Secret a Monstrous Sellout." *Now Magazine* [Toronto], February 2002. http://www.nowtoronto. com/issues/2002-02-14/news_story.php.

"Quebec Will Shelve Huge Hydroelectric Project Indefinitely." Associated Press in *Omaha World-Herald,* November 19, 1994, 7.

Roslin, Alex. "Crees Revive Hydro Project." *Montreal Gazette,* January 21, 2000. http:// www.montrealgazette.com/news/pages/010121/5036705.html.

Costo, Rupert
1906–1989 Cahuilla
Scholar, Activist, Publisher, and Journalist

The Cahuilla scholar, activist, and publisher Rupert Costo, with his wife Cherokee Jeanette Henry, exercised enormous influence in 20th-century Native American affairs with a newspaper and scholarly journal, as well as in book publishing.

Costo also entered national debate as a vocal critic of the "Indian New Deal" (the Indian Reorganization Act of 1934). In addition, he served as tribal chairman of the Cahuilla during the 1950s. Costo and Henry founded the American Indian Historical Society in 1964. Thereafter, both became important figures in American Indian scholarship and publishing. They also edited a newspaper, *Wassaja,* named in honor of Carlos Montezuma, an early 20th-century activist and physician, as well as a quarterly scholarly journal, *The Indian Historian,* and *Weewish Tree,* a magazine for Indian young people.

Costo was born in 1906 (the exact date is not known) in Anza, Riverside County, California. His father Yisdro planted the first navel orange tree in the area, which heralded the growth of the local citrus industry. As a young man, Rupert Costo was best known as an athlete, playing semiprofessional basketball. Attending Riverside City College in 1927, he met Judge John Gabbert, an enduring friend and mentor. Costo also played football, first at Haskell Institute, then at California's Whittier College. His most notable teammate there was Richard M. Nixon, who would become U.S. president in 1968, re-elected in 1972, before resigning in disgrace.

In his 20s, 30s, and 40s, Costo worked at a wide variety of jobs: as a state highway engineer, hydrologist, meteorologist, and surveyor. Only later in life did he come to the study of American Indian history, meeting and marrying Henry, an Eastern Cherokee, in the late 1950s. Henry had run away from home at the age of 17, and, by the 1930s, was working as a police reporter at the *Detroit Free Press*. She later moved to Corona, California, and again worked in newspapers, then as a public relations spokesperson for Blue Cross before meeting Costo.

Together, they coauthored several books, including *The Missions of California: A Legacy of Genocide* (1987), *Natives of the Golden State: The California Indians* (1995), *Indian Treaties: Two Centuries of Dishonor* (1977), and *A Thousand Years of American Indian Storytelling* (1981). Costo wrote other books, among them *Textbooks and the American Indian* (1970) and *Redmen of the Golden West* (1970).

As newspaper editors and publishers, Costo and Henry often advocated controversial issues involving repatriation of Native remains and protection of burial grounds. One of their favorite issues was correction of stereotypes in textbooks. Costo edited a book on the subject, *Textbooks and the American Indian* (1970).

The Indian Historical Society published 52 books, often exploring subjects that mainstream publishing houses ignored. One of the society's books, Donald A. Grinde, Jr.'s *The Iroquois and the Founding of the American Nation* (1977), explored influences of the Iroquois Confederacy on the founders of the United States, including Benjamin Franklin. Grinde's was the first book-length study of the subject, which later became an important and controversial element in debates regarding multicultural education.

Costo's writings advocated Native sovereignty via land and water rights. Costo and Henry endowed a chair in Native American studies at the University of California–Riverside (UCR) (the first chair to be endowed by an American Indian) with $400,000 from his estate shortly before his death in 1989. Costo and Henry established a library of American Indian books there. Costo also played a major role in the establishment of the UCR campus itself. In 1994, UCR named its student services building Costo Hall.

Further Reading

Costo, Rupert. *Redmen of the Golden West.* San Francisco: American Indian Historical Society, 1970.

Costo, Rupert. *Textbooks and the American Indian.* San Francisco: American Indian Historical Society, 1970.

Costo, Rupert, and Jeanette Henry. *Indian Treaties: Two Centuries of Dishonor.* San Francisco: American Indian Historical Society, 1977.

Costo, Rupert, and Jeanette Henry. *A Thousand Years of American Indian Storytelling.* San Francisco: American Indian Historical Society, 1981.

Costo, Rupert, and Jeanette Henry. *The Missions of California: A Legacy of Genocide.* San Francisco: American Indian Historical Society, 1987.

Costo, Rupert and Jeanette Henry. *Natives of the Golden State: The California Indians.* San Francisco: American Indian Historical Society, 1995.

Grinde, Donald A., Jr. *The Iroquois and the Founding of the American Nation.* San Francisco: American Indian Historical Society, 1977.

CRANDELL, BARBARA
BORN 1929 OHIO CHEROKEE
ELDER AND ACTIVIST

Born Barbara Holbrook on May 15, 1929, in Big Jenny Hollow, a small dale in the mountains near the tiny town of Davy, West Virginia, Grandmother Barbara Crandell is today the Head Mother of the Ohio Cherokees and a well-known community activist in Ohio mound preservation and repatriation.

A Bird Clan Cherokee and birth speaker of the language, Crandell grew up very poor, especially during the Great Depression. Her mother, Lora McDowell Holbrook, farmed in the old way, teaching her children traditions as much by example as by profession. The local populace, Native, black, and white, were primarily miners, whom her father, Cambell Holbrook, helped organize. One day in 1926, as Holbrook and some miners were meeting in a drift-mouth mine, company-hired thugs blew it up, with Holbrook inside. Although he survived this attempt on his life, he did not live long thereafter, leaving his wife and five children to survive as best they might through the family truck farm and local game hunting.

Marrying Frank Crandell in 1954, Crandell bought a farm dating to 1848 near Thornville, Ohio, in 1962. There, she supported her family very successfully by breeding, raising, and training standard-bred race horses for the next 35 years. An original "horse whisperer," Crandell bred numerous winning horses, the last and most favorite of them being Cragenmore. Rather than sell this magnificent horse, as is customary, Crandell kept him until his death at age 25, still, she said, as handsome as the day he raced invitational trots all over the country.

In 1980, Crandell's only son was gravely injured in a motorcycle accident, losing one leg at the hip and the use of the other. As he hovered between life and death on July 29, 1980, Crandell went out at dawn to pray at the Octagon Mound at Newark, a monument her people had built thousands of years before. She pledged "Creator" to dedicate the remainder of her life to working for Native people, if her son lived. He survived, and Crandell has since honored her promise.

Crandell has been quite famous as a thorn in the side of those who show less than proper respect for her people, their culture, and their mounds. In July 1992, when archaeologist Dr. Dee Ann Wymer came from Bloomberg University with several students to dig through the Great Circle Mound at Newark, Crandell set up camp beside the mound. When other Natives heard that "Grandma is at the mound," they joined her, eventually swelling into a large camp of more than one hundred Indians who stayed, holding vigil, through 11 days and nights. Ultimately, the governor and his men nervously came to assess the situation. The archaeologists hurriedly finished their dig, very disgruntled about the massive opposition.

In October of 1992, Crandell brought together a handful of Indians, including many people indigenous to Ohio, to form the Native American Alliance of Ohio. The organization has since grown to thousands and been very active in protecting Indian mound sites in the state of Ohio as well as Native rights to the telling of Native history and the interpreting of Native culture.

Crandell deeply protested the members-only golf course located on Newark's Circle-Octagon complex, a noted wonder of the ancient world built by her people. In June 2002, she went to the Octagon Mound to pray, and the Moundbuilders Country Club had her arrested for trespassing. She was roughed up in police custody. In the trial that followed, she was not allowed to present a defense; the judge called for a directed verdict of guilty from the jury. Crandell refused to pay the fine, but her Native friends would not allow a 72-year-old grandmother to be imprisoned. Over her objections, they paid the fine. This case made national news.

Crandell has authored one book, *Sacred Wind* (2003), which recounts the history of her maternal grandfather.

Barbara Alice Mann

Further Reading

Crandell, Barbara. *Sacred Wind.* Salt Lake City, UT: American Book Publishing, 2003.

CRUZ, JOSEPH DE LA
1937–2000 QUINAULT
POLITICAL LEADER

When long-time Quinault leader Joseph Burton de la Cruz died April 16, 2000, at age 62, *Canku Ota—A Newsletter Celebrating Native America* called him "a giant cedar of a man who helped lead his Quinault Indian Nation and other Native American tribes toward self-government" ("Joseph Burton de la Cruz," 2000). De la Cruz spent much of his life working for fishing and other treaty rights, improving health care for Native Americans, and obtaining a measure of sovereignty. He did all of these things in an often innovative and striking manner.

"Everywhere you look among Native Americans, you see Joe's imprint," said Suzan Harjo, a Cheyenne-Muskogee Indian activist in Washington, D.C. "I am in disbelief. It is a heavy blow when you lose one of those Great Cedars" (McGann, 2000). "Joe was involved in so many issues it's hard to say what his biggest accomplishment was, there's too many to choose just one," said Pearl Capoeman Baller, who followed de la Cruz as president of Quinault Indian Nation. "Everybody turns to Joe de la Cruz. He was there to protect rights for all tribes, not just Quinault. Joe was one of the greatest Indian leaders in the United States, and he worked endlessly for the Quinault people" ("Joseph Burton de la Cruz," 2000).

Reviving the Quinault Reservation

Cruz emerged from the rainforests of coastal Washington State to become a veteran of 25 years as president of the Quinault Nation. He grew up on the Quinault reservation, a local athlete from a well-known family, and son of a local labor leader. During the 1950s, he left the reservation to join the U.S. Army; after that, he worked for the federal Housing and Urban Development Administration in Portland, Oregon. Quinault elders then summoned de la Cruz home to assume leadership of a tribal economic and political revival. "When I returned home, in 1967, the fisheries were pretty much down, the timber industry was in decline, the mills that people had normally worked in were shut down. Real-estate speculators were coming onto the reservation and buying inexpensive land . . . and the tribe didn't like that," de la Cruz said (Trahant, 2006). De la Cruz initiated dramatic changes in Quinault government and took a leading position in building economic infrastructure.

De la Cruz also achieved prominence outside the reservation by serving as president of the National Tribal Chairmen's Association (1977–81) and as head of the National Congress of American Indians (1981–85). De la Cruz stepped down from Quinault leadership in 1994 to make way for Pearl Capoeman Baller, the Quinaults' first woman chief in modern times.

His niece recalled that de la Cruz once drove his truck onto a bridge to blockade logging trucks at the border of the Quinault Indian Reservation in order to protest Bureau of Indian Affairs land-use practices that discriminated against his people ("Joseph Burton de la Cruz," 2000).

De la Cruz advocated a policy by which Native reservation governments received line-item appropriations from government agencies, which placed control over important services (police, health, land use, and education, among others) in their hands. He worked to implement the Boldt decision, handed down in 1974 and confirmed by the U.S. Supreme Court in 1979, that enforced Native treaty-fishing rights.

Confrontation on a Beach

In 1969, de la Cruz ordered closure of a 26-mile-long beach on the Quinault reservation on the Pacific Ocean north of Aberdeen to all people from outside, saying that the visitors spread litter and marred local landmarks with graffiti. National television cameras rolled August 25, 1969, as CBS News anchorman Walter Cronkite described the Quinaults' confrontation with white surfers. For 10,000 years, the

Quinaults had drawn their sustenance from this beach, said Cronkite, "Then the white man came and left his mark—bottles, cans, and even abandoned cars strewn along the beach" (Trahant, 2006). Quinault volunteers then hauled away tons of garbage on flatbed trucks. "This story was much more than a beach cleanup," said Mark Trahant, a Native American himself, and a journalist who later was editorial-page editor at the *Seattle Post-Intelligencer.* "It represented a fundamental shift in the way American Indians thought about themselves" (Trahant, 2006).

De la Cruz played an active role in founding many tribal enterprises, including forestry management, land restoration, housing construction, and seafood processing. Between 1985 and 1988, de la Cruz also became influential in fisheries management on an international level as a mediator between the United States, Canada, and Native nations in the Pacific Salmon Fisheries Treaty.

De la Cruz suffered a fatal heart attack April 16, 2000, while waiting at Seattle-Tacoma International Airport to catch a flight to Oklahoma for a conference addressing Native American governance and health issues. He was survived by his wife, Dorothy, and daughters Gayle de la Cruz, Tina de la Cruz, and Lisa Kyle, as well as sons Joe de la Cruz and Steve de la Cruz. De la Cruz's extended family included seven grandchildren and two great-grandchildren.

"His whole life was dedicated to Indian welfare and Indian concerns," said Bernie Whitebear, of United Indians of All Tribes, an urban Indian organization in Seattle. "The self-governance conference that he was going to was really appropriate. He died with his boots on. A lot of the advances that the tribes are witnessing today in regard to self-governance are a result of his early involvement in that area," Whitebear said. "He was a leader in the indigenous people's efforts throughout the world, including Canada, South America" ("Joseph Burton de la Cruz," 2000; McGann, 2000).

Further Reading

"Joseph Burton de la Cruz." *Canku Ota—A Newsletter Celebrating Native America.* April 22, 2000—Issue 08. http://www.turtletrack.org/Issues00/Co04222000/CO_04222000_Delacruz.htm.

McGann, Chris. "Indian-rights Advocate Dies on Way to Conference." *Seattle Post-Intelligencer,* April 17, 2000. http://seattlepi.nwsource.com/local/joe17.shtml.

Trahant, Mark. "Peace Chiefs at Work: Stories about Remarkable American Indian Leadership in This Generation." Speech Transcript, Center for the American West. June 12, 2006. http://www.centerwest.org/events/identity/pdf/trahant.pdf.

CURTIS, CHARLES
1860–1936 KANSA AND OSAGE
U.S. SENATOR AND VICE PRESIDENT

As a Republican politician, Charles Curtis, who was one-eighth Kansa and Osage, served as a member of the U.S. House of Representatives and as the first U.S.

Senator with Native American ancestry. Curtis became a leading spokesman for some assimilationist measures, including the General Allotment Act. He also served as U.S. vice president under Herbert Hoover.

Born on Indian land that later was incorporated into North Topeka, Kansas, Curtis was the son of Oren A. Curtis (an abolitionist and Civil War Union cavalry officer) and Helen Pappan (Kaw/Osage). His mother died when he was three; he was raised under the care of his maternal grandmother on the Kaw Reservation and in Topeka. Following an attack on Kaw Indians at Council Grove by Cheyenne militants, Curtis left the Indian mission school on the Kaw Reservation in 1868 and returned to Topeka, where he attended Topeka High School. For several years as a young man, he was a jockey and worked odd jobs until he met A. H. Case, a Topeka lawyer. Studying the law and working as a law clerk, Curtis was admitted to the Kansas bar in 1881.

Entering politics as a Republican, Curtis was elected county prosecuting attorney in 1884 and 1886. From 1892 to 1906, he served eight terms in the U.S. House of Representatives. He authored the Curtis Act of 1898 that dissolved some Native American reservation governments, in an attempt to force the assimilation on American Indian peoples. The Curtis Act brought the allotment policy to the Five Civilized Tribes of Oklahoma, who had been exempted from the Dawes Allotment Act of 1887. The act also empowered the Dawes Commission, which had been created in 1893, to extinguish Native title to lands in Indian Territory. Once Native title was eliminated, the Dawes Commission allotted reservation lands to individuals. Curtis's endeavors to foster allotment and assimilation were opposed by many Native American leaders of Indian Territory. In essence, the Curtis Act paved the way for Oklahoma statehood in 1907 by destroying tribal land titles and governments there.

Curtis served in the U.S. Senate from 1907 to 1913 and 1915 to 1929. During his tenure in the Senate, Curtis was Republican party whip (1915–24) and then majority leader (1924–29). As chairman of the Senate Committee on Indian Affairs in 1924, Curtis sponsored the Indian Citizenship Act. After an unsuccessful campaign for the presidential nomination, he ran as vice president with Herbert Hoover in 1928, and served in that capacity from 1929 to 1933. Curtis was a deft politician who used his Native American ancestry for personal advantage, even as his political adversaries mocked him as "the Injun." Although

Charles Curtis, U.S. vice president, senator, and Congressional representative. (Library of Congress)

a fiscal conservative, Curtis supported veterans' benefits, farm relief, women's suffrage, and national prohibition.

The Hoover-Curtis ticket's bid for a second term was defeated in 1932 by Franklin Delano Roosevelt. Upon his retirement from politics in 1933, Curtis had served longer in the nation's Capitol than any active politician at that time. After leaving public office, Curtis headed the short-lived National Republican League and practiced law in Washington, D.C. He was also president of a gold mining company in New Mexico. In 1936, Curtis died of heart disease.

Further Reading

Johansen, Bruce E. *Native Peoples of North America.* Westport, CT: Praeger, 2005.

Schlup, Leonard. "Charles Curtis: The Vice-President from Kansas." *Manuscripts* 35 (Summer 1983): 183–201.

Unrau, William E. *Mixed Bloods and Tribal Dissolution: Charles Curtis and the Quest for Indian Identity.* Lawrence: University Press of Kansas, 1989.

D

Deer Cloud, Susan
Born 1950 Métis/Mohawk, Seneca, and Blackfeet
Writer and Poet

Susan Deer Cloud, an award-winning writer and poet, was born in Livingston Manor, New York, October 20, 1950. A Métis Indian of Mohawk (Wolf Clan), Blackfeet, and some Seneca blood, she grew up in the Catskill Mountains and still regards those mountains as her primary home.

Deer Cloud received her BA degree in general literature and creative writing (with highest academic honors) and her MA degree in English literature and creative writing from Binghamton University, where she has occasionally taught literature, rhetoric, and creative writing. In 2009, she was enrolled in an MFA program in creative writing with a concentration in poetry at Goddard College in Vermont.

Deer Cloud is the recipient of a National Endowment for the Arts Literature Fellowship in Poetry, a New York State Foundation for the Arts Literature Fellowship in Poetry, a Chenango Council for the Arts Individual Artist's Grant, and a scholarship to the

Susan Deer Cloud, Native American poet and fiction writer. (Susan Deer Cloud)

Resilience of the Human Spirit, an International Gathering of Poets. She also has served as a panelist for NYSFA.

She has received various kinds of recognition for individual poems, including first prize in the Allen Ginsberg International Poetry Contest (twice); *Prairie Schooner*'s Readers' Choice Award; a third prize from *Chiron Review*; a second prize in Eve of St. Agnes Poetry Competition; honorable mention for poems in the Winning Writers Anti-War Contest, *Many Mountains Moving* Poetry Competition; and *Artemis* Poetry Competition. Her anthology *Confluence* (2008) was given a Wordcraft Circle Editor's Award, and she has been honored with a Certificate of Achievement by Binghamton University for making "a significant contribution to advancing the awareness of women of color." She is listed in *Who's Who among American Women* and is an adviser to *Yellow Medicine Review, a Journal of Indigenous Art, Literature and Thought.*

Deer Cloud's books are *Car Stealer* (2009) and *The Last Ceremony* (2007); multicultural anthology *Confluence* (editor, 2006); *I Was Indian: Words from Turtle Island for the Next Seven Generations to Come* (2009); *Yellow Medicine Review, a Journal of Indigenous Art, Literature and Thought,* Spring 2008 (guest editor); *In the Moon When the Deer Lose Their Horns* (1993); and *The Broken Hoop* (1988).

Deer Cloud's work has been included in numerous anthologies, and her poems, stories, and essays have been published in many literary journals and magazines. She has also published under a former married name, Susan Clements.

Barbara Alice Mann

DELORIA, VINE, JR.
1933–2005 SIOUX, STANDING ROCK
EDUCATOR AND ACTIVIST

Vine Deloria, Jr., a Standing Rock Sioux, first became nationally known during the late 1960s, following publication of his book *Custer Died for Your Sins.* Deloria also rose to national prominence as a spokesman for Native American self-determination movements, becoming a widely respected professor, author, and social critic in several fields, including law, religion, and political science, as well as Native American studies. He was the best-known founder of Native American studies as a field of scholarly inquiry in the late 20th century.

By the late 1990s, Deloria was described as:

> [T]he most significant voice in this generation regarding the presentation and analysis of contemporary Indian affairs, their history, present shape, and meaning. . . . No other voice, Indian or white, has as full a command of the overall data of Indian history or affairs, and no other voice has the moral force, the honesty, to admit mistakes and to redress them, or the edge to bite through the layers of soft tissue, through the stereotypes,

myths, and outright lies, to the bone. . . . marrow of Indian affairs. (Dunsmore, 1996, 411)

A Renowned Family

Deloria was part of a renowned Sioux family that has exercised a significant impact on American life and letters. As a member of the faculty at Columbia University beginning in 1929, his aunt Ella Cara Deloria (1889–1971) gained notice as an outstanding anthropologist and linguist. She wrote *Dakota Texts* (1932), which is bilingual in Dakota and English, and *Speaking of Indians* (1944), a description of Native life before the arrival of Europeans.

Ella Cara Deloria was born in Wakpala, South Dakota. Her Dakota name, *Anbpetu Wastewin,* means "Good Woman of the Day." She attended Oberlin College and Columbia University, from which she graduated in 1915 with a bachelor's degree. After working as a schoolteacher and an employee of the YMCA (in Indian education), she returned to Columbia as a professor of anthropology, where she worked with Franz Boas on two major studies of Dakota language. She also

Vine Deloria Jr., scholar, author, and activist, shaped two generations of influential leaders, both Native and non-Indian. He died in 2005. (Courtesy Vine Deloria, Jr.)

authored a novel, *Waterlily,* during the 1940s. It was published in 1988, 17 years after her death. In her later years, she continued to write, speak, and work with reservation mission schools as she added to her Dakota grammar, fearing that it might join other Native languages in historical oblivion before she could finish.

One of the first American Indians to become an Episcopal minister, Philip Deloria (Yankton Sioux, 1854–1931) is one of about 90 historical figures whose statues surround "Christ in Majesty" at the Washington, D.C., National Episcopal Cathedral. As the long-time rector of St. Elizabeth Mission on the Standing Rock Reservation, Philip Deloria was said to have converted thousands of Sioux to Christianity. He was the father of Ella Cara Deloria and grandfather of Vine Deloria, Jr. Vine Deloria's son, Philip, is a professor of history at the University of Michigan and a renowned author and scholar.

Vine Deloria's Early Life

Vine Deloria, Jr., was born in Martin, South Dakota, on the Pine Ridge Indian Reservation, March 26, 1933. Educated in reservation schools during his early years, Deloria served in the U.S. Marine Corps between 1954 and 1956. He earned a Bachelor of Science degree at Iowa State University in 1958, and a Bachelor of Divinity at the Lutheran School of Theology in 1963. After that, Deloria served as executive director of the National Congress of American Indians. At the same time, Deloria was a member of the U.S. Board of Inquiry on Hunger and Malnutrition. Serving on this board, he found black children in the Mississippi Delta eating red clay to deal with hunger.

Early in his life as an activist, Deloria channeled his intellectual efforts into legal studies, entering the University of Colorado Law School during 1967. He took up legal studies expressly in order to advance Native rights. Deloria completed study for his law degree in 1970, and later, in 1990, joined the University of Colorado's faculty, teaching until his retirement in 2000. Deloria's home department was history, but he also was affiliated with ethnic studies, religious studies, political science, and the law school, one indication of the academic respect he commanded across many disciplines.

Common Themes of Writings

Deloria's written works (including more than 20 books and more than a hundred major articles) stressed a common theme: that sin is a major element in American history, and that "the sinners are those who have stolen and desecrated the land" (Dunsmore, 1996, 413). On this subject, Deloria quoted Curley, a Crow chief, who is best known to history as one of the scouts for George Armstrong Custer at the Battle of Little Bighorn in 1876. Curley is not known as a great Native American philosopher, but his words, spoken in 1912, evoke memories of Tecumseh, Sea'th'l, and Black Elk:

> The soil you see is not ordinary soil—it is the dust of the blood, the flesh
> and the bones of our ancestors. We fought and bled and died to keep

other Indians from taking it, and we fought and bled and died helping the whites. You will have to dig down through the surface before you find nature's earth, as the upper portion is Crow. . . . [T]he land is my blood and my dead; it is consecrated; and I do not want to give up any portion of it. (Dunsmore, 1996, 415)

As early as the 1950s, Deloria was engaging in acute criticism of the Indian Claims Commission, arguing that it was being used to avoid treaty issues (such as the nature of Native American sovereignty), not address them. He pointed out that laws and regulations announced as "help" to Indians often perpetuated colonialism. Historically, Deloria argued, the rights of Native Americans have trailed those of other ethnic groups in the United States. For example, slavery of Alaska natives was not outlawed until 1886, two decades after the Civil War.

Deloria won a broad audience among a wide variety of people for asserting, with a sharp wit, contradictions in the general cant of contemporary American life. For example, in *We Talk, You Listen* (1970), Deloria recalled a conversation with a non-Indian who asked him: "What did you [Native Americans] *do* with the land when you had it?" Deloria said he didn't understand the ecological irony of such a question until he learned that the Cuyahoga River, which runs through Cleveland, was catching fire because of pollution. "After reviewing the argument of my non-Indian friend," wrote Deloria, "I decided that he was probably correct. Whites had made better use of the land. How many Indians could have thought of creating a flammable river?" (Deloria, 1970, 9)

Deloria defined the differences between European and Native American views of the land this way:

> The tribal-communal way of life, devoid of economic competition, views land as the most vital part of man's existence. It is THEIRS. It supports them, tells them where they live, and defines HOW they live. Land does not have the simple sentimentality of purple mountains majesty. . . . Rather it provides a center of the universe for the group that lives on it. As such, the people who hold land in this way always have a home to go to. Their identity is secure. They live with it and do not abstract themselves from it and live off it. (Deloria, 1970, 175)

"It will take a continuing protest from an increasingly large chorus," wrote Deloria, "to reprogram the psychology of American society so that we will not irreversibly destroy the land we live on" (Deloria, 1992, 2). His sense of urgency at the speed of environmental deterioration during the last years of the 20th century is palpable: "Only a radical reversal of our attitudes toward nature can help us," he said (Deloria, 1992, 2). "Nor do I look forward to paying the penalties that Mother Earth must now levy against us in order for Her to survive." He continued:

> It remains for us now to learn once again that we are part of nature, not a transcendent species with no responsibilities to the natural world. As we face the twenty-first century, the next decade will be the testing ground for this proposition. We may well become one of the few species in this vast universe that has permanently ruined our home. (Deloria, 1992, 3)

Commenting on the missionaries to the Indians, Deloria sometimes condensed half a millennium of history in North America into one sentence: when the missionaries came, they had the Book [*The Bible*], and Indians had the land. Now, Deloria said, they have the land and Indians have the Book. Deloria called for adaptation of Native American land ethics to a general non-Indian society that finds itself faced with the environmental damage pursuant to 2,000 years' experience exercising the biblical commandment to multiply and subdue the earth.

Deloria was known for his sharp wit on stage. Addressing 500 students at Boise State University February 28, 1998, he jested about 19th-century pseudo-scientific assumptions that Europeans were the most intelligent race because they had the largest skulls. That was before "the discovery that Apaches had something like 100 cc's more cranial capacity than Harvard professors," Deloria joked (Etlinger, 1998, 1-B).

Throughout his life, Deloria wrote a number of books and articles that took issue with Euro-centric interpretations of reality. His early books, such as *Custer Died for Your Sins* (1969), *We Talk, You Listen* (1970), and *Of Utmost Good Faith* (1971) continued to spread to new, younger audiences. In all of his works, Deloria has asserted Native American rights of occupancy to the land. Under international law, according to Deloria, Native American nations possess an equitable title of occupancy over lands upon which they live, "and this occupancy was not to be disturbed except by voluntary and lawful sales of lands to the European country claiming the legal title to the area in question" (Lyons et al., 1992, 283).

Deloria's writings also compare the metaphysics of Native American and European points of view, especially in legal and religious matters. In *God Is Red* (first published in 1973), Deloria argued that American Indian spiritual traditions, far from being out-of-date, are more congruent with the needs of the modern world than Christianity, which he said fosters imperialism and disregard for Earth's ecological future (Johnson, 2005). In *God Is Red,* Deloria also contrasts Native American religion's melding of life with a concept of sacred place to the artifice of Old World doctrines.

Entering his late 60s by the year 2000, Deloria often walked with a cane. When people asked him about it, he was prone to joking that he had "been bitten by a rabid Republican and got a staph infection" (Wilitz, 1997, 1). Complaining about the left-leaning nature of the professoriate, Vincent Carroll, editorial page editor of Denver's *Rocky Mountain News* (and a perennial critic of Deloria), pointed out that Deloria was the only registered Republican among faculty of the History Department at the University of Colorado at Boulder. Carroll, unlike those who knew Deloria, did not realize that Deloria had registered as a Republican as a joke.

Passing Over

Political and intellectual rhetoric in Native America is usually egalitarian. Most Native tradition shies away from elevation of kings, princes, and popes. No one worthy of such a title would claim it. The passing of Vine Deloria, Jr., on November 13, 2005, however, brought forth superlatives. If Native America had a Pope, it would have been Deloria. The grief witnessed upon his passing may be compared to Poland's during May 2005, upon the passing of Pope John Paul II.

Deloria died following complications of surgery for a ruptured abdominal aortic aneurysm in Wheat Ridge, Colorado. Before the surgery complications, Deloria had struggled with recovery problems from colon cancer surgery more than a month earlier.

"The great indigenous visionary, philosopher, author and activist Vine Deloria, Jr. passed over to join his ancestors today, November 13, 2005," said a statement from the Colorado American Indian Movement ("In Honor," 2005). "The passing of Vine creates a huge intellectual and analytical void in the native and non-native worlds" ("In Honor," 2005). "It is safe to say that without the example provided by the writing and the thinking of Vine Deloria, Jr., there likely would have been no American Indian Movement, [and] there would be no international indigenous peoples' movement as it exists today. . . ." ("In Honor," 2005).

"He had the courage and the vision," the statement continued, "to challenge the dominating society at its core. He was unapologetic in confronting the racism of United States law and policy, and he was prophetic in challenging young indigenous activists to hone their strategies. He was our elder statesman and mentor. . . . For many of us, Vine was a contemporary Crazy Horse" ("In Honor," 2005). A public memorial for Deloria was held in Golden, Colorado, as a scholarship fund was initiated in his name.

University of Colorado Professor Charles Wilkinson, an expert in American Indian law, called Deloria "probably the most influential American Indian of the past century" and stated that "he was also a wonderful human being, brilliant, bitingly funny and profoundly warm and compassionate, always willing to lend a hand or lift a spirit" (Dahl, 2005).

For many days and weeks after his passing, the news rippled through Deloria's vast extended family in the United States and around the world, by e-mail and personal contact, hand-to-hand, ear-to-ear, to "all our relations," in a Native American sense. Many who knew Deloria drew comfort from the belief that he will be in the other world when they pass over.

Remembrances

University of Minnesota American Indian Studies Professor David Wilkins, who is Lumbee, wrote in *Indian Country Today* that Deloria "was never quite comfortable with the notion that he was, in fact, the principal champion of tribal nations since he wanted—no, demanded—that each Native nation express confidence in its own national identity, develop its own unique talents and together wield their collective sovereignty, that is, their dignity and integrity, in a way that enriches them and the nations around them as well." Reacting to his own influence, Deloria tried as best he could to spread his intellectual wealth around.

"Above all," wrote Wilkins, Deloria "fought tirelessly for human, not just indigenous, freedom and for ecological respect and common-sense approaches to heal the environment's many wounds. Deloria believed that America's national soul would never be cleansed until justice had been fully achieved by indigenous nations, blacks, Latinos, Asian-Americans, women, impoverished whites, any disempowered groups, and especially young people" (Wilkins, 2005).

At the memorial service with a standing-room only crowd, Deloria was remembered as an activist who, with biting satire and wit, provided intellectual muscle for the Native American civil rights revolution that began in the late 1960s, propelling Native peoples away from cradle-to-grave government supervision into a new era of self-determination and active pursuit of sovereignty and exercise of treaty-defined economic rights.

Deloria was remembered as a family man, and a lover of country music who treasured a note from Gene Autrey, dogs, professional football, and old movies, who fondly recalled his days as a U.S. Marine. The program handed out at the service called him "always a warrior, who fought the good fight until the very end [who is] even now exploring the spirit world that captivated his intellect during the course of his life" ("A Celebration," 2005).

Disrespect from the *Rocky Mountain News*

The same day that Deloria was remembered and put to rest, Vincent Carroll, editorial page editor of the *Rocky Mountain News,* still seemed to be seething over Deloria's playful response to his relentless effort to portray the University of Colorado faculty as a hotbed of political liberalism. In a column on the newspaper's editorial page, Carroll recalled Deloria as "wacky" (Carroll, 2005). Carroll condemned Deloria as antiscientific, and for maintaining, in *Red Earth, White Lies* (1995), that American Indians "existed here 'at the beginning,' probably as contemporaries of dinosaurs, and this bizarre claim only hints at his contempt for much science" (Carroll, 2005).

One can only imagine the letter to the editor Deloria might have written had he been able to reply to Carroll.

Deloria's son Philip did reply:

> Vine Deloria Jr . . . was open to any number of ideas that might be called "wacky." He was willing to step outside the boundaries of acceptable knowledge. . . . Of course, this isn't the first time the *News* has felt compelled to make light of his intellectual openness and curiosity. Who could forget the complaint a couple of years ago that the Center of the American West's Wallace Stegner Award was being given, not to a legitimate figure of some import, but to a "crank"? (Deloria, 2005).
>
> It might interest Mr. Carroll to know that the current thought regarding the peopling of the Americas is trending away from the simplicities of the Bering Straits theory—which, as you know, my father vehemently criticized—to a far more nuanced account, one open to multiple possibilities of multiple migrations. What looked wacky 10 years ago might well look quite plausible 10 years from now. Vine Deloria Jr. took seriously the possibility of an American Indian creationism, a position not so far removed from similar debates unfolding today. I trust that the *News* will be

as zealous in patrolling the power and status of "science" when the subject is Christian creationism cloaked as "intelligent design." To do otherwise would be intellectually dishonest, if not also casually racist. . . . Perhaps Carroll might have waited a day? It seems unworthy of the *News*—and egregiously so—to offer such a nasty little comment on the day when Indian people from around the country were arriving *en masse* to grieve his loss and to celebrate his life. Is this the paper's general practice when a complicated thinker and public figure passes on? It seems to me ill-mannered and indecent. (Deloria, 2005)

Beating Indian drums, and demanding a meeting with editors (which was not forthcoming), the Colorado American Indian Movement picketed the *Rocky Mountain News* the Monday after Deloria was buried. AIM's spokesman Glenn Morris said that Carroll had slurred a man who was "the equivalent of Thurgood Marshall, Frederick Douglass, and Martin Luther King rolled into one in the eyes of the Indian world" ("AIM Fire," 2005, n.p.).

The pickets at "The Rocky" (as it was called in Denver) recalled that little seemed to have changed since the newspaper, in 1863, described the Ute people as "a dissolute, vagabondish, brutal and ungrateful race" that "ought to be wiped from the face of the earth" ("AIM Fire," 2005, n.p.). The protesters also demanded that The Rocky issue an apology (which also was not forthcoming) "for its role in inciting and celebrating the Sand Creek Massacre," an 1864 assault on a peaceful Cheyenne camp in which at least 163 men, women, and children were murdered and mutilated ("AIM Fire," 2005, n.p.).

Carroll later apologized by e-mail to Philip Deloria, and then complained that he had not known that Vine Deloria was being buried the day he published his derogatory column. For a man who postured as an expert news authority, and who called his opinion column "On Point," it was a rather lame excuse.

While editors at the *Rocky Mountain News* recalled Vine Deloria, Jr., as a "crank" and a "wacko," *Indian Country Today*'s editors described the affection for him that poured from Native America at the same time:

We remember the beloved teacher for his generosity of spirit. As a professor, Deloria mentored and touched many people across all ethnic and religious persuasions while always managing to teach and guide the work of scores of Native graduate students and young activists, many of whom went on to gain success and prominence on their own. He wrote prefaces and introductions and recommendations by the dozens in careful assessments of the work at hand, but was always ready to add his considerable gravity to the work of newer hands. He would not tolerate fuzzy thinking, however, and could and would hold his students to task. . . . In every generation, to paraphrase the late Creek Medicine Man Phillip Deere, there is one who hits the click-stone just right, and sparks the fire. In his generation, Vine Deloria Jr. sparked the intellectual fire of political, legal, historical and spiritual illumination. He lighted the path to the fountainhead of knowledge, which points the way ahead. ("In Memoriam," 2005)

An obituary in the *New York Times* recalled that "While his *Custer* book, with its incendiary title, was categorized at the time as an angry young man's anthem, Mr. Deloria's real weapon, critics and admirers said, was his scathing, sardonic humor, which he was able to use on both sides of the Indian-white divide. He once called the Battle of the Little Bighorn, where Lt. Col. George Armstrong Custer and the Seventh Cavalry were defeated by a combined force of Sioux and Northern Cheyenne in 1876 in the Montana territory, "a sensitivity-training session" (Johnson, 2005). "We have brought the white man a long way in 500 years," he wrote in a *New York Times* op-ed article during 1976. "From a childish search for mythical cities of gold and fountains of youth to the simple recognition that lands are essential for human existence" (Johnson, 2005).

Further Reading

"AIM Fire: The American Indian Movement Targets the Rocky." *Denver Westword,* December 15, 2005, n.p.

Carroll, Vincent. "On Point: Vine Deloria's Other Side." *Rocky Mountain News,* November 18, 2005. http://www.rockymountainnews.com/drmn/columnist/0,1299,DRMN_23972_106,00.html#bio.

Cassirer, Ernest. *An Essay on Man.* New Haven, CT: Yale University Press, 1944.

"A Celebration of the Life of Vine Deloria, Jr." Program distributed at public memorial service, Mount Vernon Event Center, Golden, Colorado, November 18, 2005.

Dahl, Corey. "Indian Activist and Popular Author Dies; Vine Deloria Jr. Was a Retired C.U. [Colorado University] Professor." *Boulder* [Colorado] *Daily Camera,* November 15, 2005. http://www.dailycamera.com/bdc/obituaries/article/0,1713,BDC_2437_4239604,00.html.

Deloria, Philip J. "Deloria Reveled in Thinking Outside the Box." [Letter to the Editor]. *Rocky Mountain News,* November 23, 2005. http://www.rockymountainnews.com/drmn/letters/article/0,2777,DRMN_23966_4260020,00.html.

Deloria, Vine, Jr. *We Talk, You Listen: New Tribes, New Turf.* New York: Macmillan, 1970.

Deloria, Vine, Jr. *The Metaphysics of Modern Existence.* San Francisco: Harper & Row, 1979.

Deloria, Vine, Jr. "Commentary: Research, Redskins, and Reality." *American Indian Quarterly* 15, no. 4 (Fall 1991): 457–68.

Deloria, Vine, Jr. *God Is Red: A Native View of Religion.* 2nd ed. Golden, CO: North American Press/Fulcrum, 1992.

Deloria, Vine, Jr. *Red Earth, White Lies: Native Americans and the Myth of Scientific Fact.* New York: Scribner, 1995.

Deloria, Vine, Jr. "Indigenous Peoples' Literature." Deloria Web site. n.d. http://www.indians.org/welker/vine.htm.

Dunsmore, Roger. "Vine Deloria, Jr." In *Handbook of Native American Literature,* edited by Andrew Wiget, 411–15. New York: Garland, 1996.

Etlinger, Charles. "Indian Scholar Blows Holes in Theories: Deloria Says Lazy Scientists Adjust Facts to Fit Ideas." *Idaho Statesman,* February 28, 1998, p. 1-B.

George-Kanentiio, Doug. "Deloria as I Knew Him." *Indian Time* 23, no. 46 (November 17, 2005): 2–3.

Hughes, J. Donald. *American Indian Ecology.* El Paso: University of Texas Press, 1983.

"In Honor of Vine Deloria, Jr. (1933–2005)." Statement by Colorado American Indian Movement, November 14, 2005.

"In Memoriam: Vine Deloria Jr." *Indian Country Today,* November 17, 2005. http://www.indiancountry.com/content.cfm?id=1096411939.

Johnson, Kirk. "Vine Deloria Jr., 'Champion of Indian Rights,' Dies at 72." *New York Times,* November 15, 2005. http://www.nytimes.com/2005/11/15/national/15deloria.html.

Lyons, Oren, John Mohawk, Vine Deloria, Jr., Laurence Hauptman, Howard Berman, Donald A. Grinde, Jr., Curtis Berkey, and Robert Venables. *Exiled in the Land of the Free: Democracy, Indian Nations, and the Constitution.* Santa Fe, NM: Clear Light, 1992.

Wilitz, Teresa. "An Anniversary Celebration: Native American Author Exults in Gadfly Role at Newberry Conference." *Chicago Tribune,* September 15, 1997, 1 (Tempo).

Wilkins, David. "Native Visionary Spoke for All Disadvantaged Americans." *Indian Country Today,* December 1, 2005. http://www.indiancountry.com/content.cfm?id=1096412026.

Williams, Matt. "Renowned Native American Scholar Dies." *Colorado Daily,* November 14, 2005. http://www.coloradodaily.com/articles/2005/11/14/news/c_u_and_boulder/news2.txt.

DESKAHEH
1873–1925 CAYUGA
PROPONENT OF POLITICAL RIGHTS

Deskaheh (Levi General) was *Tadadaho* (speaker) of the Iroquois Grand Council at Grand River, Ontario. He presided during the early 1920s, when Canadian authorities closed the traditional Longhouse, which had been asserting independence from Canadian jurisdiction. *Deskaheh* is the title that he inherited as a league *royaner,* or chief. His given name was Levi General, and he was best known for his efforts to defend traditional governance by appealing to European authorities, notably the government of Great Britain and the League of Nations.

As Canadian authorities acted to replace the Grand River council with a governmental structure that would answer to its Indian-affairs bureaucracy, and with Canadian police poised to arrest him, Deskaheh traveled to Europe during 1921, carrying a petition for King George V. (Canada, as a member of the British Commonwealth, was technically subordinate to the British monarchy.) The petition was received

Deskaheh (Levi General), who carried the case for Iroquois sovereignty to the League of Nations. (John Kahionhes Fadden)

by Winston Churchill, the colonial secretary, and forwarded to Canada, which ignored it. Two years later, Deskaheh and George P. Decker, a lawyer, traveled to the headquarters of the League of Nations in Geneva, Switzerland, carrying a Haudenosaunee passport, with an appeal for support from the international community. The Iroquois persuaded the Netherlands to lay their petition before the League of Nations under a 17th-century mutual-aid treaty.

Several months of effort did not win Deskaheh a hearing before the international body, in large part because of diplomatic manipulation by Great Britain and Canada, governments that were being embarrassed by Deskaheh's mission. Lacking a forum at the League of Nations, Deskaheh and his supporters organized a private meeting in Switzerland that drew several thousand people who supported Iroquois sovereignty. In the meantime, Canada dissolved the Six Nations Council at Grand River that Deskaheh led, and declared him, in essence, a minister without portfolio. A Canadian court seized Deskaheh's possessions and sold them at auction.

In his last speech, March 10, 1925, Deskaheh had lost none of this distaste for forced acculturation. "Over in Ottawa, they call that policy 'Indian Advancement,'" he said. "Over in Washington [D.C.], they call it 'Assimilation.' We who would be the helpless victims say it is tyranny. . . . If this must go on to the bitter end, we would rather that you come with your guns and poison gas and get rid of us that way. Do it openly and above board" ("The Last Speech," n.d.).

As he lay dying, relatives of Deskaheh who lived in the United States were refused entry into Canada to be at his bedside. Deskaheh died two and a half months after his last defiant speech, on June 27, 1925. His funeral was well attended by the Royal Canadian Mounted Police. His brother Alexander General was then elevated to fill the position of Deskaheh on a council that continued to meet in opposition to Canadian authorities.

Levi General's ideas regarding Native sovereignty have been maintained by many Iroquois into contemporary times. The Iroquois Grand Council at Onondaga issues its own passports, which are recognized by Switzerland and several other countries, but not by the United States or Canada. Today, when Haudenosaunee (Iroquois Confederacy) passports are recognized by the United States, Deskaheh is remembered as a pioneer proponent of Native American political rights.

Further Reading

Akwesasne Notes, ed. *A Basic Call to Consciousness.* [1978]. Rooseveltown, NY: *Akwesasne Notes,* 1986.

"Deskaheh: Iroquois Statesmen and Patriot." Onchiota, New York: Six Nations Indian Museum/*Akwesasne Notes,* n.d.

"The Last Speech of Deskaheh." Centro de Medios de Informacion Aternativos de Quebee. n.d. http://www.cmaq.net/es/node/13335?PHPSESSID=c6eb1917a104b0afa2648745 65ff5600.

Rostowski, Joelle. "The Redman's Appeal for Justice." In *Indians and Europe: An Interdisciplinary Collection of Essays,* edited by Christian F. Feest. Aachen, Germany: Rader Verlag, 1987, pp. 435–53.

E

EASTMAN, CHARLES (OHIYESA)
1858–1939 SIOUX, (SANTEE AND MDEWAKANTON)
AUTHOR

Along with his contemporaries Luther Standing Bear and Gertrude Bonnin, Charles Eastman provided an historical voice for the Sioux during the generations after subjugation by the United States. Eastman also was educated as a medical doctor, and was a founder of the Society of American Indians.

Eastman was born near Redwood Falls, Minnesota. He was four years old when his family was caught up in the 1862 Sioux uprising in Minnesota. The family fled to Canada with other Santee Sioux, but Eastman's father was later turned over to U.S. authorities. His father was among the Sioux who were sentenced to hang after the Great Sioux Uprising in Minnesota during 1862–63; the father was among those pardoned by President Abraham Lincoln. His death sentence was commuted to a prison term.

Eastman was raised by relatives near Fort Ellis, in southern Manitoba. Known in adulthood by the Sioux name *Ohiyesa* ("The Winner"), Eastman attended Dartmouth College, entering the freshman class of 1883, and graduating in 1887. Eastman earned a medical degree from Boston University in 1890, at the same time that he provided eyewitness reportage of the Wounded Knee massacre. Later, he had a harrowing experience as a government physician at Pine Ridge during a time when epidemics were sweeping reservation-bound Indians. Eastman later turned to private practice, and, still later, with encouragement from his wife Elaine Goodale, to writing and lecturing.

Eastman was an unusually brilliant student as a young man. He was the person most responsible for the incorporation of Indian lore into the Boy Scouts of America. Eastman wrote nine books, some of which were translated into several languages other than English. Two of his books were autobiographical: *Indian Boyhood* (1902) and *From the Deep Woods to Civilization* (1916).

Eastman was one of a number of Sioux who watched his culture crushed in the late 19th century. His books enjoyed wide popularity early in the 1900s. In his *Indian Boyhood,* Eastman recalled how his uncle had first portrayed Euro-Americans:

> I had heard marvelous things about this people. In some things, we despised them; in others we regarded them as *wakan* [mysterious], a race whose power bordered on the supernatural. . . . I asked my uncle why the Great Mystery gave such power to the Wasi'chu . . . and not to us Dakotas.
>
> Certainly they are a heartless nation; [the uncle said] they have made some of their people servants—yes, slaves! We have never believed in keeping slaves. . . . The greatest object of their lives seems to be to gather possessions—to be rich. They desire to possess the entire world (Eastman, 1930, 282–83).

Further Reading

Eastman, Charles (Ohiyesa). *Indian Boyhood.* [1902]. New York: Little, Brown & Co., 1930.
Eastman, Charles (Ohiyesa). *From the Deep Woods to Civilization.* [1916]. Lincoln: University of Nebraska Press, 1977.
Nabokov, Peter. *Native American Testimony.* New York: Viking, 1991.

EchoHawk, John
Born 1945 Pawnee
Attorney and Indian-rights Advocate

As an attorney, and as executive director of the Native American Rights Fund (NARF) since the mid-1970s, John EchoHawk has made the organization a national force in Native legal affairs. From land rights, to water rights, to the reburial of Native bones and burial artifacts, the Native American Rights Fund has helped shape law and public opinion in late 20th-century America. EchoHawk became lead attorney in efforts to reclaim Individual Indian Monies from the U.S. government, a suit that by 2005 had become the largest class-action against the United States. NARF also has brought many crucial water-rights cases on behalf on Native peoples in the U.S. West.

The EchoHawks, a distinguished Pawnee family, are descended from John's great-grandfather, a Pawnee warrior who received the name after the Pawnees were removed to Oklahoma on a forced march from their homeland in Nebraska. The name means "the hawk whose deeds are echoed." Before their removal, the 25,000 Pawnees occupied 30 million acres of land. After removal, all but about 750 of them had died.

EchoHawk was born in Albuquerque, New Mexico, and earned a bachelor's degree from the University of New Mexico in 1967. He earned a law degree from the

John E. EchoHawk stands outside the building which houses the Native American Rights Fund in Boulder, Colorado, on March 27, 1984. (AP/Wide World Photos)

same university in 1970, the same year he began his career at the NARF as a staff attorney. He was the first attorney to be graduated from the University of New Mexico Law School in a program funded by the Office of Economic Opportunity.

Serving as senior staff attorney at the NARF is his brother, Walter EchoHawk (born 1948), who played a lead role in negotiations with the Smithsonian Institution in 1989 for the return of Native artifacts and human remains to tribes. He was a national leader in efforts to pass federal laws protecting Native graves. John EchoHawk also has been recognized as one of the 100 most influential lawyers in the United States since 1988 by the *National Law Journal.*

Further Reading

Chavers, Dean. *Modern American Indian Leaders: Their Lives and Their Works.* 2 vols. Lewiston, NY: Edwin Mellen Press, 2007.

ECHOHAWK, LARRY
BORN 1948 PAWNEE
LAWYER AND ATTORNEY GENERAL

After serving as attorney general of Idaho, Larry EchoHawk in 1994 ran for governor of Idaho as a Democrat. He lost to Republican Phil Batt in a nationwide

Republican landslide, scuttling EchoHawk's hopes to become the United States' first Native American state governor. EchoHawk advocated environmental issues, consumer protection, and crime victims' rights.

EchoHawk was born in Cody, Wyoming, and grew up in Farmington, New Mexico, one of six children of a full-blooded Pawnee father and a German mother. EcoHawk's father was a land surveyor and worked in the oil-supply business. The father was a severe alcoholic until he was converted to Mormonism.

All six of the EchoHawk children went to college and three of them graduated from law school, including Larry, John, and Walter (who are instrumental in the Native American Rights Fund). Larry EchoHawk won a football scholarship to Brigham Young University, where he earned an undergraduate degree in 1970. He also earned a juris doctor in 1973 at the University of Utah. EchoHawk's legal career began with California Indian Legal Services. After that, EchoHawk practiced law privately in Salt Lake City.

EchoHawk served as general counsel for the Shoshoni-Bannock tribes at Fort Hall, Idaho, between 1980 and 1986 and then served a term as Bannock County Prosecutor. He also served in the Idaho House of Representatives after election in 1982 and re-election in 1984. In 1991, EchoHawk became the United States' first Native American to be elected to a state-level attorney general's position. During the 1992 presidential campaign, EchoHawk was national co-chairman with Native Americans for Clinton-Gore. EchoHawk spoke to the 1992 Democratic National Convention, and was the first Native American to head a state delegation to that convention.

After his bid for Idaho's governorship, EchoHawk became the senior partner of EchoHawk Law Offices, Pocatello, Idaho. EchoHawk also is a holder of the George Washington University Martin Luther King Award for contributions to human rights. He maintains an active role in the Church of Jesus Christ of Latter-day Saints (Mormon). He was working as a law professor at Brigham Young University in May 2009 when the U.S. Senate confirmed him as President Barack Obama's nominee as Commissioner of Indian Affairs, the chief administrator of the Bureau of Indian Affairs.

Further Reading

Johansen, Bruce E., and Donald A. Grinde, Jr. *The Encyclopedia of Native American Biography*. New York: Henry Holt, 1997.

ERASMUS, GEORGES
BORN 1948 DENE
CANADIAN CIVIL RIGHTS ACTIVIST

Georges Henry Erasmus has been called "one of the most important First Nation leaders of his generation . . . who has made a paramount contribution to the welfare and community of Canada's Aboriginal peoples over the past thirty years."

As a civic and political leader, "he has dedicated his life to fighting tirelessly for the right of Canada's aboriginal peoples to control their own life and land and, in so doing, has became both a figurehead and a role model" (Renwick, 2007).

Early Life

Erasmus was born into a family of 13 at Fort Rae (*Behchoko* in Dene), North West Territories, to a father who was a hunter and trapper, and a mother who wove traditional clothing and worked as an interpreter in the Tlicho dialect of the Dene language. When Erasmus was one year of age, his family moved to Yellowknife, North West Territories. He graduated from the town's Catholic high school.

Erasmus early in life worked to address poverty and alcoholism among the Dene, as he advocated self-determination and an economic model that would reduce dependence on government. By the late 1960s, at the age of 20, Erasmus began to engage in politics with the Company of Young Canadians, which taught him organizational skills and inculcated a radical point of view in which he argued that the Dene were a colonized people who had never ceded their sovereignty to Canada. Erasmus was a key leader in the Indian Brotherhood of the NWT (IBNWT) from its founding in the 1970s, serving first as director of community development, later as president.

From Regional to National Prominence

Between 1976 and 1983, Erasmus was the Indian Brotherhood of the Northwest Territories' president, a body that became the Dene Nation, of which he then became president. Throughout his early political career, Erasmus worked to unite many groups (Native and otherwise) in favor of Dene self-determination. He also voiced Dene environmental and sovereignty objections to the Berber pipeline (proposed to convey oil through the Mackenzie River Valley) in 1974.

Rising from regional to national prominence, Erasmus was elected twice as national chief of the Assembly of First Nations, beginning in 1985, representing about 650 Canadian Aboriginal bands and nations. When he finished his second term as national chief, in 1991, the Canadian federal government appointed Erasmus as co-chair of the Royal Commission on Aboriginal Peoples with Judge René Dussault.

This body conducted a seminal study of how non-Native Canadians and their governments have treated Aboriginal peoples. The findings of the Royal Commission, most notably describing sexual abuse of many Native young people in residential schools funded by the government and run by churches, were a major embarrassment for the government. The findings provoked a wave of lawsuits that forced some churches into bankruptcy and evoked strenuous apologies from government officials.

After five years of hearings and study, the commission concluded that Native nations in Canada should be recognized legally on a par with the provinces. The commission also advised restructuring the government's bureaucracy, replacing the Department of Indian and Northern Affairs with a Department of Aboriginal Relations, separate from a Department of Indian and Inuit Services.

Following his service with the Royal Commission on Aboriginal Peoples, Erasmus took charge as president of the Aboriginal Healing Foundation, a body funded by the federal government (at $515 million as of 2007) to aid victims of abuse in the residential schools.

At the same time, Erasmus worked, as he has all his professional life, to bridge cultural gaps between majority Canadians and Aboriginal peoples. He explained that Aboriginal peoples often have had to communicate in concepts that do not relate to their perceptions. For example, the Canadian legal process requires them to pursue a "land claim," while the Aboriginal people maintain that such a thing is not needed, because "they have used and nurtured their homeland for thousands of years" (Renwick, 2007).

Erasmus received the Order of Canada in 1987, and was recognized as an Officer of Canada in 1999, both regarded as the country's highest civic awards. He also received an Aboriginal Achievement Award for Public Service in 1998. He represented Canada at the World Council of Indigenous Peoples. Erasmus, by 2007, had received eight honorary degrees in 17 years from Canadian universities, as well as an honorary degree of Doctor of Laws, from the University of Dundee (Scotland) in 2007.

Further Reading

Erasmus, Georges. *Dene Rights*. Ottawa: Privately published, 1976.

Jordan, Sheila. "The National Indian Brotherhood." Videorecording. Oakville, Ontario: Magic Lantern Communications [distributor], 1991.

Renwick, Gavin. "Laureation Address for Georges Henry Erasmus." University of Dundee [Scotland]. 2007. https://secure.dundee.ac.uk/graduation2007/erasmuslaureation.html.

Richardson, Boyce. *Drumbeat: Anger and Renewal in Indian Country*. Toronto: Summerhill Press/Assembly of First Nations, 1990.

Simpson, Jeffrey. *Faultlines: Struggling for a Canadian Vision*. Toronto: Harper and Collins, 1993.

ERDRICH, LOUISE
BORN 1954 ANISHINABE
WRITER

Native American writer and storyteller Louise Karen Erdrich, an enrolled member of the Turtle Mountain Band of Chippewa in North Dakota, is a widely read author and well loved by many critics, scholars, and the general reading public. She is often recognized as belonging to the second wave of the Native American Literary Renaissance. Erdrich's use of multiple narrators and her weaving together of different characters' stories in a fictional landscape, as well as her connection to Anishinabe oral traditions and culture, are characteristic trademarks of her fiction. Most of her stories take place in her native North Dakota.

Erdrich started her career by writing poetry. Her first collection of poems, *Jacklight,* was published in 1984, and she has published two other collections since, *Baptism of Desire* (1989) and *Original Fire* (2003). Erdrich identified herself as a fiction writer early on in her writing career as well. "I began to tell stories in poems and then realized that there was not enough room in a poem unless you are a John Milton and write enormous volumes of poetry," Erdrich explained in an interview in 1985, "I have a lot more room and it's closer to the oral tradition of sitting around and telling stories" (Coltelli, 1990, 45).

A Nickel for a Story

Born in Little Falls, Minnesota, Erdrich spent most of her childhood and youth in Wahpeton, North Dakota. As the eldest of seven children of a German American father and a French Chippewa mother, Erdrich demonstrated a keen interest in storytelling and writing from a very early age. She recalls her father paying her "a nickel for a story" to encourage her writing.

Erdrich enrolled at Dartmouth College in 1972, at a time when the college had only recently begun admitting more Native American students in accordance with its 1769 mission statement. Erdrich majored in English and Creative Writing but also took courses offered by the newly founded Native American Studies Department. At Dartmouth she met her future husband, then her teacher, Michael Dorris, director of the department. Erdrich graduated in 1976 and returned to her home state for a few years to work numerous different jobs, some more related to poetry than others. "I took a lot of weird jobs which were good for the writing," Erdrich stated of her years between studies for academic degrees (Bruchac, 1987, 78). In 1978, Erdrich enrolled in Johns Hopkins University and in 1979 she received a master's degree in Creative Writing.

Erdrich's decision to pursue a writing career was formed in college. "I told myself I would sacrifice all to be a writer," Erdrich (Louise Erdrich's, n.d.) said. However, she would not have to wait long for success.

Author Louise Erdrich. (AP/Wide World Photos)

The North Dakota Novels

Although Erdrich published her early work in magazines during her college years, she did not achieve public recognition before her collaboration with Dorris led to publication of her first novel, *Love Medicine,* in 1984. The year of their marriage, 1981, also marked the beginning of their reciprocal and creative collaboration. Their marriage was often recognized in literary circles as a perfect literary union. The couple wrote, edited, and consulted with each other throughout the marriage. "We go over every word and achieve consensus on every word," Dorris said (Coltelli, 1990, 50). Erdrich adopted the three children that Dorris had adopted as a single man, and the couple later had three daughters together.

The inspiration for *Love Medicine* came from a short story Erdrich and Dorris submitted to a contest in 1982 within a time frame of only a few weeks. The story was called "The World's Greatest Fishermen" and went on to win the competition. "We said, if it's that good maybe we ought to think about expanding this and telling that same story, because there are many stories in a story, from other points of view," Dorris said (Coltelli, 1990, 43).

Love Medicine earned Erdrich not only several book awards, including the National Book Critics Circle Award for best work of fiction that year, but also secured her a place on best-seller lists as well as on the syllabi of many college courses. The vast success of the novel was unexpected. "I thought I would live my whole life without being published and I wouldn't care, but as it turned out I was *really* happy" (Bruchac, 1987, 84, original emphasis). Erdrich published a revised edition of *Love Medicine* in 1993, which caused critics to question which edition was authoritative. Interestingly, she did not consider this a revision but rather "adding to": "There is no reason to think of publication as a final process. I think of it as temporary storage" (Chavkin and Chavkin, 1998, 1092).

The novels that followed *Love Medicine*—*The Beet Queen* (1986), *Tracks* (1988), *The Bingo Palace* (1994), and *Tales of Burning Love* (1997)—all continued to expand and weave the stories of the characters created in her debut. The sequential nature of the novels may require a new reader to begin with the first book to avoid "pick[ing] up [the story] out of sequence" (Beidler and Barton, 1999, 2), although the popularity of her works shows that she has no trouble finding readers, new or old.

Dorris and Erdrich collaborated closely on all their written work during their marriage. They edited and commented on each other's work, as well as co-wrote several books, including *The Crown of Columbus* (1991). Although often perceived in the public eye as the perfect Native American couple, they separated in 1996.

Dorris committed suicide in April 1997. Erdrich later admitted that Dorris had suffered from depression from the second year of their marriage. Their second adopted son accused Dorris of child abuse; however, as a result of Dorris's suicide, the accusations never went to court. In the dedication of *The Antelope Wife* (1998), a novel which deals in part with suicide, Erdrich included a mention that the book was written before the death of her husband and that "[h]e is remembered with love by all of his family."

Storyteller: Postmodernism and Depiction of the Chippewa Landscape

The narrative structure of *Love Medicine* led early critics to suggest that the work should be categorized as a collection of short stories instead of a novel. Erdrich's novels have been characterized as postmodern, especially with reference to her use of multiple narrators each telling their own stories and those of others, often in the form of gossip.

Erdrich herself does not see the concept of genre as defining her stories. "Perhaps short pieces become more connected, more resonant, within the context of a novel, and then again, I miss how as short stories these pieces once stood alone . . . the novels consume the short pieces while at the same time the pieces suggest additions to the novel" (Chavkin and Chavkin, 1998, 1092). She has frequently described storytelling as a very intuitive process. "You don't control the story" (Bruchac, 1987, 86).

Favoring multiple narrators also brings Erdrich's works closer to the oral storytelling tradition she values. "The town library was my teacher every bit as much as sitting in the kitchen or out under trees swapping stories or listening to older relatives. So the two are not incompatible to me" (Chavkin and Chavkin, 1998, 1094).

Another suggested designation of her work by novelist Joyce Carol Oates is that of "magical realism," due to the blending of fantastical and real elements in her stories. However, Erdrich herself is more ready to adopt the word "unpredictable" (Chavkin and Chavkin, 1998, 1092) to describe her work, as the perception of what is fantastical and what is real is not always the same for everyone. "[T]he events people pick out as magical don't seem unreal to me" (Chavkin and Chavkin, 1998, 1092). Nevertheless, the balance between the real and the fabulous continues to preoccupy Erdrich's readers. "[H]er storytelling . . . [easily navigates] the wavering line between a recognizable, psychological world and the more arcane world of legend and fable," wrote Michiko Kakutani in a recent *New York Times* review on *The Plague of Doves* (2008). Erdrich pays great attention to the use of humor, which she considers essential to American Indian life and literature (Coltelli, 1990, 46).

Erdrich's work also has received some harsh criticism, most notably in fellow Native American author Leslie Marmon Silko's 1986 review of *The Beet Queen*. In the review, Silko accused Erdrich of "postmodern, self-referential writing" that divorces language and words from their political meanings (Silko, 1998, 1108–10). Other critics have defended Erdrich against Silko's attack.

After 2000, Erdrich continued to write prolifically and to set her stories mostly in North Dakota and the Chippewa landscape for which she is most famous. The landscape of Erdrich's novels has often been compared to William Faulkner's Yoknapatawpha County. Her recent novels include *The Last Report on the Miracles at Little No Horse* (2001), *The Master Butchers Singing Club* (2003), *Four Souls* (2004), and *The Painted Drum* (2005). Her most recent novel, *The Plague of Doves* (2008), depicts a murder mystery set in the rural countryside of North Dakota in 1911 and its impact on future generations.

In addition to her adult fiction, Erdrich has written four children's books: *Grandmother's Pigeon* (1996), *The Birchbark House* (1999), *The Range Eternal* (2002), and *The Game of Silence* (2005). She has also written two nonfiction works, *The Blue Jay's Dance* (1995), a story of early motherhood, and *Books and Islands in Ojibwe Country* (2003).

In 2008, Erdrich resided in Minneapolis, Minnesota, where she was involved in a small, independent bookstore called BirchBark Books and its related press, the BirchBark Press. Erdrich's sister, Heidi, is also a poet.

Vera Martina Saarentaus

Further Reading

Beidler, Peter G., and Gay Barton. *A Reader's Guide to the Novels of Louise Erdrich.* Columbia: University of Missouri Press, 1999.

Bruchac, Joseph. *Survival This Way: Interviews with American Indian Poets.* Tucson: Sun Tracks and the University of Arizona Press, 1987.

Chavkin, Allan, ed. *The Chippewa Landscape of Louise Erdrich.* Tuscaloosa: University of Alabama Press, 1999.

Chavkin, Nancy Feyl, and Allan Chavkin. "An Interview with Louise Erdrich." [1993]. In *A Web of Stories: An Introduction to Short Fiction,* edited by Jon Ford and Marjorie Ford, 1092–94. Upper Saddle River, NJ: Prentice Hall, 1998.

Coltelli, Laura. *Winged Words: American Indian Writers Speak.* Lincoln: University of Nebraska Press, 1990.

Erdrich, Louise. *The Antelope Wife.* New York: HarperCollins, 1998.

Ford, Jon, and Majorie Ford, eds. *A Web of Stories: An Introduction to Short Fiction.* Upper Saddle River, NJ: Prentice Hall, 1998.

Jacobs, Connie A. *The Novels of Louise Erdrich.* New York: Peter Lang, 2001.

Kakutani, Michiko. "Unearthing Tangled Roots of a Town's Family Trees." *New York Times,* April 29, 2008. http://www.nytimes.com/2008/04/29/books/29kaku.html.

Louise Erdrich's Official Web Site. n.d. http://www.harpercollins.com/author/index.aspx?authorid=2905.

Postlehwaite, Diana. "A Web of Beadwork as Much a Noose as it is a Lifeline, It Holds Louise Erdrich's Characters Together." *New York Times,* April 12, 1998. http://www.nytimes.com/books/98/04/12/reviews/980412.412post.html.

Scott, Steven D. *The Gamefulness of American Postmodernism: John Barth and Louise Erdrich.* New York: Peter Lang, 2000.

Silko, Leslie Marmon: "Here's an Odd Artifact for the Fairy-Tale Shelf." [1986]. In *A Web of Stories: An Introduction to Short Fiction,* edited by Jon Ford and Marjorie Ford, 1108–10. Upper Saddle River, NJ: Prentice Hall, 1998.

Stookey, Lorena L. *Louise Erdrich: A Critical Companion.* Westport, CT: Greenwood Press, 1999.

F

FADDEN, JOHN
BORN 1938 MOHAWK
ARTIST AND EDUCATOR

John Kahionhes Fadden, his father Ray Fadden, and their families have played a major role in preserving and reviving Mohawk language and culture through artistic and educational endeavors that spanned much of the last half of the 20th century. Their efforts have reached people across the United States and in many other countries through correspondence and books, while the Faddens' major impact in upstate New York has been through the family's Six Nations Indian Museum at Onchiota.

Born into the Turtle Clan of the Akwesasne Mohawk Nation at Massena, New York, in 1938, John Fadden earned a bachelor's degree in fine art at the Rochester Institute of Technology (1961), and did graduate work at St. Lawrence University and the State University of New York at Plattsburgh. He married Eva Karonhisake Thompson and taught art in the Saranac Central School District for 32 years. As his artistic talents developed, Fadden combined with them an intense political awareness of the changes taking place at Akwesasne, his homeland, where he often illustrated for the newspaper *Akwesasne Notes*. His art also portrays worldwide indigenous and ecological themes.

John has gained considerable attention as an illustrator after his artwork first went on display at the Fadden family's Six Nations Indian Museum. His shows in galleries around the globe have included "Akwesasne: Our Strength, Our Spirit" at the World Trade Center in 1984; "Vestiges & Resurgence: The Art of the Native American" at the Lake Placid Center for the Arts in 1991; and "Onkwahwa:tsire" at the Akwesasne Cultural Center in 1997. His "Creation Story" is in the permanent collection of the Mashantucket Pequot Museum, Connecticut.

John Kahionhes Fadden (center) with his family. (Photographer: Ned Castle. Commission by ECHO Lake Aquarium and Science Center at the Leahy Center for Lake Champlain)

Fadden's illustrations have appeared in hundreds of publications, including the *Six Nations Indian Museum Series* (1955–96); *Basic Call to Consciousness* (1978); and many issues of *Akwesasne Notes* from 1969 to 1990, as well as many books. John's posters and calendars for *Akwesasne Notes* depicting the Haudenosaunee creation and other traditions have circulated worldwide. The Smithsonian Institution and the National Zoo have commissioned Fadden to produce posters depicting Native American plants and medicines. Kahionhes has served on the New York State Education Department's Haudenosaunee Social Studies Writers Committee, the New York State Museum Native Peoples Exhibition Committee, the Cornell University American Indian Program Committee, and the Board of Directors for the Tree of Peace Society.

The Six Nations Indian Museum at Onchiota has always been a family effort. John directed it after its founding by his father and mother, Christine and Ray Fadden. John's wife, Eva, was born into the Wolf Clan of the Akwesasne Mohawk Nation in 1945. Her parents were skilled artisans, and she produces traditional Mohawk black ash and sweetgrass basketry, and detailed wood carvings of animals and birds observed near her home in the Adirondacks.

Eva and John's son, David Kanietakeron Fadden, is also a gifted visual artist. His realistic images of Haudenosaunee histories have appeared in many books and periodicals, and in his children's book, *When the Shadbush Blooms.* David and other members of the Fadden family often spend time at Kawenoke, also called Cornwall Island, Akwesasne. His children will be the fourth generation of Faddens to protect the pine and spruce forest surrounding the Six Nations Indian Museum at Onchiota, as well as the animals that inhabit it. David's work, like John's, has been exhibited around the world, including the National Museum of the American Indian.

Further Reading

Whitaker, Robert. "Akwesasne Seek to Rebuild a Nation." *Plattsburgh* [New York] *Press-Republican,* January 15, 1989, n.p.

FADDEN, RAY
1910–2008 MOHAWK
EDUCATOR AND ENVIRONMENTAL ACTIVIST

"Ray Fadden," wrote Doug George-Kanentiio, one of his many students, "initiated a cultural revolution among the Mohawks by giving them reasons to be proud of who they were." "He stripped away the negative image American schools have used when referring to Indians. He led his students on amazing journeys throughout eastern North America where they visited historical sites. Met other Native people and came to appreciate the creativity and determination of their ancestors" (George-Kanentiio, 1997).

Fadden also developed methods of multicultural education a half-century before they became popular. "We would get in his old beat-up panel truck and travel all over—museums, reservations, Indian burial sites—you name it—anywhere there were Indians or some Indian history, Mr. Fadden would take us," said Ron LaFrance, one of his students during the 1950s (Barreiro, 1984, 3).

Beginning during the 1940s, Fadden told his students to research Iroquois history and create charts describing Native American contributions to the world. They thereby learned that Native Americans have had a profound effect on all of humanity. From agriculture to political science, Native peoples have transformed the way people eat and how they think, whether it is eating corn in an isolated village in Tibet or exercising democracy in the U.S. Congress.

Early Years

Ray Fadden was born on August 24, 1910, at the farmhouse of his grandfather Henry Fadden, who lived by hunting and blacksmithing, as well as farming five miles east of the hamlet of Onchiota, New York, in the northeastern Adirondack Mountains. Henry Fadden's lineage was primarily Scottish, reaching back to John McFadden, who was born in Glasgow, Scotland, in 1729, the family's first immigrant to America. A descendant may have been married to a Mohawk. The fact that Ray Fadden would marry a Mohawk and be adopted (naturalized) at Akwesasne made him Mohawk to the people who knew him best.

Fadden was raised in Onchiota and at several other locations in New York State. Carroll Fadden, Sr., his father, worked for the telephone company and traveled frequently around the state with his family, including Ray's mother Matilda. Ray began collecting Indian artifacts as a young boy, and completed his first piece of beadwork when he was 12 years old. His schooling was varied, including an informal education in the ways of the forest from his grandfather during long summer days in the Adirondacks. The elder Fadden, who some time during the late 1800s, had lived among the Menominees in the Midwest, told his grandson Ray, "Don't believe the stuff they tell you about the Indians. Most of it is lies" (Fadden, c. 1985). This observation, along with a deep, heart-felt affinity with the mountain forest, was a legacy from his grandfather that was indelibly etched in Ray's mind and soul.

As a teenager, Ray traveled to various Native American communities throughout New York State and became friends with elders from those communities. He also visited most of the museums throughout the state to view their collections of Native artifacts. During his travels, Fadden met Arthur C. Parker, a noted museum curator and authority on the Iroquois, who was Seneca, with whom Ray struck up a lasting friendship that continued until Parker's passing in 1955.

Teacher's Life

Fadden attended Fredonia Normal School, graduating in 1934 with a degree in teaching, after which he assumed a teaching position at an elementary school on the Tuscarora Reservation, near Lewiston, New York. During this time he met Christine Chubb, a young woman from Akwesasne who was living with her family in Niagara Falls, New York. Ray and Christine were married in 1935.

They moved to the Akwesasne Reservation in 1938, where Ray taught at the Mohawk School in Hogansburg and began his life's work helping to revive the Akwesasne Mohawks' culture. In 1938 Christine gave birth to their only child, John.

An Eagle Scout in his own youth, Fadden during the early 1940s began the first Boy Scout troop at Akwesasne. After encountering prejudice in the larger organization, Ray founded his own youth group. The Akwesasne Mohawk Counselor

Organization sought to educate Mohawk children in woodcrafts, Native American history, and Mohawk traditions, and in so doing, to enhance their self-image. Ray took the club members to various locations throughout the northeast to view actual sites that were historically significant in Iroquois history. The boys were awarded feathers instead of merit badges.

Fadden intended to infuse members of the Akwesasne Mohawk Counselor Organization with a knowledge base that would allow them to be employable as cultural "ambassadors," primarily as Adirondack region summer-camp counselors, to counter negative stereotypes of Native American people. He also was concerned with enabling Native young people to draw on their own culture for economic self-sufficiency. Some did become self-sufficient this way, especially in jewelry making, as multimedia artists, and in education as museum and film consultants.

According to one observer, "Multicultural education [today] regards as new theory and pedagogy the theory and teaching methods Fadden was prevented from using in the public school system in the 1930s and 1940s. Even in today's political climate, however, his use of multiple learning style approaches, his observation and subsequent application of Native instructional methods, his ability to actively involve his students in research and publication, the multiple field trips, and the establishment of a museum collection would be remarkable. The passage of more than fifty years has proven Fadden right: the people will continue" (Jennings, 1998, 171–72).

Six Nations Indian Museum Opens

On land received from Ray's parents, the structure housing the Six Nations Indian Museum was built with pine cut by Fadden. First opened to visitors in 1954, the museum initially was built to house a large number and variety of gifts given to Ray while he was teaching, along with beadwork, *gustowehs* (Iroquois chiefs' headgear), and educational charts that Ray Fadden himself had manufactured. Ray left the St. Regis Mohawk School during 1957, and began teaching seventh-grade science at the Saranac Central Junior High School in the fall of the same year. He retired in 1967.

At Onchiota, Fadden met Felix Cohen, who was working as associate solicitor at the Interior Department. Cohen was the author of the *Handbook of Indian Law,* first published in 1942, which remains a basic reference in the field. The large-format handbook ran to several hundred pages of small type and could not be easily lifted with one arm. Cohen maintained a summer cabin near the Fadden family home. John recalled that his father and Cohen walked in the woods talking of Native American contributions to general society in the early 1950s, as many Native reservations were being terminated, when such things were not in intellectual fashion. Shortly before his death in 1953, Cohen wrote of Iroquois contributions to democracy in *The American Scholar* in a seminal essay that inspired much study later in the century.

Following his retirement from full-time teaching, Ray continued to work at the museum. He was always available to tell an Iroquois legend, to describe the structure of the Iroquois government, and to point out, with his own brand of seasoned eloquence, that today's ways of life, particularly in the line of food plants, owed much to the contributions of Native American cultures.

Ray maintained an intense affinity with wild birds and animals; people often brought injured animals to him from miles around. During his retirement he was able to devote more time to preparing and maintaining feeding stations for them. Ravens, blue jays, nuthatches, and chickadees, among others, gathered sustenance at Ray's sunflower-distribution sites. Occasional raccoons, coyotes, fishers, and other animals also fed at sites built by Fadden.

By 2008, the Six Nations Indian Museum housed more than 3,000 items, ranging from a variety of arrowheads to two birch-bark canoes, as well as Iroquois pictographs and a 75-foot-long piece of beadwork, all stuffed into four small rooms, measuring, overall, 20 feet by 80 feet. Wall displays have crept to the ceilings and floors.

"The strength of my father's delivery has turned some people off," his son John said. "In a word, he's fiery." Fadden "has a nature of volatile compassion" (Thompson, 1981). When asked whether the presentation ever offended or hurt visitors, even sympathetic non-Natives, "Not as much as non-Natives have hurt Native peoples," John Fadden responded. "He's angry, and part of the reason he's angry is that when he was in the schoolroom starting in 1915, teachers said things they would never say now," explained John (Ringwald, 2001, 31). Ray grew up at a time when some non-Indians still thought of Native peoples as subhuman.

Stewardship of the Earth

In addition to revitalization of Mohawk culture, the Faddens practice an active stewardship of the Earth; until his early 90s, Ray fed local wildlife, including many birds and families of local bears, whom they know as individuals. Visitors sometimes would position themselves in Ray's screened porch in hopes of glimpsing bears at feeding time.

Large parts of Fadden's lessons were ecological: "Indians didn't worship trees. They talked to trees, they respected this form of life. The Christian, the European mentality couldn't understand that. To them trees, plants, animals, even whole mountains had no significance . . . all of that is believed to be below the human. . . . Boy, what craziness. I wonder where they got an idea like that. They say, too: Man was created in the image of God. Boy, if I were God I would be insulted. With all the destruction they have caused. How arrogant!" (Barreiro, 1984, 6).

"It makes me angry, sad, just frustrated by the stupidity of it all," he said. "They're killing everything," Ray said to all who would listen. "The fools. Every year it gets worse. Every spring I notice it, there is less life in this forest. I can tell. Maybe someone else wouldn't be able to tell. But I have known these woods all my life. I can see it happening. Every year there is less life, every year fewer insects, fewer small rodents" (Barreiro, 1984, 4).

Return to Akwesasne

In December 2003, the Mohawk Council of Akwesasne (the reserve's Canadian-side government) passed a special resolution waiving admissions policies to admit

Fadden, then aged 93, to its long-term care facility at Iakhihsohtha, "in consideration of his life-long work." *Iakhihsohtha* (pronounced "Ya-key-soh-tha"), Mohawk for "Grandparents," is a modern 30-bed home for the elderly located in Akwesasne Territory (Snye, Quebec).

By this time, Fadden was suffering from progressive dementia, which robbed him of his fiery eloquence and penetrating intellect. Because he was not Canadian, that country's government would not pay for his care and, because he was in Canada, U.S. Medicare didn't pay any of his medical bills. People at Akwesasne pitched in with regular fundraisers and silent auctions that, together with Fadden's Social Security benefits and teacher's pension, paid the bills.

Most weeks, John drove down from the mountains to visit with his father. Many times, Ray was asleep, or said nothing. Often, he did not recognize John. Every so often, however, there was a glint in his eye, recalling the Ray Fadden who had held the entire world to account.

Fadden died November 14, 2008, at Akwesasne, at the age of 98. Following his request for simplicity, Fadden was cremated and his ashes were spread on Mohawk Mountain near the family museum after a brief ceremony.

Further Reading

Barreiro, Jose. "View from the Forest: An Elder's Concern." *Indian Studies: American Indian Program at Cornell* 1, no. 3 (Fall 1984): 4–7.

Cohen, Felix. "Americanizing the White Man." *The American Scholar* 21, no. 2 (1952): 177–91.

Fadden, John Kahionhes. *Sketch of Ray Fadden's Life.* Manuscript, c. 1985.

George-Kanentiio, Doug. "Ray Fadden-Tehanentorens Is the Teacher behind Six Nations Museum." *Syracuse Herald-American,* October 23, 1997, n.p.

Golden, John. "Great White Hope of the Mohawks a Legendary Exception at Home for Elders." *Watertown Daily Times,* June 20, 2004, G-1, G-7.

Hauptman, Laurence M. *The Iroquois Struggle for Survival: World War II to Red Power.* Syracuse, NY: Syracuse University Press, 1986.

Jennings, Nadine Nelson. "In the Spirit of the Kaswentha: Cultural Literacy in Akwesasne Mohawk Culture." PhD diss., Indiana University of Pennsylvania, 1998.

Ringwald, Christopher D. "One Man Defends Six Nations; Ray Fadden Saves Iroquois Heritage." *Adirondack Explorer,* June 2001, 31–32.

Thompson, Daniel Rokwaho. *Dedication: 1981 Akwesasne Notes Calendar.* Published 1981 at Akwesasne by *Akwesasne Notes.*

FRANK, BILLY, JR.
BORN 1931 NISQUALLY
FISHING-RIGHTS ACTIVIST AND ENVIRONMENTAL ADVOCATE

Billy Frank, Jr., played a major role in Native American assertion of fishing rights in Western Washington that resulted, in 1974, in the landmark federal legal case

Billy Frank Jr., speaking as chairman of the Northwest Indian Fisheries Commission in 2006. (AP/Wide World Photos)

popularly called the "Boldt Decision." The decision reserved up to half the salmon catch for Native peoples who had signed treaties during the 1850s that ceded large tracts of land but retained the right to fish "in common with" citizens of Washington Territory at "usual and accustomed places." After that decision, Frank became influential in fisheries decision making in the Northwest, and as an environmental advocate.

Battles over Fishing Rights

For many years, despite the treaties, Washington State game and fishing police arrested Indians who attempted to fish in accordance with their terms. Frank was first arrested for exercising fishing rights at age 14, in 1945, near the mouth of the Nisqually River, a few days before Christmas. He served two years in the U.S. Marines during the Korean War, then returned to the Nisqually River, and to defense of fishing rights. During the 1960s and early 1970s, Indians militantly protected their fishing rights in the face of raids by state fisheries authorities. A nucleus of fishing-rights activists from Frank's Landing, living only a few miles from the site at which the Medicine Creek Treaty had been signed in 1854, continued to fish on the basis of the treaty, which gave them the right to fish as long as the rivers run.

Billy Frank, Sr. (Nisqually, 1880–1980), father of Billy Frank, Jr., also was active in the fishing-rights struggles. He was the original owner of Frank's Landing, a tract of land along the Nisqually River near Olympia, Washington, which became an important center of fishing-rights protests during the 1960s and early 1970s. The land was outside the bounds of the original Nisqually reservation, but, having been purchased by Frank, Sr., was given trust status after his allotted land was taken as part of the Fort Lewis Army base. The bend in the river at Frank's Landing proved to be a rich fishing ground, and thus a focus of conflict between state fish and game police and Native Americans seeking to exercise their fishing rights.

By the early 1990s, Billy Frank, Jr., then in his 50s, had become chairman of the Northwest Indian Fish Commission, and a leading spokesman for environmentalism in the Pacific Northwest. By 2007, he had headed this body for 22 years, "speaking for the salmon" on behalf of 19 treaty tribes. Frank has led a movement that evolved from activists claiming treaty rights to managers of resources.

Frank recalled:

> I went to jail when I was fourteen years old. That was the first time I ever went to jail for treaty rights. The State of Washington said I couldn't fish on the Nisqually River. So, at fourteen, I went to jail. Ninety times I went back to jail. . . . The State of Washington said 'you can't go on that river and go fishing anymore.' That's what they told us Indians. . . . 'If you go on that river, you're going to jail.' We went back fishing and we went to jail over and over until 1974. (Russo, 1992, 54)

Money Talks

Resistance to the Boldt Decision was organized among Washington State business leaders in the Washington Water Resource Committee. Frank and other fishing-rights activists decided to boycott Seattle-First National Bank, a member of the Water Resource Committee; they discussed the idea with friends at El Centro de la Raza, a Seattle social service agency. All agreed they had a good idea, with one flaw. They did not have enough money in the bank to make a boycott hurt. After a few weeks, however, they began to talk to other people. Frank recalled: "We got the Colvilles to pull out sixteen million [dollars]. . . . Then, the Washington State University kids started pulling their money out and the Teamsters Union, and other local people. . . . Then I flew up to Alaska to our native friends up there. . . . They passed a resolution and pulled out eighty million dollars" (Russo, 1992, 54).

By this time, the boycott had drawn notice at Sea-First.

> At that time, Mike Barry was the president of Sea-First. He called me up and he said, 'Bill, before I jump out of the seventeenth floor of the Sea-First bank, we got to have a meeting.' So, I brought in all my tribal leaders again. . . . He asked: 'What do you want us to do?' He said [I should] fly back to Alaska and tell the Natives to put that money back in the bank because that was only the beginning. They had another hundred fifty million that they were going to pull out. (Russo, 1992, 54)

"We know who the boss is in this country. It sure as hell isn't us," said Frank (Russo, 1992, 54). Nevertheless, the boycott was pinching the bank, the region's largest at that time, before mismanaged investments caused its near-bankruptcy. The Indians refused to restore their deposits unless Sea-First and other businesses called off their attack on the Boldt Decision.

The Washington State offensive was one part of a nationwide backlash that emerged against treaty rights during the middle and late 1970s. This movement was fueled, as expropriation of Indian resources always has been, by non-Native economic interests. During the 1980s, the battle over who would harvest how many fish continued in western Washington, and spread to other states, such as Wisconsin.

Frank became a nationally recognized leader in the co-operative effort to restore salmon runs of the Eastern Pacific. Fisheries officials returned one of the boats they had seized from him during the fish-ins, and Frank installed the old cedar dugout canoe in a spot of honor alongside the riverbank where his quest to fish in accordance with the treaties had begun.

Frank's efforts as activist and environmental advocate have been recognized internationally by many awards. In 1992, Frank was awarded the Albert Schweitzer Prize for humanitarianism by Johns Hopkins University. He also received the 2004 *Indian Country Today* Visionary Award.

Further Reading

Chavers, Dean. *Modern American Indian Leaders: Their Lives and Their Works.* 2 vols. Lewiston, NY: Edwin Mellen Press, 2007.

El Centro de la Raza 35th Anniversary. "What Kind of World Will We Leave Our Children?" Washington State Convention and Trade Center, Seattle, October 13, 2007.

Russo, Kurt, ed. *Our People, Our Land: Reflections on Common Ground,* 54–56. Bellingham, WA: Lummi Tribe and Kluckhohn Center, 1992.

G

GAGE, MATILDA JOSLYN
1826–1898
FEMINIST

With Elizabeth Cady Stanton and Susan B. Anthony, Matilda Joslyn Gage was one of the United States' three best-known feminists during the 19th century. Her radical views and opposition to organized religion caused her to be largely edited out of official histories, however. Gage believed that the vote for women would lift half of humanity from oppression by the church, state, and capitalist economy, all of which increased social pressures to remain at home, away from the professional world. Some of her ideas were adapted from her associations with the matrilineal society of the Haudenosaunee (Iroquois), where she was adopted by Mohawk clan mothers.

Matilda Gage is best remembered for collaborating with Susan B. Anthony and Elizabeth Cady Stanton on the first three volumes of the six-volume History of Woman Suffrage. *(Library of Congress)*

Activist from the Beginning

Born in Cicero, New York, east of Syracuse, March 26, 1826, Gage was raised in a home that conveyed slaves northward on the Underground Railroad. During the 1830s, as a child, Gage sought signatures on petitions opposing slavery. Her own home also became a station on the Underground Railroad during the years before the Civil War.

In 1850, Gage stated publicly that she would accept a six-month prison term and a $2,000 fine because she opposed a new fugitive-slave law, which made a criminal of anyone who assisted slaves toward freedom. "Until liberty is attained—the broadest, the deepest, the highest liberty for all—not one set alone, one clique alone, but for men and women, black and white, Irish, Germans, Americans, and Negroes, there can be no permanent peace," Gage said during the Civil War (Wagner, 2010).

Gage entered the women's rights movement with Susan B. Anthony during 1852, after the first women's rights convention in Seneca Falls four years earlier. Gage spoke in public for the first time at the third national Women's Rights Convention in Syracuse the same year. Afterward, she rapidly became a leader in the expanding women's rights movement.

Women's Rights "Triumvirate"

Gage, Anthony, and Elizabeth Cady Stanton became the triumvirate in the 19th-century woman's rights movement, with the National Woman Suffrage Association (NWSA). The NWSA used civil disobedience during the early 1870s; Gage was one of many women who broke existing laws by attempting to vote in 1871. In 1880, Gage was the first female voter in Fayetteville; she cast her vote in accordance with a state law that permitted women to vote in school board elections. Later, Gage lost a suit challenging her vote. Thus, even this limited right was removed.

Gage and Stanton wrote many of the NWSA's documents. When the United States prepared to celebrate its centennial in 1876, the NWSA said that "Liberty today is . . . but the heritage of one-half the people, the men who alone could vote." They "determined to place on record for the daughters of 1976, the fact that their mothers of 1876 had thus asserted their equality of rights, and thus impeached the government of today for its injustice towards women," as Gage wrote (Wagner, 2010).

With Stanton, Gage composed a "Declaration of Rights of Women," presented by Anthony and Gage July 4, 1876, at an official ceremony in Philadelphia they were denied permission to do so, facing arrest. Gage, who was 50 years of age at the time, declared: "We of this Centennial year must not forget that this country owes its birth to disobedience to law" (Wagner, 2010).

Writer

During the 1870s, Gage authored several articles denouncing unjust treatment of American Indians. She was adopted into the Mohawk Nation's Wolf Clan with the name *Ka-ron-ien-ha-wi* ("Sky Carrier"). She described the equality of women with men in the Iroquois system of government.

In 1879 Gage's newspaper, *The National Citizen and Ballot Box,* published portions of *A History of Woman Suffrage*, which she co-authored with Stanton and Anthony. This set also included Stanton's reports from the 1848 Seneca Falls Convention. The newspaper provided a prepublication forum for commentary before publication of the books in final form. Gage and Stanton also worked on *The Woman's Bible*; in 1893 Gage published *Woman, Church and State.*

Gage has been described "as one of the most logical, fearless and scientific writers of her day." One of Gage's primary contributions to feminist thought "was her pioneering work on the origins of woman's oppression. At a time when woman's rights advocates almost universally believed that steady progress characterized the history of woman's condition, Gage asserted that the opposite was true. She believed in the existence of prehistoric matriarchies (the 'Matriarchate' in her words) in which woman carried strong political influence" (Wagner, 1988, 32–33).

Shaped by the Iroquois' Matrilineal Society

It has been claimed that Gage was fascinated by the Haudenosaunee (Iroquois) because of their matrilineal society that was so unlike the male-dominated culture of the 19th-century United States. Gage encountered stiff resistance to her idea that women's importance in the West paralleled the rise of Christianity. She believed that ancient matriarchies were replaced (violently, in some cases) by Catholicism's Patriarchate. Steeped in the triple doctrines of obedience to authority, "woman's subordination to man, and woman's responsibility for original sin, Gage believed that organized religion was the primary enemy of women's rights" (Wagner, 1988, 32–33).

Many of Gage's contributions to the women's rights movement were literary and theoretical. Stanton said that Gage rummaged through libraries, bringing to light interesting facts that others had missed. For example, in her pamphlet, "Woman as Inventor," Gage wrote that Catherine Littlefield Greene, not Eli Whitney, had invented the cotton gin. It was Greene's idea; she had engaged Whitney to build it.

A person who always saw common interests between disparate groups, Gage argued that reform measures such as suffrage offered only partial solutions that left underlying causes of social injustice intact. Increasingly, according to Wagner, the ballot seemed to her to be an ineffective tool.

Gage died in Chicago, March 18, 1898, aged 72 years.

Gage's home in Fayetteville, New York, today is used by a nonprofit foundation in her name. The inscription on her gravestone in the Fayetteville Cemetery was her motto: "There is a word sweeter than Mother, Home or Heaven, that word is Liberty."

Bruce E. Johansen and Sally Roesch Wagner

Further Reading

Allen, Paula Gunn. *The Sacred Hoop: Recovering the Feminine in American Indian Traditions*. Boston: Beacon Press, 1986.

Anthony, Susan B., Elizabeth Cady Stanton, and Matilda Joslyn Gage. *History of Woman Suffrage*. Salem, NH: Ayer, 1985.

Brown, Judith K. "Economic Organization and Position of Women among the Iroquois." *Ethnohistory* 17, nos. 3–4 (Summer–Fall 1970): 151–67.

Carr, Lucien. *The Social and Political Position of Women among the Huron-Iroquois Tribes*. Salem, MA: Salem Press, 1884.

Gage, Matilda Joslyn. *Woman, Church and State*. [1893]. Watertown, MA: Persephone Press, 1980.

Landsman, Gail. "Portrayals of the Iroquois in the Woman Suffrage Movement." Paper presented at the Annual Conference on Iroquois Research, Rensselaerville, NY, October 8, 1988.

Wagner, Sally Roesch. "The Iroquois Confederacy: A Native American Model for Non-sexist Men." *Changing Men* (Spring–Summer 1988): 32–33.

Wagner, Sally Roesch. *The Untold Story of the Iroquois Influence on Early Feminists*. Aberdeen, SD: Sky Carrier Press, 1996.

Wagner, Sally Roesch. "Matilda Joslyn Gage: Forgotten Feminist." New York History Net. 2010. http://www.nyhistory.com/gagepage/gagebio.htm.

GEORGE-KANENTIIO, DOUGLAS
BORN 1955 MOHAWK
WRITER AND ACTIVIST

Douglas Mitchell George-Kanentiio, a member of the Bear Clan, has been a key figure in Akwesasne Mohawk political and cultural life in the late 20th and early 21st centuries. He has participated in Mohawk land-claims negotiations, was a member of the Mohawk Nation Business Committee, and a founder of the Native American Journalists Association, from which he received, in 1994, its highest kudo, the Wassaja Award for Journalism Excellence. Kanentiio was selected in 1996 to serve on the Board of Trustees for the National Museum of the American Indian. He also edited *Akwesasne Notes,* a bimonthly international journal about indigenous people worldwide, and *Indian Time,* a local newspaper at Akwesasne (Akwesasne is in parts of Quebec, Ontario, and New York State).

George-Kanentiio is chairman of Round Dance Productions, a nonprofit foundation formed with his wife Joanne Shenandoah, a renowned Oneida singer, that preserves indigenous North American language, history, music, and art. He is author of the books *Skywoman, Iroquois on Fire,* and *Iroquois Culture and Commentary,* as well as a contributor to *Treaty of Canandaigua, A Seat at the Table,* and *Sovereignty, Colonialism and the Indigenous Nations.*

As a former Mohawk Nation delegate to the Haudenosaunee Standing Committee on Burial Rules and Regulations, Kanentiio advocated return of Iroquois sacred objects from several museums. He was a member of the Mohawk Nation Land Claims Committee for seven years and was one of the founders of the Akwesasne Communications Society, which, in turn, oversaw the development of Radio

Native American author Douglas George-Kanentiio, 1999. (Joanne Shenandoah)

CKON, the only exclusively Aboriginal licensed broadcasting facility in North America.

Early Life

Kanentiio was born at Akwesasne on February 1, 1955, the fourth son and sixth child of David and Grace George. His father was a mason, a trade taught him as he carried on a family tradition reaching back many generations. The family home was located in the St. Regis Village section of Akwesasne, on the Canadian side of the reservation in the Quebec area.

The family lived across the street from the St. Regis Catholic Church, where Kanentiio helped serve mass as an altar boy. He entered the St. Regis Village School in 1961. The school was run by the Sisters of St. Anne, with religious instruction provided by a Jesuit priest, the Rev. Michael Jacobs, a Mohawk from Kahnawake. Kanentiio did well academically, scoring the highest marks in his class.

Kanentiio's mother died in 1965. Two years later, Kanentiio and 12 siblings were placed in foster homes and residential schools. He was sent to the Mohawk Institute in January 1967, remaining there until June 1968, where his experiences were unpleasant. He was placed in a foster home and entered Grade 9 at the General Vanier High School, Cornwall, Ontario, in September 1968.

Life in the Mohawk Institute

George recalled: "Count yourself lucky if you, as a Native, never had to experience the traumas of being placed, against your will, in one of Canada's residential schools. Whatever horror tales you may have heard are true. I know because I was there. I saw the beatings, listened to the weeping of the students and saw many incidents of sexual abuse. While initially shocking to an 11-year-old from Kanatakon, I learned to suppress my outrage at seeing my friends humiliated, their spirits broken, their physical selves violated by adults who were in positions of trust and had unqualified power to do to us what they willed" (George-Kanentiio, 2007).

Such treatment continued well into the 1960s. In January 1967, Doug and his brother Dean were assigned to the Mohawk Institute in Brantford, Ontario, more than 350 miles from Akwesasne (St. Regis), their family home. "We were told by the Indian Affairs social workers that the school would provide us with schooling, a warm, safe place to live and good food to eat," Doug recalled. "We should have realized the magnitude of the lie" (George-Kanentiio, 2007).

George called the Mohawk Institute "for many generations [a] the source of fear for hundreds of students, confined behind its red brick exterior" (George-Kanentiio, 2007). The institute comprised five large buildings: a four-floor residence hall with a dining hall, a school building, and two livestock barns. Most of the farm closed in 1967, although some crops were planted until the institute closed two and a half years later.

George said that students at the Mohawk Institute were fed burned toast with powdered milk and mush, a watery porridge "which slid through the stomach and bowels, hence the [school's popular] name 'mushhole.' This was our breakfast, an aberration of the food we had been assured would be ours in abundance. Another lie with many more to follow. The other daily meals were as bad and nutritionally corrupt. Forty years later, I feel the shadow pains of hunger whenever I think about the Institute; we were always scratching for the smallest of food morsels to fill growling stomachs" (George-Kanentiio, 2007).

Canada later attempted to compensate students of the boarding schools with cash payments, which he said are trivial compared to the tens of millions paid to the lawyers who represented the former student survivors: $45 million as of 2007. "Each one of us, by sickening contrast, get $10,000 for the first year of our confinements and $3,000 for each year thereafter," he said (George-Kanentiio, 2007).

George recalled how one boy, Joey Commanda, ran away from the Mohawk Institute, walking along train tracks. George wondered how much Canada would pay for the life of Commanda, an Algonquin, who was 12 years of age, after he was killed by a train near Toronto while walking along an isolated stretch of tracks, shuffling homeward hundreds of miles, "wishing his Akwesasne pals were there to show him the way" (George-Kanentiio, 2007). A Canadian federal government investigation of the institute after Commanda's death led to its closure.

School and University Life

During the next five years, George was placed in 15 foster homes across Ontario, Quebec, and New York, attending five different high schools before graduating from Massena (New York) High School in 1973. He had withdrawn from Grade 10 to take part in a land-reclamation action by the Mohawk people during 1970, but completed requirements the next year. In 1973, he attended the State University of New York at Oswego, which had a large Iroquois student body.

George did not complete a second semester in college, and went to work at various jobs at Akwesasne before moving to Los Angeles in 1974. He then worked at the University of California at Los Angeles Medical Center and enrolled at the school in 1975, but lack of financial resources compelled him to withdraw. George then lived in central California until January 1976, returning afterward to Akwesasne and Toronto, Ontario.

In 1977, he attended the University of New Mexico before transferring to Syracuse University where he organized Native American students. George played a leading role in a movement to remove the university's Indian mascot and joined with other students to advocate a Native American studies major there. He also received an internship at the Newberry Library's Native Resource Center in 1979. George took advantage of an accelerated admissions program at the Antioch School of Law in Washington, D.C., in 1980, finishing four semesters, until his support was terminated as a result of his political activism.

Returning home, George accepted the position of editor of *Indian Time,* a local newspaper at Akwesasne while serving as a committee member for a group that created a radio station, CKON. During the summer of 1984, Kanentiio joined Huston Smith, the author of *The Religions of Man* on an international tour of sacred sites from Rome to Israel, Istanbul, India, Thailand, China, and Korea. He also held an internship with the New York State Archives, worked at the Akwesasne Museum, and was selected as editor of the news journal *Akwesasne Notes* in 1986, a position he held for six years. George continued to serve the community in many capacities, as a member of the Akwesasne Emergency Team, the Akwesasne Home for the Aged, the Akwesasne Communications Society, and in various positions with the Mohawk Nation, one of which was a land-claims negotiator.

George has written numerous essays and editorials about the political divisions at Akwesasne, which is governed by three Native councils and also is subject to the jurisdictions of Canada (Quebec and Ontario) and the United States (New York State). He is an advocate for the revitalization of the ancestral Mohawk government called the Mohawk Nation Council of Chiefs. He also has attempted, with others, to create an economy based on ancestral values.

Role in "The Troubles" at Akwesasne

George has been critical of the smuggling of narcotics, tobacco, firearms, and undocumented workers through the Akwesasne territory. As a result, his newspapers were banned in some businesses, his offices firebombed twice, and his personal residence raked with machine-gun fire. He persisted in his opposition and received many threats against his life, but also received support from the Mohawk Nation Council and its supporters at Akwesasne.

George-Kanentiio played a direct role in the Mohawk civil war at Akwesasne as a newspaper editor, and ultimately as a participant, in a four-day gun battle in 1990 that resulted in the deaths of two Mohawk men. George-Kanentiio identified illicit casino gaming as the source of the violence at Akwesasne that began in 1986 and quickly expanded until the Mohawk reservation for a brief time became the fourth-largest Native American gambling center in North America. His articles traced the rise of gaming to the displacement of the Mohawks from their ancestral lifestyles of fishing and farming beginning after World War II, also related to the completion of the St. Lawrence Seaway and subsequent contamination of the Akwesasne environment by industries built along that waterway.

In March of 1990, the Akwesasne community split into two factions, resulting in an escalation of violence and terror serious enough to warrant evacuation of the reservation on April 26. Thousands fled the community, yet there were a few isolated holdouts, one of whom was David George, Jr., a brother of George-Kanentiio.

Rather than have his brother stand alone against the attacks of the pro-gaming Mohawk Sovereignty Security Force ("Warrior Society"), George-Kanentiio elected to pick up a firearm and support his brother. He, along with 11 other Mohawk men, then withstood four days of intense fighting (April 27–May 1) against greatly superior forces until Akwesasne was occupied by the New York State Police, Royal Canadian Mounted Police, and a contingent of the Canadian Army.

George was arrested by the Surete du Quebec (provincial police) and charged with the shooting death of Harold "Junior" Edwards, one of the two victims of the gunbattle. He was cleared of the killing during the preliminary hearing stage of the judicial proceedings for lack of evidence. George maintained that his arrest was a political action resulting from his severe public criticisms of the U.S. and Canadian police.

International Reputation

Kanentiio is nationally recognized as a primary source of information about Iroquoian politics and culture. His expertise has been relied upon by historians, and film producers as well as television documentary directors. His articles have been published on a regular basis in the *Syracuse Herald-American*. George's columns also have been published in the *Los Angeles Times*, the *Washington Post, Toronto Star, Rochester Democrat-Chronicle, Montreal Gazette*, the *London* (Ontario) *Free Press, Schenectady Gazette*, and the *Albany Times-Union*. He has been a columnist for *News from Indian Country*.

As advisor for a television series called *How the West Was Lost*, Kanentiio was extensively involved in the one-hour television documentary broadcast on the Discovery Channel in January and February of 1995. The specific episode is entitled

"Divided We Fall: The Iroquois and the American Revolution." From script development and review to ensuring cultural accuracy as well as on-screen interviews, Kanentiio was an important part of the project.

Kanentiio is serving as a member of the board of directors for Native American Television Network. Kanentiio was selected to be a delegate to the World Parliament of Religions in Cape Town, South Africa, in 1999, and again in 2004, at the WPR gathering in Barcelona, Spain. His experiences in Cape Town are part of the *A Seat at the Table* film released in 2004.

Kanentiio has spoken on contemporary Native American issues in such countries as Italy, Germany, Austria, Switzerland, and Luxembourg. In the United States, he has lectured at the University of Connecticut, Cornell University, Syracuse University, Colgate University, and Hamilton College.

Further Reading

George-Kanentiio, Doug. "Canada's Residential School Settlement a Bitter Disappointment." *News From Indian Country,* 2007. http://indiancountrynews.net/index.php?option=com_content&task=view&id=4044&Itemid=56.

George-Kanentiio, Doug. "Residential School Horrors Haunt Native Americans." *Rochester* [New York] *Democrat-Chronicle,* December 11, 2007. http://www.democratand chronicle.com/apps/pbcs.dll/article?AID=/20071211/OPINION02/712110317/1039/OPINION.

George-Kanentiio, Douglas M. *Iroquois on Fire: A Voice from the Mohawk Nation.* Westport, CT: Praeger, 2006.

Johansen, Bruce E. *Life and Death in Mohawk Country.* Golden, CO: North American Press, 1993.

GIAGO, TIM
BORN 1934 OGLALA LAKOTA (SIOUX)
NEWSPAPER PUBLISHER

In 1981, Tim Giago became owner of the *Lakota Times,* a newspaper serving Native Americans in South Dakota. Giago's work was part of a national trend; the number of reservation newspapers increased from 18 in 1963 to more than 220 in 1978. In 1992, Giago developed a national newspaper, *Indian Country Today.* As editor and publisher of *Indian Country Today,* Giago became one of the best-known journalists of Native American descent in North America during the 1990s. He was aided by the Freedom Forum, the charitable arm of the Gannett Corporation, which publishes *USA Today,* after which Giago modeled some of his news format. Giago was aided in this effort by Al Neuharth, publisher of *USA Today,* who is an alumnus of the University of South Dakota. Giago later sold the newspaper to the New York Oneida Indian Nation.

Giago was born at the Pine Ridge Reservation in South Dakota. His Lakota name, *Nanwica Kciji,* means "Defender." Giago attended elementary and high schools at Pine Ridge's Holy Rosary Mission. Later he served in the U.S. Navy during the Korean War. He was honorably discharged from the Navy in 1958, after which he attended San Jose Junior College, in California, and the University of Nevada at Reno.

He then began a journalistic career during the 1970s as a reporter and columnist at the *Rapid City Journal.* Giago became the first Native American to receive a Nieman Fellowship at Harvard University. He has won a number of prizes for distinguished journalism and human-rights activism. Giago was a founder, in 1984, and also the first president, of the Native American Journalists Association. The *Lakota Times* often was involved in controversies that provoked firebombings of its offices and threats on Giago's life.

For four years in a row, *Indian Country Today* so dominated the South Dakota press association's awards for weekly newspapers that the organization decided to classify it as a daily newspaper for purposes of its contests. Giago then withdrew *Indian Country Today* from the association in protest. In 1985, Giago was given the H. L. Mencken Award for editorial writing by the *Baltimore Sun.* He returned the award in 1989 after disclosure of several bigoted statements in Mencken's columns and other writings.

By the middle 1990s, *Indian Country Today* was reaching 50,000 readers a week with a circulation of 14,000 copies, before the paper was sold to the Oneida Nation of New York, under casino mogul Ray Halbritter. While the newspaper continued steadfast support of many issues that unite Native Americans (such as opposition to use of Indian images as sports mascots), it was criticized for ignoring criticism of gambling and dissent within the Oneida Nation under Halbritter's heavy-handed rule.

In addition to his publishing and writing in newspapers, Giago has authored several books, including *The Aboriginal Sin* (1978), *Notes from Indian Country* (1984), and *The American Indian and the Media* (1991). His book, *Children Left Behind,* was published in 2006. He also writes a column that is syndicated by the Knight-Ridder newspaper chain.

Giago has been outspoken in defense of Native American interests generally and Lakota concerns specifically. During South Dakota's centennial celebration in 1990, the fact that several Army officers were awarded Medals of Honor after the 1890 massacre at Wounded Knee became an issue. He asked whether the American soldiers involved in the My Lai massacre in Vietnam should also have been awarded Medals of Honor.

Further Reading

Giago, Tim. *The Aboriginal Sin: Reflections on the Holy Rosary Indian Mission School.* San Francisco: Indian Historian Press, 1978.

Giago, Tim. *Notes from Indian Country.* Pierre, SD: Keith Cochran, 1984.

Giago, Tim. *The American Indian and the Media.* Minneapolis, MN: National Conference of Christians and Jews, 1991.

Giago, Tim. *Children Left Behind.* Santa Fe, NM: Clear Light, 2006.

GORMAN, R.C.
1931–2005 NAVAJO (DINÉ)
PAINTER AND AUTHOR

Rudolph Carl ("R.C.") Gorman, a prominent Navajo (Diné) painter, was best known for lithographs, serigraphs, painted pottery, and sculptures of graceful female figures as well as other paintings. Gorman's work featured fluid lines and bright colors. He also worked in sculpture, ceramics, and stone lithography. Gorman was known for his defiance of artistic prudishness, which was reflected in the title of four cookbooks (with drawings) that he authored: *Nudes and Food.* Gorman's most familiar paintings were reproduced by the millions on posters, coffee cups, and greeting cards.

According to the *Santa Fe New Mexican,* "Gorman carved new pathways for Indian artists, who, prior to the late 1960s, often were forced into unrealistic definitions by collectors—and by a market that relied upon a stereotype of stoic

R. C. Gorman, Navajo painter and sculptor. (Dave G. Houser/Corbis)

portraits and colorful dancers rooted in the Santa Fe Indian School style" (Romancito and Clark, 2005). "I paint what I see," Gorman once said. "I don't think. I don't have any message. I think it's so phony for artists to have this huge meaning. I don't" (Baker, 2007).

Growing Up in Navajo Country

Gorman was a member of the *Clauschii'* ("Red Bottom People") Clan and the *Dibé lizhíní* ("Black Sheep People") Clan. He was born on July 26, 1931, in a traditional Navajo hogan near Chinle, Arizona, as the oldest son of Carl Nelson Gorman. The elder Gorman, who had been born in 1907, was a trader, artist, and rancher. The elder Gorman served during World War II as a Navajo code talker in the U.S. Marines. Gorman's mother was Adella Katherine Brown, an accomplished Navajo weaver. Gorman was raised by both his mother and his maternal grandmother, Zonnie Maria Brown, in and near Black Mountain, Arizona, with five brothers and sisters. Early in life, his female relatives taught Gorman Navajo traditions, including songs, prayers, and respect for the land.

Gorman was something of a child prodigy. He began painting at the age of three, encouraged by his father, who also was a painter in experimental genres. Young Gorman first painted farm animals and local scenes, including the sheep that he tended in the Canyon de Chelly with his aunts. Some of his images also included automobiles, Mickey Mouse, and Shirley Temple.

"A Taos Original"

Gorman quickly developed a style of his own that later would lead to his popular nickname in the media: "A Taos Original." In turn, Gorman's style inspired other visual artists to experiment with traditional forms in novel ways. Gorman often credited his inspiration to become a painter to encouragement by Jenny Lind, a teacher at the Ganado Presbyterian Mission School, which had been founded by his mother and father.

Before he became a well-known painter, Gorman held a number of jobs, including technical illustrator at Douglass Aircraft. Gorman later attended Northern Arizona University (1950–51 and 1955–56), in literature and art, but withdrew before he completed an undergraduate degree. Between 1951 and 1955, Gorman served in the U.S. Navy, part of that time in the Korean War. The Navajo Tribal Council gave him a scholarship in 1958 to study the art of Diego Rivera and Rufino Tamayo at Mexico City College, an experience that shaped Gorman's style for the rest of his life. Gorman moved to San Francisco during the early 1960s, where he studied art at San Francisco State University and worked in the Bay Area as a model. During 1968, Gorman moved to Taos, his home for the rest of his life, as his reputation grew.

Gorman's fame spread during the 1970s. In 1973, he was the only living artist exhibited in the "Masterworks of the American Indian" show held at the Metropolitan Museum in New York. A piece of his work was used on the cover of the exhibit catalog. By his death in 2005, Gorman's works had been collected and exhibited in more than 100 museums in the United States, Asia, and Europe. Before 1980, Gorman lived in his studio, but with fame came income that, in 1980, allowed him to build a $3 million mansion in El Prado, which he used to host "lavish, hard-drinking parties [that] were legendary" (Sharpe, 2006). At the same time, Gorman was noted for his generosity to local charities.

Gorman displayed his artistic skills in watercolor, etchings, acrylics, oils, paper casts, silk-screens, stone lithographs, as he depicted highly stylized subjects, including landscapes, spiritual beings, animals, and people, many featuring important places in Navajoland, illustrating Navajo values. His famous female figures often were drawn from friends and relatives, shown large-breasted, often barefoot, in traditional dress, including the robes and blankets that are common in the Navajo homeland and the Rio Grande pueblos.

Painting Women

"I revere women. They are my greatest inspiration," Gorman told an interviewer in 1998 ("Renowned Navajo Artist. . .", 2005). "My first art effort in school was a drawing of a naked woman. I got a whipping from my teacher and from my mother. I am not obsessed with large women or even skinny women, but I do prefer to paint women. I'm attracted to them. And larger women, they fill up the paper more. There is more space to work with. My own aunts were large women. Maybe I am reflecting them" (Baker, 2007).

Gorman's grandmother appeared often in many of his earliest paintings. As he aged, Gorman turned to writing as well as expanding his range in the visual arts. He wrote an autobiography (*The Radiance of My People,* 1992); he also wrote about various styles of art and their history, as well as cooking, one of his life-long loves. At home in his Taos studio, Gorman was known as an eccentric blender of styles in his dress as well as his art. Some called it bohemian: He favored headbands and custom-tailored Hawaiian shirts.

Gorman lived to the end of his life in El Prado, near Taos, doing business in his own gallery, the R. C. Gorman Navajo Gallery of Taos, which was the first Indian-owned fine-art gallery when it opened during 1968. Gorman also had a stake in the Nizhoni Gallery of Albuquerque, which sold his publications and prints. Gorman enjoyed sharing the monetary profits of his work; he also donated his own library (more than 1,200 books and a large number of his own works of art) to Diné College to fulfill its guiding principle, *sa'ah naaghíí bik'eh hózhóón,* to help preserve Diné culture, language, and history. The College of Ganado and Northern Arizona University presented him with honorary doctorates. In 1986, as Harvard University recognized Gorman for his contributions to art and culture, San Francisco Mayor Dianne Feinstein declared March 19 Gorman Day.

Celebrities Collect Gorman's Work

Many noted political figures and celebrities collected Gorman's work, including Elizabeth Taylor, Danny DeVito, Gregory Peck, Erma Bombeck, Barry Goldwater,

Lee Marvin, Arnold Schwarzenegger, and Jackie Onassis. Andy Warhol silk-screened a portrait of Gorman that hung in his bathroom.

In 2005, Gorman was injured in a fall at his home. He died at age 74 on November 3 after treatment for a bacterial blood infection that resulted in several complications, including pneumonia. Upon his passing, New Mexico Governor Bill Richardson, a friend of Gorman's, ordered flags in the state lowered in his honor.

The Navajo Nation's President, Joe Shirley, Jr., said that Gorman was the "Picasso of the Southwest," an apparent reference to Gorman's notoriety, not his work itself, since the two artists' painting styles were very different. The *New York Times* did Shirley one better, calling Gorman the "Picasso of American Indian art" (Romancito and Clark, 2005). Shirley also called Gorman "a child of the Navajo. . . . He afforded us the opportunity to talk about ourselves to the world. When they talked about him, they talked about us" (Shirley, 2005).

During the late 1990s, the Federal Bureau of Investigation had conducted an investigation regarding suspected pedophilia by Gorman during the previous 20 years, but no charges were filed. The FBI concluded that while some of the evidence was credible, a five-year statute of limitations had expired. Accusations that Gorman had been a pedophile resurfaced after his death. Geoffrey Francis Dunn, 51, who worked as an author, historian, and filmmaker, as well as a lecturer at the University of California at Santa Cruz, reached back to 1967 to accuse Gorman of molesting him at the age of 12. An Albuquerque television station (KRQE-TV, Channel 13) broadcast Dunn's allegation July 26, 2005, making it newsworthy because Gorman would have been 75 years of age on that date.

The station also obtained decade-old FBI reports alleging that Gorman was part of "a pedophile ring in Taos" that brought "runaways or uneducated" boys from Mexico, violating a federal law known as the White Slave Traffic Act (Sharpe, 2006). Gorman was known to have been gay, but people who knew him pointed out that sexual preference has no direct relationship to child molestation.

Virginia Dooley, who managed Gorman's career for 35 years, co-authored some of his books, and was the personal representative of his estate, said that she didn't believe the allegations of pedophilia. "It's just because Gorman was a famous person, and people like to hit on famous people," she said. "If it can't be proved, why not go with it and see what kind of mess they can make?" (Sharpe, 2006). Gorman was never legally charged with molesting a child.

Further Reading

Baker, Kris. "RIP Artist RC Gorman." *Santa Fe New Mexican,* November 3, 2007. http://www.freenewmexican.com/news/34626.html.

Brody, J.J. *Indian Painters and White Patrons.* Albuquerque: University of New Mexico Press, 1971.

Gorman, R.C. *The Radiance of My People.* Houston, TX: Santa Fe Arts Gallery, 1992.

Gorman, R.C., and Virginia Dooley. *Nudes and Food: R.C. Gorman Goes Gourmet.* Flagstaff, AZ: Northland Press, 1981.

Gorman, R.C., and Virginia Dooley. *R.C. Gorman's Nudes & Foods in Good Taste.* Santa Fe, NM: Clear Light, 1994.

Monthan, Doris. *R.C. Gorman—A Retrospective.* Flagstaff, AZ: Northland Press, 1990.

"Obituary: R.C. Gorman; Renowned Navajo Artist's Works Coveted by Celebrity Collectors." *New York Times,* November 13, 2005, n.p.

Parks, Stephen. *R.C. Gorman, A Portrait.* Boston: Little, Brown, 1983.

"Renowned Navajo Artist R.C. Gorman Dies in New Mexico." Democratic Underground.com, November 3, 2005. http://www.democraticunderground.com/discuss/duboard.php?az=view_all&address=102x1899154.

Romancito, Rick, and Virginia L. Clark. "R.C. Gorman, 1931–2005: A Taos Original." *Santa Fe New Mexican,* November 3, 2005. http://www.freenewmexican.com/news/34600.html.

Sharpe, Tom. "Child-sex Accounts Emerge after Taos Artist's Death." *Santa Fe New Mexican,* August 5, 2006. http://www.freenewmexican.com/news/47435.html.

"Shirley, Navajo Nation Honor R.C. Gorman." Gallup Independent, November 7, 2005. http://www.gallupindependent.com/2005/nov/110705rcg.html.

GREENE, GRAHAM
BORN 1955 ONEIDA
ACTOR

Graham Greene became a well-known actor who played Native American roles in some of the late 20th century's most popular movies. He was nominated for an Oscar as best supporting actor in *Dances with Wolves* (1991), in which he worked with Rodney A. Grant, an Omaha. Greene also played major roles in *Clearcut* (1992), *Last of His Tribe* (1992), and *Cooperstown* (1993).

Greene was born on the Six Nations Reserve at Grand River, near Brantford, Ontario. He began his acting career in 1974, after having worked as a carpenter, welder, rock music roadie, band manager, and music studio owner. Greene's acting career did not become his major avocation until after he had lived in England during the early 1980s and become known for his stage performances there. After returning to Canada, Greene was cast in the British film *Revolution,* starring Al Pacino. In addition to his many movie roles, Greene played in several television series in the United States and Canada, and was active in several theatrical productions in Toronto, where he was residing in the 1990s.

Made famous by his role in *Dances with Wolves,* Greene also had a leading role in the Canadian television series *Outer Limits,* for which he was nominated for a Gemini, a Canadian version of the Oscar. In 1996, the First Americans in the Arts recognized Greene's role in Twentieth Century Fox's *Die Hard with a Vengeance* as the best nontraditional role by an actor or actress.

Further Reading

Johnson, Brian D. "Dances with Oscar: Canadian Actor Graham Greene Tastes Stardom." *Maclean's,* March 25, 1991, 60–61.

Wickens, Barbara, ed. "On the Case with Greene." *Maclean's,* October 20, 1997, 74.

HALBRITTER, RAYMOND
BORN 1950 ONEIDA
BUSINESSMAN

Raymond Halbritter was among a handful of Oneidas who returned during the 1970s to the 32 acres left to the Oneidas in the Verona, New York area, about 40 miles east of Syracuse. Under treaties signed during the 18th century (most notably the Fort Schuyler Treaty of 1788), the Oneidas owned about 300,000 acres, a claim that was upheld by the U.S. Supreme Court during 1985. With no enforcement of the claim, Halbritter played a leadership role among Oneidas who decided to get some of that land back by going into business. With a large casino as their cornerstone, the Oneidas became the largest single employer in central New York State.

By the middle 1990s, about 300 Oneidas lived in the Verona area, of 1,100 on the tribal roll. Within two decades, Halbritter built a multimillion dollar economic base anchored in the Turning Stone Casino and made himself wealthy. As "tribal representative" of the Oneidas, Halbritter also was severely criticized for acting like a dictator.

Many of the Oneidas who first migrated to the Verona area lived at first in trailers, including Halbritter's aunt and uncle. One day in 1976, their trailer caught fire and burned both to death, as the local fire department refused to answer the call. Halbritter found himself organizing his neighbors to assemble a fire department of their own. "I can still smell the flesh burning," Halbritter said two decades later (Saul, 1996, A-6).

Halbritter, who worked in various construction jobs as a young man, graduated from Syracuse University in 1985 with a BS degree in business administration. The same year he became manager of a small bingo hall on the Oneida reservation. The next year, the Bureau of Indian affairs held an election to determine who should represent the Oneidas. Asserting that the election was illegitimate,

Halbritter and about 40 supporters stormed a building in which the ballots were being stored and seized them. In 1987, the BIA recognized Halbritter as Oneida "nation representative." Halbritter and his supporters became expert at applying political pressure on their behalf within the bureaucracy. He was suspended as nation representative for a time in 1993 by the BIA, and then reinstated.

In 1990, Halbritter earned a degree at the Harvard Law School. Halbritter soon applied his business acumen to the development of the Turning Stone Casino (opened in 1993) and other economic enterprises that, by the middle 1990s, allowed the Oneidas to repurchase about 3,000 acres of formerly alienated land in the Verona area. By 2006, that total was up to 16,000 acres, with a stated intent to expand to 40,000.

By 1995, the Turning Stone was drawing an estimated $200 million a year in revenues. By 2007, the casino complex's revenue had more than doubled, as it expanded and added hotel accommodations, convention facilities, and golf courses. The Oneidas do not disclose financial data, but the Turning Stone's profits were estimated by 1996 to have been at least $60 million a year (Glaberson, *New York Times,* 1996, A-1). By 2007, informed estimates of the casino's profits topped $100 million a year.

Halbritter's leadership also sparked controversy, as several Oneidas accused him of acting in a dictatorial fashion. In 1995, opponents held a "March for Democracy." Differences of opinion are especially acute between the Oneida Men's Council (established and headed by Halbritter) and the traditional Clan Mothers, whose matrilineal governing council Halbritter ignored. The traditional leadership of the Oneidas has impeached Halbritter, an action unrecognized by state and federal legal authorities. Maisie Shenandoah, a Wolf Clan mother who supported Halbritter's selection as chairman in 1987, said in 1995 that he "has turned against our people" (Glaberson, *The Guardian,* 1996, 12).

Further Reading

Chavers, Dean. *Modern American Indian Leaders: Their Lives and Their Works.* 2 vols. Lewiston, NY: Edwin Mellen Press, 2007.

Glaberson, William. "'Indian Gold' Splits Tribe; Casinos Have Made One Native American Tribe Rich but the Fight for Spoils Has Divided Families." *The Guardian* [London], June 18, 1996, 12.

Glaberson, William. "Struggle for Oneidas' Leadership Grows Bitter as Casino Succeeds." *New York Times,* June 17, 1996, A-1.

Saul, Stephanie. "Oneida Casino a Boon, but Not to the Tax Base." *Newsday,* September 24, 1996, A-6.

HALL, LOUIS (KARONIAKTAJEH)
c. 1920–1993 MOHAWK
WARRIOR SOCIETY FOUNDER

Louis Hall, whose Mohawk name is *Karoniaktajeh* (meaning "Near the Sky"), is regarded as the ideological founder of the Warrior Society in Mohawk country. The Warriors have played an important role in the Mohawk reserves of Akwesasne, in upstate New York; Kahnawake, near Montreal; and Kanesatake, near the Quebec hamlet of Oka beginning in the 1970s. Warrior advocacy of armed insurrection on the three reserves played a major role in firefights at Akwesasne that killed two Mohawk men May 1, 1990, and in the standoff with Canadian police and troops at Oka later the same summer, in which Quebec police officer Marcel Lemay was killed.

Hall was a member of the Kahnawake reserve's traditional council in 1971 when it decided to sanction a group of young men who said they wanted to revive a warrior society there. As "Keeper of the Well," Hall took the young men's request for sanction under advisement, and placed it on the council's agenda.

Unlike the Mohawk Nation Council at Akwesasne, the Longhouse at Kahnawake became an advocate of the Warrior cause, so much so that in 1973 its members sought to have non-Indian families evicted from their reserve, a move opposed by the tribal council that Canada recognizes. Following that split at Kahnawake, a group of Mohawks inspired by Hall's beliefs started the settlement at Ganienkeh to carry out their nationalistic vision of Mohawk tradition, including farms, a sawmill, cigarette sales, and high-stakes bingo.

In 1990, Hall's ideology helped provoke a rising, often emotional, debate over the future of the Haudenosaunee Confederacy. At the heart of this debate are two interpretations of history. One belongs to the members of the Iroquois Grand Council at Onondaga Territory, the Mohawk Nation Council, and many of the other national councils that make up the Iroquois' original political structure. These people reject violence, and look at the Warriors as illegitimate usurpers of a thousand-year-old history. The other interpretation, espoused by the Warriors (synthesized by Hall), rejects the governing structure as a creation of white-influenced religion, especially the Quakers, and advocates a revolution from within to overthrow it.

Some Iroquois who opposed Hall compared him with Adolph Hitler. Many of his adversaries in Mohawk country believe that his ideology is fundamentally fascist. An essay in *Indian Time,* a newspaper serving Akwesasne that analyzed Hall's ideology in June 1991, carried a small drawing of Hitler, with one difference. One has to look closely to see two Native-style braids dangling from the back of the head. Hall said that he admired Jewish people, saying that they have suffered persecution much like American Indians. Hall has been manifestly homophobic, but he is an Indian supremacist who stands the skin-deep aspect of Hitler's ideology on its head, believing that white men have hairy chests because they were born in biological union with monkeys. He was fond of pointing out that jackasses, like white men, have hair on their chests.

Hall maintains that the Warriors hold the true heritage of the Haudenosaunee, and that today's traditional council and chiefs at Akwesasne have sold out to elitism, the Quakers, the Iroquois prophet Handsome Lake, and white interests in general. Hall regards the religion of Handsome Lake as a bastardized form of Christianity grafted onto Native traditions. Hall regards its followers as traitors or "Tontos." Hall calls Handsome Lake's prophecies the hallucinations of a drunk.

"What can warrior societies do?" he asked, then answered: "Dump bridges into rivers—which are now sewers—and into the [St. Lawrence] Seaway, canceling all traffic, knock out powerhouses, high-tension power lines, punch holes in the reactors of nuclear power houses" (Hall, n.d.). By such actions, Hall measures the ascendancy of Native national liberation: "Legal extermination of the Indians as a distinct people is an act of aggression," Hall has written. "Oppression is an act of war against the people. Legislating Indians into extinction by way of assimilation is an act of war" (Hall, n.d.). Any Iroquois who does not subscribe to Hall's ideology is a racial traitor in his eyes, a sell-out to Handsome Lake and the Quakers. For following the peace-oriented path, he believes that many of the Iroquois chiefs, including the entire Onondaga council, should be executed, Mafia-style, by hit men. "They should be executing the traitors," Hall said in 1990. "But they will have to do it the way the Mafia do it, in secret and never see the victim again. No body. No case." A year later, Hall backed off the death threat, saying that the Warriors would replace the existing Grand Council by peaceful means (Johansen, 1993, 160).

Further Reading

Hall, Louis. "Rebuilding the Iroquois Confederacy." n.d. Unpaginated manuscript.

Hornung, Rick. *One Nation under the Gun: Inside the Mohawk Civil War.* New York: Pantheon, 1991.

Johansen, Bruce E. *Life and Death in Mohawk Country.* Golden, CO: North American Press, 1993.

HAYES, IRA
1923–1955 PIMA
MILITARY HERO AT IWO JIMA

Ira Hamilton Hayes, who would become a World War II hero, was born on the Pima Reservation at Sacaton, Arizona, January 12, 1923, to Pima farmers Joe E. and Nancy W. Hayes. Having joined the Marine Corps during World War II, in 1945, Hayes participated in the U.S. invasion of Iwo Jima. He was one of five soldiers who raised a U.S. flag atop Mount Suribachi on February 23 to visually confirm the end of Japanese control on the island. The flag-raising was photographed by the Associated Press, an act that changed Hayes's life.

President Franklin D. Roosevelt called the flag raisers back to the United States to promote war bonds, after which a commemorative postage stamp based on the photograph was created, along with a bronze statue in Washington, D.C. The stamp sold more copies ($137 million worth of stamps) than any other in U.S. history. The stamp, issued in spite of regulations prohibiting living people from being portrayed on U.S. postage, also helped to sell $24 billion worth of war bonds in rallies that filled stadiums with people and featured celebrities. Hayes was unhappy being sent city to city as a figurehead, and asked to be sent back to the front lines, stating that he sometimes wished the famous photo had never been taken.

At the conclusion of World War II, Hayes returned to his reservation, disoriented and weary of what he thought was unwarranted adoration. He felt guilty because most of his war buddies, including the other flag raisers, had been killed in battle. He also experienced what was then called "battle fatigue," and later Post Traumatic Stress Syndrome (PTSD). Hayes drank heavily and was arrested 51 times in 13 years (almost every arrest followed drunkenness as well-meaning friends offered Hayes drinks to celebrate his heroism). An avalanche of congratulatory mail only deepened Hayes's depression. "I was sick," he said. "I guess I was thinking of all my good war buddies. They were better men than me, and they're not coming back—much less to the White House, like me" (Chavers, 2007, 238).

Private First Class Ira H. Hayes, a Pima, stands ready to jump during an exercise at Marine Corps Paratroop School, 1943. (National Archives)

Hayes was never able to get his life into balance again. He drifted between menial jobs, usually picking cotton. The Bureau of Indian Affairs relocated Hayes to Chicago, where he quit drinking for a time, and went to work for International Harvester. Soon, however, the depression and drinking returned, and Hayes was arrested on Chicago's Skid Road, without shoes, smeared with dirt. The *Chicago Sun-Times* discovered Hayes and raised funds for rehabilitation. He started over once again in Los Angeles, then succumbed. In 1954, President Dwight Eisenhower summoned Hayes to Washington, D.C., to take part in the dedication of the 100-ton Iwo Jima Memorial near Arlington National Cemetery, the largest statue in the world. The old guilt returned and sent Hayes on a final downward spiral. When reporters asked Hayes whether he was enjoying the ceremony, he said: "I don't" (Chavers, 2007, 242).

Hayes died of exposure at the age of 33 on January 24, 1955, face down in an irrigation ditch, after a drunken episode. Hayes was honored by the Pima and regarded as a hero to everyone except himself. He was buried in Arlington National Cemetery. During the early 1960s, Johnny Cash recorded "The Ballad of Ira Hayes," as part of his album *Bitter Tears: Ballads of the American Indian,* telling the entire story in a melancholy song. The song, which was released several times on other Cash albums, recalled that "Two inches of water in a lonely ditch was a grave for Ira Hayes."

Further Reading

Chavers, Dean. *Modern American Indian Leaders: Their Lives and Their Works.* 2 vols. Lewiston, NY: Edwin Mellen Press, 2007.

HAYWARD, RICHARD ("SKIP")
BORN 1948 PEQUOT
FOUNDER OF FOXWOODS CASINO

Richard ("Skip") Hayward has been the main actor in a modern-day effort to revive the Mashantucket Pequots of Connecticut. His vehicle has been Foxwoods, the largest casino in the world.

Hayward is a son of a Navy seaman. With his mother, who was a daughter of Elizabeth George, matriarch of the Mashantucket Pequots, the family traveled the world during Richard's youth. Elizabeth George, who was born on the last remains of the reservation in 1894, lived there until her death in 1973. At one point, she was the only resident of a tract that her grandson would use to build a wildly successful casino serving gamblers in the populous Boston–New York City corridor. Elizabeth was adamant in her belief that the Pequots should retain their land.

Hayward, who had two brothers and six sisters, was the first to return to the reservation, leaving his job as a welder at Electric Boat, a military contractor, in Bridgeport, Connecticut, after Elizabeth's death. Hayward married a Chippewa, Carol, who had worked in the federal Interior Department. At the age of 27, in 1975, he came the leader of what remained of the Western (Mashantucket) Pequots. "If it hadn't been for my grandmother's tenacity and her perseverance . . . I don't think it would be here for us today," he said (Chavers, 2007, 122).

History of the Pequots

The modern-day revival of the Pequots occurs in a tragic historical context. Before they were slaughtered in the Pequot War (1636–37), the Pequots were some of the most affluent Native Americans to do business with the early English immigrants. *Pequot* is derived from the Algonquin word *Pekawatawog* or *Pequttoog,* meaning "Destroyers." Highly organized, and aggressive, the Pequot were important in Connecticut before 1637.

Massacre at Mystic

The Massachusetts Bay Colony attacked and massacred the Pequots in their fortified village near the Mystic River, on May 26, 1637. The Pequot community at Mystic had gathered for its annual Green Corn Dance ceremony. After they had assembled in a thatched fort at Mystic, mercenaries of the English and Dutch surrounded the fort and set it aflame, trapping the Pequots inside. Pequots who sought to escape the flames met Puritan muskets at point-blank range, as witnesses left descriptions of Pequot flesh sizzling as the strings on their bows melted in a holocaust of roaring fire.

Colonist William Bradford recalled: "It was a fearfull [*sic*] sight to see them thus frying" (Covey, 1966, 200). The English, Dutch, and their Indian allies held their noses against the stench of burning flesh. The entire roaring inferno burned itself out less than an hour after the torching had begun. During that hour, between 600 and 700 Pequots died.

While a few Puritans remonstrated regarding the violence, many, Bradford included, soon placed the massacre in the category of God's necessary business, along with all sorts of other things, from smallpox epidemics to late frosts and early freezes. The outcome of the Pequot War during the summer of 1636 radically altered the demographic balance in New England. Before, the English colonists had been a tiny minority. Afterward, the immigrants held a slight a majority. The terms of the peace treaty signed after the Pequot War systematically dismembered the Pequot as a people. After the Pequot War, most captured warriors were executed, and the English sold the remainder as slaves to the West Indies. Some of the women and children were distributed as servants to colonial households in New England.

Pequot Revival

The largest casino in the United States sprang from exceedingly humble beginnings. By 1935, the Mashantucket (Western) Pequot were down to 42 members and 213 acres. Mashantucket means "the Much-wooded Land." The word *Foxwoods* is a combination of the notion of forest with the Pequots' reputation as "the Fox People." By 1972, the 213-acre Western Pequot Reservation housed only one resident, Elizabeth George, Hayward's grandmother, the "Iron Lady," who died of a heart attack in 1973. Hayward, working with Native American Rights Fund (NARF) attorney Tom Tureen, sued on behalf of the Western Pequot for 800 acres sold by the state in 1855. He argued that the sale had been illegal under the Non-intercourse Acts, a series of federal laws passed in 1790 and afterward that forbade state or individual purchase of Indian land without approval of the federal government.

Hayward recruited other Pequots, many from Elizabeth's family, to return to the reservation, often not an easy task because the place had no economic base to entice people who would be giving up steady jobs. At first, some of the returning Pequots picked berries and cut firewood for sale. Hayward took the wood to town to sell, as people back home crowded into motor homes and a few other homes, often sleeping on floors.

In search of an economic base, some of the returning Pequots tried and failed at pig farming. They became attached to their 18 pigs, which eventually became pets. They raised acres of lettuce but could not break into local food markets. Tapping maple trees for syrup brought in some income, but only for a few weeks a year. A pizza restaurant also failed.

In the early 1980s, however, Hayward obtained enough federal money to build 15 houses. Until then, a new house on the reservation had not been built in more than a century. By October 1983, the Western (Mashantucket) Pequots had won the 800 acres, as well as $900,000 to pay for it, as well as federal recognition as an Indian tribe. From that point, the Mashantucket Pequots acquired more land, with an eye toward establishing businesses. At the time, the Pequot tribal roll contained

42 reservation residents and 153 other Pequots. By 2006, the Mashantucket Pequot tribal roll had grown to about 375 people.

Foxwoods

During the middle 1980s, after a decade of hand-to-mouth struggle, Hayward and his people decided to open a casino. Hayward and the other Pequots started with a small bingo parlor, because 40 or so banks had refused to loan money to them. The bingo parlor began operating in 1986 and became wildly successful. After the U.S. federal Indian Gambling Regulatory Act was passed the following year, the Pequots signed an agreement with the state of Connecticut that 25 percent of revenues would be paid in taxes. (By the fiscal year beginning July 1, 1999, and ending June 30, 2008, Foxwoods' gross gaming revenues totaled more than $1 billion.)

Foxwoods opened February 14, 1992, with its parking lot, holding 1,700 cars, full by 10:30 A.M. About 75,000 people used the facility the first day; 2,000 of them remained at closing time, 4 A.M. When it opened, Foxwoods was the only gaming establishment on the East Coast offering poker, which was banned at the time in Atlantic City. It has been noted that the Indians were cheated out of their land because, in part, of their problems with alcohol; now, their enrichment has come out of the white man's compulsion for gambling.

By the year 2000, Hayward and the Pequots found themselves with a Foxwoods complex that was drawing about 50,000 people on an average day. A reporter described his approach to Foxwoods, which "rises like a mirage out of the Connecticut forests. People from New York or Boston, traveling through scattered villages, past fields and woods, do not expect a monumental, ultramodern building complex in this rural area. Traffic lights direct the flow of vehicles into the asphalt desert of the parking lots" (Sutterlin, 2001, 32).

The Foxwoods Resort Casino complex was described by its managers as including five casinos covering 300,000 square feet, 5,842 slot machines, 370 gaming tables, and a 3,000-seat high-stakes bingo parlor with $1 million jackpots. The Foxwoods casino complex also included four hotels ranging in size from 280 to 800 rooms and suites each. In addition to gaming space and its four hotels, Foxwoods offered 23 shopping areas, 24 food-and-beverage outlets, and a movie-theater complex, as well as the Mashantucket Pequot Museum, and a Fox Grand Theater with Las Vegas–style entertainment.

Hayward's Foxwoods quickly became an integral pillar of Connecticut's economy and a multimillion-dollar contributor to Connecticut charities. The Pequots' casino even put up cash one year to help the state balance its budget. By the year 2000, the Foxwoods casino complex was paying the state of Connecticut more than $189 million a year. The Foxwoods and the Mohegan Sun casinos combined paid the state of Connecticut about 20 percent of their slot-machine profits, more than $318 million during the 1999–2000 fiscal year. The Mashantucket Pequots also became the state of Connecticut's largest single taxpayer, and, with 13,000 jobs, one of its larger employers (about 700 jobs were cut during the 2008–2009 recession). The casino employed a staff of lawyers and its own permanent lobbying office in Washington, D.C.

Hayward and his associates also developed a study of Pequot history. Revenues from Foxwoods funded a $200 million Mashantucket Pequot Museum and Research Center, which offers a model of a Pequot village, dinosaurs, and even a trailer from the 1970s reservation. More than 200 Native American artists, craftspeople, as well as consultants and contractors from roughly 50 Native American tribes and nations, lent their skills to original artwork and reproduced artifacts. Profits from Foxwoods also financed archaeological digs in the area. The archaeologists have found trace remnants of a fortified Pequot village, probably built in 1670 and abandoned in 1675, and several 18th-century dwellings. These findings are beginning to sketch the story of how the Pequots persevered after the English forbade mention of their name following the Mystic Massacre in 1637. Traces also have been found indicating that the Pequots' remote ancestors occupied the area possibly 10,000 years ago. Other Foxwoods profits have been invested in fisheries and a shipyard and used to make an annual payment to all members. The Pequots also used some of Foxwoods' profits to build fish hatcheries, jet-boat factories, and a pharmaceutical business, roads, schools, and a power plant. All of this brought economic vibrancy to the Ledyard-Mystic area that had suffered high rates of unemployment for many decades, following the decline of whaling, once the area's main industry. The Pequots became so successful that they were forced to recruit labor from outside. While many non-Indians in the area have complained about the casino, most businesses in the vicinity of Foxwoods have profited handsomely since it opened, including local suppliers, retailers, hotels, and restaurants.

Ethnic Controversies

Throughout his 2000 book *Without Reservation,* author Jeff Benedict asserts that Hayward and his associates are faux Indians. He raises ethnic questions that are common themes in Native America. How much Native blood makes one "Indian"? Based on blood quantum (a governmental definition), the most any of the present-day Mashantucket Pequots can claim is one-eighth blood. Even for those with more Indian blood, Connecticut town records often had no Native American category, so the Pequot have largely been defined out of existence. The federal government allows the Indian tribes and nations that it recognizes to set their own standards for what it calls "blood quantum."

Benedict pegs Hayward and the rest of the Western Pequots as increasingly sophisticated scam artists. "If they did pull off a scam, it's probably the most brilliant scam in American history," said Michael Bernz, who grew up in the area and hosts a morning call-in show on WBMW in Ledyard (Barry, 2000, B-1).

Remarked another observer: "Of course, if the Pequots still were selling firewood and maple syrup, nobody would be concerned about the matter. The debate isn't really about Indian rights or tribal sovereignty. It's about money. The Indians are making money—and lots of it. Some people have a hard time dealing with that fact" (Dalla, n.d.).

Hayward stepped down as tribal chairman in 1998, after 23 years on the job. He was succeeded by Kenneth Reels, who was followed, after one term, by Michael Thomas. Hayward spent his later years often advising other Native American nations and tribes on economic development.

Further Reading

Barry, Ellen. "A Question of Ancestry: In Connecticut, Casino Plans Fuel Debate over Tribal Genealogy." *Boston Globe,* May 14, 2000, B-1. http://www.citizensalliance.org/links/pages/news/National%20News/Connecticut.htm.

Benedict, Jeff. *Without Reservation: The Making of America's Most Powerful Indian Tribe and Foxwoods, the World's Largest Casino.* New York: HarperCollins, 2000.

Chavers, Dean. *Modern American Indian Leaders: Their Lives and Their Works.* 2 vols. Lewiston, NY: Edwin Mellen Press, 2007.

Covey, Cyclone. *The Gentle Radical: A Biography of Roger Williams.* New York: Mac-Millan, 1966.

Dalla, Nolan. "Tales from the Felt: Sour Grapes Growing in Connecticut." *Cardplayer Magazine.* n.d. http://www.cardplayer.com/newcp/articles/07700/dalla.html.

Dobrzynski, Judith H. "Casino Profits Help Pequot Indian Tribe Reclaim Its History." *New York Times,* September 1, 1997. http://www.dla.utexas.edu/depts/anthro/courses/97 fall/wilson_freshmen/pequot.html.

Eisler, Kim Isaac. *Revenge of the Pequots: How a Small Native American Tribe Created the World's Most Profitable Casino.* New York: Simon & Schuster, 2001.

"Pequot History." 1997. http://www.dickshovel.com/peq.html.

Sutterlin, Georg. "Handouts behind Them, Pequots Clean Up." *Neue Zurcher Zeitung* [Zurich, Switzerland], January 18, 2001, in *World Press Review,* April 2001, 32.

Herrington, John Bennett
Born 1958 Chickasaw
Astronaut

John Bennett Herrington, an enrolled Chickasaw, became the first Native American in space as a NASA astronaut in 2002. Once in space, he took part in three space walks to help build a communication system for the International Space Station. In February 2003, a crowd numbering in the hundreds welcomed him home to the Chickasaw Nation's McSwain Theater in Ada, Oklahoma.

Born September 14, 1958, in Wetumka, Oklahoma, Herrington grew up in Colorado Springs; Riverton, Wyoming; and Plano, Texas. Having graduated from Plano Senior High School, Herrington earned a bachelor's degree in applied mathematics at the University of Colorado–Colorado Springs. He joined the U.S. Navy in 1984 and worked as a test pilot for several years at bases in the United States and around the Pacific Rim. Herrington then earned a master of science degree in aeronautical engineering at the U.S. Naval Postgraduate School.

Herrington rose to the rank of Commander in the U.S. Navy and logged more than 3,300 flight hours in more than 30 models of aircraft. Herrington in 1996 was selected as an astronaut by NASA. He then joined the crew of a Space Shuttle mission to the International Space Station.

Roughly 200 elders, students, and employees of the Chickasaw Nation watched the shuttle flight carrying Herrington take off, including his parents, Joyce and Jim Herrington. NASA gave the group a tour and a dinner. During the dinner, the Chickasaw Nation Dance Troupe performed, circling Herrington's parents and presenting them with a gift. Folk singer Buffy Sainte-Marie performed "America the Beautiful" at the event, and Lee Frazier, a Chickasaw elder, prayed that the astronauts would have a safe journey—a powerful moment under-

Astronaut John B. Herrington of the Chickasaw Nation was the first Native American in space, and the first to perform a space walk, in 2002. (NASA)

scored by a moment of silence for the astronauts of the *Challenger* mission who had died in a fiery crash years earlier. The *Endeavour* mission itself was postponed twice for safety reasons.

On the three space walks during the space mission, Herrington was accompanied by astronaut Michael Lopez-Alegria of Spain. The two men installed a 45-foot 14-ton girder that spanned 300 feet to carry power, data, and temperature controls and readings for the Space Station. Aside from his space walks, Herrington also worked as *Endeavour*'s flight engineer during launch and landing.

Among the Chickasaws, Herrington often was compared to aviatrix Pearl Carter-Scott, a witness to his launch. She was taught to fly by the famous aviator Wiley Post at the age of 12. By age 13, in 1928, she became the youngest person in the United States with a pilot's license. Scott then became well known as a stunt pilot.

Herrington, who is a Sequoyah Fellow with the American Indian Science and Engineering Society, retired from both the Navy and NASA in 2005 to join Rocketplane Limited in Oklahoma City. He also served as vice president, director of flight systems, and chief test pilot.

After two years at Rocketplane, Herrington left to do public speaking and work with the Chickasaw Nation. In 2008, at the age of 50, Herrington started a bicycle ride cross-country, from Cape Flattery, Washington, to Cape Canaveral, Florida. The ride was sponsored by Pro Bike of Oklahoma City and the Chickasaw Nation, as well as Trek Bicycles and GEAR-UP South Dakota. On the bike ride, he advocated increased attention to mathematics and science by young people, stopping at several NASA Explorer schools and Indian reservations.

Further Reading

Barreiro, Jose, and Tom Johnson, eds. *America Is Indian Country: The Best of Indian Country Today*. Golden, CO: Fulcrum, 2005.

"John Herrington First American Indian to Walk in Space; First Tribally Registered Astronaut Is Member of Chickasaw Nation." U.S. State Department. December 3, 2008. http://www.america.gov/st/diversity-english/2002/December/20080512120713xlrenn ef0.6461756.html#ixzz0Kl3OUXSR&C.

"NASA Selects First Native American Astronaut; John Herrington, Chickasaw, Successfully Completes Training." Star Sailor. n.d. http://lenapelady.tripod.com/NAastronaut. html.

HIGHWAY, TOMSON
BORN 1951 CREE
PLAYWRIGHT, MUSICIAN, AND NOVELIST

Born December 6, 1951, son of a caribou hunter, on a trap-line near Maria Lake, in northern Manitoba, Tomson Highway was the 11th of 12 children born to Joe and Pelagie Philomene Highway. Highway's first language was Cree. He went on to become one of Canada's most prominent modern playwrights as well as a novelist and musician.

Following his father, who also was a sled-dog racer and fisherman, the family moved from place to place in Tomson's youth. His mother wove quilts and beads. Only five children survived infancy. The children, having no books or access to television or radio, were educated by elders telling stories. Tomson thus "fell in love with the oral tradition of storytelling" ("Tomson Highway," 2008).

At the age of six, Tomson was removed from his family by the Canadian government and placed in Guy Hill Indian Residential School, which he attended until he was 15. At the school, Tomson and his brother René were sexually abused by priests. After age 15, Highway completed high school in Winnipeg, boarding with white families.

Tomson deeply resented forcible removal from his family, but at the same time took advantage of the boarding school's offerings to learn classical music, making plans to become a concert pianist. These plans took him to London, Ontario, for a Bachelor of Arts degree in music at the University of Western Ontario, which he earned in 1975. Instead of training as a concert pianist, however, Highway, who also earned a BA in English at Western Ontario in 1977, set about organizing Native music festivals. By 1982, he had organized events in London, Ontario; a Navajoland arts festival in Window Rock, Arizona; and the World Assembly of First Nations in Regina. Highway also took several social worker jobs with Aboriginal organizations, during which time he traveled across Canada, gaining experiences that later were reflected in his writing.

Blossoming as a Playwright

Beginning in the mid-1980s, Highway blossomed as a playwright and actor, having joined Toronto's Native Earth Performing Arts Company, Canada's oldest and best-known Native dramatic troupe. With Native Earth Performing Arts Company, Highway worked with his brother René as a dancer and choreographer. Both were openly gay.

Tomson's first plays were initially unpublished: *A Ridiculous Spectacle in One Act* (1985), *New Song . . . New Dance* (1986), and *Aria* (1987). Tomson's career as a well-known playwright began with *The Rez Sisters,* in 1986, in which several women from the fictional Wasaychigan Hill Reserve in northern Ontario share their lives while experiencing the world's largest bingo hall. Highway combines Native traditions such as the Trickster figure and some Native language with European dramatic forms. *The Rez Sisters* became an important play for both Native and non-Native audiences in Canada. In 1988, it was staged at the Edinburgh International Festival in Scotland.

His second published play, *Dry Lips Oughta Move to Kapuskasing* (1989), uses the same reserve as the background, but this time features men. The two plays won the Dora Mavor Moore Award and the Floyd S. Chalmers Award. Another of Highway's plays, a musical titled *Rose,* also staged in Toronto, explores gender and race identity issues. Other plays include *Annie and the Old One* (1989), *The Incredible Adventures of Mary Jane Mosquito* (1991), and *Ernestine Shuswap Gets Her Trout* (2005). Highway's work is often sharply satirical, full of irreverent and often scatological humor.

Tomson's brother René died of AIDS in 1990, a story he developed in a novel, *Kiss of the Fur Queen* (1998). In it, Highway confronts the sexual abuse he and his brother suffered in boarding school. The novel is richly autobiographical, following the Okimasis brothers, Jeremiah and Gabriel, born in a tent on their parents' trap-line in northern Manitoba, forced to attend a Catholic boarding school where they are sexually abused. At one point, Highway characterizes European notions of God presented to him at the boarding school: "Show me the bastard who came up with this notion that who's running the goddamn show is some grumpy, embittered, sexually frustrated old fart with a long white beard hiding like a gutless coward behind some puffed-up cloud and I'll slice his goddamn balls off" (Dickinson, 2009).

Highway also has written children's books in Cree, English, and French, including *Caribou Song* (2001), which was named among the top 10 children's books by the *Toronto Globe and Mail*; *Dragonfly Kites* (2002); and *Fox on the Ice* (2003).

Highway received a Canadian National Aboriginal Achievement Award for arts and culture in 2001. The newsmagazine *Macleans* also named him as among the 100 most important people in Canadian history. In 1994, Highway became a member of the Order of Canada, the first Native writer to be included. Highway's writer-in-residence appointments have included the University of British Columbia, the University of Toronto, Simon Fraser (Kamloops campus), and Concordia University. He is trilingual, in French, English, and Cree. By 2009, Highway had presented guest lectures in more than 40 countries outside Canada.

Highway's citation for his Canadian National Aboriginal Achievement Award said that:

> Tomson Highway *is* Native theatre in this country. . . . [He has] shaped the development of Aboriginal theatre in both Canada and around the world. His plays . . . established a place and market for Aboriginal theatre in Canada. They have also been translated into numerous languages making them a window on Canada's Aboriginal reality for the rest of the world to behold. . . . The words of artistic producer Martin Bragg serve as a fitting tribute for this wonderfully creative man: "Tomson is not only a role model and inspiration for the Native community, he is a Canadian who has inspired us all to challenge ourselves both as artists and human beings." ("Arts and Culture," n.d.)

Further Reading

"Arts and Culture. Tomson Highway." *National Aboriginal Achievement Awards.* n.d. http://www.firstnationsdrum.com/Sum2001/NAAA-Highway.htm.

Bemrose, J. "Highway of Hope." *Maclean's* 102, no. 19 (May 8, 1989): 62.

Billingham, Susan. "The Configurations of Gender in Tomson Highway's 'Dry Lips Oughta Move to Kapuskasing.'" *Modern Drama* 46, no. 3 (Fall 2003): 358–80.

Dickinson, Peter. *Tomson Highway Biography.* Net Industries. 2009. http://biography.jrank.org/pages/4418/Highway-Tomson.html.

Enright, Robert, with Highway, Tomson. "Let Us Now Combine Mythologies: The Theatrical Art of Tomson Highway." *Border Crossings* 1, no. 4 (December 1992), n.p.

Filewod, Alan. "Receiving Aboriginality: Tomson Highway and the Crisis of Cultural Authenticity." *Theatre Journal* 46, no. 3 (October 1994): 363.

Hauck, Gerhard. "Roses on the Rez: Chronicle of a Failure?" *Canadian Theatre Review* 115 (Summer 2003): 47.

Honegger, Gitta. "Native Playwright: Tomson Highway." *Theatre* 23, no. 1 (Winter 1992): 88.

Johnston, Denis W. "Lines and Circles: The 'Rez' Plays of Tomson Highway." *Canadian Literature* 124 & 125 (Spring–Summer 1990): 254.

Morgan, William. *Aboriginal Voices: Amerindian, Inuit, and Sami Theatre.* Baltimore: Johns Hopkins University Press, 1992.

Moses, Daniel David. "The Trickster's Laugh: My Meeting with Tomson and Lenore." *American Indian Quarterly* 28, nos. 1–2 (Winter/Spring 2004): 107.

"Tomson Highway." Athabasca University. Centre for Language and Literature. April 29, 2008. http://www.athabascau.ca/writers/thighway.html.

Usmimani, Renate. "The Bingocentric Worlds of Michel Tremblay and Tomson Highway." *Canadian Literature* 144 (Spring 1995): 126.

HILL, CHARLIE
BORN 1951 ONEIDA
COMEDIAN

Charlie Hill, a nationally known comedian, was raised on the Wisconsin Oneida reservation. Hill honed his talents at the Comedy Store in Los Angeles, which he calls "the fastest [comedy] track in the world" (Brixey, 1993, 1-F). He also has performed in avant-garde theater in Seattle, New York, and other cities. Hill may be the most prominent contemporary Native American comedian, a master at stand-up improvisational humor with a biting ethnic wit who might remind listeners of Chris Rock crossed with Will Rogers.

Hill is Oneida, Mohawk, and Cree; growing up, he was exposed to the urban world of Detroit as well as the Wisconsin Oneidas' reservation; thus his humor has both rural and urban attributes, and appeals to a broad range of people. Hill's humor also has a national and a multiethnic character shaped, in part, by his residence as an adult in New York City, Seattle, Sacramento, and Los Angeles, where he has been a regular performer at the Comedy Store. Hill has on his resume televised appearances with Richard Pryor, Johnny Carson, David Letterman, Jay Leno, and Rosanne Carter.

"Charlie is good at making you laugh, and after you finish laughing, you think, that's really true," said Leno, host of the National Broadcasting Company's *Tonight Show,* where Hill has appeared as a guest (Charlie Hill's, 2004). Leno first met Hill during the 1970s.

On his comedy album titled *Born Again Savage,* Hill credited Dick Gregory, Lenny Bruce, and Richard Pryor for inspiring his comedic talents. "They call us 'vanishing Americans,'" Hill says. "But when was the last time you saw a Pilgrim?" (Haga, 1993, 1-R). Hill has appeared before many large audiences, among them television shows hosted by David Letterman, Merv Griffin and Mike Douglas, and Jay Leno. While Hill was performing at the La Mama Experimental Theatre in New York City, he worked with the budding Jay Leno on comedic technique. Hill says that he was inspired by Gregory because his humor had humane goals and a political dimension that "talked about the humanness of all of us" (Koch, 1990, 39-P).

Oneida Charlie Hill, Native American comedian. (Christopher Felver/Corbis)

Hill is known for humor that addresses Native American sensibilities. "I try to get people to laugh with us instead of at us," he said. "If I put on a headdress and acted stupid, I could be a millionaire in [Las] Vegas. But people who do that don't have to answer because they don't belong to Indian communities. Real Indian humor is grassroots stuff, it's about things in the community" (Price, 1998, 257).

Hill believes that if people enjoy his show, but laugh at the expense of indigenous people, they've missed the punchline. "My point was always to laugh with Indian people and not at us," he said. "Anytime I am in front of an Indian audience, I take the approach I am in front of Royalty. My favorite crowds are Indian colleges and Indian Elders. Indian Elders are fun, and they have seen it all" (Charlie Hill's, 2004).

Audiences in Los Angeles, where Hill performs most frequently, often include many Latinos, who share indigenous heritage. He readily incorporates Latino historical themes into his routine, with Davy Crockett a favorite target: "Since there's Latinos here tonight I need to thank them for kicking Davy Crockett's ass!" Inverting the image of Davy Crockett as a heroic figure, Hill jokes, "They always say, 'Oh, Davy Crockett he was a famous Indian fighter.' That means, oh, he murdered people, in fact, he was a terrorist. What are we going to have fifty years from now?" Hill breaks into a song, to the tune of "Davy Crockett," "'Oh Omar, Oh Omar Khadaffi!'" (Price, 1998, 261–62).

Hill's humor has a very serious political edge; he works to establish common interests between various indigenous peoples, meanwhile tweaking everyone's nose. "They talk about the American holocaust, but they just call it Manifest Destiny," he said. Hill jokes that he watched the movie *1492* backward so it would have a happy ending. "It's my job to get people to laugh with us [Native Americans] instead of at us" (Koch, 1990, 39-P).

Hill is an expert at putting the moccasin on the other foot. Observing that European American tourists who visit reservations often ask naive questions such as, "What Indian tribe was the fiercest?" or "Can I take your picture?" Hill exclaims, "We Indians ought to be tourists in the suburbs in a white neighborhood and see how they like it: 'Are you really white people? Godamn! Can I take your picture? How do you survive in these suburbs? My god!'" (Price, 1998, 266).

Further Reading

Brixey, Elizabeth. "Laugh It Up for Indians." *Wisconsin State Journal* [Madison], February 26, 1993, 1-F.

"Charlie Hill Offers a Taste of Indian Humor." *American Indian* 2, no. 2 (Spring 2001): 30.

Charlie Hill's Official Web Page. 2004. http://www.american-entertainment.net/artists/hill.

Haga, Chuck. "How Many Comedians Does It Take to Battle Oppression?" *Star-Tribune* [Minneapolis], February 26, 1993, 1-R.

Koch, John. "Comic Stands Up for Native Americans." *Boston Globe,* November 21, 1990, 39-P.

Price, Darby Li Po. "Laughing without Reservation: Indian Standup Comedians." *American Indian Culture and Research Journal* 22, no. 4 (1998): 255–71.

Hobson, Geary
Born 1941 Cherokee
Writer and Scholar

Born June 12, 1941, in Dermott, Chicot County, Arkansas, writer, scholar, social critic, and organizer Geary Hobson (Cherokee—Arkansas Quapaw) grew up culturally Cherokee while maintaining ties to his Quapaw relatives. He is legally "white," however, under Arkansas law. The Hobson home in rural Desha County was built on the Amos Bayou Road on Highway 138, which is considered the oldest road in Arkansas, having originated as a pre-Columbian trace that predated the Quapaw occupation of the area.

Hobson's father was a surveyor, and both of his grandfathers were active outdoorsmen who taught Hobson fishing, hunting, and trapping. As a young man, he took on a variety of jobs including farm labor and semiprofessional baseball. Like others in his large extended family, Hobson studies and speaks several indigenous and colonial languages reflective of the history of the Southeast, including English, Cherokee, French, Spanish, and Quapaw. Partly because he is not fluent in either Cherokee or Quapaw, he supports the active preservation and publication of indigenous languages. Hobson's extensive knowledge of the Southeast as a region shaped by diverse histories, languages, and cultures is clearly evident in his body of scholarly and creative works.

Hobson joined the U.S. Marines during the early years of the Vietnam conflict, serving as a radioman and machine gunner with the Marines from 1959 to 1963, followed by reserve duty between 1963 and 1965. "For several years after I came back from Southeast Asia, and after I got out of the Marine Corps, I didn't really think of myself as a Vietnam veteran because I was in Southeast Asia before there really was a Vietnam War. . . . I didn't consider myself a Vietnam veteran until they began to classify the war as being from 1959 to 1975, covering a 16-year period. . . . So, in one sense, I am a Vietnam veteran although I wasn't in Vietnam as a combat participant, only in Laos" (Hobson, "Vietnam," 2008).

Back in the United States, Hobson became active in the antiwar movement and joined the Veterans against the War, which paid his way to the 1968 Democratic Convention in Chicago. Hobson's involvement with the movement was short-lived due to disillusionment over the growing influence of nonveterans.

A Writer and a Teacher

Hobson earned both his BA (1968) and MA (1969) in English at Arizona State University, and completed his PhD in American Studies (1986) at the University of New Mexico. Early on in his career, he became a specialist in American literary greats such as Emerson, Thoreau, and Melville while marking the absence of many Native American authors in mainstream literary scholarship. Hobson returned to graduate studies and completed his dissertation *Indian Country: A Critical Examination of Native American Literature since 1968.*

He has held a variety of teaching and administrative duties at several universities in the disciplines of English and Native American Studies. At the University of New Mexico, Hobson assisted in establishing the Native American Studies program and served as its coordinator from 1976–78. He is currently an Associate Professor of English at the University of Oklahoma and a member of the Native American Studies faculty, another program he helped to establish.

Hobson has served on several editorial advisory boards, including the *American Indian Quarterly, Wicazo Sa Review,* University of Arizona Press Sun Tracks Series, and Intercultural Alliance of Artists and Scholars.

Separate Anglophone Literature

In the late 1960s, many American critics began to comment on a "new, emerging" body of Native American writing. Hobson responded that this "flurry of literary activity, in the years 1968–1970" was "a renascence and not simply a 'boom,' or a 'fad,'. . . . It is renewal, it is continuance—and it is remembering" (Hobson, *Remembered Earth,* 1979, 2).

Hobson has frequently called for mainstream recognition of Native American literature as a significant presence within American history and literature. Many American literature courses now integrate Native American authors, however, Hobson believes that to fully appreciate the diversity, scope, and quality of Native American literature, a separate area of Anglophone literary studies needs to be created that embraces the multiplicity of indigenous languages, varied tribal histories, regional environments, customs, values, and aesthetics.

Writing during the 1970s

Hobson's return to civilian life in the late 1960s mixed academics with activism, a recipe that would continue throughout the 1970s. While a graduate student at the University of New Mexico, Hobson witnessed the politically volatile times as a member of the Kiva Club, an American Indian student organization. He also participated in protest marches in Albuquerque and Gallup, New Mexico. Hobson also worked for Gus Blaisdell, who owned the Living Batch Bookstore in Albuquerque, a regionally famous hangout for writers including Edward Abbey, Joy Harjo, Lucy Tapahonso, Allen Ginsberg, Leslie Silko, Maurice Kenny, and Simon Ortiz, among others.

During this time, Hobson was invited to guest edit the University of New Mexico American Studies graduate student publication *New America.* Hobson's *Special Native American Issue* for Summer/Fall 1976 included both established and new writers on the theme of contemporary Indian life. One reviewer noted, "The focus on contemporary Indian reality makes for a bitter pill at times, but one which provides necessary medicine for readers whose interest in Native literature hasn't passed the Noble Savage illusion" (Castro, 1979).

Working on *New America* fueled the idea of an anthology of contemporary Native American writing. *The Remembered Earth* was first published by Albuquerque's Red Earth Press in 1979, then by the University of New Mexico Press in 1981. It includes contributions from 75 Native American writers, poets, and artists, some from the *New America: Special Native American Issue*. The anthology of poetry, short fiction, and critical essays is considered an important contribution to the dissemination and study of Native American writing.

In his introduction, Hobson addressed the question "Who are Native American writers anyway?" stating he tried to "include as broad a spectrum of definition as possible . . . including writers of mixed-blood, even those who would probably have difficulty producing a Certificate of Indian Blood or tribal enrollment number, as well as those who were born full-bloods and raised on reservations" (Hobson, *Remembered Earth,* 1979, 8).

As the decade waned, Hobson worked in an advisory role for the 1978 TV miniseries *The Awakening Land,* starring Jane Seymour, Hal Holbrook, and Elizabeth Montgomery, based on the trilogy of novels by Conrad Richter.

Themes in Writing

Hobson's writing is noteworthy for his inclusion of traditional values that emphasize respectful relationships to others and to the land. Stylistically, his work ranges from quiet intimacy to biting satire or tongue-in-cheek wit. His creative projects are deeply informed by tribal histories, tribal languages, genealogical research, and personal experiences. Likewise, his military experiences shape his poetry as in "Central Highlands, Viet Nam, 1968" and his as yet unpublished short novel, *Plain of Jars,* about the conflict in Laos.

In his scholarly works, Hobson remains devoted to disseminating Native American literature while voicing sharp criticism for appropriation and misuse of Indian culture. His influential essay, "The Rise of the White Shaman as a New Version of Cultural Imperialism" (1976), revealed how neo-romanticism created by Jerome Rothenberg, Gary Snyder, Gene Fowler, and others often prevents readers from understanding works by writers with authentic tribal experiences.

He continues to do extensive research concerning Southeastern tribes, the Arkansas Quapaw in particular. In his essay, "The Folks Left Out of the Photographs" (2004), written for the anthology *Beyond the Reach of Time and Change* edited by Simon Ortiz, Hobson reflects on his mother's family history that is frequently cited in the folk history of his childhood home but has been erased from the official histories of the same region. He questions what might have been had Southeastern Indians been "seen" as Indians rather than subjected to what he calls "enwhitening" or "enblackening."

The process of identity erasure in all manner of documents, including the census, turned people of mixed ancestry into categories that policy makers could easily classify as white or black. "In the American South, Indian people, mixed-bloods as well as full-bloods, who elected to remain in their traditional homelands, no matter the reasons, were designated by American (i.e. white) census-takers and public officials as legally white—not so that such Indian remains might have better access to the white world but rather to facilitate these people's further disenfranchisement and exploitation" (Hobson, "Folks," 2004, 111).

His novel, *The Last of the Ofos* (2000), situates protagonist Thomas Darko at important moments of American 20th-century history. Darko struggles to retain Ofo identity and human dignity in contexts where an Indian is an "indigenous informant," an antique object of academic study.

Native Writers' Circle of the Americas

Among Native American writers, discussion of an international writers' gathering grew throughout the 1980s. In 1990, Hobson joined the Steering Committee for such an event. Hobson's wife, Barbara, was hired as Project Coordinator and the international festival of Native American writers "Returning the Gift" was held in Norman, Oklahoma, in July 1992. The festival extended over five days and resulted in the establishment of two organizations, the Native Writers' Circle of the Americas (NWCA), which maintains three awards for Native American writers, and an apprentice mentoring organization called Wordcraft Circle of Native Writers and Storytellers. Hobson served as the NWCA's Project Director from 1992–2007 and his essay, "On a Festival Called Returning the Gift," in *Returning the Gift* (1994) relates the history of the gathering.

Awards

Hobson has received several awards, including a Rockefeller Grant for minority group scholars (1981), a National Endowment of the Arts grant (1982), Wordcraft Circle's Mentor of the Year Award (1998), University of Oklahoma Presidential Professor Award (1998, the first American Indian faculty to receive this award), and the Lifetime Achievement Award from the Native Writers' Circle of the Americas (2003).

Barbara K. Robins

Further Reading

Castro, Michael. *"New America: A Review: Special Native American Issue." ASAIL Newsletter* 3 (1979). http://oncampus.richmond.edu/faculty/ASAIL/SAILns/31.html.

Hobson, Geary. "The Folks Left Out of the Photographs." In *Beyond the Reach of Time and Change: Native American Reflections on the Frank A. Rinehart Photograph Collection,* edited by Simon Ortiz, Tucson: Arizona University Press, 2004, pp. 109–23.

Hobson, Geary. "Native American Literature: Remembrance, Renewal." *U.S. Society & Values: Electronic Journal of the Department of State* 5 (February, 2000). usinfo.state.gov/journals/itsv/0200/ijse/toc.htm.

Hobson, Geary. "Vietnam Narrative." *More Indian Voices from Vietnam.* Robert Sanderson, ed. Sequoyah Research Center and American Native Press Archives. September 19, 2008. http://anpa.ualr.edu/digital_library/narratives/SanViet2.html.

Hobson, Geary, ed. *The Remembered Earth: An Anthology of Contemporary Native American Literature.* Albuquerque: University of New Mexico Press, 1979.

J

JAMES, JEWELL (TSE-SEALTH, PRAYING WOLF)
BORN 1953 LUMMI
ENVIRONMENTAL ACTIVIST AND ARTIST

Jewell Praying Wolf James became known in the late 20th century as an artist of international standing as well as an advocate of worldwide environmental restoration. James called for creation of a "world court of the environment" that would publicize the behavior of "environmentally criminal activity" around the world. In 1994, James played a major role in convening leaders of more than 300 Indian tribes at the White House, with President Bill Clinton, the first time that a pan-tribal summit had been conducted there.

The proposal for a world court of the environment was originally contained in a declaration by the "Group of 100," a group of writers, scientists, and environmentalists who met during 1991 in Morelia, Mexico, in which James took part.

James is a lineal descendant of Chief Seath'tl (after whom the city of Seattle was named). He has been coordinator of the Lummi Tribe's Treaty Protection Task Force. He has extensive experience in law, environment, and politics at the state, national, and international levels. He has chaired the board of the Florence R. Kluckhohn Center and is the founder and served as director of the Indian-in-the-Moon Foundation. He also has been treasurer of the National Tribal Environmental Council.

James is a master carver of totem, or healing poles, which have been presented around the world. For example, the Lummis presented two totem poles carved from red cedar trees to the Pentagon to support the families of the 184 people who died there September 11, 2001. The Liberty and Freedom totem poles were the "sacredness of love joining us together," said James. "The totem pole isn't a sacred thing, it's the sacredness of love joining us together," said James, who wore a coned straw hat over long, black, braided hair and a black vest with a shadowy gray wolf's head on the back as he presented the poles September 19, 2004 (Robins, 2007, 201).

Further Reading

Robins, Barbara K. "Healing Poles: Traditional Art for Modern Grief." *The International Journal of the Humanities* 5, no. 9 (2007): 201–8.

Williams, Rudi. "Pentagon Presented 9/11 'Healing Poles'." American Forces Press Service. U.S. Department of Defense, September 20, 2004. http://www.defenselink.mil/news/newsarticle.aspx?id=25256.

JEMISON, G. PETER
BORN 1945 SENECA
ARTIST

G. Peter Jemison, an eighth-generation descendant of Mary Jemison, is a Heron Clan Seneca from Cattauraugus; he was born in Silver Creek, New York. Jemison has directed the American Indian Community House Gallery in New York City. He has been the long-time manager of Ganondagan, an historic Seneca village site (designated as a state and federal historic site) 25 miles southeast of Rochester, New York. Jemison has been active in national efforts to advocate the return of Native American remains and funerary objects from museums and other non-Indian archives. Jemison also is an influential administrator, curator, editor, and writer. In 2004, he was elected Board Member at Large of the American Association of Museums.

Jemison describes himself as a "faith-keeper," who organizes dance performers and banquets. "Members of your clan ask you to become a faith-keeper, and the only choice you have is to say you are ready, or not yet," says Jemison. "I was only ready when I was 50" (Kandell, 2006). Jemison's work, according to one observer, "draws upon the concept of *orenda,* the traditional Haudenosaunee (Iroquois Confederacy) belief that every living thing and every part of creation contains a spiritual force. Presenting a challenge to reductive and exclusionary art historical structures, Jemison synthesizes the dual traditions of academic and traditional Native American arts" (Eight Modern, 2007).

Jemison has served as Chairman of the Haudenosaunee Standing Committee on Burial Rules and Regulations. "What we see objectively is when you ask a museum like the New York State Museum what remains could be identified as Caucasian, that number is zero, or very close to zero," he has said. "When you ask about Native American [remains], that's all there is. Isn't there something strange about this?" (Crowe, 1995, A-3).

Jemison, whose media as an artist include acrylics, pen and ink, charcoal, and colored pencils, began drawing as a boy. Encouraged by his parents and art teachers, he attended the State University of New York at Buffalo in art (1962–67). He also studied art at the University of Siena, Italy, during 1964.

In addition to his reputation as an artist, Jemison is well known in Haudenosaunee country as an organizer of shows for other artists. One example of many such shows that Jemison has organized was "Where We Stand: Contemporary Haudenosaunee Artists," which showed August 15–December 21, 1997, at the New York State Historical Association Fenimore House Museum (renamed, in 1999, the Fenimore Art Museum). This show featured a number of Haudenosaunee artists active in a wide array of forms, from painting to basketweaving, silversmithing, prints, and sculpture.

Jemison and fellow Senecas erected a full-scale replica of a longhouse and opened it to the public at Ganondagan in 1998. "We wanted to give people a sense of how our ancestors had lived," he said. The longhouse, about 65 feet long, 20 feet wide, and 25 feet high, has been equipped with four roof smoke holes. It was described in *Smithsonian* magazine thusly: "Elm bark covers outer and inner walls and the roof. The floor is made of pounded earth. Dozens of raised platform beds line the walls. An assortment of gourd bowls, baskets woven from wood strips, corn-husk mats, fur blankets, snowshoes and lacrosse sticks are stored on ledges reached by notched wooden ladders. A bark-skin canoe hangs from the ceiling" (Kandell, 2006).

Jemison is also widely known as a curator of Native American arts. Some of Jemison's curatorial projects include Pan-American Exposition Centennial: Images of the American Indian at the Burchfield-Penney Art Center in Buffalo, New York; and Stan Hill: The Spirit Released/A Circle Complete at the Fenimore Art Museum, Cooperstown, New York. He co-edited *The Treaty of Canandaigua 1794: 200 Years of Treaty Relations between the Iroquois Confederacy and the United States* (2000).

Jemison's work has been collected by many museums worldwide, including the Heard Museum, Phoenix, Arizona; the Institute of American Indian Arts Museum, Santa Fe, New Mexico; the Denver Art Museum; the British Museum, London; and the Museum der Weltkultern, Frankfurt, Germany.

Further Reading

Crowe, Kenneth C. "Museums Work to Restore Tribal Heritage." *Albany Times Union,* December 10, 1995, A-3.

Eight Modern. 2007. http://www.eightmodern.net/artists/bio/4250.

Jemison, Peter, and Anna M. Schein, eds. *The Treaty of Canandaigua 1794: 200 Years of Treaty Relations between the Iroquois Confederacy and the United States.* Santa Fe, NM: Clear Light, 2000.

Kandell, Jonathan "Steeped in History: New York's Breathtaking Finger Lakes District Has Inspired American Notables from Mark Twain to Harriet Tubman." *Smithsonian Magazine,* September 2006. http://www.smithsonianmag.com/travel/fingerlake. html?c=&page=2.

K

Kauffman, Hattie
Born 1955 Nez Perce
Television Broadcaster

Hattie Kauffman became known to millions of Americans in the late 20th century as a national correspondent for the Columbia Broadcasting System and as a feature reporter for the American Broadcasting Company's *Good Morning America.* For her earlier television news reporting at KING-TV in Seattle, Kauffman, who is of German and Nez Perce ancestry, won four Emmy awards.

Kauffman was born on a Nez Perce Reservation. She earned a BS degree at the University of Minnesota. She then attended the Graduate School of Journalism there on a WCCO-TV Minorities in Broadcasting Scholarship. She began to broadcast on radio while a student in Minneapolis. Kauffman became the first Native American journalist to report on a national broadcast in 1989 while working at KING-TV in Seattle. She was a reporter and anchor at KING-TV Seattle (1981–87).

Between 1987 and 1990, Kauffman was a special correspondent for *Good Morning America.* In 1990, she was a consumer-affairs reporter for CBS News, a job that took her from a Hawaiian leper colony to interview deep-sea hunters of sunken treasure, and to a woman's shooting range. Kauffman early in her network career was a frequent substitute on CBS *This Morning,* and she reported regularly for CBS' *48 Hours* and *Street Stories.* She then became a regular correspondent for CBS *This Morning* between 1990 and 1999. In 2007, Kauffman was a veteran national news correspondent for *The Early Show,* based in Los Angeles, a job she began in 1999.

Kauffman covered breaking news, celebrity profiles, and features about ordinary people. She covered the Oklahoma City federal building bombing, the death of John F. Kennedy, Jr., and the saga of Elian Gonzales, the child who was returned to Cuba after an international incident. In 2007, she covered wildfires that ravaged southern California. Kauffman also has reported on unique (and physically challenging) vacation ideas, such as rock climbing, whitewater rafting, and race-car driving, scuba diving (with dolphins), ski jumping and luge riding at Lake Placid, New York, as well as rodeo riding.

Kauffman has been described as having "a unique style of reporting human interest stories [that] has earned her acclaim throughout her career" (Hattie Kauffman, 2007).

Further Reading

Hattie Kauffman: National News Correspondent. CBS News. *The Early Show.* 2007. http://www.cbsnews.com/stories/2002/05/21/earlyshow/bios/main509679.shtml.

KAWAGLEY, ANGAYUQAQ OSCAR
BORN 1934 YUPIAQ, ALASKA NATIVE
SCIENTIST

Angayuqaq Oscar Kawagley, a prominent interpreter of Alaska Native traditions in modern science, was born in Mamterilleq (Bethel), Alaska, during 1934. Both of his parents died during his infancy, so he was raised by his grandmother from the age of two. During Kawagley's life, his Yupiaq people have endured cultural change on fast-forward, emerging from the upper stone age to the jet age. Yupiaq was Kawagley's first language. His grandmother told him of the Bear Woman's and nature's reciprocity, as the boarding schools taught him Western science. He learned from both.

Kawagley earned a bachelor's degree in education, majoring in biological sciences, followed by a master's of education, both at the University of Alaska–Fairbanks. Kawagley then earned a PhD in social and educational studies at the University of British Columbia.

Kawagley is professor emeritus of education in the College of Liberal Arts at the University of Alaska–Fairbanks. His specialty is the integration of indigenous and Western knowledge in a renewed educational system, an effort he explains in his book, *A Yupiaq Worldview: A Pathway to Ecology and Spirit.* He also has advised the Intergovernmental Panel on Climate Change (IPCC) on Native Alaskan points of view and global warming.

A man of many talents, Kawagley played a role as "Butch" in *Salmonberries,* a story of life in a remote Alaskan village on the North Slope, which was voted best film at the 1991 Montreal Film Festival. The *New York Times'* Janet Maslin, however, panned the film as an "amateurish" and "halting, awkward" effort suffering from the "stilted direction of Percy Adlon" (Maslin, 1994). Maslin characterized Kawagley as part of "a cast of nonchalant Alaskans," in the film, which starred k.d. Lang and Chuck Connors (Maslin, 1994).

Kawagley has served as executive director of many nonprofit corporations that focus on health, science, education, and health. He also was working, in 2009, on Haskell University's American Indian and Alaska Native Climate Change Working Group. Between 1980 and 1986, Kawagley served on the Inuit Circumpolar Conference's Executive Committee.

Interpreting Native Alaskan Views

Kawagley is known mainly as a person whose ideas have shaped non-Native Alaskans' views of the world. He often has explained to them a basic difference between European and Yupiaq worldviews with regard to ownership of land:

> I recently watched a television program titled "You Own Alaska." My first reaction was that this was an expression motivated by political and economic interest. But the more I thought about it, the more it grated on my worldview. How could anyone "own" Alaska? According to my ancestral traditions, the land owns me! Thus began my reflections on how my Yupiaq worldview differs from that of the dominant society. (Kawagley, 2009)

With regard to a changing climate, Kawagley provides a Native Alaskan view, which relies on signposts from nature, shorn of the Christian ethic that humankind's duty is, as the book of *Genesis* says, to multiply and subdue the Earth. In the Yupiaq worldview, "The cold defines my landscape. . . . The cold made my language, my worldview, my culture, and technology. Now, the cold is waning at a very fast rate, and as a result, it is changing the landscape" (Kawagley, 2009).

The Yupiaq once used the alder tree's leafing to tell them when the smelt would run, providing them with food. Usually, the king salmon arrived when the alders budded. However, "These indicators are no longer reliable when spring arrives two to four weeks earlier than usual" (Kawagley, 2009).

"The encroachment of Western civilization in the Yupiaq world changed a people that did not seek changing," Kawagley has written. "The Yupiaq peoples' systems of education, governance, spirituality, economy, being and behavior were very much in conformity with their philosophy of life and provided for harmonious living. The people were satisfied with the quality of their life and felt that their technology was in accord with it. The culture- and nature-mediated technology was geared to a sustainable level of self-sufficiency," wrote Kawagley (1999).

Merging Views of Education

Kawagley wrote on the ethos of assimilation, especially in the boarding schools. "From the late 1960s and up to the present," he stated, "Native people have been working diligently to change education so that it accommodates their languages, worldviews, culture, and technology. This is a slow healing process for the village" (Kawagley, 2009).

Kawagley believes that the two worlds will merge: "In the Eurocentric world of science and technology exist many alternative approaches that are nature-friendly and sustainable," he has written. "They await the time when the global societies evolve from consumerism and materialism to ones that are oriented to conservation and regeneration" (Kawagley, 1999).

Further Reading

Kawagley, Angayuqaq Oscar. *A Yupiaq Worldview: A Pathway to Ecology and Spirit.* 2nd ed. Long Grove, IL: Waveland Press, 1995.

Kawagley, Angayuqaq Oscar. "Alaskan Native Education: History and Adaptation in the New Millennium." *Journal of American Indian Education* 39, no. 1 (Fall 1999). http://www.ankn.uaf.edu/curriculum/Articles/OscarKawagley/ANEHistory.html.

Kawagley, Angayuqaq Oscar. "My Place, My Identity." *EJournalUSA.* Washington, DC: U.S. State Department. June 2009. http://www.america.gov/st/peopleplace-english/2009/June/20090617113323wrybakcuh5.195254e-02.html.

Maslin, Janet. "K. D. Lang's Debut, in an Alaskan Chill." *New York Times,* September 2, 1994. http://movies.nytimes.com/person/239029/Oscar-Kawagley.

L

LaDuke, Winona
Born 1959 Anishinabe (Ojibwa)
Environmental Activist and Political Figure

Ask Winona LaDuke what she does for a living, and she may say "rural economic development." That's what they called it at Harvard, where LaDuke took her undergraduate degree during the late 1970s. The sum of those three words is more than its parts, however. LaDuke is engaged in a reservation revolution, changing the ways that Native Americans (and many other people as well) think about how and where they get and use their energy, food, and other basics of daily life. In 2007, LaDuke was inducted into the National Women's Hall of Fame in Seneca Falls, New York.

LaDuke is a passionate advocate of direct action, quoting Malcolm X, "by any means necessary." "Sometimes," LaDuke said at the University of Nebraska at Omaha November 6, 2007, "You have to put your body on the line." LaDuke, whose Anishinabe name is *Benaysayequay,* meaning "Thunderbird Woman," says: "I have a fervent belief that Native people should own land. Want a wind turbine on your reservation? At White Earth they have plans to go carbon neutral with five of them. Buy the land from a non-Indian farmer or rancher and get busy." That's rural economic development, LaDuke style.

A charismatic, dynamic speaker with a long face and expressive eyes, LaDuke meets audiences one-on-one. She has written several books, lectured around the world, and twice, in 1996 and 2000, ran for vice president of the United States on the Green Party ticket with Ralph Nader. Most of her days are spent at home on the White Earth Anishinabe (also known as Chippewa or Ojibwa) Reservation about 200 miles northwest of Minneapolis, Minnesota. On the reservation, LaDuke leads the White Earth Land Recovery Project, started in 1989. She founded the recovery project to reclaim Anishinaabeg lands (originally 837,000

Native American activist, environmentalist, and author, Winona LaDuke. (AP/Wide World Photos)

acres) promised by a federal treaty signed in 1867 that had been sold or stolen, often by logging companies. By 2007, the project was buying back real estate, installing wind and solar power, harvesting wild rice for home use and export, and feeding elders buffalo meat instead of commodity cheese (among many other things) on a $1.7 million annual budget. Anyone who can fix a reservation car, she insists, can build and install solar panels.

The White Earth Land Recovery Project has become the largest reservation-based nonprofit organization in the United States. In addition to working toward recovery of the White Earth Indian Reservation's original land, the group advocates land stewardship, language fluency, community development, and spiritual and cultural traditions.

With a $20,000 award from the first Reebok Human Rights Award, LaDuke founded the White Earth Land Recovery Project on the reservation, where she had moved during the early 1980s. The project's major goal has been to regain a land base in Native lands on a reservation that by 1990 was 92 percent owned by non-Indians.

LaDuke's brand of economic development relies heavily on creation of employment that produces real goods and services, keeping money at home. She disparages government programs on reservations that leave more people engaged in job training than in jobs. For example, she helped create Native Harvest, which provides food for domestic consumption and sale over the Internet. By 2007, Native Harvest's wild rice alone was bringing in $500,000 a year. "To be sovereign," she said at the University of Nebraska, Omaha, event, "You have to have an economy that is internal—grow your own food, produce your own energy."

Early Years

LaDuke was born in Los Angeles, daughter of Vincent LaDuke, an Indian activist during the 1950s, and Betty LaDuke, a painter and art professor. LaDuke says that her parents gave her an animating activist spirit. While studying at Harvard, she met Cherokee activist Jimmy Durham; soon she became involved in Native American environmental issues.

By her teenage years, LaDuke was engaged in debate at school, and, as a member of her high school's championship team in Oregon, was recruited to Harvard (she graduated in 1982), surprising nearly everyone in her community. At the age of 18, she was involved in researching the effect of uranium mining on Navajos as part of her debating activities, which led to environmental advocacy that, decades later, helped lead to a ban on such mining on the reservation. "There is no safe way to mine uranium," LaDuke said in a speech at the University of Nebraska at Omaha, November 5, 2007. "Most of the Navajos' uranium miners have died."

LaDuke has tirelessly lectured, written, and pressed authorities for answers on environmental issues, from the Navajo uranium mines, to Hydro-Quebec's construction sites at James Bay, to toxic waste sites on Native Alaskan and Canadian land along the Arctic Ocean. LaDuke's assertions have been confirmed by environmental scientists. As if to illustrate just how pervasive pollution of the entire Earth has become, studies of Inuit women's breast milk in the late 20th century revealed abnormally high levels of PCBs. Studies around the rim of Hudson's Bay, conducted by Eric Dewailly of Laval University in 1988, found that nursing mothers' milk contained more than six times the level of PCBs considered safe by the Canadian government. The fish that most Inuit eat bioaccumulate PCBs, dioxins, mercury, and other toxic materials in the food chain.

LaDuke publicized her findings in numerous newspaper and magazine articles, and as a founder of the Indigenous Women's Network and a board member of Greenpeace. She also initiated a national Native environmental advocacy group, Honor the Earth, that raises money for economic development projects on reservations. She was named by *Time* magazine in 1995 as one of 50 "Leaders for the Future."

Green Party Campaign

Under ordinary circumstances, Winona LaDuke says unabashedly that she is not inclined toward electoral politics. She would rather be farming and caring for her children and grandchildren on the White Earth Reservation. During the late summer of 1996, however, an extraordinary circumstance arose for LaDuke when Ralph Nader, who had been nominated to run for president by the Green Party, tapped her for vice president. The Nader-LaDuke ticket received 0.6 percent of the popular vote in the November 5 general election that year. Four years later, the same ticket was influential enough in some states to be accused by liberals of diverting just enough votes from Democrat Al Gore to put Republican George W. Bush in the White House.

The Green Party was listed on the general election ballot in 22 states, under other names in some of them, such as the Liberty, Ecology, and Community Party in Louisiana, and the Pacific Party in Oregon. The Green Party, which began organizing in 1984, by late 1996 had 29 elected officials in 10 states. The party platform focuses on increased grassroots democracy and break-up of corporate power. The platform also puts an emphasis on environmentally correct economic policy, nonviolence, and social justice.

In the 1996 election, the Green Party felt slighted after the Sierra Club endorsed Bill Clinton and Al Gore as an environmentally friendly alternative to Republican candidates Bob Dole and Bill Kemp. However, a sizable number of dissidents argued that the Sierra Club should have endorsed Nader and LaDuke. The dissidents were led by former Sierra Club president David Brower.

"It is shameful that the Sierra Club would endorse someone of so many environmental promises and so little environmental protection," said LaDuke (LaDuke, 1996, 38–45). She characterized President Clinton as an environmental opportunist, who said in 1992 that he would not allow any weakening of the Endangered Species Act, but who in 1994 signed legislation that froze addition of species to that list. The Sierra Club's internal conflict was reflected in the November/December 1996 edition of its magazine, where Clinton was endorsed at the bottom of page 60, while LaDuke appeared on the cover riding a horse for a special issue on Native Americans and the Environment. She also wrote the cover story.

LaDuke said her campaign brought American Indian issues into the national campaign. LaDuke favors a constitutional amendment that would protect the air and water as common property, to be maintained free from contamination. "The rights of the people to use and enjoy air, water, and sunlight are essential to life, liberty, and the pursuit of happiness," LaDuke wrote in *Indian Country Today,* October 14, 1996.

"A Remarkable Figure"

In the waning days of the national campaign, John Nichols, an editorial writer for the Madison, Wisconsin, *Capital Times,* summarized LaDuke's contribution, saying that she "is a remarkable figure whose history of American Indian, environmental, and economic justice activism makes her uniquely qualified to participate in a national debate that desperately needs her insights. Yet, in an age of sound-bite politics, LaDuke and Nader have been largely neglected." Nichols continued: "As we move into the final stages of a campaign that has been as vapid as any in this nation's history, Winona LaDuke stands out as a lonely voice of substance" (Johansen, 1996, 4).

Most of LaDuke's initiatives are more basic than national politics. She helped (with Margaret Smith, a former teacher) to build Mino-Miijim, to give wild rice and other traditional foods, including buffalo meat and hominy, to elderly people with Type 2 diabetes on the reservation.

LaDuke maintains that "The essence of the problem is about consumption, recognizing that a society [the United States] that consumes one third of the world's resources is unsustainable. This level of consumption requires constant intervention into other people's lands. That's what's going on" ("Americans," n.d.).

On November 16, 2008, LaDuke's home on the White Earth Reservation burned to the ground because of an electrical fire. LaDuke, five children, and three grandchildren escaped injury, but art, books, music, photographs, and other collectibles from LaDuke's travels around the world, as well as furniture and other possessions, were destroyed. Many friends banded together to replace some of the memorable pieces.

Further Reading

"Americans Who Tell the Truth: Winona LaDuke." n.d. http://www.americanswhotellthetruth. org/pgs/portraits/Winona_LaDuke.html.

Bowermaster, Jon. "Earth of a Nation." *Harper's Bazaar,* April 1993, 99–101.

Johansen, Bruce E. "Running for Office: LaDuke and the Green Party." *Native Americas* 18, no. 4 (Winter 1996): 3–4.

Kummer, Corby. "Going with the Grain: True Wild Rice, for the Past Twenty Years Nearly Impossible to Find, Is Slowly Being Nurtured Back to Market." *Atlantic Monthly,* May 2004, 145–48.

LaDuke, Winona. "The Growing Strength of Native Environmentalism: Like Tributaries to a River." *Sierra,* November/December 1996, 38–45.

LaDuke, Winona. *All Our Relations: Native Struggles for Land and Life*. Cambridge, MA: South End Press/Minneapolis, MN: Honor the Earth, 1999.

LaDuke, Winona. *Last Standing Woman (History and Heritage).* Stillwater, MN: Voyageur Press, 1999.

LaDuke, Winona. *The Winona LaDuke Reader: A Collection of Essential Writings*. Stillwater, MN: Voyageur Press, 2002.

LaDuke, Winona. *Recovering the Sacred: The Power of Naming and Claiming*. Cambridge, MA: South End Press, 2005.

Melmer, David. "Winona LaDuke Inducted into National Women's Hall of Fame." *Indian Country Today,* October 15, 2007. http://www.indiancountry.com/content. cfm?id=1096415916.

LaFlesche, Susan
1865–1910 U'ma'ha (Omaha)
Physician

Daughter of Omaha principal Chief Joseph LaFlesche, Susan LaFlesche Picotte blazed a career of genius through a number of white schools, then became a doctor on the Omaha Reservation during a time when cholera, influenza, tuberculosis, and other diseases were reaching epidemic proportions. She nearly worked herself to death serving the Omahas as a government physician.

In 1884, after two and a half years at the Elizabeth Institute for Young Ladies in Elizabeth, New Jersey, LaFlesche enrolled at the Hampton Normal and Agricultural Institute in Hampton, Virginia. This vocational school had been started by General Samuel C. Armstrong to educate freed slaves. A number of Indians also attended, and the school played a role in the designs of Lt. Richard Henry Pratt, who started Carlisle Indian School. LaFlesche graduated from Hampton May 20, 1886, at the top of her class. Between 1886 and 1889, she attended the Women's

Susan La Flesche Picotte, first female Native American physician in the United States. (Nebraska State Historical Society)

Medical College of Pennsylvania on a scholarship raised by her friends, many of whom were non-Indian, again graduating at the top of her class.

LaFlesche thus became one of a handful of Native American physicians in the 19th century, a group that includes Charles Eastman and Carlos Montezuma. She was the only Native American woman to become a medical doctor during that century. For five years, LaFlesche fought pervasive disease on the Omaha Reservation, making some progress.

In December 1891, LaFlesche wrote that influenza "raged with more violence than during the two preceding years. Some families were rendered helpless by it. . . . Almost every day I was out making visits. . . . Several days the temperature was 15 to 20 degrees below zero, and I had to drive [a horse-drawn buggy] myself" (Mathes, 1985, 73). During that winter, she treated more than 600 patients.

By 1892, the intensity of her work was costing LaFlesche her own health. She was beset by a number of debilitating illnesses for the rest of her life, as she ministered to the ever-present ills of the Omahas. At one point she wearily departed for Washington, D.C., to testify for the Omahas because people had threatened to convey her bodily, her mission was of such importance to them.

Back on the Omaha reservation, LaFlesche waged a tireless campaign against alcoholism, recounting stories of how Indians craving liquor used their rent money and even pawned their clothes in winter to obtain it. She wrote about Harry Edwards, who, on a winter's night in 1894, "fell from a buggy, was not missed by his drunken companions, and in the morning was found frozen to death" (Mathes, 1985, 75). From a medical point of view, LaFlesche believed that alcoholism was at the root of many of the physical, mental, and moral ills facing the Omahas and other American Indians.

In 1894, her health improving, LaFlesche married Henri Picotte, who was part French and part Sioux; she also began a new medical practice for Indians and whites at Bancroft, Nebraska. LaFlesche practiced medicine there for the rest of her life, as her own health permitted. After LaFlesche's death on September 18, 1915, the *Walthill Times* added an extra page (in its September 24 issue) and filled it with warm eulogies to her. Friends recalled that hundreds of people in the area, Indian and Euro-American, owed their lives to her care.

The hospital that Susan LaFlesche built at Walthill has since been declared a national historic landmark. Since 1988, her memory has been celebrated at an annual festival there.

Further Reading

Ferris, Jeri. *Native American Doctor: The Story of Susan Laflesche Picotte.* Minneapolis, MN: Carolrhoda Books, 1991.

Mathes, Valerie Sherer. "Dr. Susan LaFlesche Picotte: The Reformed and the Reformer." In *Indian Lives: Essays on Nineteenth-and Twentieth-century Native American Leaders,* edited by L. G. Moses and Raymond Wilson, 61–89. Norman: University of Oklahoma Press, 1985.

Tong, Benson. *Susan La Flesche Picotte, M.D.: Omaha Indian Leader and Reformer.* Norman: University of Oklahoma Press, 1999.

Wilkerson, J. L. *A Doctor to Her People: Dr. Susan LaFlesche Picotte.* Kansas City, MO: Acorn Books, 1999.

LaFlesche, Susette (Inshta Theamba, Bright Eyes)
1854–1903 U'ma'ha (Omaha)
Native-rights Advocate and Journalist

Susette LaFlesche became a major 19th-century Native-rights advocate through the case of the Ponca Standing Bear (*Standing Bear v. Crook,* 1879), the first legal proceeding (decided in Omaha Federal District Court) to establish Native Americans as human beings under the U.S. law of *habeas corpus*. Susette also accompanied her brother Francis and Standing Bear on a lecture tour of Eastern cities in 1879 and 1880 to support the Poncas' case for a return of their homeland. Newspaper articles about the Poncas' forced exile by Omaha journalist Thomas H. Tibbles helped ignite a furor in Congress and among the public.

LaFlesche was born near Bellevue, Nebraska, the eldest daughter of Joseph "Iron Eye" LaFlesche and Mary Gale LaFlesche, daughter of an Army surgeon. Like her sister Susan, LaFlesche attended the Presbyterian mission school on the Omaha Reservation. Both sisters were among the most brilliant students ever to attend the school. Susette also studied art at the University of Nebraska.

Defending Standing Bear

In the late 1870s, LaFlesche traveled with her father to Indian Territory (later Oklahoma) to render rudimentary medical attention to the Poncas with Standing Bear, whose people had been forced to move there from their former homeland along the Niobrara River in northern Nebraska. When the Poncas attempted to escape their forced exile and return to their homeland, they marched for several weeks in midwinter, finally eating their moccasins to survive, arriving at the Omaha Reservation with bleeding feet. The Omahas, particularly the LaFlesche family, granted them sanctuary and sustenance.

Tibbles, an editor at the *Omaha World-Herald,* was the first journalist to interview Standing Bear while the LaFlesche family sheltered the Poncas. Tibbles's accounts were telegraphed to newspapers on the East Coast. In the meantime, LaFlesche and Tibbles fell in love and married in 1882. Both also toured the East Coast with Standing Bear, "armed with news clippings on the Ponca story and endorsements from General [George] Crook, the mayor of Omaha, and leading Nebraska clergymen," raising support for the restoration of Ponca lands (Tibbles, 1880, 129).

In Boston, where support for Standing Bear's Poncas was very strong, a citizens' committee formed that included Henry Wadsworth Longfellow. While Susette LaFlesche was visiting Boston with Standing Bear, Longfellow said of her, "*This* is Minnehaha" (Tibbles, 1880, 130).

In Boston, Tibbles, LaFlesche, and Standing Bear first met Helen Hunt Jackson. The Poncas' story inflamed Jackson's conscience and changed her life. Heretofore known as a poet (and a childhood friend of Emily Dickinson), Jackson set out to write *A Century of Dishonor,* a best-selling book that described the angst of an America debating the future of the Native American peoples who had survived the last of the Indian wars. Jackson became a major figure in the Anglo-American debate over the future of Native Americans. Standing Bear and his people eventually were allowed to return home to the Niobrara River after Congress investigated the conditions under which they had been evicted.

Reporting at Wounded Knee

Following the massacre at Wounded Knee in 1890, LaFlesche became one of the first female war correspondents to be employed by any American newspaper, and America's first female Native American war correspondent. While LaFlesche interviewed Native Americans, other reporters spun imaginative tales as they read conspiracies of intrigue and impending violence into expressions on the faces of Indians returning home after performing in Buffalo Bill Cody's Wild West Show.

The *World-Herald* often published LaFlesche's accounts of events at Wounded Knee under the headline "What Bright Eyes Thinks." Unlike most other correspondents, LaFlesche stressed the common humanity of the Ghost Dancers: "The causes that brought about the 'Messiah scare' may seem to be very simple if one stops to think, first of all, that the Sioux are human beings with the same feelings, desires, resentments, and aspirations as all other human beings" (Reilly, 1997, 198).

The *Omaha World-Herald* treated the conflict as a massacre rather than a battle (as the U.S. Army calls it to this day) under headlines such as "All Murdered in a Mass." The newspaper's accounts emphasized the difference in the amount of firepower available to each side and the large number of women and children in the Native camp. Editorially, the *World-Herald* called what had happened at Wounded Knee "A Crime against Civilization." The paper asked: "What sentiment dignifies and raises it from the low estate of murder to that of war. . . . On a field on which there can be no honor" (Reilly, 1997, 211–12).

While other newspapers railed against "murderous Redskins," LaFlesche, under the headline "Horrors of War," described the sufferings of Indian women and children who had been seriously wounded in the shooting. This account, as compiled by Hugh Reilly, makes for wrenching reading. LaFlesche was nearly alone in reporting the suffering of the Native people at Wounded Knee. Reilly wrote, "Bright Eyes' anger was palpable. The Sioux believe that they have been made to suffer because the whites want their land, she wrote. 'If the white people want their land and must have it, they can go about getting it some other way than by forcing it from them by starving them or provoking them to war and sacrificing the lives of innocent women and children.'" (Reilly, 1997, 215).

LaFlesche also co-authored a memoir with Standing Bear, *Ploughed Under: The Story of an Indian Chief*. In ensuing years, LaFlesche and Tibbles also toured the British Isles. The couple lived in Washington, D.C., but eventually LaFlesche returned to Lincoln, Nebraska, where she died in 1903. She was buried in Bancroft, Nebraska. In 1994, LaFlesche was inducted into the National Women's Hall of Fame.

Further Reading

Jackson, Helen Hunt. *A Century of Dishonor: A Sketch of the United States Government's Dealings with Some of the Indian Tribes.* [Boston: Roberts Bros., 1888]. St. Clair Shores, MI: Scholarly Press, 1972.

Massey, Rosemary. *Footprints in Blood: Standing Bear's Struggle for Freedom and Human Dignity.* Omaha, NE: American Indian Center of Omaha, 1979.

Reilly, Hugh. *Treatment of Native Americans by the Frontier Press: An Omaha, Nebraska Study, 1868–1891.* Master's thesis, University of Nebraska at Omaha, 1997.

Tibbles, Thomas Henry. *The Ponca Chiefs: An Account of the Trial of Standing Bear.* [1880]. Lincoln: University of Nebraska Press, 1972.

Wilson, Dorothy Clarke. *Bright Eyes: The Story of Suzette LaFlesche.* New York: McGraw-Hill, 1974.

LITTLEFEATHER, SACHEEN
BORN 1947 APACHE, YAQUI, PUEBLO
ACTRESS AND ACTIVIST

Sacheen Littlefeather was the stage name of a movie actress and activist who rejected an Oscar on behalf of Marlon Brando at the March 27, 1973, Academy Awards. Littlefeather's given name is Maria Cruz, and she is of mixed ancestry (Apache, Yaqui, Pueblo, and Caucasian). Brando refused the Oscar for Best Actor in *The Godfather* in protest of the movie and television industries' stereotyping of American Indians, and to emphasize grievances associated with the ongoing occupation of Wounded Knee.

At the awards ceremony, Littlefeather said: "Marlon Brando . . . has asked me to tell you, in a very long speech which I cannot share with you presently—because of time [the producer had given her only 45 seconds]—that he . . . very regretfully cannot accept this very generous award. . . . I beg at this time that I have not intruded upon this evening and that we will, in the future . . . our hearts and our understanding will meet with love and generosity. Thank you on behalf of Marlon Brando" (News of the Odd, 1973).

Brando said of American Indians: "We murdered them. We lied to them. We cheated them out of their lands. We starved them into signing fraudulent agreements that we called treaties which we never kept. We turned them into beggars on a continent that gave life for as long as life can remember" (Brando, 1973).

A few people in the audience applauded, but many more jeered until Littlefeather walked off the stage. Later in the evening, Clint Eastwood wondered aloud whether he should present the award for Best Picture "on behalf of all the cowboys shot in John Ford westerns over the years," and Raquel Welch said, "I hope the winner doesn't have a cause," before announcing the winner of the Best Actress Oscar. Co-host Michael Caine criticized Brando for "Letting some poor little Indian girl take the boos," instead of "[standing] up and [doing] it himself" (News of the Odd, 1973).

Littlefeather's brief appearance on behalf of Brando produced a few film roles for her, as well as an appearance in *Playboy*. Littlefeather continued her activism after the incident that made her famous, as she advocated Native Americans' work in roles suitable for them in movies. She also fought obesity, alcoholism, and diabetes, and cared for Indians with AIDS, including her brother.

Further Reading

Brando, Marlon. "The Godfather: That Unfinished Oscar Speech." *New York Times,* March 30, 1973. http://www.nytimes.com/packages/html/movies/bestpictures/godfather-ar3.html.

News of the Odd. March 27, 1973. http://www.newsoftheodd.com/article1027.html.

LUCAS, PHIL
1942–2007 CHOCTAW
FILMMAKER

The Choctaw filmmaker Phil Lucas was among the first American Indians to receive national acclaim behind the filmmaker's camera. He specialized in films that showed Native reality in cities and on reservations, portraying problems, such as alcoholism, in the context of searches for solutions.

Lucas wrote, directed, or produced more than 100 films, documentaries, and TV series episodes. Lucas also wrote widely, rebutting negative stereotypes of Native

Americans in television and film. Lucas won an Emmy Award in 1994 for co-directing *The Native Americans* on the Turner Broadcasting System. Lucas's work was screened in several venues, including the Sundance and Cannes film festivals. He also had a consulting role on mainstream television shows, including *Northern Exposure* and *MacGyver.*

"He is definitely one of the pioneering creative forces in American Indian life," said Hanay Geiogamah, a professor of theater and American Indian studies at the University of California–Los Angeles. "He probably is our foremost [Native American] film documentarian" (Frey, 2007). "His life could make a great film just in itself," said Mike Korolenko, a friend and faculty member at Bellevue, Washington, Community College ("Phil Lucas," 2007). "He was a teacher in his films as well as in the classroom," said Korolenko (Frey, 2007).

Lucas was born in Phoenix, Arizona. He recalled that as a young Choctaw he had seen signs that said: "No dogs or Indians allowed." Prejudice propelled his life's plans to tell his people's story in film. Such early prejudice helped inspire his film career. "He worked toward racial equality in any way he could," said Gary Robinson, Lucas's production partner and close friend (Bach, 2007). Lucas also learned to play the guitar despite the fact that he had lost a thumb in an accident during his childhood.

Having earned a degree in visual communication at Western Washington State University in Bellingham, Lucas traveled widely before establishing a home and family. He tried a variety of jobs during his travels, as a musician in New York City, advertising agent in Honduras, and freelance photographer in Managua, Nicaragua, where he survived the devastating earthquake during December 1972. He also became active in the Bahá'í faith.

Lucas taught courses in film at the Institute of American Indian Arts, Santa Fe, as well as the University of Lethbridge in Alberta. Close to his home in Issaquah, Lucas also taught film at Bellevue Community College, where he founded and hosted an American Indian Film Festival, bringing several Native American filmmakers to campus. "He was the kind of guy who you wanted to run back to and tell about your success," said Travis Sterner, who runs a film-production company in Bellevue ("Phil Lucas," 2007).

Lucas produced and directed *Images of Indians,* a series broadcast during 1980 on PBS that examined portrayals of Native Americans in the media. He was especially direct on the use of Indians as stereotypical sports mascots. In 1980, on the pages of *Four Winds,* he asked how whites would react to a team named the "Cleveland Caucasians." What would European Americans think, Lucas asked, if Indians adopted racial names (such as the "Window Rock Negroes" or the "Tahlequah White Boys") for their sports teams? (Lucas, 1980).

In *The Honour of All,* Lucas described how members of British Columbia's Alkali Lake band resisted alcoholism. A village that was almost totally alcoholic during the 1960s nearly entirely went sober within 20 years. "*The Honour of All* was the most powerful thing you'd ever want to see," said Robinson (Frey, 2007). Lucas also co-produced the early 1990s film *The Broken Chain* starring Pierce Brosnan. Lucas received the Taos Mountain Award for lifetime achievement at the Taos

Talking Picture Festival in 1999. His film *Restoring the Sacred Circle* won the Best Public Service Award at the 2002 American Indian Film Festival in San Francisco.

Lucas died at age 65, February 4, 2007, in Issaquah, Washington, of complications following heart surgery. Survivors included his wife, Mary Lou Lucas, and sons Josh of Tacoma and Jason of Seattle, as well as daughters Amra Lucas of Seattle and Sara Lucas of Issaquah.

Further Reading

Bach, Ashley. "Phil Lucas' Films Told Real Stories of Native People." *Seattle Times,* February 7, 2007. http://seattletimes.nwsource.com/html/localnews/2003560250_lucaso bit07e0.html.

Frey, Christine. "Phil Lucas, 1942–2007: Native American 'a Teacher in His Films and Classroom.'" *Seattle Post-Intelligencer,* February 7, 2007. http://seattlepi.nwsource.com/local/302643_obitlucas07.html.

Lucas, Phil. "Images of Indians." *Four Winds: The International Forum for Native American Art, Literature, and History* (Autumn 1980): 69–77.

"Phil Lucas, Award-winning Choctaw Filmmaker, Dies." Indianz.com, February 7, 2007. [Reprint of Bach, 2007]. http://www.indianz.com/News/2007/000785.asp.

LUNA, JAMES
BORN 1950 LUISEÑO
PERFORMANCE ARTIST

With a daring sense of conception and cultural irony, performance artist James Luna has shaken up the world of Native American art. Having been called "one of the most dangerous Indians alive," Luna replies: "At times the message can be potent. One of my subjects is with ethnic identity—how people perceive us and how we perceive ourselves. Not everybody can talk about that, so I guess that makes me a dangerous character" (Fletcher, 2008).

Luna's work "confronts and challenges commonly held stereotypes about Native Americans, museums, art, and life, and does it with irony, humor, sorrow, and a strong sense of story-telling in motion" ("James Luna," 2004). Much of Luna's work is bicultural (tricultural, if one includes his Latino heritage), and he is comfortable with it: "I'm a man of two worlds [and] I do it with ease," he has said (Durland, 1998).

Early Life

Luna was born in 1950 in Orange, California. His mother was Luiseño and his father Mexican. Luna graduated in 1976 with a BA in art from the University of California–Irvine at a time when that school's art faculty and students were known for their daring approaches to conceptual and performance art. In 1983,

Luna earned a master's degree in counseling at San Diego State University. He has long worked as a counselor at Palomar College, San Marcos.

He can be critical of other artists: In college, Luna said, "I didn't go to a lot of shows and I didn't hang out with the art crowd" (Durland, 1998). He took the job as a counselor for financial security unavailable to most artists, and also to give him a connection to people outside the world of art, which he sometimes finds rather removed from reality.

In the mid-1980s, Luna went into semiseclusion. In 1986, however, David Avalos, curator at San Diego's Centro de la Raza and Philip Brookman realized the potential of Luna's work, providing financial support and a studio.

Expanding His Range of Expression

Luna began his artistic life as a painter. With painting, however, he felt confined, unable to express emotions. Painting also limited his ability to express transition, or motion. Luna has said that he "stumbled" into performance art while working with instructors Bas Jan Ader (from the Netherlands) and Jim Turrell at UC–Irvine. Luna quickly expanded his range of expression to the design, installation, and performance of work that may include several media, including video, to challenge cultural and historical assumptions about Native Americans.

While painting usually involves an audience in a passive way, Luna enjoys performance art because the audience takes part in the act of expression with him. "I involve the audience," Luna said in an interview. "People give you control of their imagination. I can have them outraged one moment and crying the next. That's the power the audience gives you. It's knowing that and knowing how to use it effectively" (Fletcher, 2008).

Luna resents being pigeonholed as an ethnic artist, "to be called upon only when his ethnicity is timely—as during the Christopher Columbus anniversary in 1992" (Durland, 1998). He would rather be known as "James Luna, artist. Period. James Luna, artist who happens to be an Indian." To the avalanche of engagements offered in 1992, he replied, "Call me in '93" (Durland, 1998).

While Luna does not want to be rat-holed as an "Indian artist," he draws freely on Native American traditions and cultural practices as a major component of his artistic persona. He reserves the right, however, to be sharply critical of all assumptions, including those expressed in Native American cultures. "Authenticity," for example, to Luna, becomes a stereotype of a kind, a set of expectations beyond which Native people are not allowed to grow and change.

Confronted with an occasional critic who accuses Luna of exploiting his own cultural background, he replies that all artists draw from their own experiences.

While Luna says that his work is not political, some members of his audience disagree. His strikingly original design and execution cannot help but involve political context, no matter how it is categorized. Some of Luna's work is autobiographical, as when he illustrates his own battle with alcoholism as part of a culturewide problem. Some of the work is cathartic, perhaps reflecting his academic preparation as a counselor.

Mimicry and Parody

One of Luna's favorite targets is faux (i.e., "plastic") medicine men. In "Capitalists?" he combined a "high technology" peace pipe mounted on the chassis of a desk telephone, a portrait of himself in beads and fringe, and a poem parodying a shaman who said he was from a long line of Cherokee holy men who completed a session in a commercial sweat lodge by singing a Lakota song, who "gave you a Seminole medicine pouch and a Kiowa name" (Dubin, 2002, 53).

Luna parodies stereotypes, as with his "End of the Frail," a modern take on James Earle Fraser's iconic turn-of-the-20th century *End of the Trail,* that displays a bowed, exhausted Indian on a weary horse, his spear pointed earthward. The original was displayed on a huge scale at the 1915 Panama-Pacific Exposition in San Francisco. In his tableau variation on *End of the Trail,* "Luna mimics the same lifeless pose, but the pony has been replaced by a weathered sawhorse, and the spear by a bottle of liquor. Nobility has been replaced by pathos. The exhaustion is no longer that of effort but that of despair" (Durland, 1998).

In one performance, Luna asks members of the audience to take photographs with him as a "real live Indian." Reactions of the audience become part of the art, Luna believes. He takes risks, depending on an unscripted audience to take part, aiming to "create a conversation" that will leave people changed in ways that a more passive exhibition would not. Sometimes the conversation takes directions ("shock and dismay, sadness, empathy, association") that surprise even the artist (Fletcher, 2008). Once again, Luna's experience as a counselor comes into play as he appears once in Native regalia, then in typical non-Indian street clothes:

> There was an Indian in a breechcloth with everybody going "Oh wow, there's an Indian." Then I came out in my street clothes and they said "Oh, there's a guy." But when I came out in my regalia, I knew that it would get that response from the audience. Everybody went for it. There was a big ooh and aah when I stepped up on that pedestal with my war dance outfit. They forgot about all the rest and really lined up to have their picture taken. This is the memento that they really wanted. Even people that were art savvy fell for it. (Fletcher, 2008)

Artist under Glass

Luna's work often parodies the display of Native "artifacts" in museums. Luna is an iconoclast who will introduce one to oneself. Perhaps his best-known performance is *The Artifact Piece,* introduced in 1987 at the San Diego Museum of Man. It features a glass case in which *he* is the artifactual "Indian," confronting stereotypes. In this work, *he* is the object, "the other." Luna filled the display case with sand and "artifacts," some of his favorite music and books, legal papers, and labels describing scars acquired during his life.

According to one source, "Few works of contemporary Indian art have been so perfectly conceived and executed. Outrageous and brilliant, *The Artifact Piece* rumbled across Indian Country in the late 1980s like a quiet earthquake, making fine work by other Native artists suddenly look obsolete and timid. . . . Luna brought danger into the equation, and in the new atmosphere, anything seemed possible" (Smith, 2009, 95).

Performances around the World

As an artist, Luna reserves the right to be inconsistent. Occasionally, having said that his work is specific to North America, Luna does take his show on the road—far afield. In 2005, at the invitation of the National Museum of the American Indian, he took part in the Venice Biennale. In Belo Horizonte, Brazil, in 2005, Luna's work appeared at the Hemispheric Institute.

Luna continues, as he has since 1975, to live and work on La Jolla Indian Reservation, a Luiseño community near Mount Palomar, north of San Diego.

Luna's work has been portrayed on film, including a segment of *Race Is the Place,* a Public Broadcasting Service television magazine. He has taught on the faculty of Palomar College and San Diego State University, and lectured at Harvard University and other colleges and universities. Luna received an award at the American Indian Film Festival for best live short performance, as well as a Dance Theater Workshop of New York Bessie Award, and an Eiteljorg Fellowship for Native American Fine Art. Luna also collaborated with filmmaker Isaac Artenstein on *The History of the Luiseño People.*

Further Reading

Dubin, Margaret, ed. *The Dirt Is Red Here: Art and Poetry from Native California.* Berkeley, CA: Heyday Books, 2002.

Durland, Steven. "Call Me in '93: An Interview with James Luna." In *The Citizen Artist: 20 Years of Art in the Public Arena: An Anthology from High Performance Magazine 1978–1998,* edited by Linda Frye Burnham and Steven Durland. New York: Critical Press, 1998. Reading Room. Community Arts Network. http://www.communityarts.net/readingroom/archivefiles/2002/09/call_me_in_93_a.php.

Fletcher, Kenneth R. "James Luna Is Known for Pushing Boundaries in His Installations, Where He Engages Audiences by Making Himself Part of a Tableau." *Smithsonian Magazine,* April 2008. http://www.smithsonianmag.com/arts-culture/atm-qa-james-luna.html.

Inventing "the Indian": The West as America: Reinterpreting Images of the Frontier, 1820–1920. Washington, DC: Smithsonian Institution, 1991.

"James Luna." Native Networks: National Museum of the American Indian. 2004. http://www.nativenetworks.si.edu/eng/rose/luna_j.htm.

Luna, James. *Encuentro: Invasion of the Americas and the Making of the Mestizo.* A catalog for a show of the same name presented at SPARC (Social and Public Art Resource Center), Los Angeles, 1991.

McHugh, Kathleen. "Profane Illuminations: History and Collaboration in James Luna and Isaac Artenstein's *The History of the Luiseño People.*" *Biography* 31, no. 3 (Summer 2008): 429–60.

Nottage, James H., ed. *Diversity and Dialogue*. Seattle: University of Washington Press, 2008.

Smith, Paul Chaat. *Everything You Know about Indians Is Wrong*. Minneapolis: University of Minnesota Press, 2009.

"Urban (Almost) Rituals." Soundings Theatre, Te Papa, Wellington, Massey University College, New Zealand. May 14, 2009. http://www.onedaysculpture.org.nz/ODS_artist detail.php?idartist=12.

Lyons, Oren
Born 1930 Onondaga
Political Leader, Artist, Lacrosse Player, and Philosopher

Oren Lyons, whose Onondaga name is *Joagquisho* ("Bright Sun"), became known worldwide during the last half of the 20th century as an author, publisher, and crisis negotiator, as well as spokesman for the Haudenosaunee (Iroquois) in several world forums. He is an accomplished graphic artist as well as a renowned lacrosse player and coach. Lyons's father also was a well-known lacrosse goalkeeper. During 1990, Lyons organized an Iroquois national team that played in the world lacrosse championships in Australia. In addition, Lyons worked as a professor of Native American Studies at the State University of New York at Buffalo. As an author, Lyons is known most notably as lead author of *Exiled in the Land of the Free* (1992).

Lyons was educated in art at Syracuse University (1954–58). After graduating, Lyons enjoyed a successful career as a commercial artist at Norcross Greeting Cards in New York City for more than a decade (1959–70). Lyons began as a paste-up artist at Norcross; in a dozen years at the firm, he worked his way up to head planning director for seasonal lines.

Iroquois Faith-keeper

During 1970, Lyons abandoned his career in greeting cards and returned home to the Onondaga territory, where he was condoled (installed) as faithkeeper of the Iroquois Grand Council. Lyons also was part of a negotiating

Oren Lyons, Iroquois Faithkeeper, 2007. (AP/Wide World Photos)

team from the Iroquois Confederacy that helped resolve the 1990 standoff between Mohawks and authorities at Kanesatake (Oka), Quebec. The confederacy's negotiators occupied a crucial middle ground between the Mohawk Warrior Society and Canadian officials during the months of negotiations that preceded the use of armed force by the Canadian Army and police at Kanesatake and Kahnawake. The Iroquois negotiators urged both sides to concentrate on long-term solutions to problems brought to light by the summer's violence. They recommended a fair land-rights process in Canada, the creation of viable economic bases for the communities involved in the crisis, and the recognition of long-standing (but often ignored) treaty rights, including border rights.

Lyons has been involved in a number of other Iroquois-rights issues, most notably the return of wampum belts to the confederacy by the State of New York. He has spoken on behalf of the Haudenosaunee in several international forums, including the United Nations, where he said: "I see no seat for the eagles. We forget and we consider ourselves superior, but we are after all a mere part of the creation" ("Chief Oren Lyons," n.d.).

Lyons has been active in uniting religious peoples of differing traditions. On April 28, 1997, he took part in an interfaith service at Saint Bartholomew's Church in New York City in support of the United Nations with leaders from Christian, Jewish, Buddhist, Sikh, Jainist, Islamic, and Hindi clergy. One aim of the service was to diminish international tensions based on religious differences.

Lyons has faced harsh criticism by some merchants in the Iroquois Confederacy for his belief that some of their profits should go back to the nations on which they do business. This criticism reached a peak in the late winter of 1998, when Lyons and other supporters of the traditional council burned and bulldozed four smoke shops on Onondaga Territory. Lyons and other members of the council have long maintained that sovereignty is a collective right to be exercised by a governing body, not a license to make profits because merchants on Native American territories may avoid paying New York State sales tax.

"Who represents the sovereignty of the United States?" Lyons and co-author John C. Mohawk asked in *Cultural Survival Quarterly* (Lyons et al., 1992, 58). "Is it the New York Yankees? Bloomingdales? the *Los Angeles Times*? William F. Buckley?" Just as private enterprises do not speak for the United States, wrote Lyons and Mohawk, private Iroquois businesspeople cannot exercise national sovereignty as individuals, especially when it is used as a cover for socially debasing activities such as smuggling illegal drugs.

Speaking for the Natural World

The Haudenosaunee (Iroquois) have an enduring relationship with the United Nations. During the organization's early years, a delegation of Haudenosaunee chiefs visited its headquarters in New York City, usually about once a year, drawing parallels between the world body and their own "league of nations." Since 1977, Lyons, and other indigenous representatives, have approached the United Nations to speak on behalf of the natural world.

"We had alarming news from the Four Directions about fish, wildlife and birds, contaminated, sick and disappearing," says Lyons. "And today we continue to speak on their behalf. Today, they are more endangered than ever, and if anything, their conditions are worse. . . . As long as you make war against *Etenoha* (Mother Earth), there can never be peace" (Lyons Web Site D).

Lyons has sounded warnings in a number of international environmental forums. The venues differ, but the message is always similar: "We were told that there would come a time when we would not find clean water to wash ourselves, to cook our foods, to make our medicines, and to drink," Lyons says. Today, Lyons peers into the future with great apprehension. "We were told that there would come a time when, tending our gardens, we would pull up our plants and the vines would be empty. Our precious seed would begin to disappear. . . . Can we withstand another 500 years of 'sustainable development?' I don't think so." "It is not too late," Lyons told the United Nations General Assembly, "we still have options. We need the courage to change our values to the regeneration of families, the life that surrounds us" (Lyons Web Site B).

Lyons has become a social and political activist on a worldwide scale. He has, for example, spoken out against policies of the World Bank that have an adverse impact on indigenous peoples, usually through the backing of development projects that impinge on traditional lifeways by destroying environmental balance and stimulating in-migration of nonindigenous peoples. Lyons cited from a statement by Survival International, dated September 20, 1994: "The World Bank and the IMF make decisions every day that affect the lives of hundreds of thousands of tribal peoples. The tribes are hardly, if ever, consulted. In the last fifty years the World Bank has approved projects that have had catastrophic results for indigenous people worldwide. According to the Bank's own figures, by 1996 it will have evicted 4 million people, many of them tribal" (Lyons Web Site C).

Lyons believes that human beings can be productive and supportive of nature, or we can be parasites. "Right now we are parasites," Lyons argues. We are, by sheer numbers and behavior, extinguishing other species of life. "The natural laws say that no one entity can grow unchecked," Lyons believes. "There are forces that will check this unbridled growth, such as disease and lack of food and water. Privilege will not prevail. There can be no peace as long as you make war on Mother Earth" (Lyons Web Site C).

Further Reading

"Chief Oren Lyons." n.d. http://fraktali.849pm.com/text/lyons/oren1.html.

Lyons, Oren. Web Site A. "Opening Address for the Year of Indigenous Peoples, United Nations, New York City, 1993." http://www.indians.org/walker/onondaga.htm.

Lyons, Oren. Web Site B. "Address . . . to the United Nations Organization, 'The Year of Indigenous Peoples,' . . . New York City, December 10, 1992." http://www.ratical.com/many_worlds/6Nations/OLatUNin92.html.

Lyons, Oren. Web Site C. "Ethics, Spiritual Values and the Promotion of Environmentally Sustainable Development. Fifty Years of the World Bank, Over 50 Tribes Devastated." October 3, 1995. http://www.ratical.com/ratville/OrenLyons.html#development.

Lyons, Oren. Web Site D. "Opening Remarks." Working Group on Indigenous Peoples, United Nations, Geneva, Switzerland. Document: E/CN.4/Sub.2/1997/1415th Session: July 28–August 1, 1997. http://www.docip.org/anglais/update_en/up_en_19_20.html#opst.

Lyons, Oren, John Mohawk, Vine Deloria, Jr., Laurence Hauptman, Howard Berman, Donald A. Grinde, Jr., Curtis Berkey, and Robert Venables. *Exiled in the Land of the Free: Democracy, Indian Nations, and the Constitution.* Santa Fe, NM: Clear Light, 1992.

M

MacDonald, Peter (Hoshkaisith Begay)
Born 1928 Diné (Navajo)
Political Leader

Peter MacDonald served four terms as chairman of the Diné (Navajo) Nation, with a territory the size of West Virginia, encouraging economic development. Before the end of his fourth term, he was removed from office by the nation council in 1989 for accepting bribes. MacDonald's policies also engendered considerable opposition from many Navajo, who called him "MacDollar," especially regarding coal strip mining and uranium excavation from small mines called "dog holes." MacDonald often was criticized for acting as a front for corporate energy-development interests.

Uranium mining, which began before MacDonald was elected, was controversial because of the many deaths from lung cancer. By the time MacDonald left office, several hundred cases of lung cancer had been diagnosed among a people who had no word for the disease in their indigenous language. The Navajo Nation also had suffered the largest uranium waste spill in the history of the United States in 1979. After MacDonald left office, the mining of uranium on Navajo land was outlawed.

Early Life

MacDonald was born December 20, 1928, with the Navajo name *Hoshkaisith Begay* ("Peter MacDonald" was assigned to him in a government boarding school). His father died when he was two years of age. MacDonald's early years with his mother and maternal grandfather were deeply impoverished.

MacDonald herded sheep as a young man and attended a Bureau of Indian Affairs school at Teec Nos Pos in northeastern Arizona. He later transferred to another boarding school at Shiprock, New Mexico, on the reservation, but ran away twice rather than suffer taunts and humiliation. He said later that he had trouble accepting the portrayal of Navajos by teachers at the schools as "superstitious savages. . . . We were made to feel that our parents, our grandparents, and everything else that had come before us, was inferior" (MacDonald, 1993, 49). Fed up with the boarding schools, he dropped out in the sixth grade.

MacDonald at age 15 lied about his age during World War II and was drafted into the U.S. Marine Corps, serving in the South Pacific and China. He became one of the famous Navajo code talkers who used their language to confuse the Japanese military. He was honorably discharged from the Marines in 1946. Later, he found short-term employment on railroads and in sawmills.

In 1948, MacDonald enrolled in Bacone College, a Baptist school for Indians in Oklahoma. Earning a general-equivalency degree (GED) and majoring in sociology, MacDonald later transferred to the University of Oklahoma on a scholarship, where he earned an electrical engineering BS degree in 1957.

MacDonald used his degree to get a job with Hughes Aircraft in Los Angeles, in the company's defense contract wing, and worked his way up to director of the Polaris missile project, an executive position with a high salary. In 1963, however, he resigned that position and took a sizable reduction in pay to go to work with the Navajo Nation as Director of Management, Methods, and Procedures. In 1965, he became Director of the Navajo Office of Economic Opportunity, part of President Lyndon B. Johnson's War on Poverty.

Navajo Leader

In 1970, MacDonald won the chairmanship of the Navajo Nation and was inaugurated in January 1971, as several thousand people braved bitterly cold weather at the Navajo rodeo grounds to hear his first major speech in office. He promised a new day of political self-control for Navajos, increased prosperity, and better educational opportunities. He was elected again in 1974, 1978, and 1986.

MacDonald also played a major role in the early days of the Council of Energy Resource Tribes (CERT), during 1974, and served as its chairman for a time. The organization represents American Indian tribes and nations that hold energy resources (mainly coal, oil, and natural gas) vis à vis the interests of the federal government and major corporations.

MacDonald was unpopular with some Navajos. The Coalition for Navajo Liberation (CNL) formed in 1974 with the expressed purpose of seeking his resignation, mainly on environmental grounds related to coal and uranium mining. On May 18, 1976, CNL assembled several hundred people in Window Rock, the seat of Navajo government, to demand his ouster.

MacDonald set out to transfer many Bureau of Indian Affairs programs to Navajo government control. He also pledged to expand Navajo resource development and to negotiate better terms for it. MacDonald became embroiled in many disputes: with the Hopis, over land claims; with other Navajo, after he packed the nation's courts with his supporters; and with Arizona Senator Barry Goldwater, whom he accused of being insufficiently attentive to the Navajos' needs in the land dispute with the Hopis. Many Navajo traditionalists also bitterly opposed uranium and coal mining.

Prison

MacDonald went to federal prison in 1990 for helping to provoke a riot by supporters following his conviction for federal fraud, racketeering, burglary, and conspiracy. They had stormed tribal offices in an attempt to restore MacDonald to power when they were met by Navajo police, two of whom were injured in the melee. MacDonald was pardoned by President Bill Clinton in 2001.

MacDonald married Rubye Wallace, a Comanche whom he met during college, and they had two children, Linda and Peter, Jr.

MacDonald continued to be active in Navajo politics. He was a Republican but was sharply critical of Arizona Senator John McCain. When McCain was nominated for U.S. president in 2008, MacDonald changed his party affiliation and advocated a Navajo Nation's endorsement of Barack Obama. McCain had been co-chair of the Senate Subcommittee for Indian Affairs during a hearing on MacDonald's business dealings that preceded his removal from the Navajo Nation's chairmanship.

Further Reading

Bland, Celia. *Peter MacDonald: Former Chairman of the Navajo Nation.* New York: Chelsea House, 1995.

"Former Navajo Leader Convicted." *New York Times,* November 15, 1992. http://www.nytimes.com/1992/11/15/us/former-navajo-leader-convicted.html.

Johansen, Bruce, and Roberto Maestas. *Wasi'chu: The Continuing Indian Wars*. New York: Monthly Review Press, 1979.

MacDonald, Peter. *The Last Warrior: Peter MacDonald and the Navajo*. London: Orion Books, 1993.

MANKILLER, WILMA
BORN 1945 CHEROKEE
POLITICAL LEADER

Wilma Pearl Mankiller, long-time chief of the Oklahoma Cherokees and the first woman to lead a major Indian nation in the United States in modern times, became well known nationally to the extent that she was inducted into the National Women's Hall of Fame. The author Alice Walker said that "Wilma Mankiller is someone I feel I've known in this lifetime and many lifetimes before. I recognize in her the greatest beauty, dignity, and truthfulness—an honesty that embraces, a candor that heals, a radical love for people and empathy with the earth" (Trahant, 2000).

The first woman to become chief of the Cherokee Nation, Wilma P. Mankiller is perhaps the best-known female Native American activist in the United States. (University of Utah Women's Week Celebration)

Mankiller received the United States' highest civilian honor, the Presidential Medal of Freedom, in 1998. She also was named American Indian Woman of the Year in 1986 and Woman of the Year by *Ms.* magazine in 1987. She has published two books: an autobiography, *Mankiller: A Chief and Her People* (1993), and *Every Day Is a Good Day: Reflections of Contemporary Indigenous Women* (2004).

The name "Mankiller" is an occupational title among the Cherokees, a military title given to a person who protects a village. Mankiller lives near Tahlequah, Oklahoma, on land allotted to her paternal grandfather, John Mankiller, shortly after Oklahoma statehood in 1907.

Early Life

Mankiller was born in Rocky Mountain, Oklahoma, November 18, 1945, to Charley Mankiller, a full-blooded Cherokee, and Clara Irene Sitton Mankiller, who was Dutch-Irish. She was the 6th in a family of 11 children in a home with no running water or electricity. In 1956, when she was 11, after crops failed on the family farm, the family was relocated by the Bureau of Indian Affairs to the San Francisco area. They lived in Hunter's Point, an impoverished, mainly African American neighborhood, where Mankiller completed high school. The family may have been poor, but Mankiller recalled that the family never lacked books. "This love of reading came from the traditional Cherokee passion for telling and listening to stories" (Chavers, 2007, 139).

What kept the family together during that period, said Mankiller, "was the Indian center, which was a place where many other families like ours, sort of refugees, I guess you could say in the city, gathered at the San Francisco Indian Center and shared our experiences and kind of tried to build a community there" (Mankiller, "Rebuilding," 1993). Relocation was meant to eradicate Native American traditions and land base, but soon Mankiller found herself working in preschool and adult education programs with California's Pit River Tribe. Mankiller became interested in helping the Pitt River Tribe regain its ancestral land, so she volunteered for seven years.

During the late 1960s, living in the Bay Area enabled Mankiller to play a vital role in the Red Power movement. Mankiller married Hugo Olaya, an Ecuadorian, and they had two children during their 11 years together. Mankiller directed the American Indian Youth Center in East Oakland, California. Although family responsibilities prevented Mankiller from being present on Alcatraz Island herself when American Indian activists occupied the former federal prison site in 1969, she raised money to support the protestors, and frequently visited "The Rock."

Return to the Cherokee Nation

In 1977, Mankiller completed a bachelor of arts degree at Union College. Shortly thereafter, she returned to her family's ancestral lands in Oklahoma, in large part as a Native activist, dealing with issues that affected peoples' everyday lives, such as availability of clean water and decent housing. By 1979, she had earned a master's degree in community planning at the University of Arkansas.

Mankiller's career with the Cherokee Nation began with a job as an economic stimulus coordinator; she became a program development specialist in 1979. Returning home from class at the University of Arkansas one day, Mankiller was almost killed in a head-on collision in which one of her best friends died. She barely avoided amputation of her right leg and endured 18 operations. While hospitalized, Mankiller also was diagnosed with systemic *myasthenia gravis,* a chronic neuromuscular disease that causes varying degrees of weakness in the voluntary muscles, requiring more surgery. She recovered, and served as founder and director of the Cherokee Community Development Department in 1981.

In 1983, Ross O. Swimmer, principal chief of the Cherokees, stood for re-election and included Mankiller as his running mate, in the position of deputy principal chief. His inclusion of a woman on the ballot and Mankiller's acceptance of the role caused both to receive death threats and hate mail. Her tires were slashed. "I expected people to challenge me because I had an activist background, or challenge me because I was going around talking about something called grass-roots democracy, and because my husband and I were organizing these rural communities, and so I thought people would challenge me on my ideas when I began to run for election in 1983, but they didn't. The only thing people wanted to talk about in 1983 was my being a woman. That was the most hurtful experience I've ever been through," Mankiller recalled later (Mankiller, "Rebuilding," 1993). Despite the threats, the Swimmer-Mankiller ticket won the election. Swimmer resigned to lead the Bureau of Indian Affairs in December of 1985, and Mankiller filled his job as acting principal chief.

Cherokee Principal Chief

In 1987, Mankiller became the first Cherokee woman to be elected principal chief, winning with more than 80 percent of the vote. She thus became leader of the second-largest Native nation in the United States (the largest is the Diné, or Navajo). The Cherokee Nation of Oklahoma has a tribal roll of more than 140,000 members.

The government that Mankiller supervised had more than 1,200 employees and an annual budget of $75 million.

Following her election as principal chief, a young man asked her how he should address her. He seemed uncomfortable with "chief," which he took to be a male term of address. "Should we address you as chieftainess?" he asked. Mankiller did not reply. Then, after hearing the suggestion "chiefette," she responded. "I told him to call me 'Ms.-Chief' or 'misChief'" (Trahant, 2000).

Mankiller's leadership was characterized by attention to issues that are basic to everyday life, such as employment, education, health care, and economic development, a strategy that made her very popular with constituents. Mankiller governed even as health problems plagued her. She had a kidney transplant in 1991; Her brother, Don Mankiller, donated a kidney. Mankiller was re-elected to a second term and served to the end of it in 1995. She declined to run again, but remained politically active, living in Tahlequah, Oklahoma, the capital of the Cherokee Nation, with her Cherokee second husband, Charlie Soap. She had married Soap, then director of tribal development, in 1986.

Her philosophy involved "rebuilding the Cherokee Nation community by community and person by person":

> I can't tell you how many every-day Americans that I've talked with who've visited a tribal community in Oklahoma or in other places, and they've looked around and they saw all the social indicators of decline: high infant mortality, high unemployment, many, many other very serious problems among our people, and they always ask, "What happened to these people? Why do native people have all these problems?", and I think that in order to understand the contemporary issues we're dealing with today and how we plan to dig our way out [we need to also explain] how indeed we *are* digging our way out. (Mankiller, "Rebuilding," 1993)

"We are a revitalized tribe," said Mankiller, "After every major upheaval, we have been able to gather together as a people and rebuild a community and a government. Individually and collectively, Cherokee people possess an extraordinary ability to face down adversity and continue moving forward. We are able to do that because our culture, though certainly diminished, has sustained us since time immemorial. This Cherokee culture is a well-kept secret" (*Wilma Mankiller,* n.d.).

Mankiller died April 6, 2010 of pancreatic cancer at the age of 64.

Further Reading

Champagne, Duane, ed. *Native America: Portrait of the Peoples.* Canton, MI: Visible Ink Press, 1994.

Chavers, Dean. *Modern American Indian Leaders: Their Lives and Their Works.* 2 vols. Lewiston, NY: Edwin Mellen Press, 2007.

Janda, Sarah Eppler. *Beloved Women: The Political Lives of LaDonna Harris and Wilma Mankiller.* DeKalb: Northern Illinois University Press, 2008.

Mankiller, Wilma. "Rebuilding the Cherokee Nation." [A Speech] by Wilma Mankiller, Former Chief of the Cherokee Nation, April 2, 1993—Sweet Briar College. http://gos.sbc.edu/m/mankiller.html.

Mankiller, Wilma. *Every Day Is a Good Day: Reflections of Contemporary Indigenous Women.* Golden, CO: Fulcrum Publishing, 2004.

Mankiller, Wilma, and Michael Wallis. *Mankiller: A Chief and Her People.* New York: St. Martin's Press, 1993.

Trahant, Mark. "Wilma Mankiller Talks Straight but Makes Mischief, Too." *Canku Ota— A Newsletter Celebrating Native America.* Issue 11, June 3, 2000. Reprinted from the *Seattle Times,* date unknown. http://www.turtletrack.org/Issues00/Co06032000/CO_06032000_Mankiller.htm.

"Wilma Mankiller Former Principal Chief of the Cherokee Nation." n.d. http://www.powersource.com/gallery/people/wilma.html.

MANN, BARBARA ALICE
BORN 1947 SENECA, OHIO
SCHOLAR, AUTHOR, AND ACTIVIST

Barbara Alice Mann, who teaches at the University of Toledo, is notable across the United States and internationally in Native American studies and women's studies. She is also known for her work on the "Indian" novels of James Fenimore Cooper. Mann co-authored *Sign in the Sky* that has subsequently played an important role in revising scholarship vis-à-vis the founding date of the Haudenosaunee (Iroquois) Confederacy from roughly 1450 C.E. to 1142 C.E., by tracking an eclipse of the sun at the site of the Senecas' ratification of the confederacy.

She is known for writing about other controversial subjects, including George Washington's role in Native American genocide and whether disease was spread intentionally to exterminate Native peoples. Mann has composed a body of historical writings that is searingly realistic and corrective of omissions caused by past denial and ignorance. Much of her work also is instructive in the field of women's studies. Mann possesses a rare combination of talent and diligence.

Despite heavy pressures on scholars within academia to move nomadically about the country to enhance employment opportunities and reputation, Mann has remained in northwest Ohio, her Iroquoian homeland. She believes that her obligation "to feed the living and the ancestors and to honor the spirits of place" outweigh any personal advantages to be gained from moving away. "We evaded Jacksonian Removal," she said, "so I'm damned if they're going to get me with Academic Removal" (Mann, 2007).

Born in Toledo, August 4, 1947, Mann spent her earliest years on her family's absentee allotment farm in Metamora, Ohio, the old Seneca stomping grounds. In 1942, her parents married in Toledo instead of the small nearby town of Swanton (where everyone knew that her mother was an Indian) because interracial marriage was still illegal, even if she was Indian rather than black (the main race policed at the time). The family was relatively poor. Mann's father had a silk-screen art business.

Native American scholar, author, and activist Barbara Alice Mann. (Courtesy Barbara Mann)

Mann joined the Air Force three days before her 18th birthday in 1965. She served in Wiesbaden, Germany, having enlisted mainly to access GI Bill benefits, because she saw no other way of paying for college. Despite having earned straight As throughout her years at Rogers High School, she was told point-blank that scholarship committees had no intention of "wasting a scholarship on a girl" (Mann, 2007). The GI Bill worked better on paper than it did in reality, however. To survive after her enlistment, Mann was forced to work rather than study. By 1980, she was a divorced, single mother and sole support of her daughter Nastassia, working 50-hour weeks at the Toledo Metropolitan Area Council of Governments as a public information assistant.

Completely unable to afford four-year college tuition, Mann took three semesters of classes at the University of Toledo, maintaining a 4.0 average. She then took college bypass tests through the College-level Examination Program, gaining two years' worth of undergraduate credits (all that were possible). With these two years of credits, Mann received a full scholarship for her remaining two years of undergraduate studies. The scholarship required full-time attendance along with her 50-hour-a-week job. Mann finished her BA degree in 1982 with a 3.901 GPA and was valedictorian of her class.

In 1985, Mann married Alan Epstein. She had been born with problematic lungs and kidneys and in 1994 she had a heart attack. Her husband suggested that she earn a higher degree and teach, because university faculty enjoyed more flexible work schedules than other workers. Mann received a Regents' scholarship for her first quarter and then went on to land a teaching assistantship, finishing her PhD at UT during 1997.

Despite chronic health problems, by 2007 Mann had compiled a serious publishing record, including seminal research in all three of her fields, while teaching full-time at the University of Toledo, with no released time for research. By 2008, she had produced eight books and dozens of articles. Active in the indigenous community of Ohio, Mann serves as northern director of the Native American Alliance of Ohio and on the Grandmothers' Council of the Native American Commission of Ohio.

Further Reading

Mann, Barbara A. "*The Last of the Mohicans* and *'The Indian*-haters'; Forbidden Ground: Racial Politics and Hidden Identity in James Fenimore Cooper's Leather-Stocking Tales." PhD diss., University of Toledo, 1997.

Mann, Barbara Alice. *Iroquois Women: The Gantowisas.* New York: Peter Lang, 2000.

Mann, Barbara Alice. *George Washington's War on Native America.* Westport, CT: Praeger, 2005.

Mann, Barbara Alice. *Daughters of Mother Earth: The Wisdom of Native American Women.* Westport, CT: Praeger, 2006.

Mann, Barbara Alice. Personal communication, August 8, 2006.

Mann, Barbara Alice. Personal communication, November 20, 2007.

Mann, Barbara A., and Jerry L. Fields. "A Sign in the Sky: Dating the League of the Haudenosaunee." *American Indian Culture and Research Journal* 21, no. 2 (1997): 105–63.

McCloud, Janet (Yet Si Blue)
1934–2003 Puyallup
Activist

Janet McCloud, who was initially well known as a fishing-rights activist in the Pacific Northwest, became a worldwide Native American advocate. She was "a master orator, prolific writer and political activist—a woman who helped shape state history, resurrected Indian spirituality for many and empowered the civil rights movement of native peoples worldwide" (Kamb, 2003).

Early Life

McCloud was born into the family of Chief Seath'l (Seattle) as Janet Renecker on March 30, 1934, on the Tulalip Reservation, the oldest of three girls. Raised in abject poverty, at the age of six, she was panhandling on the Skid Road of the city named for her ancestor. "Mom told us how she panhandled at such a young age and that that was the reason she never passed a panhandler by without giving them something," said her son, Don McCloud, Jr. ("Janet McCloud," 2003). Her step-father was an alcoholic who held few steady jobs, so few that the children often were shuttled between foster homes and churches.

Having attended public schools near Seattle, at the age of 13 Renecker was placed in a boarding school. She married and divorced at an early age, then, in the early 1950s, married Don McCloud, Sr., a Puyallup Indian truck driver, electrical lineman, and fisherman. They had eight children (two boys and six girls). He died of cancer in 1985.

The McClouds moved to Frank's Landing on the Nisqually River, where Don's stepfather, Billy Frank, Sr., and his family had fished for decades, fending off state agents. The Franks' treaty-rights stand extended to at least 1937, when state agents arrested Billy Frank, Sr., and several other Indians for illegal fishing. Don also worked at odd jobs, including a dog food factory. The family also hunted and fished to feed itself.

Fishing-rights Activism

The McClouds quickly became involved in the fishing-rights struggles along the Nisqually River that had become part of the Franks' daily life, as Native peoples in western Washington maintained their treaty rights to fish in the face of arrests by state game agents. By 1965, Janet and several other fishing-rights advocates were going to jail on a routine basis for fishing, as the Medicine Creek Treaty of 1854 specified, in their "usual and accustomed places." The McClouds and other Native Americans set their nets at Frank's Landing along the Nisqually River and watched game wardens surround, beat, and arrest them.

In January of 1961, state game wardens burst into the McClouds' home search-ing for deer meat. McCloud asked them, "Do you have a search warrant?" They did. It said "John Doe." "That was my first experience with game wardens," she said. " It made me so mad, but that's the way they treated us back then" (Trahant, 1999).

In the beginning, she said, "We were just fishing people. We didn't have any councils, we didn't have any lawyers, we didn't have any money, and we just saw ourselves as kamikazes. All we had was us, so we'd go out there and they'd beat us up, they'd mace us, they'd throw us in jail, terrorize our kids and come and ha-rass us at our homes, terrorize our kids in school. . . . We were the front line" ("The Great Janet McCloud," 2006).

The fish-ins continued until federal courts in the 1970s upheld the Indians' rights to take fish on a basis equal to sports and commercial fishermen in the area. In jail, the Indians often fasted in protest. "I didn't mind going to jail so much until Edith, my sister-in-law, said, 'And we're not eating either.'" She said later: "That was my first fast and we went six days without eating. They'd bring lima beans with ham, fried potatoes, and everything I loved. She could smell those good foods but wouldn't eat them. It made the fast more difficult" ("Janet McCloud," 2003).

McCloud said that, at the time, she experienced a vision: "I heard a voice that sounded like Crazy Horse telling me not to be afraid. It said I wasn't alone and that I was being protected. I felt the voice so strong that all my fear and sadness went away. It's where I got my strength to face hostile audiences and all the adversity" ("Janet McCloud," 2003). During the fish-ins, McCloud was given the name *Yet Si Blue* ("Woman Who Speaks Her Mind"), signifying her advocacy of human rights.

Conflict over Fishing Intensifies

As the fishing struggle intensified, McCloud and other fishing-rights activists formed the Survival of the American Indians Association (SAIA) in 1964. Soon their ambit also broadened to cultural programs for Native American inmates at McNeil Island prison near Tacoma that became a national model as the Brotherhood of American Indians.

The McClouds, the Franks, and other fishing-rights activists began to build the case that resulted in the Boldt Decision of 1974 that enforced the treaties, in which U.S. District Judge George Boldt ruled in favor of 14 treaty tribes. Famous people (two examples were Marlon Brando and Dick Gregory) came to fish alongside the Indians.

One of the most violent reactions by game agents occurred October 13, 1965, as several dozen state agents surrounded about 50 fishing Indians, most of them women and children. Within minutes after the Indians put their nets in the water, state agents in speedboats rushed the gathering and agents rammed the Indians' boats. On shore, Native women and children reacted to the rammings by pelting state officers with debris. The agents then beat some of them.

"Wardens were everywhere and they all seemed to be eight feet tall," McCloud wrote in the SAIA's newsletter, which she edited. "They were shoving, kicking, pushing clubs at men, women and children. We were vastly outnumbered yet we were all trying to protect one another." Six Indians, including McCloud, were taken into custody and charged with resisting arrest. They were acquitted when films indicated that the confrontation had been provoked by the agents, not the Indians.

In the meantime, Dick Gregory was arrested for illegally fishing with the Indians, convicted and then, having been sentenced to 90 days in jail, started fasting. "Here this man is going to jail for us, living on distilled water," McCloud said. "So I collected kids off the rez and said, 'Let's go demonstrate'" (Trahant, 1999). They erected a tipi near the jail, and tourists began to gather as the state derided Gregory as a publicity hound. The state turned on sprinklers under the tipi and then arrested McCloud and her children. Eight days later, state troopers demolished the tipi.

National Leader

McCloud became a national leader after the fishing-rights issue was adjudicated. Late in the 1960s, McCloud met Thomas Banyacya, the Hopi spiritual leader; she also came to know the Iroquois clan mother Audrey Shenandoah, who taught her

Earth-centered religious beliefs. In the 1970s, she helped form the Northwest Indian Women's Circle that worked to develop leadership skills in the context of traditional values. McCloud was active in the American Indian Movement (AIM) on national issues and worked with the Native American Rights Fund on legal issues, often using experience gained during the conflict over fishing rights. In 1985, she was instrumental in the founding of the Indigenous Women's Network. She adamantly opposed forced sterilization of Native American women by federal Indian Health Services, after roughly 70 percent of Native women in the United States were sterilized (Johansen, 1998, 44). With Lorelie Means, Madonna Gilbert, and others, McCloud also started the Women of All Red Nations (WARN).

McCloud, who farmed her family's 10 acres near Yelm, Washington, south of the Nisqually River, compared life to a garden. She told people to sow their best seeds and then care for what they produced. The McClouds taught their children to fish, put up food, and provide for anyone who came to their door in need. Traditional economy and ceremony were a path out of poverty, she believed.

McCloud characterized her home as "a place to which people come for a traditional Native American ceremony, or as the first step when beginning a sojourn, or to join a tribute to the Winter Moon at the solstice. 'The elders have said this is a spiritual place. For over 30 years, we've used this land to teach our traditional ways,' McCloud said. 'When all is going crazy . . . our people can come back to the center to find the calming effect; to reconnect with their spiritual self'" (Trahant, 1999).

In 1985, McCloud hosted 300 women from many countries for five days on her 10 acres, which she calls *Sapa Dawn,* to talk about shared concerns regarding social, economic, and family problems that gave birth to the Indigenous Women's Network. They put up tipis to accommodate the participants. Dennis Banks, Russell Means, and other leaders of AIM spent time camping at Sapa Dawn, using its sweat lodge, before their occupation of Wounded Knee, South Dakota, in 1973.

McCloud expressed her philosophy:

> We have to help the Indian mother . . . present the women's view. . . . We can raise the consciousness of the men and the family. We view ourselves as facilitators, not leaders, to provide a framework for our traditions and history. We provide role models for leadership . . . we are trying to take responsibility. . . . Women are coming together . . . The root of the problem is genocide but how are we dealing with this? . . . The best thing to do is to organize. . . . It is impossible to organize disorganized women. . . . Indian women suffer from double doses of racism and sexism . . . it manifests itself in being mentally dependent . . . we know the history. ("The Great Janet McCloud," 2006)

Passing On

As she grew older, McCloud suffered complications from diabetes as well as high blood pressure. For two months before her passing on November 25, 2003, family and friends gathered at Sapa Dawn as her body failed. A report in the *Seattle*

Post-Intelligencer stated, at the time, that "Pots and pans clanked, babies cried, phones rang, doors opened and closed. Footsteps paraded across floorboards as her children, grandchildren and great-grandchildren joined a veritable who's-who in Indian country to gather here over the past two months and accompany 'Yet-Si-Blue' on her final journey" (Kamb, 2003). McCloud's granddaughters dressed her in traditional clothing and wrapped her body in a handmade quilt.

After McCloud passed away, her family hosted an honoring in her memory with the Puyallup Tribe that drew about 200 people. Sally, one of her daughters, chuckled as she recalled: "They said we had to be tough and if we were going to be dumb, we had to be real tough." Janet's eight children stood right beside her as she fought for the fishing rights of the Natives. They remember her strength and her generosity" ("Janet McCloud," 2003). McCloud was survived by 8 children, 25 grandchildren, 28 great-grandchildren, and 10 adopted children.

Further Reading

"The Great Janet McCloud." Indigenous Women's Network. March 28, 2006. http://indig enouswomen.org/Articles/The-Great-Janet-McCloud.html.

"Janet McCloud. 'Yet Si Blue'." *Indian Country Today,* December 5, 2003. http://indig enouswomen.org/Our-Founding-Mothers/Janet-McCloud.html.

Johansen, Bruce E. "Reprise: Forced Sterilizations." *Native Americas* 15, no. 4 (Winter, 1998): 44–47.

Kamb, Lewis. "In Memory of Janet McCloud; Janet McCloud, 1934–2003: Indian Activist Put Family First." *Seattle Post-Intelligencer,* November 27, 2003. http://www.worldwidefriends.org/janetmccloud.html.

Trahant, Mark. "The Center of Everything—Native Leader Janet McCloud Finds Peace in Her Place, Her Victories, Her Family. It Has Taken Many Years to Get There." *Seattle Times* (Northwest People), July 4, 1999. http://community.seattletimes.nwsource.com/archive.

McNickle, D'Arcy
1904–1977 Métis; Salish and Kootenai
Novelist, Historian, and Activist

Writing both fact and fiction, William D'Arcy McNickle's positions on Native American rights and sovereignty anticipated decades of popular activism during the last half of the 20th century, into the 21st. As author of three important novels and several works of nonfiction, McNickle is studied today as an important figure in several academic fields. Outside academia, he also was a government worker, activist, and advocate.

Early Life

McNickle was born on January 18, 1904, in St. Ignatius, Montana, to Philomena Parenteau, a Cree who had fled from Canada after a Métis revolt failed in 1855.

She was then adopted by the Salish and Kootenai (Flathead), and married a Scots-Irish rancher, William McNickle. D'Arcy, their son, was educated at St. Ignatius, a Catholic boarding school. After that, the young McNickle was forced to attend a Bureau of Indian Affairs boarding school in Chemawa, Oregon. Then McNickle, at 17 years of age, enrolled at the University of Montana in classical literature and languages.

McNickle's professors recognized his talent as a writer, leading to his acceptance into Oxford University. To pay for his studies and travel to Great Britain, McNickle sold his land allotment in 1925, but trouble with academic credit transfer from Montana precluded his plans. McNickle then moved to Paris, wrote, and experimented with music before returning to the States, settling in New York in 1928.

McNickle worked at several editing jobs in New York City (including work on the *Encyclopaedia Brittanica* and the *National Encyclopaedia of American Biography*) as he took classes at the New School for Social Research and Columbia University. In addition, he wrote short stories and his first novel, *The Surrounded,* was published in 1936. *The Surrounded* described the life of a mixed-blood, Archilde Leon, who finds himself in conflict between family in his Native culture and changes forced on all of them by Anglo-America's invasion. The novel described the real-world difficulties faced by many, if not most, Native people.

As is often the case for many writers, McNickle's stories and novel did not bring in much money. During the 1930s and the Depression, he took a job with the Federal Writers' Project in Washington, D.C., to pay his bills. From there, he went to work in the Bureau of Indian Affairs under the reformist administration of John Collier, President Franklin D. Roosevelt's Commissioner of Indian Affairs. He worked at the BIA 16 years, outlasting Collier's tenure and Roosevelt's Administration, charged with the implementing the Indian Reorganization Act (IRA) of 1934.

Advocacy of Treaty Rights

McNickle advocated federal enforcement of treaties to protect Native lands, as well as policies that encouraged democracy in reservation governments. Some local people did not see eye-to-eye with the government's definition of democracy, however. Unlike Collier, McNickle transcended the bounds of government-instituted Native governments, and saw an increasing value in Native Americans' own organizing efforts aimed at the kind of self-determination that was becoming popular as he aged.

In 1944, McNickle helped to found the National Congress of American Indians. As the BIA shifted from Roosevelt-era reformist focus to termination and relocation during the 1950s, he left government employment in 1954 and advocated Native economic development at the American Indian Development Corporation. McNickle was a member of the United States Civil Rights Commission during the 1960s as well. In 1966, he became a professor at the University of Saskatchewan and developed an anthropology department there.

McNickle addressed Native American issues, but also aimed his message at non-Native audiences. McNickle published a number of historical and ethnographic works, including *They Came Here First: The Epic of the American Indian* (1949), *Indians and Other Americans: A Study of Indian Affairs* (with Harold Fey, 1959), and *The Indian Tribes of the United States: Ethnic and Cultural Survival* (1962). In 1954, McNickle published *Runner in the Sun: A Story of Indian Maize* with Apache visual artist Allan Houser, a novel for young adults that is probably the first book set in precontact America written by an American Indian.

They Came Here First was the first general history of indigenous peoples in North America to be written by a Native scholar. This book "emphasized the ability of Native communities to adapt to new circumstances and to survive the consequences of American conquest and colonization" (Hoxie, 2007, 17). McNickle moved discourse on Native American history past the era of the Vanishing American, and placed it in the context of long-lasting cultures long before the arrival of Europeans. He emphasized that Native Americans had identities of their own, not simply as "wards" of the government, and that these traditions had survived enormous oppression. In other words, he set an intellectual basis for self-determination and "nation building" that followed.

Inspiring a New Generation

In 1960, McNickle convinced the Agency for International Development (AID) to sponsor six-week workshops at the University of Colorado for American Indian students aimed at enabling them to complete college degrees and return to their communities with new skills. His purpose was to inspire a new generation of leaders. McNickle wanted to counteract the destruction of Native communities by termination policies. The workshops provoked many of the students to think about Native American peoples as subjects of "internal colonization," a theme that echoed through the movements instigated a few years later by the American Indian Movement. In 1961, McNickle played a leading role in convening the American Indian Conference at the University of Chicago, which is often looked at today as the single most important event in launching a new era of American Indian resurgence.

Treaty rights assertions in the 1960s such as those for fishing rights in the Pacific Northwest (among others) were spurred, in part, by McNickle's ideas, and those of many readers and students whom he inspired. The heritage McNickle provided for Native American activism resembled Vine Deloria, Jr.'s ideas a few years later. The two were close friends. Both McNickle and Deloria placed growing Native American activism in an international context, arguing that the way that non-Indians in America received rising aspirations of Native peoples would influence how many peoples of the Third World view the United States.

McNickle retired from the University of Saskatchewan in 1971, the same year that he published *Indian Man: The Story of Oliver La Farge*. The next year, he played a major role in founding the Center for the History of the American Indian at the Newberry Library in Chicago, and served as its first director. After his death, the center was named in McNickle's honor.

Having married three times during his adult life, McNickle had two daughters. While working on *Wind from an Enemy Sky,* in October of 1977, McNickle died of a heart attack in Albuquerque.

Further Reading

Cobb, Daniel M. "Talking the Language of the Larger World: Politics in Cold War (Native) America." In *Beyond Red Power: American Indian Politics and Activism since 1900,* edited by Daniel M. Cobb and Loretta Fowler, 161–77. Santa Fe, NM: School for Advanced Research, 2007.

Hoxie, Frederick E. "Missing the Point: Academic Experts and American Indian Politics." In *Beyond Red Power: American Indian Politics and Activism since 1900,* edited by Daniel M. Cobb and Loretta Fowler, 16–32. Santa Fe, NM: School for Advanced Research, 2007.

MEANS, RUSSELL
BORN 1939 OGLALA LAKOTA
ACTIVIST

One of the two best-known founders of the American Indian Movement (AIM) during the 1960s and 1970s (with Dennis Banks), Russell Means parlayed his notoriety into work as an actor, author, and activist into the 21st century.

Early Life

Means was born on November 10, 1939, on the Pine Ridge Reservation in South Dakota. Both of Means's parents were educated at Indian boarding schools. Theodora Louise Feather Means, Means's mother, and Walter "Hank" Means, his father, moved the family to Vallejo, California, in 1942. Walter worked as a welder in the Mare Island Naval Shipyard. The home was unstable into Russell's teenaged years, with his father's chronic alcoholism and his own petty thefts, school truancy, and drug as well as alcohol abuse. Means graduated from San Leandro High School in 1958.

Russell Means, leader of the American Indian Movement, February 18, 1974. (AP/Wide World Photos)

Means became an Indian activist during the early and middle 1960s. A symbolic take-over of Alcatraz Island took place in 1964 (five years before the better-known occupation during 1969) and included Means and his father. Russell later confided that his father's willingness to stand up for Indian treaty rights "made me proud to be his son, and to be a Lakota" (Means, 1995, 105). Federal statutes give Native Americans first option on closed federal facilities, the same laws that were used in Seattle to establish the Daybreak Star Center at the former Fort Lawton, a U.S. Army outpost during World War II. Means was 26 years of age at the time and had been recently fired from a security job at the San Francisco Cow Palace.

Founding the American Indian Movement

By 1969, when the second occupation of "The Rock" took place, Means took part in the 19-month seizure. The year before, he had founded AIM with two Anishinabe (Ojibwa) activists from Minnesota, Clyde Bellecourt and Dennis Banks. Means was AIM's first national director, starting in 1970. "Here was a way to be a *real* Indian, and AIM had shown it to me," declared Means. "No longer would I be content to 'work within the system.' . . . Instead, like Clyde and Dennis and the others in AIM, I would get in the white man's face until he gave me and my people our just due. With that decision, my whole existence suddenly came into focus. For the first time, I knew the purpose of my life and the path I must follow to fulfill it. At the age of thirty I became a full-time Indian" (Means, 1995, 153).

The founders of AIM developed a talent for high-profile public events that utilized popular symbols that attracted media attention. One such event took place on Thanksgiving Day of 1970, when Means and Banks led a group from AIM that, with local Wampanoag activists in Plymouth, Massachusetts, declared a "day of mourning" for Native peoples while the rest of the United States was celebrating the 350th anniversary of the Pilgrims' arrival at Plymouth Rock, Massachusetts. Means gave a passionate speech as he stood before a statue of Chief Massasoit, who had befriended the Pilgrims. AIM actions also often involved considerable muscle and bravado. In this case, they assumed control of a replica of the *Mayflower* and lathered Plymouth Rock in red paint as TV news cameras filmed.

The campaigns of AIM soon expanded to include a symbolic "seizure" of the presidential carvings atop Mount Rushmore to dramatize the fact that the Black Hills are still legally owned by the Sioux (the U.S. government's land-claims payment has never been accepted). AIM raised the stakes with a caravan that crossed the United States. The Trail of Broken Treaties culminated in Washington, D.C., a week before the 1972 national elections with the seizure and ransacking of the Bureau of Indian Affairs headquarters building. Means, Banks, and others then organized the occupation of Wounded Knee, on the Pine Ridge Reservation, to commemorate the massacre there in 1890, and to accentuate treaty rights by forming what they called an independent Lakota nation. As they faced off with FBI agents and U.S. Army troops, AIM seared its image into American consciousness. The occupation lasted 71 days and made Means and Banks world famous as AIM's leaders.

After the Wounded Knee occupation ended, the federal government besieged Means and Banks with a legal assault that tied them up in court for years. Means alone endured a dozen trials on a potpourri of charges. The FBI also infiltrated AIM with informers, through its Counter Intelligence Program (COINTELPRO), creating fear and dissension, splitting the group into factions that eroded its effectiveness as a national force, although local chapters continued to operate in many areas. COINTELPRO was a factor in the killing of Anna Mae Aquash and other AIM activists.

Political and Artistic Activities

In 1974 Means ran for the Oglala Sioux tribal chairmanship against the incumbent, Dick Wilson, and lost narrowly, in a contested election that the U.S. Civil Rights Commission found was marred by widespread vote fraud. This election was part of an ongoing conflict between AIM and the Wilson government on the reservation that included the murder of at least 65 AIM activists in three years (1973–76), many at the hands of reservation police heavily armed with weapons acquired with federal money. In 1976, Means was acquitted of the murder of Martin Montileaux in Scenic, South Dakota. In 1978, he began serving 12 months of a 48-month sentence for his role in a riot during 1974.

Over the years, Means evolved something of an eclectic taste in politics. He joined *Hustler* magazine publisher and pornographer Larry Flynt in a campaign for the Republican presidential nomination in 1984. Disgusted and annoyed at Flynt's tactics, however, Means withdrew his support in the midst of the campaign. Means became friends with activist Ward Churchill, who nominated him for president during the 1988 U.S. national campaign on the Libertarian Party ticket. Means lost the nomination to former Republican congressman Ron Paul. During 2001, Means also started an unsuccessful campaign for the governorship of New Mexico but dropped out after missing a filing deadline. He ran again in 2002 for leadership of the Oglala Sioux tribe at Pine Ridge. He won a primary but lost the general election to incumbent John Yellow Bird Steele.

In the meantime, Means traveled the world in support of various indigenous groups. He supported the Miskito Indians of Nicaragua against the Sandinistas during the 1980s, a stand that was controversial among AIM members who looked at the Sandinista regime as a political advance following the Somoza dynasty. Means was criticized for naively supporting the Reagan Administration's efforts, including a trade embargo and "Contra" insurgent warfare, to topple the Sandinista regime. Means also undertook a speaking tour during 1986 that was funded by Reverend Sun Myung Moon and his Unification Church (the "Moonies").

Means's career as an actor and author has been more successful than his political aspirations. In 1992, Means played Chingachgook in *Last of the Mohicans*. He provided the voice of Chief Powhatan in Disney's *Pocahontas* (1995). He had acted in 10 other films by 2006, as well as many guest appearances on television dramas. He published an autobiography, *Where White Men Fear to Tread*, in 1995, as well as two music CDs and several works of art.

Means continued to be notable for his fiery rhetoric. In a speech delivered to several thousand people at the Black Hills International Survival Gathering in 1980, titled "For America to Live, Europe Must Die," he criticized all European ideologies, capitalism and Marxism alike: "Capitalists, at least, can be relied upon to develop uranium as fuel only at the rate at which they can show a good profit," he said. "That's their ethic, and maybe that will buy some time. Marxists, on the other hand, can be relied upon to develop uranium fuel as rapidly as possible simply because it's the most 'efficient' production fuel available. That's their ethic, and I fail to see where it's preferable. Like I said, Marxism is right smack in the middle of the European tradition. It's the same old song" ("For America," 1980).

"There is another way," Means said. "There is the traditional Lakota way and the ways of the other American Indian peoples. It is the way that knows that humans do not have the right to degrade Mother Earth, that there are forces beyond anything the European mind has conceived, that humans must be in harmony with all relations or the relations will eventually eliminate the disharmony. A lopsided emphasis on humans by humans—the European's arrogance of acting as though they were beyond the nature of all related things—can only result in a total disharmony and a readjustment which cuts arrogant humans down to size, gives them a taste of that reality beyond their grasp or control and restores the harmony" ("For America," 1980).

Further Reading

Caldwell, Christopher. "The Antiwar, Anti-Abortion, Anti-Drug-Enforcement-Administration, Anti-Medicare Candidacy of Dr. Ron Paul." *New York Times Magazine,* July 22, 2007. http://www.nytimes.com/2007/07/22/magazine/22Paul-t.html.

"For America to Live, Europe Must Die." Speech by Russell Means at Black Hills International Survival Gathering, 1980. http://www.dickshovel.com/Banks.html.

Means, Russell. *Where White Men Fear to Tread.* New York: St. Martin's Griffin, 1995.

Smith, Paul Chaat, and Robert Allen Warrior. *Like a Hurricane: The Indian Movement from Alcatraz to Wounded Knee.* New York: New Press, 1996.

MILLS, BILLY
BORN 1938 OGLALA LAKOTA
DISTANCE RUNNER

After entering the race as a virtual unknown, Billy Mills won the 10,000-meter run at the 1964 Olympic Games in Tokyo. His victory, the first by an American in an Olympic long-distance track event, is often recalled as one of the most astounding upsets in the history of the games. Mills later distinguished himself as an inspirational speaker and advocate of Native American causes.

Billy Mills throws his arms into the air as he hits the finish line to win a surprise gold medal for the United States in the Olympic 10,000 meter run in Tokyo, October 14, 1964. (AP/Wide World Photos)

Career as a Runner

William M. Mills, of mixed ancestry, was born in 1938 on the Pine Ridge Indian Reservation in South Dakota. He was named *Makata Taka Hela,* meaning "Love Your Country" and "Respects the Earth." His mixed ancestry caused Mills to feel isolated and rejected at times. Additionally, he was orphaned at age 12. Athletics came to offer him a release and an avenue of acceptance and distinction.

Mills attended Haskell Institute in Lawrence, Kansas, graduating from high school in 1957, having participated in boxing and running. He had wanted to play football, but at 5-foot-2 and 104 pounds, admitted he was not built for that sport. Eventually, Mills devoted himself exclusively to running, performing well enough to secure an athletic scholarship at the University of Kansas. Mills developed as a runner under Kansas track coach Bill Easton. At the University of Kansas, he was a three-time all-American, as he won the Big Eight conference cross-country championship in 1960. The team that Mills led won two national NCAA outdoor team championships in 1959 and 1960. At that point, Mills tried out for the U.S. Olympic Team, but did not make the cut.

After college, Mills quit running competitively and joined the U.S. Marine Corps on an officer's commission. Fellow officers urged Mills to begin running again, and he won a 10,000-meter run in interservice competition. The Marines then sent Mills to the Olympic Trials for the 1964 games, and he made the team. Mills had to borrow shoes for the Olympics because U.S. officials believed he had little chance of doing well, so they spent their limited funds on other athletes.

Mills qualified in the 10,000-meter run a minute slower than Australian Ron Clarke, whom most observers expected to run a close race for first place with Tunisian Mohammad Gammoudi. Mills came out of the pack to win the gold medal in what was regarded at the time as one of the most stunning upsets of Olympic history. He passed both Clarke and Gammoudi on the last lap. Mills not only won the race; he also set an Olympic record in the event. He became the first Olympian from the United States to win a gold medal in long-distance track in the modern games. (The only person to come close was Louis Tewanima, a Hopi, who won a silver medal in the 10,000 meters at the 1912 Olympiad.)

Mills's victory was such a surprise that some sports reporters did not even know Mills's name. Mills also placed 14th in the marathon at the Tokyo Olympics. He later was inducted into the United States Olympic Hall of Fame. On his return to Pine Ridge, the Oglalas gave Mills a large pow-wow and a ring made of Black Hills gold.

Mills continued to compete in long-distance events after the Olympics, becoming one of the fastest distance runners of all time. During 1965, he set U.S. records for the 10,000-meter and three miles, as well as a world record of 27 minutes, 12 seconds in the six-mile run. This record has not been beat.

Life Off the Running Track

Off the track, living in Sacramento, California, Mills has been married to Patricia for more than four decades, as they raised three daughters. After leaving the Marines, he worked as a life insurance salesman. For many years, he has been in demand as an inspirational speaker across the United States. Later in his life, Mills became a businessman. He remained active in causes that benefit Native Americans, especially athletes. Mills also took a leading role in the empowerment of indigenous peoples. As the spokesperson for Running Strong for American Indian Youth, a division of Christian Relief Services, he has worked to help people in American Indian communities meet fundamental needs of food, clothing, and shelter.

Mills has received many awards. He also was the subject of a feature film, *Running Brave,* starring Robby Benson, that was released in 1984.

Further Reading

Chavers, Dean. *Modern American Indian Leaders: Their Lives and Their Works.* 2 vols. Lewiston, NY: Edwin Mellen Press, 2007.

Mills, Billy, and Nicholas Sparks. *Wokini: A Lakota Journey to Happiness and Understanding.* Carlsbad, CA: Hay House, 2003.

Mohawk, John C.
1944–2006 Seneca
Educator and Author

John C. Mohawk (*Sotisisowah*), one of the foremost Haudenosaunee (Iroquois) scholars and activists, combined the roles and talents of university professor, elder statesman, historian, master storyteller, international negotiator, and cultural revivalist. Mohawk was "intensely steeped in the spiritual ceremonial traditions of the Haudenosaunee people through his foundational longhouse culture at the Cattaraugus Reservation in western New York," wrote José Barreiro in *Indian Country*

Today. "Mohawk was one of those rare American Indian individuals who comfortably stepped out into the Western academic and journalistic arenas. He was an enthusiastic participant in his own traditional ways, a legendary singer and knowledgeable elder of the most profound ceremonial cycles of the Haudenosaunee. As a scholar, he represented the Native traditional school of thought in a way that was as authentic as it was brilliantly modern and universal" (Barreiro, 2006).

Mohawk's long-time friend and former student Lori Taylor wrote, "John Mohawk talked about himself as a person who bridged worlds. We need people who can bridge those worlds, and translate each to the other. This is precisely what drew me to study with him. [Mohawk] could explain the flow of world history, mediate violent battles, and still talk to his neighbors on the reservation about corn, beans, squash, and diabetes." John was the heart of the Native Studies program at the University of Buffalo," said friend and university colleague Bruce Jackson. "Other people taught it, but he was the one who always provided the focus, the compassion and the guiding intelligence," said Jackson. "In addition, the students really loved him" (Jackson, 2006).

"John had a wonderful connection with the elders [of] the Haudenosaunee (Iroquois), and they invested in him truly to hold the culture in place," said Barry White, a friend of Mohawk's for more than 30 years. "His dad, Ernie, was one of his major mentors in the thought and philosophy of the Iroquois, and people from across the Six Nations invested in him like he was a conduit for the transmission of their culture to the next generation" (Jackson, 2006).

A Peacemaker Above All

Mohawk was born into the Seneca Turtle Clan during 1944 to Ernie and Elsie Mohawk. After graduating from Gowanda High School, Mohawk earned an undergraduate degree in history at Hartwick College during 1968 and started graduate studies at the University of Buffalo two years later.

Mohawk received his MA degree (1989) and PhD (1994) from the American Studies Program at the University of Buffalo (now the State University of New York at Buffalo), after which he joined the school's faculty. Mohawk also directed UB's indigenous studies program. Mohawk became known as a skilled crisis negotiator who not only helped reconcile differences between Iroquois factions, but also, during 1980, played a role in negotiating U.S.-Iranian relations.

Mohawk was editor of *Akwesasne Notes* between 1976 and 1983. In 1987, he helped found *Daybreak* magazine, and served as one of its editors until 1997. He also was an opinion columnist for *Indian Country Today*. Among Mohawk's best-known books are *Utopian Legacies* (2000) and *Exiled in the Land of the Free* (1992), which he co-edited with Oren Lyons.

Above all, Mohawk was a peacemaker. In "The Warriors Who Turned to Peace," which came out in the Winter 2005 issue of *Yes!* magazine, he described the history of the Haudenosaunee Confederacy's Peacemaker, who introduced a political system that enabled them to stop killing one another in bouts of blood revenge:

According to the Great Law, peace is arrived at through the exercise of righteousness, reason, and power. You have the power to make peace with an enemy only if you acknowledge that the enemy is human. To acknowledge that they are rational beings who want to live and who want their children to live enhances your power by giving you the capacity to speak to them. If you think they are not human, you won't have that capacity; you will have destroyed your own power to communicate with the very people you must communicate with if you are going to bring about peace. (Mohawk, 2004)

Food Is Life

Mohawk was passionately interested in food. "He loved to eat and he loved finding ways to make eating more rational," said Jackson. He became an advocate of the Slow Food movement. He saw health benefits that would help Indians as they battled obesity, diabetes, and heart and circulation problems. Food was an expression of life to Mohawk. Jackson recalled: "When he invited me down to his mother's house on the Cattaraugus Indian Reservation for the tenth day of his mother's funeral, he said, 'You should come. Somebody's bringing bear stew. You've probably never had bear stew.' Late that day he filled a plate with the bear stew and lots of other things and he carefully carried the plate into the woods behind the house, where he left it for her" (Jackson, 2006).

Mohawk initiated and led the Iroquois White Corn Project, which produced and marketed traditional Seneca corn to restaurants, part of a larger effort by Mohawk to help maintain small-scale sustainable agriculture. Originally called the Pinewoods Community Farming Project, the white corn project was initiated in 1997. It began with the hope that Native Americans and other people as well would revitalize the use of traditional Iroquois foods. This corn is renowned for its slow-released carbohydrates. These carbohydrates can be crucial in the fight against diabetes, a disease that has reached epidemic proportions in the Native American community.

The white corn project grew quickly from one restaurant, the Pinewoods Café on the Cattaraugus Indian Reservation in Irving. The corn is hulled and milled there after being collected by various Iroquois farmers. The menu at the Pinewoods Café includes corn and bean soups, as well as chili made with buffalo meat. Diners also sample meals with all of the three components of the Iroquois diet represented—the "Three Sisters": beans, corn, and squash.

Mohawk realized that if Iroquois corn is healthy for Native Americans, there also would be a market among non-Indians. Not only have the health benefits warranted interest, but its earthy aroma and unusual flavor appeals to many people. Americans expect corn to be so unnaturally sweet, but this corn has been such a sensation that the project has recently attained national coverage and praise on the pages of *Gourmet* magazine.

Iroquois white corn may be used in many ways. Two flours can be milled from it, according to Mohawk. The flour may be used as a healthy substitute for white and wheat bread. The corn can be used in essentially every dish as common sweet corn. It also adds a unique flavor that can bring new life to ordinary dishes.

Utopian Legacies

Mohawk was best-known outside New York State has an author. His histories ranged the world, combining Native American and European themes. In *Utopian Legacies,* for example, he examined Western ideological thought as a provocation of political oppression. "Nazism was a revitalization movement, complete with its own vision of utopia, its rationalizations for conquest and plunder, and an ability to disarm ordinary people's sense of morality and to plunge an entire nation . . . into an orgy of violence and murder," wrote Mohawk (2000, 210).

To Mohawk, the legacy of utopianism is one of the defining tenets of several Western European cultures. Mohawk found utopian assumptions operating in some of the most powerful ideological forces shaping Christianity, Islam, and capitalism. He notes that the Christian creation story begins with the expulsion of the original human couple (Adam and Eve) from a notable Western utopia, the Garden of Eden. Mohawk described some of the common elements of utopianism: "Utopian ideologies enable plunderers to claim—even to believe—that they are in pursuit of noble goals" (2000, 3). Thus, the Spanish conquests was propelled by a triple-set of utopian myths, which have since been condensed to "God, gold, and glory." "Inherent in utopian thought . . . is a notion of progress," wrote Mohawk (2000, 4). Devotees of any given ideology labor for a promised land that is never attained, whether as the fabled Seven Cities of Cibola, a workers' paradise, or life after death.

Aspirations of utopia inevitably create myths by which a "chosen people" attempt to elevate themselves above the rest of humanity. Witness Hitler's eugenic Aryan "superman," or Stalin's New Socialist Man. In turn, a "chosen people" justify seizure of victims' land and resources as required by the conqueror's plunder-enabling utopian vision. When one utopian vision collides with another, the results sometimes have bathed Eurasian history in blood. Mohawk describes the brutality of the Christian Crusades. In these wars, as in many others, brutality was excused by perpetrators who characterized their enemies as subhuman.

Passing

Mohawk died suddenly at his home in Buffalo December 10, 2006, at age 61. Mohawk's sudden departure reminded some who knew him of Vine Deloria, Jr.'s passing 13 months earlier. Like Deloria, Mohawk was not nearly finished with life's tour—his journey came to a sudden halt while still very much a work in progress.

A funeral ceremony was held in the Longhouse at the Cattaraugus Indian Reservation, after which Mohawk was buried in the Seneca Nation Cemetery, next to his wife, Yvonne Dion-Buffalo, of the Samson Cree Band, who had died in June 2005.

Further Reading

Barreiro, Jose. "John Mohawk, Beloved Man of Wisdom, Passes On." *Indian Country Today,* December 15, 2006. http://www.hanksville.org/NAresources/news/2006/12/john-mohawk-beloved-man-of-wisdom.html.

Jackson, Bruce. "Saying 'Oh!': John Mohawk 1944–2006." December 20, 2006. http://buffaloreport.com/2006/061220.jackson.mohawk.html.

Lyons, Oren, and John C. Mohawk. *Exiled in the Land of the Free: Democracy, Indian Nations, and the U.S. Constitution.* Santa Fe, NM: Clear Light, 1992.

"Mohawk, John C., Professor; a Foremost Iroquois Scholar and Activist." *Buffalo News,* December 15, 2006. http://www.legacy.com/buffalonews/DeathNotices.asp.

Mohawk, John. "The Warriors Who Turned to Peace." *Yes! Magazine,* November, 2004. http://www.yesmagazine.org/issues/healing-resistance/the-warriors-who-turned-to-peace.

Mohawk, John C. *Utopian Legacies: A History of Conquest and Oppression in the Western World.* Santa Fe, NM: Clear Light, 2000.

MOMADAY, N. SCOTT
BORN 1934 KIOWA
WRITER, ARTIST, AND TEACHER

Navarre Scott Momaday, a Kiowa novelist, poet, visual artist, and professor, came to the attention of a worldwide audience in 1969, after he became the first American Indian to win a Pulitzer Prize in fiction for *House Made of Dawn.* Momaday's work arrived at about the same time that American Indian activism was stirred by the founding of the American Indian Movement and other activities, such as publication of Dee Brown's *Bury My Heart at Wounded Knee. House Made of Dawn* helped to initiate a modern rebirth of American Indian literature. In addition to working with words, Momaday often illustrates his books with sketches. His etchings and paintings also have been widely exhibited.

Early Life

Momaday was born February 27, 1934, in Lawton, Oklahoma, to Alfred Momaday (a full-blooded Kiowa), a painter, and Natachee Scott Momaday, who was French American and Cherokee and a writer. "I grew up in a creative household and followed in my mother's footsteps, to begin with. My father was a great storyteller and he knew many stories from the Kiowa oral tradition," Momaday said during a Public Broadcasting Service (PBS) documentary about him that was aired during 2001. "He told me many of these stories over and over because I loved them. But it was only after I became an adult that I understood how fragile they are, because they exist only by word of mouth, always just one generation away from extinction. That's when I began to write down the tales my father and others had told me" ("Keeper," 2001).

N. Scott Momaday, professor and author, winner of a Guggenheim fellowship and a Pulitzer Prize for fiction. (AP/Wide World Photos)

At the age of six months, a Kiowa storyteller gave Momaday a Kiowa name, *Tsoaitalee* ("Rock-Tree Boy"), referring to a location near Devil's Tower, in Wyoming. Within two years of his birth, Momaday's family moved to the Navajo reservation in New Mexico for seven years. In 1946, both parents became teachers at a school on the Jemez Pueblo in New Mexico. Life in New Mexico later would fundamentally flavor Momaday's novels and poetry. At Jemez, Momaday watched life change quickly following the return of veterans from World War II. Its population increased as Anglo-American ways of life became more commonplace. Veterans returning from World War II brought outside experiences home.

"I grew up in two worlds and straddle both those worlds even now," Momaday said. "It has made for confusion and a richness in my life. I've been able to deal with it reasonably well, I think, and I value it" ("Keeper," 2001). Momaday developed a keen eye for the impact of such changes on Native people, some of whom left the reservations for jobs. Others became suicidal as familiar signposts of traditional life vanished. Many turned to alcohol or other drugs. While Momaday became an acute student of personal identity crises in his writing, he seemed to thrive from change himself.

Education, Teaching, Writing

Momaday earned a bachelor's degree in political science at the University of New Mexico (1958), then taught for a time on New Mexico's Jicarilla Apache Reservation, where he began to write. His talents were recognized quickly; in 1959, he received a Wallace Stegner Creative Writing Scholarship for poetry. At Stanford University, he worked with his mentor, poet Yvor Winters. Momaday earned a master's degree at Stanford in 1960 and a PhD three years later, after which he began to teach at the University of California–Santa Barbara. There, he began to work on *House Made of Dawn,* which captured the search for Native American identity in a rapidly changing world that Momaday had observed at Jemez. Abel, the main character, leaves the reservation for World War II, then struggles with his identity upon return. A Navajo and a Kiowa help Abel rediscover his Native

American heritage, an experience that resonated with many people on reservations and in cities who were engaged in the same sort of struggle and change.

Following *House Made of Dawn,* Momaday wrote several other books that address Native American people's attempts to maintain traditions in the 20th century, including *The Way to Rainy Mountain* (1969), a work that combines some of his own past with Kiowa history and myth; a childhood memoir (*The Names,* 1976); a book of poems (*The Gourd Dancer,* also 1976); and *The Ancient Child* (1989). He authored *In the Presence of the Sun* (1991), *Circle of Wonder: A Native American Christmas Story* (1993), and *The Native Americans: Indian Country* (1993), as well as other, later titles. He also scripted a play, *The Indolent Boys* (2007).

In addition to his work on Native American themes, Momaday is a scholar of Emily Dickinson and Frederick Goddard Tuckerman. He has been awarded a Guggenheim Fellowship, a National Institute of Arts and Letters Award, and the Premio Letterario Internationale Mondello, Italy's highest literary award. He is also a Fellow of the American Academy of Arts and Sciences and a founding trustee of the National Museum of the American Indian.

Momaday has held tenured appointments at the Santa Barbara and Berkeley campuses of the University of California, Stanford University, and the University of Arizona, where he was named regents professor. At Berkeley, Momaday was Professor of English and Comparative Literature. He also designed a graduate program of American Indian Studies. Momaday moved from Berkeley to Stanford in 1973. In 1982, he moved again, to Tucson, at the University of Arizona.

He has lectured at several other universities, including Princeton and Columbia. His teaching credits also include the University of Moscow, in Russia, where he was the first to teach Native American literature. In 2007, Momaday received the National Medal of Arts.

Surveying Native American experience over the last century, Momaday sees reasons to be optimistic. "The turn of the century was the lowest point for the devastation of Indian culture by disease and persecution, and it's a wonder to me that they survived it and have not only maintained their identity, but are actually growing stronger in some ways. The situation is still very bad, especially in certain geographical areas, but there are more Indians going to school, more Indians becoming professional people, more Indians assuming full responsibility in our society. We have a long way to go, but we're making great strides" ("Keeper," 2001).

Momaday is a member of the Kiowa Gourd Dance Society. He also visits sacred places such as Devil's Tower, which, he told PBS, "are important to me, because they've been made sacred by sacrifice, by the investment of blood and experience and story. So I have a keen sense of that and a great appreciation of it. And I think that the greatest deprivation that the Native American suffers today is the theft of the sacred" ("Keeper," 2001).

Further Reading

"Keeper of the Flame: N. Scott Momaday." New Perspectives on the West. Public Broadcasting System. 2001. http://www.pbs.org/weta/thewest/program/producers/momaday.htm.

Momaday, N. Scott. *House Made of Dawn.* New York: Harper & Row, 1968.

Momaday, N. Scott. *The Names.* Tucson: University of Arizona Press, 1976.

Schubnell, Matthias. *N. Scott Momaday: The Cultural and Literary Background.* Norman: University of Oklahoma Press, 1985.

Schubnell, Matthias, ed. *Conversations with N. Scott Momaday.* Jackson: University Press of Mississippi, 1997.

Montezuma, Carlos (Wassaja)
c. 1867–1923 Yavapai
Native-rights Leader and Physician

Among the Yavapai, Carlos Montezuma was known as *Wassaja,* translated from the Yuman language as meaning "Gesturing," or "Beckoning," a name that later was taken as the title of a well-known Native American newspaper. Montezuma combined activism with a career as a surgeon.

He was born in the *Ka Veecum Gahkwoot'th* (Superstition Mountains) of central Arizona in 1866 or 1867 into the Yavapai Indian nation, which translates as "Almost-People to the East," one of 13 bands of *Pai* or *Pa'a* (the People) in present-day central Arizona. His father was called Cocuyevah. No record of his mother's name exists. At about the age of five (probably during 1871), during a raid, O'odham soldiers from the Salt River area, allied with U.S. Army General George Crook, kidnapped Wassaja. He lived with them on the Gila River for a short time, after which Carlos Gentile, a photographer and prospector, bought him for about $30.

Wassaja's mother, defying an Indian agent's order not to leave her reservation, went out to search for her son and was shot by an Indian scout in the nearby mountains. Gentile took the young Wassaja to the eastern United States, where he was baptized as a Christian and given the name Carlos Montezuma. Young Carlos received some education in Chicago, then attended Carlisle Indian School. Gentile's photography business failed, and he committed suicide in 1893. Before his suicide, Gentile had given Carlos to a Baptist missionary, George W. Ingalls, who soon turned him over to the Reverend W. H. Stedman of Urbana, Illinois.

Carlos Montezuma, U.S. American Indian rights leader and physician. (National Library of Medicine/National Archives)

For two years after that, Montezuma received private tutoring. After one year of preparatory school, he enrolled at the University of Illinois. In 1884, Montezuma received a bachelor of science degree (cum laude). Subsequently, he attended the Chicago Medical College at Northwestern University with a partial scholarship, while working as a pharmacist. In 1889, Montezuma received a medical degree.

Medical Practice

Montezuma tried private practice in Chicago for a short time, then accepted a one-year appointment at the Fort Stevenson Indian School in North Dakota as a physician and surgeon. After that, he worked at Indian agencies in Washington State and Nevada. In 1894, he accepted an appointment at the Carlisle Indian School in Pennsylvania and came to know Carlisle's founder and chief administrator, Col. Richard Henry Pratt. Montezuma also came to know Zitkala-sa (Gertrude Simmons Bonnin), a well-known Sioux writer and Indian-rights activist.

Montezuma returned to Chicago in 1896 and began a private medical practice specializing in gastrointestinal disorders that became very successful. He was invited to teach at the College of Physicians and Surgeons as well as at the postgraduate level at Chicago Medical School.

Traveling with the Carlisle football team in the U.S. Southwest during 1901, Montezuma made contact with his Yavapai family. In 1903, the Yavapai gained rights to 24,680 acres on the former Fort McDowell Military Reserve, near Phoenix, part of their homeland. Montezuma helped his Yavapai family to successfully resist removal from their homelands to the Pima Salt River Reservation. The government sought to build a dam on the Verde River on their reservation. For many years afterward, Montezuma represented his people as he advocated Yavapai land and water rights.

Throughout his adult life, Montezuma opposed the reservation system and its administration by the Bureau of Indian Affairs. He remembered the humiliation of his mother having to ask the Indian agent's permission to leave her homeland to search for him after he was kidnapped. Governmental caprice and insensitivity to American Indians fueled Montezuma's fight for Indian rights. Montezuma considered the fact that Native Americans were not legally enfranchised by the United States an insult, especially after black former slaves were granted citizenship following the Civil War.

Published Works

Although he encouraged citizenship and assimilation, Montezuma also advocated Native American ethnic pride. He authored *Let My People Go* (1914) and two other books on Indian political issues. He established the Indian rights magazine *Wassaja* (in this context, "Wassaja" meant "Let My People Go") during 1916. In 1906, President Theodore Roosevelt offered to appoint Montezuma Commissioner of Indian Affairs, but he refused. In 1917, Montezuma was arrested and jailed for opposing the drafting of American Indians into military service during World War I. President Woodrow Wilson released Montezuma and then again offered him the position as head of the Bureau of Indian Affairs. Once again, he declined, knowing that holding such a position would compromise his crusade for Indian rights and abolition of the BIA.

Montezuma was a long-time advocate of collective action. During 1904, with Luzena Choteau, an Oklahoma Wyandotte, he played a role in the founding of the National Indian Republican Association. With Thomas L. Sloan (Omaha) and Walter Battice (Sac and Fox from Oklahoma) in 1909, Montezuma formed the Indian Progressive Organization. Two years later, with Laura Cornelius (an Oneida from Wisconsin) and Henry Standing Bear (a Lakota from the Rosebud Sioux Reservation), he organized meetings in Columbus, Ohio, that laid a basis for the Society of American Indians.

Wassaja was published monthly from April 1916 until November 1922. It was only one of several venues in which Montezuma addressed Indian-rights issues. He was a tireless author of newspaper and magazine articles, as well as lectures. Countering the "vanishing Indian" thesis (an assumption commonly repeated by non-Indians, at the time) in a piece entitled "Changing Is Not Vanishing," Montezuma wrote: "The Indian race vanishing? No, never! The race will live on and prosper forever" (Montezuma, 1987).

Montezuma became a Mason in the late part of his life and became Master Mason. Montezuma's first wife was Romanian; his second wife was Marie Keller. Montezuma returned home to live with his relatives at Fort McDowell. Beset by diabetes and tuberculosis, he passed on January 31, 1923, on the reservation. Montezuma was buried in the Fort McDowell Indian Cemetery.

Wassaja was revived by Rupert Costo and Jeannette Henry in 1972 to honor Montezuma's Indian-rights activities.

Further Reading

Iverson, Peter. *Carlos Montezuma and the Changing World of American Indians.* [1982]. Albuquerque: University of New Mexico Press, 2001.

Montezuma, Carlos. "Changing Is Not Vanishing." *The Papers of Carlos Montezuma, M.D.* [1916]. Edited by John W. Larner, Jr. New York: Primary Source Microfilm and Scholarly Resources, 1987.

Speroff, Leon. *Carlos Montezuma, M.D.: A Yavapai American Hero.* Portland, OR: Arnica, 2003.

N

Nampeyo
c. 1859–1942 Hopi-Tewa
Artist

Nampeyo was born at Hano, Arizona, about 1859. Nampeyo ("Snake Girl"; *Tcumana, Nampayu, Nampayo*), an internationally notable Hopi-Tewa potter, was a daughter of father Qotsvena, of the Snake Clan, and mother Qotcakao, of the Tobacco Clan. As a young girl, she watched her grandmother make the large *ollas* (Spanish for water pots) and other vessels used in traditional Hopi village life. Her village, Hano, was adjacent to Walpi on First Mesa and was set up by Tewa people fleeing Spanish oppression in the Rio Grande Valley after Pope's Rebellion in 1680. Although the Tewas intermarried with the Hopis, they retained much of their language and distinctive ceremonies into the 19th century.

Contemporary accounts describe Nampeyo as a stunning young woman. In 1879, she married her first husband, Kwivioya, who left her soon afterward because he believed that he could not keep other men away from her. In 1881, Nampeyo married a second and final time to Lesou from the neighboring village of Walpi.

About 1892, she began to revive the designs and forms present in Hopi ancient pottery because she thought that they were superior to contemporary styles. Initially, other Hopi artists scorned Nampeyo's work, but when they saw that her pottery sold at high prices, they began to copy her designs and techniques. When the archeologist Jesse Walter Fewkes employed her husband in excavations at *Sikyatki* (an early Pueblo ruin) in 1895, old pottery shards unearthed there provided her with a treasure trove of ancient designs. Nampeyo also visited other archeological sites at nearby *Awatovi, Payupki,* and *Tsukuvi* to expand her knowledge of ancient styles. Using bits of broken ancient pottery, she created her own motifs rooted in ancient Hopi forms. As Nampeyo's pottery improved, it took on a fluid, bold style that is still distinctive of her work.

Nampeyo, a Hopi potter, builds her kiln, ca. 1906. (Library of Congress)

By the end of the 19th century, Nampeyo had become a prominent Indian artist. In 1898 and 1910, she journeyed to Chicago to promote her work. In 1904 and 1907, she was employed by the Fred Harvey Hotel Company at its Grand Canyon Lodge. Her partnership with Fred Harvey made Nampeyo a figure of international renown. The Smithsonian Institution also began to collect her work.

Through Nampeyo's efforts, Hopi pottery was elevated to a commercially viable art form. When Nampeyo began her work, few Hopi women still produced pots, but she single-handedly revived the craft and enhanced its esthetics. By the 1930s, Nampeyo began to go blind and she could no longer create the remarkably precise, fine and fluid decorations that became her hallmark. Her husband helped to create Nampeyo's pottery during her declining years, until he died in 1932. Her four daughters (Annie, Cecilia, Fannie, and Nellie) were also renowned potters in their own right. Nampeyo died at her home on July 20, 1942.

Further Reading

Heller, Jules, and Nancy G. Heller. *North American Women Artists of the Twentieth Century—A Biographical Dictionary*. New York: Garland, 1995.
Sonneborn, Liz. *A to Z of Native American Women*. New York: Facts On File, 1998.

ORTIZ, SIMON J.
BORN 1941 PUEBLO, ACOMA
POET

Simon J. Ortiz is an Acoma Pueblo writer who is recognized by scholars of Native American literature as one of the most significant voices to come out of the Native American renaissance of the 1960s and 1970s. His writing accomplishments include poems, short stories, essays, and children's books, but he is primarily known as a poet. Ortiz's interest in preserving the oral tradition of his Acoma ancestors combines a blend of traditional forms and themes with an acknowledgment of the contemporary world. Ortiz has been writing for more than 30 years, producing 19 books of poetry and prose. He occasionally writes in a combination of prose and verse.

Growing Up in Navajo Country

Born May 27, 1941, in Albuquerque, New Mexico, Ortiz was raised in the Eagle Clan in the Acoma village of McCartys (*Deetseyamah*). Ortiz had close family ties, most notably with his father and elder sisters, relationships that also were strengthened by clan relationships. Drawing on these ties, Ortiz spoke the Acoma language (*Aacpumeh dzehni*), mixed with English and Spanish.

His father, Joseph, was a railroad worker and was often away from home for long periods. Due to his father's work, the family moved to Arizona when Ortiz was in the fifth grade. Ortiz recounts that both his parents were good storytellers and singers and that both of these qualities influenced him. He often says that his first writings were songs, and his simple and direct poetic style is similar to storytelling. In fact, Ortiz describes himself more as storyteller than a poet. It has been noted that "His poetry is narrative in style, because he feels each work *must* tell a story" (Cullum, 2004, 228).

Ortiz received his elementary education in the U.S. government McCartys Day School and published his first poem—for his mother, Mamie—in the school newspaper while he was in the fifth grade. In the McCartys school, students were required to learn and speak English. In the 1950s, it was traditional for Indian children to be sent to boarding schools, so for Grades 7 through 12, Ortiz lived at Catherine's School, an American Indian boarding school in Albuquerque.

"As early on I associated reading with oral stories, it was not difficult to learn to read" or write, Ortiz said. He stated that it was exciting "to go to school" even though he has a critical opinion regarding government boarding schools. Native American people have been faced with assimilationist boarding schools since the 1870s and the policy, Ortiz said, "was to break or sever ties to culture, family, and tribe, to change indigenous people into 'Americans.'" Those schools didn't allow students to speak in their native languages—that was "punishable with a hard crack by the teacher's ruler" (Ortiz, 1992, 8).

Ortiz obtained his first typewriter as a pre-adolescent, having sold mail-order hand cream for a local company to pay for it. He began to write poetry, inspired by a mix of feelings—both loneliness and love—and country-western and folk songs, "Strangely, not Aacquemeh songs which I had grown up with" (Ortiz, 1992, 13). He also kept diaries and journals. In the seventh grade, inspired by fiction writers, young Ortiz started writing stories.

Becoming a Writer

In 1962, at the age of 21, Ortiz committed himself to becoming a writer. He attended Fort Lewis College for two years, majoring in chemistry, then enlisted in the U.S. Army from 1963 to 1966. He returned to his studies (in English), at the University of New Mexico (1966–68) and then was enrolled in the prestigious Writers' Workshop at the University of Iowa, where he earned an MFA in 1969. "It was remotely because what I really wanted to do was read, think and write," he explained ("American Author," n.d.). Ortiz's developing identity as a writer also included a sense of his people's history and present-day reality. Ortiz admired his grandfather, a spiritual leader and healer. This new awareness of his culture's plight in America would lead to a darker time in Ortiz's life.

Ortiz taught at San Diego State University and the Institute of the American Indian Arts in 1974, at Navajo Community College from 1975 to 1977, and at the College of Marin from 1976 to 1979. In 1979, he joined the faculty of the University of New Mexico. In 2002, that institution awarded Ortiz an honorary Doctor of Letters. Ortiz was a professor of American Indian Studies in the Department of English at Arizona State University in Tempe, Arizona. He also has been a faculty member at the University of Toronto, and he is a summer faculty member of American Indian Language Development Institute (AILDI). He remains politically active.

In addition to teaching, Ortiz has worked as a journalist, public-relations director, editor of a community newspaper, and consulting editor of the Pueblo of the Acoma Press. He also served as lieutenant governor of the Acoma Pueblo.

Ortiz has been married and divorced four times. He often dedicates his poetry to his children—a son Raho Nez and daughters Rainy Dawn and Sara Marie. He has eight grandchildren.

Themes and Concerns

Ortiz places all his work within the limits of his own lifetime, speaking of people's every-day lives. He speaks of American Indian culture's role in the world today. Ortiz is best known for several themes. The most frequent one is the land and a sense of place. "If anything is most vital, essential, and absolutely important in Native cultural philosophy," it is an interdependence between the land and the people, writes Ortiz in his book of writers' essays *Speaking for the Generations.* The concept of interdependence is "the fact that without land there is no life, and without a responsible social and cultural outlook by humans, no life-sustaining land is possible" (Ortiz, 1998, xii).

In the *Woven Stone,* Ortiz "advocates an increased role for Indian cultures to provide non-Indian culture with the benefit of their thousands of years of experience so that it can avoid destroying itself and the rest of the world." Ortiz's images "vividly demonstrate the results of the white culture's lack of concern with the destruction caused by the quest for profit under the capitalist system" (Graber, 2000, 19–21). Ortiz's writings serve to provide context as well as understanding of anti-Indian racism. Ortiz recalls his former wife's (Marlene, an Anglo-American) complaint that she was never included in his writing due to racism. However, Ortiz explains that so-called Indian racism is rather ethnocentrism among Native Americans that is a result of racism and colonialism. "In effect it comes from fighting racism which has taken away the positive feeling; it is an effort to reverse racism's result by regaining belief in self," he said (Ortiz, 1992, 30). Through his poetry, Ortiz continues to preserve American Indian traditions and cultures, "confident that they will survive due to the efforts of those who, like himself, will continue to document and celebrate their culture" (Cullum, 2004, 228).

Ortiz says that occasional awkwardness of language in his poetry may be traced to the period when he learned English fluently and "felt awkward" when he started translating from the Acoma language of his family home and community to English. The Native American people to whom Ortiz belonged had a secure cultural and linguistic integrity. However, they had to be "constantly on the defensive," protecting their culture, livelihood, rights, land, language, spirit, "everything." "The Acoma language was a vital link to the continuance of the *hanoh,* the people, as a whole" (Ortiz, 1992, 6).

Stressing the importance of language, Ortiz states that the language from "birth to six years of age in the Acoma family and community was the basis and source of all I would do later in poetry, short fiction, essay, and other works" (Ortiz, 1992, 6). He concludes with sadness that such support and connectedness does not exist now as it did then. The importance of language goes beyond just oral tradition—the language through oral tradition presents the "consciousness of the people" and "evokes and expresses a belief system." In his book of poetry, *Woven Stone,* Ortiz even states that it is his boyhood experience, that closeness to a specific Native American way of life, that was a prelude to the alcoholism that he suffered later. Alcoholism—another theme that he attributed as one of the political and social ills—was, according to Ortiz, an outcome of the way Native Americans were treated by the colonizer—dispossessed, oppressed, and poor.

Major Works

Ortiz's major works include *Going for the Rain* (1976), *A Good Journey* (1977), *Fight Back* (1980), *From the Sand Creek* (1981), and *After and Before the Lightning* (1986).

In *Going for the Rain,* Ortiz provides a picture of what is like for a Native American to be raised in his own traditions, to go out to the larger American culture, and return to his Place, where he feels he belongs. *A Good Journey* is the journey of the generations through life, from grandparents to parents to children, while *Fight Back* commemorates the 300th anniversary of the 1680 Pueblo Revolt against the Spanish colonists. The revolt is compared to the exploitative treatment of Native Americans by the U.S. government where large uranium deposits are on Indian land. That was the time when Ortiz worked in the mining industry.

From the Sand Creek was written while Ortiz was being treated for alcoholism at the Veterans Administration Hospital in Colorado. Fort Lyon Veterans Hospital coincidentally was built on the site where, in 1864, U.S. troops massacred one-fifth of the Cheyenne and Arapaho people after promising them peace and safety. Ortiz parallels the same sadness and hopelessness between Vietnam veterans and Indians who were in the same place more than a hundred years ago.

In *After and Before the Lightning,* Ortiz recounts another of his life experiences, this time as an assistant professor at Sinte Gleska College on the Lakota Sioux Reservation in South Dakota. The poet writes of humankind's place in the universe and how quickly life can be taken away.

Besides these major works, Ortiz has published other poetry, including *Naked in the Wind* (1971), *A Poem Is a Journey* (1981), *Woven Stone* (1992, a collection of poetry and prose), and *Telling and Showing Her: The Earth, The Land* (1995). Ortiz's fiction and short stories include *Many Farm Notes* (1975), *Fightin': New and Collected Stories* (1983), and *Men on the Moon: Collected Short Stories* (1999).

Ortiz lives in the Acoma Pueblo, New Mexico. Among other awards, he has held a New Mexico Humanities Council Humanitarian Award, the Lila Wallace Reader's Digest Writer's Award, a National Endowment for the Arts fellowship, and the National Endowment for the Arts Discovery Award. Ortiz also received a Lifetime Achievement Award from the Returning the Gift Festival of Native Writers, and in 1981 was an Honored Poet at the White House Salute to Poetry.

Milica Vukovljak

Further Reading

"American Author: Simon J. Ortiz." Answers.com. n.d. http://www.answers.com/topic/simon-j-ortiz.

Cullum, Linda. *Contemporary American Ethnic Poets: Lives, Works, Sources.* Westport, CT: Greenwood Press, 2004.

Graber, Gregg. "Something Wicked This Way Comes: Warnings by Simon Ortiz and Martin Cruz Smith." *Wicazo Sa Review* 15, no. 2 (2000): 17–25.

Oakes, Elizabeth H. *American Writers.* New York: Facts On File, 2004.

Ortiz, Simon J. *Woven Stone.* Tucson: University of Arizona Press, 1992.

Ortiz, Simon J. *Speaking for the Generations.* Tucson: University of Arizona Press, 1998.

OWENS, LOUIS
1948–2002 CHOCTAW AND CHEROKEE
SCHOLAR AND NOVELIST

Louis Owens was one of the second wave of Native American scholars and novelists to come to prominence after the Native American literary Renaissance of the 1960s. Of mixed-blood heritage, Owens used literature and scholarship to navigate the complicated waters of racial politics in academia during the 1980s and 1990s. Owens did not shy away from his European ancestry, yet he also did not deny his Native American identity. He confronted the issues of mixed-blood identity in most of his novels and several of his works of scholarship. To Owens, the terminology was important since his identity could not be expressed by the usual terms, such half-breed, or half-blood.

Owens's own experience drove him as a scholar. Professor James Woodress, a noted biographer of Willa Cather, was Owens's mentor and dissertation director while at the University of California–Davis. He explained the connection between Owens's life and experience. "Because Louis came from very poor parents who were farm laborers, novels like *The Grapes of Wrath* [sic] moved him a great deal" ("In Memoriam," n.d.) Owens saw literature as a way to understand the multiple identities and experiences of his youth. Literature provided Owens with a way for identity to be transformed into understanding.

An obituary of Owens stated:

> Louis used his fiction as a means of reinventing himself, of reconstructing his past. [He was] a fabulist, a surrealist, a spinner of myths [. . .] He has written of the bedrock human compulsion to weave fictionalized accounts of ourselves, to acknowledge the "hybrid monster of self" that is the source of all stories. (Martin, 2002)

Owens had said that his fiction was always written for himself, never with an audience in mind. "Trying to figure [an audience] out would probably drive you crazy, or make you write what they want instead of what you want. That's probably one of the few benefits of having a job, to have the luxury of writing what I want to write" (Purdy, 1998). In essence, Owens wanted to make the act of writing a way to challenge the dominant view of ethnic identity and create conflict with the reader and within the writer (Owens) himself.

Early Life and Academic Career

Owens was born July 18, 1948, in Lompoc, California, of migrant farm workers who traveled between Mississippi, Oklahoma, and the Central Valley of California. He was one of his mother's nine children; his father was her second husband. Owens's mother was an Oklahoma Cherokee, and his father was Mississippi Choctaw and Irish. His family left Mississippi and Oklahoma during the Depression to make a living picking vegetables. They were unable to earn a living wage in California, and, as a result, Owens and the rest of the children spent much of their childhoods in extreme poverty. In the most stereotypical way, he lived the life of an "Okie."

In the Owens family, Louis was a first-generation college student. After attending Cuesta (Community) College, in San Luis Obispo, California, from 1966 to 1968, Owens received his BA in 1971 from the University of California at Santa Barbara and his MA, in 1974, from the same school. Owens also worked as a ranger in the U.S. Forest Service from 1969 to 1974 in Washington State. Owens earned his PhD in English at the University of California at Davis in 1978. The same year he received his master's degree, Owens married Polly Pipkin with whom he had two daughters: Elizabeth, born in 1983, and Alexandra, born in 1985.

Published Works

Owens authored five novels, often classified as mysteries: *Wolfsong* (1991); *The Sharpest Sight* (1991), which won the 1995 Roman Noir Prize for Outstanding Mystery Novel in its French translation; *Bone Game* (1996); *Nightland* (1996), which won a 1997 Before Columbus American Book Award; and *Dark River* (1999).

His most notable nonfiction work was *Other Destinies: Understanding the American Indian Novel* (1994). Other important nonfiction works include *Mixed-blood Messages: Literature, Film, Family, Place* (1998), which won him the Wordcraft Circle Writer of the Year Award in the category of Prose—Personal and Critical Essays; and *I Hear the Train: Reflections, Inventions, Refractions* (2001). He wrote a number of other nonfiction volumes, such as *John Steinbeck's Re-Vision of America* (1985). Owens is also the author of more than 100 critical essays, nonfiction essays, and book reviews.

The Sharpest Sight

The Sharpest Sight is usually regarded as Owens's greatest literary success, although it did receive censure from some critics. The University of Oklahoma

Press believed the book was strong enough to nominate for the Pulitzer Prize, but reviewers from *Publishers Weekly* and *Kirkus* were less thrilled by it, possibly because it was misunderstood. The story of a Chicano/Native American deputy sheriff investigating the death of his mentally disturbed, former Vietnam platoon mate lives in a California that Gabriel Garcia Marquez and Raymond Chandler would have created together. While it does explore the issues of racism, borders, and borderlines with complex and intriguing symbolism, it was criticized for having juvenile characters. Critics saw the novel's combination of magical realism and hard-boiled detective fiction as a revolutionary narrative move.

Other Destinies

Other Destinies is paramount among Owens's nonfiction because it reveals the literary heritage of those of mixed blood and examines what literature written about and by mixed-bloods says not only about indigenous peoples and Anglo populations but also about America and its perception of racial identity. Using the Bakhtian concepts of image, self, and performance, Owens created a jargon-free collection of essays by authors who cannot "play" Indian but are instead forced to "be" Indians. In their decision to accept their "Indian-ness," all of the authors in the collection faced marginalization or ridicule of their work. The collection is often criticized for its lack of readability. Many critics found it difficult to read the book from start to finish. Critics also viewed Owens as light on his criticism of the authors he discussed. As Arnold Krupat, an ardent supporter of Owens and admirer of his novels, explained in his review for the *Journal of American History,* "The tendency is to offer descriptive accounts that sometimes mask what the reading of a given novel actually feels like; for example, Momaday's *The Ancient Child* (1989), for all its conceptual brilliance and structural ingenuity, has stretches (to my mind) of bombastic, self-parodying prose" (Krupat, 1993, 1090).

The collection went on to win Owens the 1993 PEN-Josephine Miles Award for "a new perception of multicultural literature that did not seek validation from the literary establishment, but created its own standards and models of literature" (PEN Oakland, n.d.).

Teaching Career and Accolades

Owens's teaching career lasted more than 20 years, beginning at the University of Pisa, Italy, where he taught through the Fulbright program during 1980 and 1981, lecturing on American literature. From 1981 to 1982, Owens was a visiting lecturer in English at the University of California at Davis. He then moved to California State University at Northridge as an assistant professor in English from 1982 to 1984. He became an assistant professor at the University of New Mexico after leaving Northridge, and he was promoted in 1986 to associate professor of English.

Owens moved to the University of California at Santa Cruz as a professor of literature from 1989 until 1994. While at Santa Cruz, in 1989, Owens received a National Endowment for the Arts Creative Writing Fellowship. He also was named honored alumnus of the year by his junior college in 1993. Owens won both the University of California at Santa Cruz Alumni Association Distinguished Teaching Award and the Student-Alumni Council Favorite Professor Award. He was described by his colleagues at UCSC as "a charismatic and inspiring classroom figure and a dedicated mentor" ("In Memoriam," n.d.).

Owens returned to the University of New Mexico in 1995, where he won the University of New Mexico Alumni Award for Teaching Excellence and was named a Presidential Lecturer. Owens returned to teach English and Native American studies at the University of California at Davis beginning in 2000, to his suicide two years later. He also led the creative writing program there.

Owens was at the peak of his career among the foremost Native American scholars in the United States when he committed suicide in Albuquerque, July 26, 2002, after leaving home to attend a Native American writing conference in Bellingham, Washington. Owens shot himself in the chest near his pickup truck at the Albuquerque airport parking garage. A passerby heard the shot, found him next to the truck, and called police. Owens died the next day in an Albuquerque hospital.

In 2004, the Western Literature Association established the Louis Owens Award, which provides graduate students of underrepresented ethnic or sexual orientation minorities financial support to attend the organization's annual meeting. The award honors Owens's belief in the voice of minority and underprivileged students in the study of Western literature.

Jason R. Gallagher

Further Reading

Colonnese, T., and Owens, L. *American Indian Novelists: An Annotated Critical Bibliography*. New York: Garland, 1985.

Contemporary Authors Autobiography Series. Vol. 24. Farmington Hills, MI: Gale, 1991.

"In Memoriam: Louis D. Owens: Professor of English and Native American Studies. University of California–Davis. 1948–2002." University of California. n.d. http://www.universityofcalifornia.edu/senate/inmemoriam/LouisD.Owens.htm/.

Kilpatrick, J. *Louis Owens: Literary Reflections on His Life and Work*. Norman: University of Oklahoma, 1999.

Krupat, Arnold. Review of *Other Destinies*, by Louis Owens. *Journal of American History* 80, no. 3 (December 1993): 1089–1090.

LaLonde, C.A. *Grave Concerns, Trickster Turns: The Novels of Louis Owens*. Norman: University of Oklahoma, 2002.

"Louis Owens, 54, American Indian Novelist and Literary Critic." *New York Times*, August 3, 2002. http://query.nytimes.com/gst/ fullpage.html?res=9F01E4DD153BF930 A3575BC0A9649C8B63.

"Louis Owens, 1948–2002." Internet Public Library. Native American Authors Project. n.d. http://www.ipl.org/div/natam/bin/browse.pl/A73.

Martin, G. "Suicide: The Aftermath." *San Francisco Chronicle*, October 6, 2002. http://www.sfgate.com/cgi-bin/article.cgi?file=/chronicle/archive/2002/10/06/LV55853.DTL.

"Native American Critic and Novelist Louis Owens Dies." July 30, 2002. http://www.news.ucdavis.edu/search/news_detail.lasso?id=6137&title=Native%20American%20Critic%20and%20Novelist%20Louis%20Owens%20Dies.

PEN Oakland. n.d. http://www.penoakland.org/.

Purdy, J. "Clear Waters: A Conversation with Louis Owens." 1998. http://www.ac.wwu.edu/~purdy/OWENS.html.

"UNM Professor Dies from Gunshot Wound." *New Mexico Daily Lobo,* August 18, 2002. http://media.www.dailylobo.com/media/storage/paper344/news/2002/08/19/News/Unm-Professor.Dies.From.Gunshot.Wound-260679.shtml.

P

PARKER, ARTHUR (GAWASOWANEH)
1881–1955 SENECA
WRITER AND MUSEUM CURATOR

Arthur Caswell Parker (whose Iroquois name *Gawasowaneh* means "Big Snow-snake") became one of history's leading Native Americans in anthropology and museum directorship, as well as a prolific author. Parker also coined the word "museologist." He was the long-time curator at the Rochester Municipal Museum, later known as the Rochester Museum and Science Center, in New York.

Born on the Cattaraugus Seneca Reservation April 5, 1881, the one-quarter-blood Parker was a great-nephew of Ely S. Parker, secretary to U.S. Grant during the Civil War, as well as a distant relative of the Iroquois prophet Handsome Lake. After studying at Dickinson Seminary, Pennsylvania, Parker came to know Frederick Ward Putnam, a leading museum director, while studying at Harvard.

Parker never finished his degree at Harvard, but he became a field archaeologist for Harvard's Peabody Museum in 1903. Parker also worked

Arthur C. Parker, 1918. (Parker, Arthur C. The Life of General Ely S. Parker, Buffalo Historical Society, 1919)

part-time at the American Museum of Natural History before he was appointed state archaeologist for the New York State Museum, Albany, in 1906. Parker took the lead in excavating several Iroquois sites, and organized the New York State Archaeological Survey as he built the state museum into a major center for archaeological study. In the meantime, Parker also authored *The Archaeological History of New York.*

In 1925, Parker was appointed Director of the Rochester Museum of Arts and Sciences, a role that he filled for almost two decades. While Parker was best known as a museum director, he also was a prolific writer, with roughly 500 pieces during his lifetime that ranged from books to journal and magazine articles, radio scripts, plays, and other works. His bibliography eventually included 14 books, among them *Erie Indian Village* (1913), *Code of Handsome Lake* (1913), *Life of General Ely S. Parker* (1919), *Seneca Myths and Folk Tales* (1923), and *Last of the Senecas* (1952).

In *To Be Indian* (2001), the first full-scale biography of Parker, Jay Porter brings him to life:

> Although not tall, at perhaps five feet six inches, he cut a dignified figure in his smart clothes with his dark hair and hazel eyes winking out from under his trademark fedora. Some thought he looked quintessentially "Indian;" others thought of him as "white." However they encountered him, people seemed to have warmed to Parker because of his skill at putting them at ease. A lover of puns and word games, he was friendly, with a charming sense of humor. (Porter, 2001, xvii)

Porter's portrait of Parker is richly detailed, delineating a man walking the cusp of Indian and non-Indian worlds, a person always acutely aware of the interplay between the two. He was a 33rd degree Freemason as well as an adopted member of the Seneca Bear Clan.

The biography describes a man who was intensely aware of prevailing ideological winds, with special attention throughout much of his life to a eugenic point of view that went severely out of intellectual fashion after Hitler's Nazis took its tenets to especially cruel extremes between 1933 and 1945. Before the Meriam Report (1928) and the Indian Reorganization Act (1934), Parker voiced doubts that Native Americans could maintain their cultural identity in the midst of popular demands for a breakdown of reservation land bases (through the Allotment acts and other measures) and suffocating policies of assimilation.

As Parker sometimes favored restrictions on immigration to reduce the proportion of the "less fit," it has been posited that he was "simply following a fashion" (Porter, 2001, 30). After all, Woodrow Wilson and George Eastman (of the Eastman-Kodak fortune) made similar statements at the same time. He continued to struggle with the racial question during the Nazi years and beyond and came to believe in "the preservation of racial type—that of the Aryan white man." He held forth against "indiscriminate blood-blending and inharmonious race contacts" (Porter, 2001, 137).

In the 1950s, the intellectual wind had begun to shift, and Parker started to shift with it. Native self-determination and preservation of identity became fashionable by the 1930s. Parker ended his professional life best known for popular innovation in museums, which he called "the university of the common man." On his death in 1955, Parker was recalled warmly by Mohawk culture bearer Ray Fadden who wrote that Parker "was a great person, desiring nothing for himself, and ever ready to do good for everyone, no matter who" (Porter, 2001, 241). Obscuring his earlier doubts about Native American cultural survival and his eugenic ruminations, Parker's affectionate personality won out in the end—a tribute to his essential humanity.

Parker died January 1, 1955, in Rochester.

Further Reading

Johansen, Bruce E. Review of *To Be Indian: The Life of Iroquois-Seneca Arthur Caswell Parker,* by Joy Porter. *American Indian Culture and Research Journal* 26, no. 3 (2002): 167–68.

Parker, Arthur. *Parker on the Iroquois.* Edited by William N. Fenton. Syracuse, NY: Syracuse University Press, 1968.

Parker, Arthur. *The Code of Handsome Lake, the Seneca Prophet.* New York State Museum Bulletin No. 163. Albany, 1913.

Parker, Arthur. *The History of the Seneca Indians.* [1926]. Port Washington, NY: Ira J. Friedman, 1967.

Porter, Joy. *To Be Indian: The Life of Iroquois-Seneca Arthur Caswell Parker.* Norman: University of Oklahoma Press, 2001.

PELTIER, LEONARD
BORN 1944 ANISHINABE, OJIBWA, CHIPPEWA
AMERICAN INDIAN MOVEMENT ACTIVIST

An activist in the American Indian Movement (AIM) during the 1973 confrontation at Wounded Knee, Leonard Peltier was caught in a shootout with Federal Bureau of Investigation agents and state police at the Jumping Bull Ranch on the Pine Ridge Indian Reservation during June 26, 1975. Peltier later was convicted of killing two FBI agents, Ronald Williams and Jack Coler, during that confrontation. Peltier's initial trial, which was held in Fargo, North Dakota, Federal District Court in 1977, has since become the focus of an international protest movement aimed at obtaining a retrial.

Peltier's defense characterized his conviction as a textbook example of a manufactured verdict, a major reason that Amnesty International declared Peltier a political prisoner. On October 15, 1985, the government admitted in open court that it did not have proof of who killed the two agents.

Pine Ridge Political Murders, 1973–1976

The killings of FBI agents for which Peltier was convicted occurred at a time when the Pine Ridge Reservation had been turned into an armed camp by supporters and

Leonard Peltier (shown here in prison in 1986), serving two life sentences for killing two FBI agents, continues to assert his innocence. (AP/Wide World Photos)

opponents of tribal chairman Richard Wilson. From the early 1970s until his defeat for the chairman's office by Al Trimble in 1976, Wilson outfitted a tribal police force with weapons purchased with money from the federal government. The local context of the occupation included an effort to publicly confront Wilson's policies, which often favored non-Indian ranchers, farmers, and corporations.

Wilson's police answered his detractors by increasing assaults on his opponents, examples of which were described in a chronology of murders between 1973 and 1976 kept by the Wounded Knee Legal Defense-Offense Committee. Following the occupation of Wounded Knee during 1973, more than 60 AIM members and supporters were killed on and near the Pine Ridge Reservation for political reasons.

Using only these documented political deaths, the yearly murder rate on Pine Ridge Reservation between March 1, 1973, and March 1, 1976, was 170 per 100,000, the highest in the country. The U.S. average was 9.7 per 100,000, with the range for large cities as follows: Detroit, 20.2; Chicago, 15.9; New York City, 16.3; Washington, D.C, 13.4; Los Angeles, 12.9; Seattle, 5.6; and Boston, 5.6. An estimated 20,000 persons were murdered in the United States in 1974. In a nation of 200 million persons, a murder rate comparable to that of Pine Ridge between 1973 and 1976 would have left 340,000 persons dead for political reasons in one year; 1.32 million in three.

Many of the political murders were carried out by the tribal government's "Guardians of the Oglala Nation" (GOON) squad, militarized police. During this period there was essentially no law enforcement or prosecution of the murders. One of the GOON's favorite weapons was the automobile. Officially, such deaths could be reported as traffic accidents.

Shootout at the Jumping Bull Ranch

On June 26, 1975, two unmarked cars chased a red truck onto the ranch, which was housing several families being defended by AIM. The agents shot at the ranch and its residents shot back in self-defense. Minutes later, more than 150 FBI SWAT-team members, Bureau of Indian Affairs police, and Pine Ridge police surrounded the ranch and a firefight erupted, with those inside taking the brunt. The two FBI agents were fatally wounded. A Native American man, Joe Stuntz, aged 23, also died of a shot in the head by an unidentified government agent's sniper bullet that day. Like the murders of several dozen other Native peoples on the reservation during those tumultuous years, the FBI did not investigate Stuntz's death.

The same FBI that complained that lack of manpower kept it from investigating the wave of political murders at Pine Ridge between 1973 and 1976 had enough agents to assign Coler and Williams to pursue a pair of purloined cowboy boots to the Jumping Bull Ranch on June 26, 1975—as well as hundreds of agents who mounted a nationwide dragnet for the killers of Coler and Williams in the firefight there, for which Leonard Peltier later was convicted with questionable evidence.

In *The Unquiet Grave* (2006), writer Steve Hendricks described the firefight with uncommon acuity, in part based on his mining of FBI records under the Freedom of Information Act. He is also sensitive to the records' limitations. At Jumping Bull, for example, the FBI reports imagined bunkers where there were root cellars and machine guns in hands that held old hunting rifles. The FBI itself was not short of firepower. Bad blood still is very evident, enduring over the years, as when, during 2000, former South Dakota Governor Bill Janklow stepped in with all his then-formidable political power to block requests that might have led to a pardon of Peltier by President Bill Clinton.

Peltier's Pursuit and Prosecution

Following the shootout at the Jumping Bull Ranch, Peltier escaped to Canada knowing that he would never get a fair trial. He was captured in Canada on February 6, 1976. Peltier subsequently was put on trial before an all-white jury in Fargo, North Dakota, Federal District Court before a hostile judge, Paul Benson. The FBI created a climate of fear during the proceedings to convince jurors that Peltier was a terrorist.

The FBI contributed to the conviction of Peltier by faking evidence, finding a compliant judge, and drilling the fake evidence into the heads of an all-white jury, meanwhile denying the defense even the pretense of fair treatment. Peltier was sentenced to two life terms in prison. Even after the United States Tenth Circuit Court of Appeals, in November 2003, condemned the fact that the government withheld evidence and intimidated witnesses, the conviction stood.

Even before Peltier's trial started, however, the prosecution's case began to fall apart. Discovery proceedings produced an affidavit, signed by government witness Myrtle Poor Bear dated February 19, 1976 (before two others known to the defense, dated February 23 and March 31), which said that the woman had not been on the scene of the June 26, 1975, gun battle in which the two FBI agents had been shot to death. This information, contained in an affidavit that had not been sent to Canada by the U.S. government during Peltier's extradition hearing, contradicted the other two statements attributed to Poor Bear.

More important, Poor Bear herself recanted. On April 13, out of earshot of the jury, Poor Bear told the court (having been called by the defense) that she had never seen Peltier before meeting him at the trial. Furthermore, Poor Bear said that she had not been allowed to read the three affidavits implicating Peltier in the murders that bore her name, and that FBI agents David Price and Bill Wood had threatened physical harm to herself and her children if she did not sign them.

Judge Benson refused to let the jury hear Poor Bear's testimony, ruling it "irrelevant" to the case. The next day the judge changed his mind and ruled the testimony relevant, but still would not let the jury hear it. He ruled this time that Poor Bear's testimony was prejudicial to the government's case, and, if believed, could confuse the jury.

Prosecution testimony, which occupied the first five weeks of the trial, ranged far from events on the day of the shootings. The prosecution was allowed to bring up extraneous charges against Peltier on which he had not been tried and testimony that ran counter to the federal rules of evidence. The defense's planned two weeks of testimony was reduced to two-and-a-half days by Judge Benson, who limited defense testimony to events directly connected with the shootings themselves. Virtually every time the defense challenged the government, and before every attempt by the defense to present its case, Benson had the jury removed from the courtroom. The jury heard only parts of the defense's case.

Impossible Sighting

The only evidence that directly linked Peltier to the killings of Coler and Williams (other than that fabricated in Poor Bear's name) came from Frederick Coward, an FBI agent, who said he had recognized Peltier from half a mile away through a seven-power rifle sight. The defense team replicated the sighting and found that the feat was impossible through such a sight at such a distance, even for a person with excellent vision. In court, defense attorneys offered to duplicate their experience for the jury, so that its members could judge for themselves the veracity of the FBI agent's statement. Judge Benson refused the request. "Finally," said Bruce Ellison, a member of the defense team, "we brought in someone from a gun shop, who said that an idiot could tell you that it is impossible to recognize someone, even someone you know, from a half-mile away through a seven-power sight" (Johansen and Maestas, 1979, 114).

The prosecution, its eyewitness testimony in dispute, linked Peltier to the use of an AR-15, a semiautomatic rifle, which was not introduced as evidence because it had been blown apart during a Kansas freeway explosion on September 10, 1975. FBI Agent Evan Hodge testified at the Fargo trial that the AR-15 was the weapon used to kill Agents Williams and Coler. However, the weapon tested by Agent Hodge did not match the ballistic evidence. That weapon, alleged by the government as having been used by Peltier, did not kill the agents. Nonetheless, the prosecution used this weapon in court as a prop in its argument to convince the jury that Peltier shot Williams and Coler at point-blank range.

Three Native juveniles also testified that they had seen Peltier at the scene. Each of them also testified, under cross-examination, that their testimony had been coerced by the FBI. One of them testified that he had been threatened with beating. Another said that he had been tied and handcuffed to a chair for three hours to elicit his statement. The third swore that he was told that if he did not cooperate he "would never walk the Earth again" (Johansen and Maestas, 1979, 115).

Demands for a New Trial

Following his conviction, Peltier became the object of a growing popular movement demanding a new trial. Peltier's request for a new trial was rejected by the Eighth U.S. Circuit Court in St. Louis in 1978; hearings on his appeal also were declined by the U.S. Supreme Court in 1978 and 1986. In the meantime, Peltier's support spread to the Soviet Union and Europe. In the Soviet Union, by 1986, an estimated 17 million people had signed petitions in his support.

Peter Matthiessen's *In the Spirit of Crazy Horse* was readied for publication in the early 1980s, making a case for Peltier's innocence. The publisher, Viking, withdrew the book after former South Dakota Governor Janklow threatened to sue for libel over passages in the book that linked him to the rape of a young Native American woman. Bootlegged copies of the book began to circulate, and it was published in the late 1980s after Janklow's case was dismissed by the South Dakota Supreme Court. *In the Spirit of Crazy Horse* presents, in an epilogue appended after the book had been suppressed for eight years, a case that Peltier was not the murderer of the two FBI agents. In an interview, a Native man known only as "X" confesses to the murders. In the meantime, the FBI had withheld from the public 6,000 pages of documents on the case, for reasons the agency associated with national security.

During the 1980s and 1990s, as Peltier's appeals for a new trial were denied several times by U.S. federal courts, he was serving two life terms at Marion Federal Penitentiary, Illinois, and at Leavenworth Federal Penitentiary in Kansas, developing his talents as an artist, creating posters, paintings, and designs for a line of greeting cards that were sold nationwide. Peltier's case also became the focus of the feature film *Thunderheart* and a documentary, *Incident at Oglala*.

Peltier's case came to the attention of Amnesty International and the government of Canada, from which Peltier was extradited to face trial on the basis of the Poor Bear affidavits. Peltier's appeals were directed by several well-known legal personalities, including former U.S. Attorney General Ramsey Clark and attorney

William Kunstler. His third appeal for a new trial was turned down by the Eighth Circuit Court of Appeals (St. Paul, Minnesota) in 1993, for the third time, exhausting his remedies within the U.S. legal system. In August 2009, Peltier, who by then had been imprisoned 32 years, was denied parole. He will be eligible for another parole hearing in 2024, at age 79.

Even 30 to 35 years after the shootout at Jumping Bull, an electronic poll conducted in 2005 by "Native America Calling" and *The Native American Times* asked "Who do you think is the greatest Native American?" Of the nearly 7,000 votes registered, the most-often named person was Leonard Peltier ("Greatest Native," 2005).

Further Reading

American Indian Movement. "Free Peltier." n.d. http://www.aimovement.org/peltier/.

Banks, Dennis, and Richard Erdoes. *Ojibwa Warrior: Dennis Banks and the Rise of the American Indian Movement*. Norman: University of Oklahoma Press, 2004.

Churchill, Ward, and Jim Vander Wall. *Agents of Repression: The FBI's Secret War against the Black Panther Party and the American Indian Movement*. Boston: South End Press, 1990.

"Greatest Native American Poll." Native America Calling and *The Native American Times*. October 15, 2005. http://terrrijean.smartwriters.com/index.2ts?page=greatestpoll.

Hendricks, Steve. *The Unquiet Grave: The FBI and the Struggle for the Soul of Indian Country*. New York: Thunder's Mouth Press, 2006.

Johansen, Bruce. "Peltier and the Posse." *The Nation,* October 1, 1977, 304–7.

Johansen, Bruce E., and Roberto F. Maestas. *Wasi'chu: The Continuing Indian Wars*. New York: Monthly Review Press, 1979.

Matthiessen, Peter. *In the Spirit of Crazy Horse*. New York: Viking, 1991.

R

REIFEL, BEN
1906–1990 BRULE SIOUX
U.S. CONGRESSMAN

Ben Reifel, who would become a congressman from South Dakota, was born in Parmelee, South Dakota, son of a German father and a Sioux mother. Reifel did not pass the eighth grade until he was 16 and did not go to high school because his father could see no reason for it. The elder Reifel told Ben he was needed on the farm. The young man read whatever he could find. His passion for education grew to a point where he ran away from home, hiking 250 miles, so he could enroll in high school.

Despite his late start in formal education, Reifel earned a BS degree from South Dakota State University (1932). He joined the Army Reserves as a commissioned officer while in college and was called to duty in World War II. At the end of the war, he was appointed Bureau of Indian Affairs (BIA) superintendent at the Fort Berthold Agency, North Dakota. Reifel returned to college at Harvard for a master's in public administration, and then became one of the first American Indians to earn a PhD, also

Ben Reifel, Native American Congressman from South Dakota, as a young man. (Nebraska State Historical Society)

at Harvard. Reifel then returned to the Dakotas, and held several BIA posts, including the superintendent post at Pine Ridge, where he was the first Indian agent of Native ancestry. His career at the BIA culminated when he was appointed area director of the office in Aberdeen, South Dakota.

In 1960, Reifel retired from the BIA to run for Congress. He won on his first run for public office (as a Republican) and served five terms before retiring in 1970. On his retirement, Reifel, who had fought so hard to get a formal education, was awarded an honorary degree from the University of South Dakota.

Reifel died of cancer in 1990 in Sioux Falls, South Dakota, at the age of 83.

Further Reading

Reifel, Benjamin. (1906–1990). Biographical Dictionary of the U.S. Congress. n.d. http://bioguide.congress.gov/scripts/biodisplay.pl?index=R000152.

REYNOLDS, ALLIE
1917–1994 CREEK OR CHEROKEE
MAJOR LEAGUE BASEBALL PITCHER

Allie Pierce Reynolds, who had Creek ancestors, pitched more than 11 years in major league baseball, with the New York Yankees and Cleveland Indians. In 1951, on his way to winning 182 games in the majors, he became the third pitcher in the history of major league baseball to pitch two no-hitters in one season.

Reynolds, who was one-quarter Creek (a minority of sources say he was Cherokee), was born February 10, 1917, in Bethany, Oklahoma, the son of a fundamentalist preacher. His baseball career began as a star pitcher at Capitol Hill High School, Oklahoma City, under Coach Jim Lookabaugh. Early in his high school baseball career, Reynolds and a teammate, Odassus McCutcheon, decided to prepare for games with what they said was a Creek ritual that involved burning items of household furniture. The two young men said that they were warding off "shart demons." Reynolds later incorporated the same ritual, in modified form, as he prepared to pitch in the major leagues.

Reynolds accepted a football and track scholarship to Oklahoma Agricultural & Mechanical College (now Oklahoma State University), where he also ran track and continued playing baseball, this time coached by the renowned Henry P. Iba. Reynolds joined the Cleveland Indians after graduating from OSU.

Reynolds's major league debut was in 1942, with the Indians, where he played four years, followed by seven years with the Yankees. He was named an all-star in 1945, 1949, 1950, and 1952 through 1954; he led the American League in strikeouts in 1943 with 151 and 1952 with 160. In 1952, Reynolds maintained the best earned-run average (ERA) in the American League, at 2.06, and he led the same league in shutouts with seven in 1951 and six in 1952.

Allie P. Reynolds, a recipient of the Henry J. Bennett distinguished service award, and Richard W. Poole, Oklahoma State University, 1988. (OSU Photograph Collection, Courtesy of Special Collections and University Archives, Oklahoma State University Libraries)

Reynolds pitched for the Yankees in the World Series in 1947, 1949, 1950, 1951, 1952, and 1953, maintaining an ERA of 2.79. A plaque in Reynolds's honor hangs in Monument Park at Yankee Stadium, which calls him "One of the Yankees' greatest right-handed pitchers." Having retired from baseball with the Yankees after the 1954 season, Reynolds became a well-known business executive as president of Reynolds Petroleum and Atlas Mud Companies. He also directed the Oklahoma City 89ers in minor league baseball. Reynolds was president of the American Indian Hall of Fame. He received the Creek Nation's Medallion Award in 1986. Oklahoma State University's baseball stadium was named in 1982 to honor Reynolds and his late wife, Earleen.

Reynolds died December 26, 1994, in Oklahoma City, after which the Jim Thorpe Association established the Allie Reynolds Award, for "Oklahoma's outstanding high school senior, based on accomplishments, sports, civics, character and leadership."

Further Reading

"Allie Pierce Reynolds: Businessman, Civic Leader, Renowned Sports Personality." Henry G. Bennett Distinguished Service Award, Oklahoma State University, 1988. http://www.library.okstate.edu/about/awards/bennett/reynolds.htm.

ROGERS, WILL
1879–1935 CHEROKEE
HUMORIST

Today's one-word characterization of Will Rogers usually is "humorist." During his life, which ended suddenly in an Alaska plane crash, he was much more than that. Drawing on his Cherokee roots, Rogers was very nearly a moral compass of the nation during the 1920s and 1930s. During a life that ranged the world, Rogers frequently called upon his Cherokee upbringing with a style of humor that was wry and instructive. Cy Eberhart, who does re-enactments of Rogers, recalls him as a plainspoken man who held no official position, even as his opinions shaped debates on national and world issues. He was as comfortable visiting with presidents and European royalty as he was riding with cowboys on the range, said Eberhart, who recalls Rogers as "a soul of America" (Eberhart, 2007, 5).

Rogers was well known and admired to a degree that is difficult to convey to anyone who was not alive at the time, as a movie actor, and as a columnist in 600 newspapers with a circulation of 40 million readers (more than half the reading-age population of the United States at that time). Rogers was not merely a stand-up comedian. The words "vaudevillian, actor, writer, orator, and humanitarian" were used to describe him as often as "humorist." He may have been the best-known celebrity of his time, but he managed to retain an extraordinary humility and empathy for ordinary people. Rogers was immensely popular in the world of entertainment, and he shared his celebrity. He taught Tom Mix, who later became Hollywood's best-known movie cowboy, how to rope and ride. Rogers also suggested that Gene Autry, who was then a telegraph operator in Oklahoma, audition for an acting role in Hollywood. Autry went on to become a household word as a cowboy actor after Rogers's death. Rogers himself acted in 72 movies.

Rogers's humor often was rooted in a Native American tradition, as described by American Indian scholar Vine Deloria, Jr.:

For centuries before the white invasion, teasing was a method of control of social situations by Indian people. Rather than embarrass members of the tribe publicly, people used to tease individuals they

Will Rogers. (Library of Congress)

considered out of step with the consensus of tribal opinion. In this way egos were preserved and disputes within the tribe of a personal nature were held to a minimum. (Deloria, 1969, 147)

Early Life

William Penn Adair Rogers was born in Oologah, Indian Territory (now Oklahoma) November 4, 1879 to a Cherokee ranching family, as an enrolled member of the Cherokee Nation. Raised as a rancher on the Cherokee Territory, Rogers became an expert horseman and trick roper, an ability that would serve him on stage most of his professional life.

Rogers wanted to work as a cowboy in the style that he had experienced as a young man but found his opportunities restricted as Indian Territory was invaded by whites seeking land. Rogers was impressed by a photograph in a geography book that showed large grazing ranges in Argentina. At age 23, Rogers sailed to Argentina by way of London (a more direct route did not exist at the time) with a friend, Dick Parris. Once in Argentina, the two young men found no free land. Rogers paid his friend's way home and then lived destitute for a time in Buenos Aires, until he found a stockyard job roping cattle. After that, he got a job "chaperoning" a shipload of livestock bound for South Africa.

Once he had arrived in South Africa, Rogers was among cowboys who drove stock inland 200 miles to a ranch, where he then spent several weeks working as a hired hand. Later Rogers was employed with a crew that moved a herd of several hundred mules 250 miles to Ladysmith, also in South Africa, where he joined Texas Jack's Wild West Show. Texas Jack was so impressed by Rogers's quick hand with a rope that he was hired on the spot for his first job as an entertainer. As Rogers and Texas Jack became friends, the Wild West Show toured South Africa, playing before mixed audiences—blacks, Kaffirs, Englishmen, Afrikaners, and East Indians. Rogers soon was being advertised as "the Cherokee Kid." He wrote his sister, "I am going to learn things while with him that will enable me to make my living without making it by day labor" (Yagoda, 1993, 59–60).

Rogers later decided to work his way around the world, returning home. Sailing to Australia, he worked for a time with the Wirth Brothers Circus, which also toured New Zealand, after which he continued across the Pacific Ocean to the United States. Traveling the world, he came to identify as an American as well as a Cherokee.

Rogers began his career in vaudeville during 1904, adding political humor to his trick roping. Soon he was better known as a political philosopher and humorist than as a cowboy. In 1918, Rogers joined the Ziegfeld Follies as one of its few male performers—and absolutely the only one ever to bring a horse, Teddy (and rider Buck McGee), onstage during the troupe's performances. President Woodrow Wilson attended some of his performances and was spoofed by Rogers. Other presidents maintained close ties to Rogers. Calvin Coolidge invited him to stay at 1600 Pennsylvania Avenue, and Franklin D. Roosevelt frequently communicated with him.

Rogers married Betty Blake (1879–1944) in 1908 after an eight-year courtship. They had four children, including Will Rogers, Jr. (1911–93), who became an actor, a decorated combat veteran, and a member of the United States Congress. Mary Rogers (1913–89) acted on Broadway; Jim Rogers (1915–2000) played bit parts in a few movies, but mainly followed in his father's footsteps as a rancher and horse breeder. Fred Rogers, born in 1918, died of diphtheria at age 2.

Fame Spreads

Rogers's reputation as a political commentator and humorist spread rapidly during his vaudeville days. By the early 1920s, Rogers also was writing one of the most widely distributed weekly newspaper columns in the United States for the McNaught Syndicate. Over the course of his life, Rogers wrote enough newspaper columns to fill 10 bound volumes. As a popular writer, Rogers's ambit swept the spectrum of political commentary, but he also commented frequently on the abuse of American Indian peoples by the U.S. government. Rogers's commentaries were so popular that his name was mentioned as a possible candidate for president of the United States in 1924, 1928, and 1932.

While he did not accept invitations to run for high office, Rogers did master the new communication technologies of his time, radio and film, spreading his fame still more widely. Eventually he starred or appeared in 71 films—exceeding the number of roles played by Clark Gable, Shirley Temple, and Mae West by 1934. His radio shows were heard by millions of people.

Rogers traveled the world his entire adult life. During 1926, he sailed to Europe to write "Letters of a Self-Made Diplomat to His President" for the *Saturday Evening Post*. The next year found him in the Soviet Union and Mexico.

Legendary Generosity and Character

Rogers's generosity was legendary. He donated $5,000 for earthquake relief in Managua, Nicaragua, during the early 1930s, and visited the city. He was fond of saying that people don't want their taxes lowered. People want just taxes, with everyone paying a proportionate share according to wealth.

Eberhart remarked: "A special vitality is present when people matter. We see its presence in Rogers. In him humane became a verb. He brought the humanness of his Indian heritage to life for all to witness. It was an action part of his life: His fairness, caring and respect of others" (Eberhart, 2007, 43). In one occasion, the filming of a movie starring Rogers ended ahead of schedule, so he paid the crew for their lost time. Later he worked it out with the studios that such pay would be forthcoming in any such future event.

Columnist George Matthews Adams recalled Rogers:

> Today I sat a few feet from Will Rogers and saw him chew his gum and spread his jokes and "gags" so thick that they blew up the room with laughter—the kind of laughter that covers your face with tears. If anybody

else had said the things he said in a serious mood they would have sent for the police. But Will Rogers never hurts people. But he packs wisdom there just the same. He is one of the wisest thinkers in America. He is tremendously much of all that America is.

I studied the face of this man. It is set in rough cast like Lincoln's. His eyes are unusually keen. He has a fine nose and a splendid chin. His mouth is rather large so that he is able to get great smiles from it to permeate into the great crowds that roar from his jibes and also to facilitate his ability to throw his gum in unison with his cowboy rope. Will Rogers' hands are big, bold and brown. His forehead is very striking in its suggestion of intelligence. But the biggest thing about this American product is his heart. Will Rogers is loyalty and squareness to the core. (Day, 1962, 168–69)

Gene Buck, Zeigfeld's chief writer, said that Rogers "possessed the genius to write and to say out loud what most of us thought, but didn't dare say, about people, affairs, and conditions. With his grand sense of humor he possessed a great mind with an uncanny knowledge of human beings and their motives" (Payne and Lyons, 1936, 196).

Rogers was a consummate student of the news, and the human essence of it. Rogers's nightly routine after each *Follies* appearance was to buy every newspaper he could lay his hands on, go to the Friars Club, and "peruse them carefully at a table in a secluded corner. While reading he would jot down notes. These formed his next day's act" (Payne and Lyons, 1936, 35).

World Travels during the 1930s

During the early 1930s, Rogers's ports of call were in Asia, "dining with the emperor of Manchuria and sipping tea with Japan's minister of war." A year before the plane crash that killed him, Rogers toured the world a final time, with his family, including wife Betty and his three children, Bill, Mary, and Jim. By the 1930s, Rogers was using some of the first passenger aircraft in his travels. His friends included pioneer aviators Charles Lindbergh and Wiley Post.

Rogers died August 15, 1935 when a plane carrying him and Post went down in a bay near Point Barrow. A family of hunters camped nearby sent a runner to Barrow to report the accident. News of Rogers's and Post's deaths dominated front pages the next day. Following his death, the United States mourned Rogers. A hundred thousand people visited his casket in Glendale, California, 15,000 an hour.

Roosevelt, who was president of the United States when Rogers was killed, paid him this homage: "The first time that I fully realized Will Rogers' exceptional and deep understanding of political and social problems was when he came back from his long European trip a good many years ago. While I had discussed European matters with many others, both American and Foreign, Will Rogers' analysis of affairs abroad was not only more interesting but proved to be more accurate than any other I had heard" (Payne and Lyons, 1936, 7).

The Shrine of the Sun in Colorado was erected in Rogers's honor, and a statue of him was installed in National Statuary Hall of the U.S. Capitol. Today a Will

Rogers Memorial Museum, with extensive archives and exhibits, is maintained in Claremore, Oklahoma. Visitors to the museum enter beside a plaque presented by the Cherokee Nation with a seal of the nation, noting Rogers's Cherokee heritage, inscribed: "We honor the memory of Oklahoma's beloved native son. A modest, unspoiled child of the plains, cowboy, actor, humorist and world traveler whose homely philosophy and superior gifts brought laughter and tears to prince and commoner alike. His aversion to sham and deceit, his love of candor and sincerity, coupled with abounding wit and affable repartee, won for him universal homage and an appropriate title, 'Ambassador of Good Will'" (Eberhart, 2007, 12).

Rogers's ranch at Pacific Palisades, California, is now a public park. The Dog Iron Ranch, on the shores of Lake Oologah, Oklahoma, on which he was born, is also a public park and a memorial. The Oklahoma City airport was named for Rogers.

Further Reading

Chavers, Dean. *Modern American Indian Leaders: Their Lives and Their Works.* 2 vols. Lewiston, NY: Edwin Mellen Press, 2007.

Croy, Homer. *Our Will Rogers.* New York: Duell, Sloan, and Pearce, 1953.

Day, Donald. *The Autobiography of Will Rogers.* Boston: Houghton Mifflin, 1962.

Deloria, Vine, Jr. *Custer Died for Your Sins.* Norman: University of Oklahoma Press, 1969.

Eberhart, E. T. (Cy). "Rediscovering the Soul of America, or Playing along with Will Rogers." Unpublished manuscript, 2007.

Justice, Daniel Heath. "Our Fires Survive the Storm: Removal and Defiance in the Cherokee Literary Tradition." PhD diss., University of Nebraska, 2002.

Payne, William, and Lyons, Jake, eds. *Folks Say of Will Rogers: A Memorial Anecdotage.* New York: G. P. Putnam's Sons, 1936.

Rogers, Betty. *Will Rogers.* Norman: University of Oklahoma Press, 1941.

Rogers, Will. *The Writings of Will Rogers.* 21 vols. Stillwater: Oklahoma State University Press, 1973–83.

Wertheim, Arthur, ed. *Will Rogers at the Ziegfeld Follies.* Norman: University of Oklahoma Press, 1992.

Yagoda, Ben. *Will Rogers: A Biography.* New York: Alfred A. Knopf, 1993.

S

SAINTE-MARIE, BUFFY
BORN 1941 CREE
FOLKSINGER

The popular folksinger and songwriter Buffy Sainte-Marie, one of the best-known voices of the North American folk-music revival during the 1960s, was born February 20, 1941, on the Piapot Cree Indian Reserve in the Qu'Appelle Valley of Saskatchewan in Canada. She was raised by relatives, Albert and Winifred Sainte-Marie, in Maine and Massachusetts. As a teenager, Sainte-Marie taught herself to play the guitar and piano. Sainte-Marie returned to the Piapot Cree Reserve for a pow-wow in 1964 and found a warm welcome, after which she was adopted by Chief Piapot's youngest son, and taught Cree culture and history.

A Singing Career Starts Early

By her early 20s, Sainte-Marie was touring Canada, singing in small venues, most often at folk festivals, pow-wows, and coffeehouses of Toronto's Yorkville district. After playing her music in several Greenwich Village clubs, Sainte-Marie turned professional, and, by 1965, she was performing at Carnegie Hall and the Newport (Rhode Island) Folk Festival. She had

Buffy Sainte-Marie, Cree singer-songwriter, January 23, 1978. (AP/Wide World Photos)

no formal voice training until after the beginning of her professional career. Soon she was traveling across Europe, Canada, Australia, and Asia.

Sainte-Marie earned a BA in philosophy from the University of Massachusetts (1963), after having become a U.S. citizen. She also earned a PhD in Fine Arts there in 1983. By the mid-1970s, she had become active in the Bahá'í faith, singing at several Bahá'í events, including its 1992 World Congress.

Sainte-Marie recorded several albums of popular and American Indian music, often mixing traditional and modern themes. Her singing career included several hit singles, such as "Universal Soldier," which was inspired by the return of injured soldiers from the Vietnam War. That song was recorded by Donovan, among others. Her song "Until It's Time for You to Go" was recorded not only by Elvis Presley, but also by Cher, Neil Diamond, Barbara Streisand, Roberta Flack, Bobby Darin, and Arthur Fiedler and the Boston Pops Orchestra. Some of her other song were recorded by Janis Joplin, Taj Mahal, and other notable musicians.

Sainte-Marie was named best new artist by *Billboard* magazine in 1964 for her debut album, *It's My Way,* released by Vanguard Records, along with the many performances of her songs by other artists. At the same time, she continued to record music that publicized the wretched conditions faced by Native Americans, such as "My Country 'Tis of Thy People You're Dying." (1964). Her 1992 song "Bury My Heart at Wounded Knee" mentions the Leonard Peltier case.

During the 1960s, the Federal Bureau of Investigation sought to suppress her music, along with that of several other activist performers. She recovered, however, and went on to record 17 albums, while appearing on *Sesame Street* with her son Dakota Starblanket Wolfchild for five years. Her song "Up Where We Belong" (co-written with Will Jennings and Jack Nitzsche) and sung by Joe Cocker and Jennifer Warnes in the film *An Officer and a Gentleman* received a 1982 Academy Award for Best Song.

Sainte-Marie acted in several movies, including the Turner Network's *The Broken Chain* (1993). She also wrote prose and poetry for several American Indian publications and served as an associate editor of *The Indian Voice* (Vancouver, British Columbia).

By the 1990s, Sainte-Marie had performed in most of the world's major countries, and the larger urban areas of the United States and Canada. In 1992, she released a collection of recordings, *Confidence and Likely Stories,* which departed from her earlier work by including instrumental music. She also wrote a children's book, *Nokosis and the Magic Hat* (1986). While her mass appeal ebbed after the 1980s, Sainte-Marie continued an active musical career, including a studio album, released in 2008, *Running for the Drum.*

Sainte-Marie married Dewain Bugbee, a Hawaiian surfing teacher, in 1968, but divorced him in 1971. Four years later, she married Sheldon Wolfchild of Minnesota. They had a boy (Dakota "Cody" Starblanket Wolfchild) before separating. During the early 1980s, she married Jack Nitzsche, but by 1993, she had a relationship with Hawaiian Chuck Wilson.

Sainte-Marie has received several honorary doctoral degrees in Canada, among them from the University of Regina Emily Carr Institute of Art and Design in Vancouver, British Columbia; Canada Carleton University, in Ottawa; and the University of Western Ontario in 2009 in London. She also has taught digital music at several colleges. In 2008, the Canadian Aboriginal Music Awards honored her lifetime contributions. She was inducted into Canada's Walk of Fame in 1999.

Further Reading

"Buffy Sainte-Marie." Creative Native. n.d. http://www.creative-native.com/biograp.htm.

Buffy Sainte-Marie Home Page. n.d. http://www.buffysaintemarie.co.uk.

Buffy Sainte-Marie: A Multimedia Life. Documentary film produced by CineFocus-Paquin Pictures. Montreal, Quebec, 2008.

Churchill, E. Richard, and Linda Churchill. *45 Profiles in Modern Music*. Portland, ME: J. Weston Walch, 1996, 110–12.

Rheingold, Howard. *Folk Songs, Digital Art, and Indian Empowerment. Brainstorms*. n.d. http://www.well.com/~hlr/tomorrow/buffy.html.

SHENANDOAH, JOANNE (TEKALIHWA:KHWA) BORN 1957 ONEIDA MUSICIAN

Joanne Lynn Shenandoah (*Tekalihwa:khwa*), a Wolf Clan member of the Haudenosaunee (Iroquois Confederacy's) Oneida Nation, by the early 21st century became a major presence in Native American folk music, fusing traditional Iroquois social songs with Western music and other styles, including rock, techno, gospel, and folk. By 2008, her music had appeared on 14 individual recordings as well as 40 collections with other artists, including Neil Young and Bruce Cockburn. She has sung around the world, from Australia (on stage with the Dalai Lama), to Spain, South Korea, Turkey, Belgium, and many other places.

Shenandoah's remarkable voice combined traditional Iroquois songs with today's melodies and themes.

Native American singer Joanne Shenandoah at the ancient Oneida Indian village site known as Nichols Pond near Canastota, New York. Shenandoah's music fuses ancient melodies and chants with contemporary styles. (AP/Wide World Photos)

Musician Neil Young has said that he considers her songs "the best tributes to Native American music" (Shenandoah, 2007).

Shenandoah has won more Native American Music Awards than any other musician, and shared a Grammy. She was honored with a Lifetime Achievement Award at a Native American Music Awards ceremony in Niagara Falls, New York, in 2007. The same year, the American Indian Film Festival in San Francisco presented her with the Best Music Video Award while the film *Our Land, Our Life,* in which Shenandoah wrote and sang the entire music score, was acknowledged as Best Documentary. The subject of the documentary, Carrie Dann, an elder of the Western Shoshone Nation, was given the Eagle Spirit Award for her courage in preserving her nation's heritage.

Shenandoah is a daughter of Maisie Shenandoah, an Oneida Wolf Clan mother, singer, and music teacher, and the late Clifford Shenandoah, an Onondaga chief as well as an accomplished jazz guitarist. Clifford Shenandoah was one of a line of Oneida chiefs reaching back to the Shenandoah, or *Skennandoah* (the two names are variants of the same word, meaning "Deer" in Oneida). Skennandoah organized Oneidas to feed General George Washington's Continental Army during a bitter winter at Valley Force, Pennsylvania, in the midst of the Revolutionary War.

As a girl, Shenandoah "played almost anything I could get my hands on, starting with piano, guitar, clarinet, and percussion" (Shenandoah, 2007). Later, she learned to play other instruments, such as the harp. Shenandoah was urged to study music and to make use of her beautiful voice from her earliest years. The enrapturing nature of her voice, even as a child, was reflected in her Oneida name, *Tekalihwa:khwa,* which means "She Sings." Instrumentation on her songs may vary from violin to water drum, cello, and glass harmonica, among many others.

She at first made a living as an architectural designer for 14 years, but rediscovery of her people's stories and songs prompted Shenandoah to begin a singing career. Shenandoah married Mohawk editor and activist Doug George in 1991, and, with him, formed Round Dance Productions of Oneida, New York. George and Shenandoah produced films, books, and other media that combined entertainment with themes emphasizing Native American rights and history.

Shenandoah is internationally known as well, with, among others, a single ("Nature Dance") in Germany, and a collection of dance music in Spain. She has toured across the United States, in Turkey, South Korea, France, Spain, and Germany, among other countries. In 1993, she was recognized by the First Americans in the Arts Foundation as its Musician of the Year.

Shenandoah opened the 1994 concert at Woodstock before an audience of about 250,000 people. Shenandoah also has appeared on stage at Carnegie Hall, the White House, Kennedy Center, Earth Day on the Washington, D.C. Mall, and the Special Olympics. She contributed to an album in defense of Leonard Peltier and helped organize a concert of Native American women singers at the White House. Her music was featured on the Canadian Broadcasting Corporation's documentary *The War against the Indian,* and several local and national Public Broadcasting documentaries in the United States.

Shenandoah also had a role in the musical score of the commercial television series *Northern Exposure,* and sang a song about the repatriation of Native American remains that was played on *Larry King Live.* "Hopefully," Shenandoah said after the song was played on the talk show, "my listeners, Indian or not, can begin to see the human side of Indian problems" (Shenandoah, 2007).

At home, Shenandoah's family has been involved in a long-term dispute regarding abuse of Iroquois democratic traditions by Nation Representative Ray Halbritter, who has built extensive casino and business venues on New York Oneida land. The family believes that Halbritter took office as a nation leader without consent of the people. Halbritter has retaliated by depriving the Shenandoahs and other protesters of services and membership in the tribe, as well as by ordering Nation police to demolish some of their homes.

Further Reading

Johansen, Bruce E. "The New York Oneidas: A Case Study in the Mismatch of Cultural Tradition and Economic Development." *American Indian Culture and Research Journal* 26, no. 3 (2002): 25–46.
Shenandoah, Joanne. Personal communication, November 20, 2007.

SHENANDOAH, LEON
1915–1996 ONONDAGA
IROQUOIS CONFEDERACY TADADAHO (SPEAKER)

Leon Shenandoah served as *Tadadaho* ("Firekeeper," or Speaker) of the Iroquois Confederacy during much of the late 20th century, from his initiation in 1969 to his death from kidney failure July 22, 1996, at age 81. Shenandoah, a "gentle, soft-spoken, humble holy man," held the oldest continuous political office in North America, and one of the oldest in the world (Yarrow, 1996). The Iroquois Confederacy has seated a *Tadadaho,* or speaker, since at least about 1100 C.E. Shenandoah was the 235th *Tadadaho* of the confederacy. Sid Hill was elevated to the role after Shenandoah's passing.

Survivors included his wife, Thelma, and six sons (Duane, Leon, Jr., Raymond, Gary, Irwin, and Jerome); a daughter, Lorie; a brother, Edward; two sisters, Alice Papineau and Phoebe Hill, all of the Onondaga Nation; 34 grandchildren, and 20 great-grandchildren.

Shenandoah lived on the Onondaga reservation south of Syracuse most of his life. His modest home was heated with a wood stove, situated close to the site of his birth, May 18, 1915, a cabin on Hemlock Creek. Born into the Eel Clan of the Onondaga, he was the youngest of five siblings.

As an infant, he almost died after a pot of scalding water was poured over nearly his entire body. Nursed back to health by a traditional healer, Shenandoah was told that his life had been preserved so that he could serve his people in a high office.

Shenandoah spent much of his life being groomed for the position of *Tadadaho,* an office he held for three decades, until his death.

Custodian

Shenandoah's formal schooling ended at eighth grade. With his wife Thelma, Shenandoah raised seven children, meanwhile maintaining his fluency in the Onondaga language, and his intense interest in Haudenosaunee (Iroquois) traditions, including the Code of Handsome Lake. As a young man, Shenandoah was a lacrosse player. To support his family, he worked for decades as a custodian at Syracuse University until he retired in the mid-1980s.

On the Onondaga Nation, Shenandoah was a custodian of another kind—keeper, as *Tadadaho,* of the "fire that never dies," the central council of the Haudenosaunee Confederacy. Shenandoah was regarded as both a political and spiritual leader. When asked about Iroquois influences on American democracy, Shenandoah said that the United States' founders made a mistake when they divorced state and church. "When the United States copied our form of government in the 1750s, they left out spirituality," Shenandoah said. "This is what I learned as a child. . . . Our religion is within the government and our government is within our religion. It is entwined. If the government goes off to one side . . . the religion will then pull you back in line. . . . [One] counteracts the other. . . . But when the United States joined the 13 colonies and copied our form of government, they held their meetings in one house, and their church (their beliefs) in another house. . . . It's not under the same roof like we do" (Austin, 1986, 177–78). Interviewed in *New Age* magazine, Shenandoah was asked, "What is the greatest power?" He paused a few moments, then replied slowly, "The greatest power is the Creator. But if you want to know the greatest strength, that is gentleness" (Yarrow, 1996).

In 1987, Shenandoah led the Grand Council when it banned the sale of Fourth of July fireworks on the reservation. "We decided that it's not really our way," Shenandoah explained, adding, "It's not really independence for us."

Shortly after he assumed office, Shenandoah visited the Museum of the American Indian in New York City. When a receptionist asked "May I help you?," he quietly said: "Yes. You can give us back our wampum belts" (Fadden, 1997). For three decades, Shenandoah played an important role in a campaign to have the wampum belts, which are records of the confederacy, returned from several museums and from New York State. His last official act July 4, 1996, was presiding over the return of 74 wampum belts from the same museum where he had greeted the receptionist many years earlier. Even though Shenandoah was ailing and had resigned office the previous fall due to illness, he "donned his feather hat and assumed his office for the return of these precious belts" (Yarrow, 1996).

Shenandoah steadfastly opposed gambling, a controversial issue among the Iroquois. He maintained that it fostered greed. He was a frequent international representative of the confederacy, speaking at the Earth Summit in Brazil during 1992, and, twice, before the United Nations. At home, Shenandoah was a quiet, traditionally minded man who drove an old Pontiac that someone had given to him, and smoked a corn-cob pipe.

Practicing Sovereignty

Shenandoah presided over a Haudenosaunee council that construed sovereignty strictly. A practical example (one of many) was provided by sanctuary offered Dennis Banks, American Indian Movement leader who was fleeing federal prosecution. Facing several federal criminal charges, Banks and compatriots slipped out of Wounded Knee near the end of the siege in 1973, taking sanctuary for a time in California, where officials refused to extradite him to South Dakota, in part because Attorney General Bill Janklow, who was given to bombast, had pledged to kill AIM members. Later, Banks took shelter on the Onondaga Nation in New York State, where FBI jurisdiction was not accepted by the Haudenosaunee (Iroquois) Confederacy. Banks met with Shenandoah, who placed his request for sanctuary before the confederacy's council. The council debated the issue, and accepted Banks's residency. "You are safe under the wings of the Onondaga Nation," Shenandoah told Banks (Banks and Erdoes, 2004, 332).

Speaking before the United Nations in 1985, Shenandoah outlined the principles of Iroquois leadership: Quoting from the Great Law of Peace, the Iroquois' guiding law, he said that the Haudenosaunee chiefs "shall be mentors of the people for all time. The thickness of their skins shall be seven spans; which is to say that they shall be proof against anger, offensive action and, criticism. Their hearts shall be full of peace and good will, and their minds full of a yearning for the welfare of the people. With endless patience, they shall carry out their duty. Their firmness shall be tempered with a tenderness for their people. Neither anger nor fury shall find lodging in their minds, and all their words and actions shall be marked by calm deliberation" ("Address," 1985).

Shenandoah's decisions were suffused with an environmental focus: "When people cease to respect and express gratitude for these many things," he told the United Nations, "then all life will be destroyed, and human life on this planet will come to an end. These are our times and responsibilities. Every human being has a sacred duty to protect the welfare of our Mother Earth, from whom all life comes. In order to do this we must recognize the enemy—the one within us. We must begin with ourselves."

Shenandoah continued: "We must live in harmony with the Natural World and recognize that excessive exploitation can only lead to our own destruction. We cannot trade the welfare of our future generations for profit now. We must abide by the Natural Law or be victim of its ultimate reality" ("Address," 1985).

Waging Peace

More specifically, Shenandoah called upon world leaders to abolish nuclear and conventional weapons of war. "When warriors are leaders, then you will have war," he said. Leaders must be taught to wage peace, he said. "We must unite the religions of the world as the spiritual force strong enough to prevail in peace. It is no longer good enough to cry, 'Peace.' We must act peace, live peace, and march [for] peace in alliance with the people of the world" ("Address," 1985).

Further Reading

"Address to the General Assembly of the United Nations Delivered October 25, 1985, by Leon Shenandoah, Tadodaho, Haudenosaunee." http://www.earthportals.com/Portal_Messenger/shenandoah.html.

Austin, Alberta. *Ne'Ho Niyo' De:No': That's What It Was Like*. Lackawanna, NY: Rebco Enterprises, 1986.

Banks, Dennis, and Richard Erdoes. *Ojibwa Warrior: Dennis Banks and the Rise of the American Indian Movement*. Norman: University of Oklahoma Press, 2004.

Stout, David. "Leon Shenandoah, 81, Leader of the Iroquois Confederacy." *New York Times,* July 23, 1996. http://www.nytimes.com/1996/07/23/nyregion/leon-shenandoah-81-leader-of-the-iroquois-confederacy.html.

Yarrow, David. "Native American Wisdom. The Tree of Peace: New World Symbol of Freedom. Leon Shenandoah. Tadodaho, Onondaga Nation Indigenous Wisdomkeeper." 1996. http://www.earthportals.com/Portal_Messenger/shenandoah.html.

SILVERHEELS, JAY
1919–1980 MOHAWK
ACTOR

Born Harry J. Smith on the Six Nations Reserve near Brantford, Ontario, in Canada, May 26, 1919, the Mohawk who acquired the stage name "Jay Silverheels" became well known as the Lone Ranger's television sidekick Tonto on the long-running series, *The Lone Ranger.* Silverheels also acted in a film version of the same plot, as well as in other films, including *The Prairie* (1947), *Broken Arrow* (1950), and *War Arrow* (1953). In 1979, Silverheels became the first Native American to have a star set on Hollywood Boulevard's Walk of Fame. Silverheels (he changed his name legally in 1971) probably played more American Indian roles than any other actor.

As a young man, Silverheels was best known as an athlete—a boxer, wrestler, lacrosse player, and harness racer. He won two wrestling championships as a teenager, and was a silver medalist in the Eastern Shore finals of the Golden Gloves, boxing in Madison Square Garden. He also was a member of Canada's national lacrosse team. By 1938, he became the highest-paid player on the team, which stopped in Hollywood, California, for a match, where the actor Joe E. Brown suggested that Smith take up acting. Adopting the stage name Silverheels, he first worked as a waiter, then broke into acting with bit parts and stunts.

Silverheels acted in 30 movies, as well as many television shows, including *The Virginian, Wagon Train,* and *Daniel Boone.* He resented having to play a stereotyped Indian as the Lone Ranger's sidekick Tonto, but little else was offered to Indian actors at the time. In 1962, he joined other Native actors in the Indian Actors Workshop. Silverheels also served on the Screen Actors Guild's Board of Directors, where he advocated Indians' portrayal of Native American roles in the movies and on television.

Appearing on Johnny Carson, Silverheels characterized his time as the Lone Ranger's sidekick as "lousy years" (Chavers, 2007, 589). In 1963, he was the first Native American to be inducted into the Screen Actors' Hall of Fame. He died at age 60 March 5, 1980, at the Motion Picture Home in Woodland, California, leaving a wife, Mary, and three children: Karen, Pamela, and Jay Anthony.

Actors Jay Silverheels (left) and Clayton Moore pose as Tonto and the Lone Ranger. The television series The Lone Ranger *ran from 1949 to 1957. (AP/Wide World Photos)*

Further Reading

Chavers, Dean. *Modern American Indian Leaders: Their Lives and Their Works.* 2 vols. Lewiston, NY: Edwin Mellen Press, 2007.

SIXKILLER, SONNY
BORN 1951 CHEROKEE
FOOTBALL PLAYER

Born in Tahlequah, Oklahoma, in 1951, Alex (Sonny) Sixkiller, who is Cherokee, played football at the University of Washington as a star quarterback from 1970 to 1972, when he graduated. He excelled despite his relatively small size at 5-foot-10 and 153 pounds, setting passing records that stood for more than 30 years.

Sixkiller's family migrated to Oklahoma in 1838 on the Trail of Tears. When he was one, Sixkiller's family moved to Ashland, Oregon, in the Rogue River Valley. He spent hours a day playing sandlot football with friends, later becoming a star on the Ashland High School team, from which he was recruited by the University of Washington.

Sixkiller became one of the University of Washington's most notable quarterbacks, setting several game, season, and career records. During his sophomore year, Sixkiller was the best college-level passer in the United States, and his photo appeared on the cover of *Sports Illustrated*. That year, 1970, he averaged 18.6 completions and 227 yards per game. His 2,303 yards in a season stood as the team record until 2003, when Cody Pickett surpassed it. In three years, Sixkiller completed passes for 5,496 yards at a time when the ground game received more emphasis than today.

As a sophomore, Sixkiller assumed a leadership role on a team that had won only one game and lost nine the previous season. The Huskies turned into winners, going 6–4, 8–3, and 8–3 the next three years. At a time before many Native Americans had assumed professional leadership roles, Sixkiller endured racial taunts so severe that, according to one account, "team captains wrote to the Seattle media imploring them to stop focusing on [his] race" (Trower, 2004). On the other hand, at a time when Indian fishing rights were controversial in the Pacific Northwest, Native American groups sought Sixkiller's support.

Sixkiller later played professional football for a time, but his career was cut short by injuries. In 1974, he played briefly with Toronto in the Canadian Football League, and with Philadelphia and Hawaii in the World Football League.

He was inducted into the American Indian Hall of Fame in 1987. He also co-authored an autobiography, *Sonny Sixkiller's Tales from the Huskies' Sideline.*

Actor Burt Reynolds (who is one-eighth Cherokee) invited Sixkiller to play a part in *The Longest Yard* (1974), a movie about a prison football team. In the movie, Sixkiller played a halfback on the inmate team that took on the guards. Sixkiller also briefly played a boat captain in the television series *Hawaii Five-O.*

Sixkiller later worked as a broadcast analyst for University of Washington football games on Fox Sports Net Northwest. Sixkiller and Denise, to whom he had been married 30 years in 2004, live in Seattle, having raised three sons. Casey, a Dartmouth graduate, worked as an aide to Washington Senator Pat Murray. Jesse also attended Dartmouth, while Tyson was a student at the University of Washington.

A pop-punk band was named for Sixkiller in 1997: the Philadelphia-based Sonny Sixkiller, featuring Kara Lafty, formerly of Moped, and guitarist Matt Kelley.

Further Reading

Oxendine, Joseph B. *American Indian Sports Heritage.* Lincoln: University of Nebraska Press, 1995.

Sixkiller, Sonny, with Bon Condotta. *Sonny Sixkiller's Tales from the Huskies' Sideline.* Champaign, IL: Sports Publishing, 2002.

Trower, Tim. "Where Are They Now? Sonny Sixkiller. Ashland High School, 1969." *Mail Tribune,* September 17, 2004. http://archive.mailtribune.com/archive/2004/0917/sport/stories/04sport.htm.

SNAKE, REUBEN
1937–1993 WINNEBAGO (HO-CHUNK)
POLITICAL AND SPIRITUAL LEADER

Given all that he accomplished during his brief life, one could imagine Reuben Snake (1937–93) as having been an overly busy person. He was a Roadman of the Native American Church, Chairman of the Winnebago (Ho-Chunk) Tribe, as well as a shaper of Native American history through leadership in the American Indian Movement, the National Congress of American Indians, and many other groups.

Snake, who signed his letters "your humble serpent," also served as an international representative of Native America in diplomatic circles, and as a major advocate of the legalization of "Grandfather Peyote" for use among the 300,000 members of the Native American Church. Snake served 28 years in Winnebago reservation governance, first as a council member, later as vice chairman and chairman. A friend of Snake's observed: "He gave a little bit of himself to everyone he met" (Johansen, 1996, 60).

Snake compiled such a rich record of accomplishments, and, at the same time, never seemed to desire the recognition of leadership. He also never seemed to be in too much of a hurry. This incongruity sharpens when one realizes that Snake had little more than a quarter century for serious work between the time he swore off skid road alcoholism at the age of 28, and his death at 56. In a stressed-out and overscheduled world, Snake always had time to tell a story. Self-described as a 350-pound "militant Teddy Bear," Snake's stories were told with considerable humor (Fikes and Echo-Hawk, 1996, 115).

Early Life

Born January 12, 1937, on Winnebago Reservation Indian Hospital in eastern Nebraska, Snake was given the Winnebago name *Kikawa Unga,* which means "Rising Up." Snake began adulthood as a member of the U.S. Army Green Berets between 1954 and 1958. He was educated at Northwestern College, Orange City, Iowa; the University of Nebraska at Omaha; and Peru (Nebraska) State College. From early in his life, Snake had a keen sense for hypocrisy, beginning at an Indian boarding school in Neillsville, Wisconsin, during the early 1940s. The white schoolmaster, a German immigrant, had encouraged his children to learn and speak the Winnebago language. At the same time, Snake and other Winnebago students were forbidden to speak their own language.

Later, Snake served in the U.S. Army Special Forces and met Indian hobbyists in Germany. In Berlin, he met the first European-descended people who treated him with respect. After his army duty ended, back in the United States, Snake and a brother knocked around at several odd jobs, living on various urban skid roads. One day, Snake decided to go sober after the odor of his brother's feet nearly knocked him out. He moved to Omaha, started a family, and took a stable job in a manufacturing plant. The company helped finance college classes in mechanical engineering for him at the University of Nebraska at Omaha. Snake also practiced as a Mormon until segregation of church services (whites in one, Indians in another) provoked him to quit. He then took up full-time practice in the Native American Church, becoming a Roadman in 1974.

Throughout his life as an activist, Snake searched for spiritual meaning in life, and he found it in the Native American Church. He was active in efforts to legalize use of peyote in Native American Church ceremonies. Following a Supreme Court ruling in 1990 denying legal use of peyote, Snake became a leader in an effort to persuade Congress to legalize it. He also played a major role in creating a documentary film called *Peyote Road* (1996), distributed by Kifaru as part of its Native American Relations Series. President Bill Clinton signed into law an amendment to the American Indian Religious Freedom Act legalizing peyote's use a year after Snake died.

Humor as a Leadership Tool

Noted for humor that kept him in demand as a conference speaker, Snake was active in efforts to broaden the scope of Native American religious freedom, as well as tribal economic development. Snake often used humor to drive home the point that Native American philosophy, especially the idea that all natural phenomena move in cycles and that all things are related, could help ameliorate Europeans' alienation from nature. During a speech in Seattle in 1991, at an event sponsored by the Lummis, Snake proposed that "every Indian person in this nation of ours . . . go out and adopt 250 white people. Bring them into the family. Teach them the right way to do things" (Russo, 1992, 41).

Snake used humor in his activism as well. He explained, for example, how he became an admiral of the Winnebago Navy. The Army Corps of Engineers was preparing in 1970 to condemn 627 acres of Winnebago land to build a resort complex. Snake and a number of other Winnebagoes decided to protest the condemnation by fording the Missouri River, west to east, onto the land in question. "We discovered that there wasn't one Indian on the Winnebago reservation who owned a boat," Snake recalled. Two small boats (one 12-footer and another 14 feet long) were borrowed from friends at the University of Nebraska. "This was the magnificent fleet of the Winnebago Navy," said Snake (Fikes and Echo-Hawk, 1996, 150).

> Our fearless leader, Louie LaRose, was standing . . . with a war bonnet on. Of course we Winnebagoes are woodlands Indians so we never were familiar with wearing war bonnets. War bonnets are a tradition among the Plains Indians. Louie forgot to tie the drawstring on the back of his war bonnet, so when we hit the main channel, the breeze . . . caught his eagle feathers and turned them inside out. Instead of looking like a fierce Winnebago warrior, he wound up looking like a Mormon pioneer woman in a sun bonnet. (Fikes and Echo-Hawk, 1996, 150)

War bonnets aside, the Winnebagoes took the Army Corps of Engineers to federal court, and won. Later, the tribe's "WinneVegas" casino was built on some of the land.

Snake's forte was consensus building and conflict resolution. "Three things that characterized Reuben were strength, clarity, and patience," said Susan Harjo, Director of the Morning Star Institution. "He always had a very good way of bringing people to consensus. No matter how long it took, how contentious the issue was, he was prepared to stay for however long it took" (Little Eagle and Reynolds, 1993, n.p.).

"Reuben always imparted a message of respect, describing a faithful vision of a loving world—'a world of relatives,'" said the editors of *Akwe:kon Journal,* published by Cornell University's American Indian Program. "Reuben Snake could explain things better than anyone, and he was very funny and pleasant to be with. . . . [He] encouraged communications that were not normally possible" (Little Eagle and Reynolds, 1993, n.p.).

Snake's body aged rapidly in his mid-forties, when he suffered the first of two heart attacks. He also suffered from diabetes. On June 28, 1993, Snake passed into the spirit world following a heart attack complicated with diabetes, on the Winnebago Reservation. Snake had assembled his family for a last Native American Church service. One of Snake's six children and 16 grandchildren, Abigail Snake, said that shortly before his death, Snake had a vision in which a long-deceased brother came to him, burning sage and smudging him with its residue, a Winnebago rite of passage. "I'm not afraid," he told Abigail. "I'm ready" (Johansen, 1996, 61).

A report in *Indian Country Today* characterized Snake by noting "a warmhearted bear of a man noted for his leadership in spiritual circles and the political arena was called home by his creator. . . . Reuben Snake will be mourned by people across the nation who remember his booming voice, his ever-present wit, and his dauntless dedication to Indian people of many tribal nations" (Little Eagle and Reynolds, 1993, n.p.).

Further Reading

Chavers, Dean. *Modern American Indian Leaders: Their Lives and Their Works.* 2 vols. Lewiston, NY: Edwin Mellen Press, 2007.

Fikes, Jay C., and Walter E. Echo-Hawk. *Reuben Snake: Your Humble Serpent.* Santa Fe, NM: Clear Light, 1996.

Johansen, Bruce E. "Reuben Snake: A True Leader." Review of *Reuben Snake: Your Humble Serpent,* by Jay C. Fikes and Walter E. Echo-Hawk. *Native Americas* 13, no. 2 (Summer 1996): 60–61.

Little Eagle, Avis, and Jerry Reynolds. "Tribute to Reuben Snake: 'Humble Serpent' Journeys On." *Indian Country Today,* June 30, 1993, n.p.

Russo, Kurt, ed. *Our People, Our Land: Reflections on Common Ground: Perspectives on the Columbus Quincentenary.* Bellingham, WA: Lummi Tribe, 1992.

"Your Humble Serpent: The Wisdom of Reuben Snake." Videotape. 70 minutes. Produced and directed by Gary Rhine. Kifaru Productions, San Francisco, 1995.

Louis Sockalexis, a Penobscot, played for the Cleveland Indians between 1897 and 1899. (AP/Wide World Photos)

SOCKALEXIS, LOUIS 1875–1913 PENOBSCOT MAJOR LEAGUE BASEBALL PLAYER

Louis Sockalexis, once an outfielder with the Cleveland Indians, is the supposed "honoree" for the team's Chief Wahoo mascot that has become the subject of protests by many Native Americans who are wary of stereotypes. The Cleveland Indians' official media guide states that the "Indians" name was adopted in honor of Sockalexis, a Penobscot who played for the Cleveland Spiders (the team's previous name) between 1897 and 1899. He played three seasons and batted .313. Whatever the origin of the team name, Sockalexis is widely believed to have been the first Native American to play major league baseball.

The story of Sockalexis allows many Cleveland Indians fans to boast that the team's name was an honor, not an insult. The team's media guide first mentioned the Sockalexis story in 1968, just as the new American Indian Movement started protesting.

Cleveland entered professional baseball late in the 19th century with a team named the Spiders. In the team's first year, the Spiders lost 134 games. Later, the team was called the "Naps." The Cleveland Indian name was adopted by a vote of the fans during 1914. Chief Wahoo was created by a *Cleveland Plain Dealer* columnist during the 1940s. Chief Wahoo's image was first sewn onto Cleveland Indian uniforms in 1947.

In 1999, the Cleveland Indians' media guide devoted an entire page to the Sockalexis rationale for the team's name, which was coyly declared bogus a year later. In 2000, the wording of the guide was changed, with the reference to Sockalexis taken as "legend." The old version was proved factually inaccurate by Ellen Staurowsky, a professor at Ithaca College, New York, who maintains that the team should drop its Indian moniker. Any change could cost the baseball club a lot of money, because Chief Wahoo is among the best-selling sports icons on clothing and other merchandise.

Sockalexis began playing baseball at Holy Cross College, Worcester, Massachusetts, less than five years after the 1890 massacre at Wounded Knee. He had grown up on the Indian Island Reservation in Old Town, Maine. By 1897, he was playing baseball at Notre Dame, from which he was expelled after only a month because of public drunkenness. The Cleveland Spiders signed him for $1,500.

At first, Sockalexis experienced something of a hitting streak. By the middle of his first season with the Spiders, he was hitting .335. It has been said that some fans "took to wearing Indian headdresses and screaming war whoops every time Sockalexis came to bat" (Nevard, n.d.). During July of 1897, however, Sockalexis got drunk and injured himself. He spent most of the rest of his baseball career on the bench, before being released by the Spiders in 1899. For a decade after that, Sockalexis performed manual labor in Cleveland as he continued to suffer from alcoholism. He died in 1913, at the age of 38. A 1992 novel based on his life (*The Cleveland Indian: The Legend of King Saturday*) was penned by Luke Salisbury.

In 1972, in the context of a lawsuit against the Cleveland Indians, Native activist Russell Means openly critiqued the Chief Wahoo image: "That Indian looks like a damn fool, like a clown and we resent being portrayed as either savages or clowns." Means did not content himself with an attack on stereotypes, but turned to racial analogy to advance his argument against mascots. "Take the Washington Redskins. . . . Redskin is a derogatory name . . . what if we called them the Washington Niggers, or Washington Rednecks, or Washington Pollacks?" (King, 2004, 195).

An essay in the University of California student newspaper following the 1995 World Series between the Atlanta Braves and the Cleveland Indians described a purported basketball game between the Philadelphia Amish and the New York Jews. "Do you find this tasteless and degrading?" the writer asked. "Do you feel as ludicrous reading it as I do writing it? If the answer is 'yes' to either of these questions, then you should feel very uncomfortable about this year's World Series" (Bulwa, 1995).

Further Reading

Bulwa, Demian. "Tomahawk Chop the Indian Mascots." *Daily Californian* (University of California–Berkeley), October 20, 1995. muse.jhu.edu/journals/new_centennial_review/v004/4.1king.html.

King, C. Richard. "Borrowing Power: Racial Metaphors and Pseudo-Indian Mascots." *The New Centennial Review* 4, no. 1 (Spring 2004): 189–209.

Nevard, David. "Wahooism in the USA." No date. Accessed January 12, 2010. http://webpages.charter.net/joekuras/bhxi3d.htm.

Salisbury, Luke. *The Cleveland Indian: The Legend of King Saturday*. Mill Creek, WA: Black Heron Press, 1992.

SOHAPPY, DAVID
1925–1991 WANAPAM
FISHING-RIGHTS ACTIVIST

The 1974 Boldt decision (*U.S. v. Washington*) restored recognition of treaty rights regarding salmon fishing west of the Cascade Mountains in Washington State. East of the Cascades, during the 1980s and 1990s, however, the fishing-rights battle continued in a form that reminded many people of the fish-ins of the 1960s. Many

Native people along the Columbia River and its tributaries also fished for a livelihood long before European Americans migrated to their land, but they had no treaties protecting their right to do so. For years, David Sohappy, his wife Myra, and their sons erected a riverbank shelter and fished in the traditional manner.

The Sohappys' name came from the Wanapam word *souiehappie,* meaning "Shoving Something under a Ledge." Sohappy's ancestors had traded salmon with members of the Lewis and Clark Expedition. The Wanapams never signed a treaty, wishing only to be left in peace to live as they had for hundreds, if not thousands, of years. By the early 1940s, Sohappy's family had been pushed off its ancestral homeland at Priest Rapids and White Bluffs, which became part of the Hanford Nuclear Reservation. Hanford was located in the middle of a desert that Lewis and Clark characterized as the most barren piece of land that they saw between St. Louis and the Pacific Ocean. Still, Sohappy fished, even as his father, Jim Sohappy, warned him that if he continued to live in the old ways, "The white man is going to put you in jail someday" (Johansen and Grinde, 1997, 363).

State Harassment

During the 1950s, development devastated the Celilo Falls, which once was one of the richest Indian fishing grounds in North America. Most of the people who had fished there gave up their traditional livelihoods and moved to the nearby Yakama reservation, or into urban areas. Sohappy and Myra moved to a sliver of federally owned land called Cook's Landing, just above the first of several dams along the Columbia and its tributaries. They built a small longhouse with a dirt floor. Sohappy built fishing traps from driftwood. As the fish-ins of the 1960s attracted nationwide publicity, Sohappy fished until state game and fishing officials raided his camp, beat members of his family, and, in 1968, had him jailed for fishing illegally. Sohapppy then brought legal action, and the case, *Sohappy v. Smith,* produced a landmark federal ruling that was supposed to prevent the states of Washington and Oregon from interfering with Indian fishing, except for conservation purposes.

The state ignored the ruling and continued to harass Sohappy and his family. Under cover of darkness, state agents sunk their boats and slashed their nets. In 1981 and 1982, the states of Washington and Oregon successfully but quietly lobbied into law a federal provision that made the interstate sale of fish taken in violation of state law a felony—an act aimed squarely at Sohappy. Eight months before the law was signed by President Ronald Reagan, the state had enlisted federal undercover agents in a fish-buying sting that the press called "Salmonscam," to entrap Sohappy. He was later convicted in Los Angeles (the trial had been moved from the local jurisdiction because of racial prejudice against Indians) of taking 317 fish, and sentenced to five years in prison. During the trial, testimony about the Sohappy's religion and the practice of conservation was not allowed.

Sohappy became a symbol of Native American rights across the United States. Myra Sohappy sought support from the United Nations Commission on Human Rights to have her husband tried by a jury of his peers in the Yakama Nation's

Tribal Court. The new trial was arranged with the help of Senator Daniel Inouye, Chairman of the Senate Select Committee on Indian Affairs. The Yakama court found that the federal prosecution had interfered with Sohappy's practice of his Seven Drum religion.

Prison Kills

Released after 20 months in prison, Sohappy had aged rapidly. Confinement and the prison diet had sapped his strength. Sohappy suffered several strokes during the months in prison, when he was even denied the use of an eagle prayer feather for comfort (it was rejected as "contraband" by prison officials). Back at Cook's Landing, Sohappy found that vindictive federal officials had tacked an eviction notice to his small house. Sohappy took the eviction notice to court and beat the government for what turned out to be his last time.

He died in a nursing home in Hood River, Oregon, in 1991. A few days later, Sohappy was buried, as his Wanapam relatives gathered in an old graveyard. They sang old songs as they lowered his body into the earth, having wrapped it in a Pendleton blanket. He was placed so that the early morning sun would warm his head, facing west toward Mount Adams. Tom Keefe, Jr., an attorney who had been instrumental in securing Sohappy's release from prison, stood by the grave and remembered. "And while the sun chased a crescent moon across the Yakima Valley, I thanked David Sohappy for the time we had spent together, and I wondered how the salmon he had fought to protect would fare in his absence. Now he is gone, and the natural runs of Chinook that fed his family since time immemorial are headed for the Endangered Species Act list" (Keefe, 1991, 6).

Further Reading

Johansen, Bruce E., and Donald A. Grinde, Jr. *The Encyclopedia of Native American Biography.* New York: Henry Holt, 1997.

Keefe, Tom, Jr. "A Tribute to David Sohappy." *Native Nations,* June/July 1991, 4–6.

United States v. Washington: 384 F. Supp. 312 (1974).

Standing Bear
c. 1830–1902 Ponca
Political Leader

The story of Standing Bear and his Ponca band combines some unusual elements: two cruel treks from a government-mandated exile; a frontier city's people and a federal judge outraged by their treatment; the U'ma'ha (Omaha) LaFlesche family working in league with a newspaperman; and a U.S. Army general, George Crook,

Standing Bear, a Ponca chieftain, filed suit against U.S. policy, which ultimately resulted in the United States legally recognizing Native Americans as human beings. (Library of Congress)

who, unknown to most of his peers, had been inducted into the U'ma'has' Soldier Lodge through a Sundance, including chest piercing.

Standing Bear became nationally famous in the late 1870s, during a time of forced removal for the Ponca and other Native peoples on the Great Plains. Standing Bear led some of his people on two 500-mile marches from Indian Territory (now Oklahoma) back to Nebraska. When the group reached Omaha, Standing Bear was involved in the first court case to result in a declaration that American Indians should be treated as human beings under the law of *habeas corpus*. Thus, the army could not relocate Standing Bear's party by force without cause. The case of Standing Bear's people was so compelling that General Crook volunteered as main defendant in the case.

The landmark legal case *Standing Bear v. Crook* never would have occurred if Standing Bear had not possessed an overriding drive that transcended the rest of his life: he sought, against all U.S. government directives, to bury his deceased son in the ancestral earth of the Poncas' traditional homeland. This need compelled him to walk until hunger forced him and his companions to eat their moccasins, and to continue walking as their bare feet bled in the snow.

Poncas' Own Trail of Tears

By every Anglo-American measure, the Poncas led by Standing Bear were "good Indians," before they were sent packing on their own trail of tears. They did what the Great White Father thought was good for them. Before their forced removal in 1877 by the U.S. Army from the Niobrara River country in northernmost Nebraska, the Poncas had begun the transition to farming in the Jefferson yeoman image that reformers insisted was, along with education and Christianity, the Indian's key to the future. The Poncas also had endeavored to maintain friendly relationships with the United States. In 1858, they ceded part of their homeland, trading it for nearby land that was then said, by treaty, to be theirs forever.

The Poncas' adaptation to civilization was rudely interrupted by a bureaucratic mistake in Washington, D.C. When the United States signed the Treaty of

Fort Laramie in 1868, a bureaucratic mistake by sloppy cartographers ceded the Poncas' homeland to their enemies, the Great Sioux Nation. The U.S. Army was thus compelled to enforce the treaty against the Poncas at the behest of the Sioux. In late January 1877, Indian inspector Edward C. Kemble told the Poncas they had to leave home for Indian Territory.

Standing Bear and nine other Ponca chiefs were forced to visit Indian Territory to inspect the lands that the government proposed as their new home. Dissatisfied with the new land, the chiefs who were young enough to walk home decided to do so; the rest stayed in Oklahoma, under protest. Having walked almost 500 miles, Standing Bear and the other chiefs were provided shelter among the Omahas. After a few days of rest, Standing Bear and the other chiefs traveled to Sioux City to telegraph President Rutherford B. Hayes about their opposition to removal. On his return to Ponca Agency (in northern Nebraska), Standing Bear was arrested for leaving the reservation without permission and sent to Yankton for a military trial. A sympathetic commander freed Standing Bear, but Secretary of the Interior Carl Schurz demanded that the Poncas, as a group, be compelled to move to Indian Territory.

A few months later, paying no heed to the Poncas' objections, federal troops removed 723 of them at bayonet-point from three villages along the Niobrara River to Indian Territory, "just as one would drive a herd of ponies," said the Poncas' paramount chief White Eagle (Dando-Collins, 2004, 34). After the Poncas were forced out of the Niobrara Valley, troops tore down all 236 log houses, plus barns, a grist mill, sawmill, and blacksmith shop, church, and schoolhouse. The only building left standing was the government's Indian agency.

Standing Bear protested that his people were being removed from their homeland illegally: "This land is ours," he said. "We have never sold it. We have our houses . . . here. Our fathers and some of our children are buried here. Here we wish to live and die. We have harmed no man. We have kept our treaty. We have learned to work. We can make a good living here. We do not wish to sell our land, and we think no man has a right to take it from us. Here we will live, and here we will die" (Tibbles, 1880, 6).

Standing Bear later described the scene as federal troops arrived to escort the Poncas southward:

> They took our reapers, mowers, hand-rakes, spades, ploughs, bedsteads, stoves, cupboards, everything we had on our farms, and put them in one large building. Then they put into the wagons such thing as they could carry. We told them that we would rather die than leave our lands; but we could not help ourselves. They took us down. Many died on the road. Two of my children died. After we reached the new land, all my horses died. The water was very bad. All our cattle died. Not one was left. I stayed until one hundred fifty eight of my people had died. Then I ran away with 30 of my people, men, women, and children. Some of the children were orphans. We were three months on the road. We were weak and sick and starved. . . . Half of us were sick. (Jackson, 1888, 203–4)

During a cold April 1877, a first group of Poncas endured a 51-day march southward, under the direction of Indian Agent James Lawrence. A second group departed in May under agent E.A. Howard. The second march, 65 days in length, was dogged by heavy rain, a tornado, and several deaths. Once both groups reached Indian Territory, malaria weakened and killed many of the Poncas who had survived the forced marches.

Agent Howard left behind a taciturn diary that provides an outline of the daily sufferings of the people who were being forced to march southward. Nearly every day brought news of death (usually of children), illness, bad roads, and an unusually large number of severe thunderstorms, especially during May and June of 1877. Once the Poncas arrived in Indian Territory, their most immediate problem became intense humid heat and swarms of biting insects. Suddenly, they also realized that no one had appropriated a single dollar or expended an hour of effort providing them with shelter from the cruelties of the elements in this new land.

Excerpts from Howard's diary sketched the cruelties of the Poncas' forced removal, as it was experienced by Standing Bear and others:

> **May 21st.** Broke camp [at] seven o'clock and marched to Crayton, a distance of thirteen miles. . . . The child that died yesterday was here buried by the Indians. . . . **May 24.** Buried the child that died yesterday in the cemetery at Neligh, giving it a Christian burial. . . . **May 27.** . . . Several of the Indians were found to be quite sick, and, having no physician . . . they gave us much anxiety and no trouble. The daughter of Standing Bear . . . was very low of consumption, and moving her with any degree of comfort was almost impossible. . . . **June 5.** Daughter of Standing Bear . . . died at two o'clock. . . . **June 6.** Prairie Flower, wife of Shine White and daughter of Standing Bear . . . was here given a Christian burial . . . at Milford, Nebraska. . . . (Jackson, 1888, 207–13)

An unusually volatile spring on the prairie compounded the journey.

> **June 7.** . . . A storm, such as I never before experienced . . . blew a fearful tornado, demolishing every tent in camp, and rending many of them into shreds, overturning wagons, and hurling wagon-boxes . . . through the air in every direction like straws. Some of the people were taken up by the wind and carried as much as three hundred yards. Several of the Indians were quite seriously hurt, and one child died the next day. . . . (Jackson, 1888, 214)

Howard's daily record of the entire march has been preserved in the archives of the Bureau of Indian Affairs.

> **June 16.** . . . During the march a wagon tipped over, injuring a woman quite severely. Indians out of rations, and feeling hostile. . . . **June 18.** . . . Had coffin made for dead Indian. . . . A fearful thunder-storm during the night flooded the camp-equipage. **July 2.** . . . During the last few days of the journey, the weather was exceedingly hot, and the teams [of horses]

terribly annoyed and bitten by green-head flies, which attacked them in great numbers. . . . The people are all nearly worn out from the fatigue of the march. . . . (Jackson, 1888, 216)

During their marches to Indian Territory, 158 of the Poncas died of starvation and disease.

During the fall of 1877, Standing Bear and other Ponca leaders met with President Hayes and Secretary Schurz in Washington, D.C., to request that the Poncas be allowed to leave Indian Territory. They would have found either of two options acceptable: repatriation along the Niobrara on the land from which they had been forced to move, or a home on the Omaha Reservation. The Omahas and Poncas were related by family ties. The appeal was rejected because it conflicted with Interior Department policy to concentrate Native peoples on larger reservations (which were said to be easiest to administer) in the Indian Territory. In the meantime, nearly half of the Poncas who had made the journey south had died, including Standing Bear's only remaining son, who died of malaria.

In Indian Territory, the Poncas found illness and death dogging their every step. Standing Bear commented:

> It was now in the fall, and the sickness was worse than ever. Families had settled on separate tracts of land, and were scattered around. The whole family would be sick and no one would know it . . . [S]ome of the female[s] . . . would die and the others would not be able to bury them. They would drag them with a pony out on the prairie and leave them there. Men would take sick while at work and die in less than a day. . . . There were dead in every family. . . . I lost all my children but one little girl. I was in an awful place, and I was a prisoner there. (Tibbles, 1880, 14–15)

A year after their removal, at least a third of the Poncas had died, including two of Standing Bear's children, a daughter, Prairie Flower (who died of pneumonia on the march), and a son, Bear Shield. Following Bear Shield's death, Standing Bear, determined to bury the bones of his son in the lands of his ancestors, escaped north with about 30 other Poncas.

Standing Bear's group walked for 50 days during the worst of winter with no money, eating raw corn until it gave out, and sleeping in haystacks under thin, tattered blankets. "When their moccasins ran out, they walked barefoot in the snow. Barely able to stand on their bloodied feet, they struggled into the Otoe agency in southern Nebraska" (Mathes, 1989, 45). Their accounts, later given to the press in Omaha and distributed nationally by wire, indicated that friendly whites often helped them during their winter trek northward. The Poncas arrived at the Omaha Agency, where they were offered food, lodging, and seed for use, if they wished to stay.

Making His Case

In March of 1879, troops under General Crook arrested Standing Bear and his party, and conveyed them to Fort Omaha, just north of the growing frontier city of the same name. Enriched by its status as a new railroad terminus, Omaha had already grown to 150,000 residents, many of them liberal emigrants from the East Coast and Europe. When Crook arrived at the fort, which was serving as his head-quarters, he called Omaha newspaperman Thomas Henry Tibbles.

Tibbles was filling in for the editor of the *Herald*. He walked to Fort Omaha the next morning, about four miles, and interviewed members of Standing Bear's group. As Tibbles returned to town, running part of the way, he stopped at every church he could find, asking pastors if he could address their congregations about the travail of the Poncas. At a Congregational Church, the pastor, Rev. Mr. Sherill, allowed him to speak "between the opening hymns" (Tibbles, 1880, 27). After hearing Tibbles's account, two churches passed resolutions to the Interior Department and Secretary Carl Schurz on the Poncas' behalf. By the next day, Tibbles was preparing wire dispatches for newspapers in Chicago, New York, and other cities, as he searched for attorneys who would represent Standing Bear and his people in Omaha Federal District Court.

Tibbles was 39 years of age at the time, and had been an outspoken abolition-ist, a scout in the Civil War, and a circuit-riding preacher before he was hired as an assistant editor at the liberal *Omaha Daily Herald* (today part of Omaha's only daily newspaper, the *Omaha World-Herald*). Using the then-new technology of the telegraph, Tibbles spread the story to the East Coast. In Omaha, Tibbles pro-vided pages of coverage and provocative front-page headlines, such as "Criminal Cruelty—The History of the Ponca Prisoners Now at the Barracks," and "A Tale of Cruelty That Has Never [Been] Surpassed." Tibbles's dispatches were wired to major East Coast newspapers, and a flurry of protest letters to Congress on the Poncas' behalf resulted.

Crook already had announced his disgust at how Standing Bear's party was being treated and became a major conduit of a legal case (*Standing Bear et al. v. Crook*) that he had every intention of losing. Following a trial during the spring of 1879 that included a speech by Standing Bear that provoked tears from the bench, Federal District Court Judge Elmer Dundy ruled during 1879 that Indians were people within the meaning of the law, and no law gave the army authority to forc-ibly remove them from their lands.

By the time the case went to court in May of 1879, Standing Bear and the rest of the Poncas drew a large audience to Judge Dundy's courtroom, many of whom ignored Judge Dundy's instructions not to applaud the chief's remarks.

> [Standing Bear] claimed that, although his skin was of a different hue, yet he was a man, and that God made him. He said he was not a savage, and related how he had saved the life of a soldier whom he had found on the Plains, starved, and almost frozen to death, and of a man who had lost his way on the trackless prairie, whom he had fed and guided to his destina-tion. In spite of the orders of the court and the efforts of the bailiffs, he was greeted with continual rounds of applause. (Tibbles, 1880, 93)

Shortly after, Standing Bear's older brother Big Snake tested the ruling by mov-ing 100 miles in Indian Territory, from the Poncas' assigned reservation to one occupied by the Cheyennes. He was arrested by troops and returned. Big Snake did not know that Judge Dundy had restricted the scope of his ruling to Standing Bear and his party. After William H. Whiteman, the Ponca Indian Agent, ordered that he be imprisoned, Big Snake protested and said he was not guilty of any crime. When he became unruly, he was shot to death. The Interior Department maintained that the shooting was an accident, but many of the Poncas believed that Big Snake was murdered.

Within a few months of Judge Dundy's ruling, the Standing Bear case became famous in the press across the United States as an instance by which even the most cooperative of small Native nations could be grievously wronged by U.S. Indian policy. Everyone except the most obtuse Indian haters believed the Poncas had been wronged legally and morally. General Crook, whose name appears as respondent in the court case, was convinced that the Poncas should be able to go home. Even Secretary of the Interior Carl Schurz admitted in 1879 that "The Poncas were grievously wronged by . . . a mistake in making the Sioux treaty" (Armstrong, 1971, 119).

Campaign to Restore the Poncas' Homeland

Following the trial, the Poncas toured the East Coast with Tibbles and Susette LaFlesche, Tibbles's wife, in a campaign to pressure the federal government to restore the Poncas' homeland along the Niobrara. They took news clippings and had endorsements from prominent people, such as General Crook, the mayor of Omaha, and Nebraskan ministers. (In Boston, where support for Standing Bear's Poncas was strong, a citizens' committee formed that included Henry Wadsworth Longfellow.) They met Helen Hunt Jackson and the Poncas' story inflamed Jackson's conscience and changed her life. Heretofore known as a poet, Jackson set out to write *A Century of Dishonor,* a best-selling book that described the angst of an America debating the future of the Native American peoples who had survived the last of the Indian wars.

Senator Henry Dawes, who later would become known as the primary author of the Allotment Act, reportedly strongly supported the Poncas' cause. The Ponca chief White Eagle, who had lost his wife and four children to removal, who was dying of malaria contracted in the Indian Territory, came to Washington, D.C., and testified eloquently, after which the Congress restored the Poncas' homeland.

The *New York Times* joined the popular newspaper crusades for restoration of Ponca lands after the trial of Standing Bear in Judge Dundy's Omaha federal court. An editorial February 21, 1880, provided a short summary of the Poncas' troubles with their picturesque homeland along the Niobrara in northernmost Nebraska, beginning with the United States' blunder of ceding to the Sioux land already guaranteed them by a previous treaty. "To this robbery of the tribe was added the destruction of their houses, movable property, and farms," the *Times* editorialized. "A citizen of the United States would have redress in the courts for such outrage as this" (Hayes, 1997, 37–38). The Poncas had done their best to become farmers as the Great Father had instructed them, and they had been wronged at every turn.

The *Times* described Helen Hunt Jackson's advocacy of the Poncas' case along the East Coast as she took *A Century of Dishonor* to press. Jackson compared Judge Dundy's ruling to Abraham Lincoln's signing of the Emancipation Proclamation.

The *Times* was a consistent supporter of both Jackson and the Poncas, writing on one occasion that "In the history of the blunders and wrongs characterizing the so-called Indian policy of the United States (which is no policy), we find no darker page than that on which is recorded the wrongs of the Ponca Indians. . . . They ought to have their lands again at any cost to the Government under whose authority they have been so tyrannically despoiled" (Hayes, 1997, 221, 223).

Following all of this popular pressure, in 1890 Standing Bear and his people finally were allowed to return home to the Niobrara River after Congress investigated the conditions under which they had been evicted. Standing Bear's efforts produced a victory, but nearly his entire family died.

Further Reading

Armstrong, Virginia Irving. *I Have Spoken: American History through the Voices of the Indians*. Chicago: Swallow Press, 1971.

Dando-Collins, Stephen. *Standing Bear Is a Person: The True Story of a Native American's Quest for Justice*. New York: Da Capo Press, 2004.

Hayes, Robert G. *A Race at Bay:* New York Times *Editorials on the "Indian Problem."* Carbondale: Southern Illinois University Press, 1997.

Jackson, Helen Hunt. *A Century of Dishonor: A Sketch of the United States Government's Dealings with Some of the Indian Tribes.* [Boston: Roberts Bros., 1888]. St. Clair Shores, MI: Scholarly Press, 1972.

Massey, Rosemary, et al. *Footprints in Blood: Standing Bear's Struggle for Freedom and Human Dignity.* Omaha, NE: American Indian Center of Omaha, 1979.

Mathes, Valerie Sherer. "Helen Hunt Jackson and the Ponca Controversy." *Montana: The Magazine of Western History* 39, no. 1 (Winter 1989): 42–53.

Tibbles, Thomas Henry. *The Ponca Chiefs: An Account of the Trial of Standing Bear.* [1880]. Lincoln: University of Nebraska Press, 1972.

STUDI, WES
BORN 1947 CHEROKEE
ACTOR AND ACTIVIST

Full-blooded Cherokee actor Wes Studi (Wesley Studie), who has starred in several major motion pictures, spoke Cherokee until primary school, and today has taken an activist role in the revitalization of Native languages as a spokesperson for the Indigenous Language Institute in Santa Fe, New Mexico. He also teaches Cherokee. Studi has been characterized as "a soft-spoken, gentle man, easy to talk to, interesting and interested in the one to whom he is talking. His modesty belies the depth of his passion and abilities" (Kettler, 2004).

Early Life and Acting Career

Studi was born in Nofire Hollow, Oklahoma, between Stillwell and Tahlequah, December 17, 1947, the eldest of four sons of a ranch hand. He lived for most of his childhood in northeastern Oklahoma, attending Chilocco Indian School in northern Oklahoma through Grade 12, where a vocational teacher advised him to stick to low-paid menial work and ignore his aspirations for risky careers, such as acting. That advice haunted Studi for many years after he was drafted into the U.S. Army in 1967 and sent to Vietnam for 18 months during the war there with the 9th Infantry Division, mainly in the Mekong Delta.

Actor Wes Studi in Geronimo. *(Bureau L.A. Collection/Corbis)*

Studi returned from Vietnam horrified by the cruelty of the war and the callous treatment of veterans at home. He traveled rather aimlessly for a few years, until he used the GI Bill to enroll at Tulsa Junior College. Although Studi did not act professionally until much later, he took a role at Tulsa Junior College in the play *Royal Hunt of the Sun* with the American Indian Theater Company.

Soon after that, Studi was drawn to political activism in the American Indian Movement (AIM), taking part in the 1973 occupation of Wounded Knee, on the Pine Ridge Reservation in South Dakota. Later he attended Tahlequah University, worked with the Cherokee Nation, and worked as a reporter for *The Cherokee Advocate*.

After 1980, well into his third decade, Studi began acting professionally. Studi's ability to speak a Native language, ride a horse, and handle a rifle qualified him for historical roles. He took a role in the Nebraska PBS production *The Trial of Standing Bear,* which was broadcast in 1988.

Moving to Los Angeles, Studi acted first in minor parts for television. Soon thereafter, he began landing roles in Hollywood films. Studi has played strong Native American characters who are proud of their heritage, often with an edgy swagger. His first film role was in *Pow Wow Highway* (1989). He was the toughest Pawnee in *Dances with Wolves* (1990) and Magua in *Last of the Mohicans* (1992). Studi then starred in *Geronimo: An American Legend* (1993) and acted with Al Pacino and Robert De Niro in *Heat* (1995). He also played in *Crazy Horse* (1996) and *Deep Rising* (1998). In 1999, Studi was cast in *The Sphinx.* He played

Joe Leaphorn, a Navajo police officer, in PBS productions of Tony Hillerman's novels *Skinwalkers* (2002), *Coyote Waits* (2003), and *A Thief of Time* (2003). Studi played Opechancanough, a Powhatan uncle of Pocahontas, in Terrence Malick's film, *The New World* (2005).

A critic wrote that "Studi flourished in his new calling, finding frequent work with his expressive features and warm sense of humor" (Wes Studi, n.d.) Studi has won many awards for his acting. In 2000, he was named Artist of the Decade at the First Americans in the Arts Awards.

By 2009, Studi had appeared in more than 50 television shows and movies. One of the most recent was the five-part PBS historical series *We Shall Remain,* in which he played the 19th-century Cherokee leader Major Ridge in a top hat and tailored suit. "One thing I really appreciated was that there was no stick with feathers hanging off of it," he said of the role. "You know what you usually see, with eagles screaming in the distance?" The role, he said, "was therapeutic to myself as a Cherokee" (Lloyd, 2009, D-2).

Broader Life

After his first marriage failed, Studi married Rebecca Graves, a teacher, and they had two children, Daniel and Leah. He married a third time to Maura Dhu. They have had a child named Kholan and live in Santa Fe, New Mexico.

Studi has many talents in addition to acting. He is a horseback rider and trainer, author of two children's books, and a soapstone sculptor. He plays bass guitar in a six-person band, Firecat of Discord, with Dhu, who is lead singer. His brother plays rhythm guitar or drums. Firecat has played in Ryman Auditorium, the original home of the Grand Ole Opry in Nashville, Tennessee.

Studi's books for children are titled *The Adventures of Billy Bean* and *The Further Adventures of Billy Bean,* both written for the Cherokee Bilingual/Cross Cultural Education Center. The books were first drafted as short stories for Cherokee Nation periodicals, then adapted as books on request of the Cherokee bilingual program in which Studi was working at the time.

Studi talked about his legacy: "I would like to be remembered as a man who was capable of taking care of his family, and any more than that would be to have been effective in a positive way, not only for the younger generation, but even for my peers," Studi told a writer for *Oklahoma Woman/Oklahoma Man* magazine in 2004 "I would hope to have been a good man. I would hope to be remembered as a good man who maybe had his faults but was capable of overcoming some of them in order to live a productive life and leave some sort of legacy that is positive" (Kettler, 2005).

Further Reading

Banks, Wendy. "In Both His Prolific Acting Career and His Extraordinary Life, Wes Studi Has Proved to Be a Perceptive Student of Both Human History and Human Behavior." *Smithsonian American Indian Magazine,* Fall 2005. http://www.thestudigroup.com/bibliography.html.

Kettler, Jim. "A Man of Depth and Determination." *Oklahoma Woman/Oklahoma Man* [Magazine]. November 2004. http://www.thestudigroup.com/biojimkettler.html.

Lloyd, Janice. "Not Victims, Not Warriors." *USA Today,* April 13, 2009, D-1, D-2.

Studi, Wes. Biography, n.d. Accessed March 15, 2010. http://www.answers.com/topic/wes-studi.

Studie, Wesley. *The Adventures of Billy Bean.* Tahlequah, OK: Cherokee Bilingual/Cross Cultural Education Center, 1982.

Studie, Wesley. *More Adventures of Billy Bean (also known as The Further Adventures of Billy Bean).* Cherokee Bilingual/Cross Cultural Education Center, 1983.

T

THORPE, JIM
1888–1953 SAC AND FOX/POTAWATOMI AND CHIPPEWA ATHLETE

Born in a one-room log cabin near Prague, Oklahoma Territory, of Irish, French, Sac-Fox, and Potawatomi descent, James Frances Thorpe (*Wathohuck,* "The Bright Path") became an outstanding college and professional football player, and a gold medal Olympic athlete. Thorpe excelled at so many different sports that some sports historians have called him one of the greatest all-around athletes of any era.

Thorpe had a twin brother Charles, who died at age nine. They were the second and third children of six. The father, Hiram Thorpe, was Irish and Sac-Fox. His mother, who was one-quarter French and three-quarters Chippewa, was a granddaughter of the notable Sac-Fox leader, Black Hawk.

The family moved to a 160-acre farm during the Oklahoma land rush of 1889, an example of Native Americans competing with non-Indians for

Jim Thorpe is greeted by Mayor William Jay Gaynor (third from left) and other dignitaries in an Olympic ceremony in New York City, 1912. (Library of Congress)

255

land that had once been under Indian title. On the farm, Thorpe was known as a child who could not sit still. He quickly learned to ride horses, swim, and hunt. He attended the Sac-Fox reservation school, then at the Haskell Institute in Lawrence, Kansas, and finally the Carlisle Indian School in Pennsylvania. Hiram Thorpe was a large (6 feet and 230 pounds) and frequently violent man. After being beaten by his father at one point in his youth, Thorpe ran away to the Texas Panhandle and spent some time as a cowhand, breaking horses, mending fences, and doing other chores for room and board. Thorpe's mother died in 1900, when he was 13 years of age.

Carlisle School

Thorpe entered Carlisle with plans to become an electrician but learned to be a tailor instead. Carlisle also was Thorpe's gateway to sports, particularly football. Thorpe's abilities drew the attention of Carlisle's athletic coach, Glenn S. "Pop" Warner, who trained young Thorpe in track and football. Very quickly, Thorpe became a varsity player.

In the summer of 1909, Thorpe went to North Carolina to work on a farm under the Carlisle School's outing program that was meant to integrate Native American boys and girls into the working world of mainstream society. Thorpe also played baseball there, joining the Carolina League. He played professional baseball for Winston-Salem, Fayetteville, and Rocky Mount, during the 1910 and 1911 seasons, with no idea that this later might conflict with his future career as an Olympian. He had not even contemplated competing at Stockholm until Coach Warner suggested he try out the following fall.

Thorpe was an All-American college football player in 1911 and 1912, as Coach Warner turned Carlisle Indian School into a national football power. Thorpe's accomplishments on the gridiron were legendary. In one game, he scored 17 points in 17 minutes. His average kick-off return was 70 yards. In one game against Army, he ran 90 yards for a touchdown, and had the play annulled for a penalty. Very shortly after that, he ran 95 yards for another touchdown. Dwight D. Eisenhower, who much later would be elected president, was playing on the Army team against Thorpe. Later, Eisenhower said: "On the football field, there was no one like him in the world" (Coppock, 2007, 60). While at Carlisle, Thorpe won letters in 10 sports besides football: baseball, track, boxing, wrestling, lacrosse, gymnastics, swimming, hockey, handball, and basketball. He also was a prize-winning marksman and excelled at golf.

U.S. Olympic Team

Thorpe made the 1912 Olympic team and represented the United States well, winning both the decathlon (100-meter dash, running broad jump, shot put, running high jump, 400-meter race, discus throw, 110-meter high hurdles, pole vault, javelin throw, and 1,500-meter race) and the pentathlon (running broad jump, javelin throw, 200-meter race, discus, and 1,500-meter race), the first time one person won both events in a modern Olympic games. This was the apex of Thorpe's career as an athlete, and a summer around which the rest of his life would revolve. Thorpe placed first in four out of the five events in the pentathlon, an unusually strong performance. In the decathlon, Thorpe's score set a record that stood for 15 years. When King Gustav V of Sweden told Thorpe he was "the greatest athlete in the world," he replied, "Thanks, King" (D'O'Brian, 1992).

A year after his victories, the now-famous Thorpe's professional baseball activities came to light, causing a scandal. The fact that he had been paid was a violation of Thorpe's amateur standing, making him ineligible for the Olympics. The Amateur Athletic Union stripped Thorpe of his Olympic medals and his record was struck from the Olympic archive.

Life after the Olympics

In 1913, Thorpe married Iva Mille, the first of his three wives. They had three daughters and a son before divorcing in 1924. Thorpe played college football one more year at Carlisle, and was named to the All-American team. Thorpe then played professional baseball between 1913 and 1919 for the New York Giants, Cincinnati Reds, and Boston Braves, most often as a right fielder. New York Giants manager John McGraw once spit out a racial slur that caused Thorpe to bristle. Advancing on McGraw, Thorpe was ready to punch out the manager. The entire team was just sufficient to hold him down. In the 1920s, Thorpe began another professional sports career in football, with the Chicago Cardinals and other teams. In 1920, Thorpe helped organize the American Professional Football Association (which became the National Football League in 1922), and was its first president. At the same time, Thorpe played for football teams in Canton, Ohio, New York, and St. Petersburg, Florida. Thorpe recruited an all-Indian team (the Oorang Indians), and the team played two seasons. In 1921, the team won two games and lost six; in 1922, before the team was disbanded, the Oorang Indians won one game and lost 10.

Thorpe married Freeda Kirkpatrick in 1924. Thorpe left football in 1929, and he had two sons with Kirkpatrick. The family then moved to Hollywood, where Thorpe set out to sell the film rights to his life story. Metro-Goldwyn-Mayer (MGM) bought rights but did not produce anything. In 1932, Thorpe published a book, *Jim Thorpe's History of the Olympics* (1932) in time for the games in Los Angeles the same year.

He worked on construction jobs (earning only 30 cents an hour) and appeared in a few minor film roles. He played a supporting character in Errol Flynn's *The Green Light* (1937).

Returning to Oklahoma in 1937, Thorpe became active in tribal politics. In 1940, Thorpe took a national lecture tour on the importance of sports in American life and his career. Thorpe briefly served in the Merchant Marine during World War II.

Thorpe divorced a second time in 1949, then quickly married Patricia Gladys Askew. Also in 1949, Warner Brothers picked up rights to his life story from MGM, which led to *Jim Thorpe, All-American* (1951), starring Burt Lancaster.

In 1950, a poll of about 400 Associated Press sports writers named Thorpe the greatest athlete (and football player) in the first half of the 20th century, ahead of Babe Ruth, Ty Cobb, Red Grange, and Jack Dempsey, and others. Thorpe was inducted into the college and professional football halls of fame.

Thorpe died of a heart attack in Lomita, California, in 1953, as he was sitting down to dinner at home. The next year, two villages in Pennsylvania, Mauch Chunk and East Mauch Chunk, merged and named themselves after him, providing $10,000 for a public monument, after Oklahoma Gov. Johnston Murray refused to approve a legislative bill that would have provided $25,000 for a memorial. Eisenhower, then serving his first term as president, endorsed the memorial.

In 1982, the Jim Thorpe Foundation was established to work for restoration of his Olympic medals. Replicas of the medals were presented to Thorpe's family in 1983. A year later, Dennis Banks and other members of the American Indian Movement helped organize The Longest Run, during which Indian runners saluted Thorpe with a relay across North America. The run began at Onondaga, New York, and ended at the site of the 1984 Summer Olympics in Los Angeles, where the return of his medals was celebrated.

Further Reading

Coppock, Mike. "Jim Thorpe: NFL Star and Athlete Extraordinaire." *Native Peoples: Arts & Lifeways* 20, no. 6 (November/December 2007): 60–62.

D'O'Brian, Joseph. "The Greatest Athlete in the World." *American Heritage Magazine* 43, no. 4 (July/August 1992). http://www.americanheritage.com/articles/magazine/ah/1992/4/1992_4_93.shtml.

Thorpe, James, and Thomas F. Collinson. *Jim Thorpe's History of the Olympics*. Los Angeles: Wetzel Publishing Co., 1932.

Wheeler, Robert W. *Jim Thorpe: The World's Greatest Athlete*. Norman: University of Oklahoma Press, 1981.

TINKER, CLARENCE ("TINK")
1887–1942 OSAGE
ARMY AIR CORPS GENERAL

The mixed-blood Osage Clarence "Tink" Tinker, after whom Tinker Air Force Base in Oklahoma is named, was one of the pioneers of military aviation as a leader in the Army Air Corps during the 1920s and 1930s. He was the first U.S. military officer to die in combat during World War II in air operations in the Pacific. His wife, Madeline Tinker, played a role in choosing the official song of the U.S. Air Force, which is still sung today.

Tinker has been widely characterized as a daring aviator who played an important role in the strategic development of aviation for military purposes. Tinker was the first Native American to become a major general, with two stars in the U.S. Army. He was known as an "enlisted man's general," an outstanding leader and teacher.

Family Roots

Tinker's family was well known in Osage country. His father, George Edward Tinker, was born in 1868 at present-day St. Paul, Kansas, to George Edward Tinker and Genevieve "Jane" Revard Tinker. George, who was one-fourth Osage, served on the Osage Tribal Council from the Strike Axe District. He co-founded and edited *The Wah-shah-she News,* a weekly in Pawhuska. In 1909, Tinker co-founded

Major Clarence L. Tinker, right, and his aide, First Lieutenant J. C. Crosthwaite, February 14, 1934. (AP/Wide World Photos)

The Osage Magazine, later titled *The Oklahoma Magazine.* A major emphasis of Tinker's journalism was graft and corruption associated with the Osages' rich oil and gas holdings. He died October 31, 1947.

Clarence was born at Osage Mission November 21, 1887. His mother was Sarah Ann "Nan" Schwagerty. He grew up in Pawhuska, the main town on the Osage Nation of the Indian Territory, which later became Osage County, Oklahoma. Tinker went to Catholic schools in Hominy and Pawhuska, Oklahoma, as well as public school in Elgin, Kansas. He spent a short time at Haskell Institute at Lawrence, Kansas, but did not graduate. His high school studies were completed at the Wentworth Military Academy, Lexington, Missouri, in 1908. After graduation, Tinker was posted to the occupation forces in the Philippine Islands as a newly commissioned third lieutenant. He served in the Philippine Constabulary between 1908 and 1912, after which he received a commission as a second lieutenant in the U.S. Army Infantry.

In 1913, Tinker married Madeline Doyle, who had lived in Nova Scotia, and in Waikiki, Hawaii. Their son, Clarence L. Tinker, was born in Honolulu in 1916.

Tinker rose to the rank of captain by 1920, serving in Hawaii and along the U.S. border with Mexico, as well as in California. He was posted with the 25th Infantry Regiment, a unit of the "Buffalo Soldiers," a name applied by the Apaches to U.S. Army units that were mainly black because the Apaches thought their heads looked like buffalo. Officially, they were called "United States Colored Troops."

Military Career

Following World War I, Tinker was assigned to the Polytechnic High School in Riverside, California, as a professor of military studies and tactics. Here he began his career as a developer of military air power. About 1920, Tinker transferred to the Army Air Service and began flight training. Between 1922 and 1926, he commanded the 16th Observation Squadron and 7th Air Service Division at Ft. Riley, Kansas, one of the U.S. Army's first aviation units.

By 1926, Tinker, now a major, was assigned to the U.S. Embassy in London as an assistant military attaché for aviation, working with the British to apply aviation to the practice of war. In September 1926, Tinker and an assistant naval aviation attaché crashed while flying in Surrey, about 15 miles south of London. Their aircraft burst into flames. Tinker escaped and helped the attaché, although both suffered extensive burns.

Tinker was assigned as the first commander in 1930 of the 20th Pursuit Group at Mather Airfield in Sacramento, California. *Time* magazine of March 5, 1934, in an article entitled "Army's First Week," reported that Major Tinker was commanding the Western Zone from San Francisco. Tinker was quoted pondering the difficulties of military aviation:

> Commercial air pilots have from a year to a year and a half special training over the routes which they are to take before they are allowed to go alone. The large new land planes used by the commercial transports are fitted with many automatic control instruments for blind flying in darkness and fog which are not seen on planes used by the military units. Also, closed and warmed cockpits and cabins prevent pilots from having to expose themselves to dangerous temperatures. Army pilot training, on the other hand, is the direct opposite. There are no radio beams or lights to show him where the enemy is. . . . The army pilot is used to flying in formation, to bombing, to fighting ships in the air, to pursuit and attack. . . . If the weather is bad, there is no object in sending an army plane up. In war we must see our objective. ("General Clarence Tinker," 2007)

Later Career and Death at Sea

Tinker continued to develop military aviation through the 1930s, investigating bombing techniques at Muroc Dry Lake in 1936, along with other strategies. By 1940, he was stationed at Southeast Air Base, Tampa, Florida (later MacDill Air Force Base), commanding a garrison of 600 men with 15 aircraft.

In 1940, Tinker was promoted to brigadier general. In January 1942 he was assigned to command the Hawaiian Air Force following Japanese attacks on Pearl Harbor. Tinker was faced with defending the islands with aircraft and crews that had been devastated by the attacks during a buildup for war in the Pacific.

Tinker rallied his airmen to take an important part in the Battle of Midway in mid-1942, during which the United States' forces began to turn the tide in the war. The U.S. forces destroyed several Japanese aircraft carriers and battleships. The

Japanese lost 4,800 troops in the battle as they were driven from Midway. Tinker, who flew air missions during the battle, was unaccounted for at its conclusion. His compatriots hoped he would be found on the island when they reached it, but he was not and was declared dead June 9, 1942.

In 1939, Madeline Tinker and another Army Air Corps' general's wife were asked to pick a song for the corps. They chose a zippy one by Robert Crawford that began with the well-known words "Off we go, into the wild blue yonder" and named it "The Air Force Song." Madeline Tinker, who became known as the "Matron of MacDill" remarried after the war and died in 2000, at age 104. "The Air Force Song" was played quietly at her funeral. Clarence, Jr. ("Bud") also served in the Army Air Corps. He died in combat during World War II in Europe.

Further Reading

Crowder, James L. *Osage General: Major General Clarence L. Tinker.* Washington, DC: U.S. Government Printing Office, 1987.

"General Clarence Tinker, Hap Arnold's Daring Go-to Guy." *Talking Proud! A Magazine about Service and Sacrifice.* July 2, 2007. http://www.talkingproud.us/HistoryTinker-ClarenceA.html.

George E. Tinker: Biography. Sequoyah Research Center. American Native Press Archives. n.d. http://anpa.ualr.edu/digital_library/Osage_Sketch/osage_sketch_1.htm.

TOHE, LAURA
BORN 1952 DINÉ (NAVAJO)
POET AND SCHOLAR

The Diné (Navajo) poet and essayist Laura Tohe was born in Fort Defiance, Arizona, of the *Tsenabahilnii* (Sleepy Water People) and *Tódich'iinii* (Bitter Water) clans. Raised near the Chuska Mountains, along the Navajo Nation's eastern reaches, Tohe attended boarding schools and public schools in Albuquerque.

Tohe has written that her mother dropped out of high school, then ran away to the Grand Canyon in Arizona, meeting her father, who had just returned to the United States from World War II. They married and had several children. The marriage then

Navajo writer Laura Tohe. (Julaire Scott)

failed, after which "my mother gathered all us kids up, and we went to live near her mother, who was teaching on the Navajo reservation in Arizona" (Tohe, 2000, 103). By the early 1950s, Tohe's mother, along with four boys and one girl, were living in a Diné hogan with no electricity or plumbing. She supported the family with a job cooking at a Bureau of Indian Affairs boarding school.

Daily life was a struggle. Not only did the family live without modern conveniences, but Tohe's mother had to negotiate 30 miles of rutted, muddy (sometimes icy) roads to buy groceries. Female relatives sometimes provided financial aid. An aunt would "put on her old cowboy boots and saddle up her horse and drive in the cattle that we branded and vaccinated according to her instructions" (Tohe, 2000, 105).

Tohe earned a psychology BA at the University of New Mexico in 1975, followed by an MA (1985) and a PhD (1993) at the University of Nebraska, in English, on a Regents Fellowship. Her dissertation was titled: "No Parole Today. A Creative Dissertation of Poetry and Short Stories of the Indian School Experience."

Hired to teach in the Department of English at Arizona State University in 1994, she is cross-listed in women's studies and Native American studies. Tohe is conversant as a poet and as an academic who writes for several journals, such as *Calyx* and *Callaloo*. Her work has been set to modern dance by the Moving Company, at the University of Nebraska at Omaha.

Tohe has been a member of advisory boards for the Native American literary journal *Wicazo Sa Review* as well as the National Caucus Board of the Wordcraft Circle of Native Writers and Storytellers. Tohe was named Writer of the Year (1999) for poetry for her collection *No Parole Today* by the Wordcraft Circle of Native Writers. She wrote a children's play, *The Story of Me,* commissioned by Emmy Gifford Children's Theater, Omaha (1993). She also received the Faculty of the Year Award of the ASU College of Extended Education in 2000.

A Critique of Feminism

Tohe has been critical of Western feminist ideology that devalues a woman's role in the home in favor of career employment. In "There Is No Word for Feminism in My Language," she wrote that Navajo women can fill a traditional role in the home while also being strong and courageous. "In the Diné world," Tohe has written, "a young person grows up knowing that the women are quite capable of being in charge" (Tohe, 2000, 105).

> As long as I can remember, the Diné (or Navajo, as we are also referred to) women in my life have always shown courage, determination, strength, persistence, and endurance in their own special way. My female relatives lived their lives within the Diné matrilineal culture that valued, honored, and respected them. These women passed on to their daughters not only their strength, but the expectation to assume responsibility for the family, and therefore were expected to act as leaders for the family and the tribe.

> Despite five hundred years of Western patriarchal intrusion, this practice continues. . . . The Diné women continue to possess the qualities of leadership and strength and continue to endure and ultimately to pass on those qualities to their daughters, even though there is no word for feminism in the Diné language. (Tohe, 2000, 103, 104)

Tohe admires the qualities that this culture attributes to a good Diné woman: "generosity, wisdom, strength of character, and one who is respected by her community." She finds it natural to "show generosity, cheerfulness, and respect to my guests in the manner of Changing Woman. . . . My stories are not unusual within the Diné world because we know the strength of the women" (Tohe, 2000, 103–4, 110).

"Like my mother and other Indian women who grew up in a matrilineal culture, when we cross into the Western world, we see how that world values women differently," Tohe has written. "Young girls were forced to leave home and learn not only an alien culture but also a vocational skill that would supposedly enable them to make a living in the white man's world" (Tohe, 2000, 105).

In college, first encountering the concept of "feminism" in a women's studies class, Tohe struggled to reconcile the concept with her traditional beliefs. She found that feminist issues were defined overwhelmingly in a European American framework. The issues were different; most Native American families were struggling to survive, and unable to engage in an ideological dialogue. She quipped: "How could Indian women discourse in the feminist dialogue of the 1970s or participate in the symbolic act of burning their bras? Some probably owned only one bra and would not even consider burning it" (Tohe, 2000, 105).

Diné women draw strength from a matriarchal culture that defines its identity as female, through its origin story. Changing Woman, the major deity in the Diné worldview, provided their first clan structure and instructions on proper conduct of life. Women define and transmit culture, and the household is important, not an inferior gender role from which to escape. "Mother" is an important role bestowed after birth of the first child.

Further Reading

Erdrich, Heidi, and Laura Tohe, eds. *Sister Nations: Native American Women Writers on Community.* St. Paul: Minnesota Historical Society, 2002.

Harjo, Joy, and Gloria Bird, eds. *Reinventing the Enemy's Language: Contemporary Native Women's Writing of North America.* New York: W. W. Norton, 1997.

Tohe, Laura. *No Parole Today: Poetry and Stories.* Albuquerque, NM: West End Press, 1999.

Tohe, Laura. "There Is No Word for Feminism in My Language." *Wicazo Sa Review: A Journal of Native American Studies* 15, no. 2 (2000): 103–10. http://muse.jhu.edu/journals/wicazo_sa_review/v015/15.2tohe.html.

Tohe, Laura. *Tséyi': Deep in the Rock, Reflections on Canyon de Chelly,* with Stephen E. Strom (photographer). Tucson: University of Arizona Press, 2005.

Trafzer, Clifford E., ed. *Blue Dawn, Red Earth: New Native American Storytellers.* New York: Anchor Books, 1996.

Journalist Mark Trahant. (Courtesy Mark Trahant)

TRAHANT, MARK N. BORN 1957 NORTHERN SHOSHONE AND BANNOCK NEWSPAPER EDITOR AND COLUMNIST

Mark N. Trahant, who is Shoshone and Bannock, is a syndicated columnist and editor with a career in both Native American and mainstream newspapers. In 2003, he was appointed as editorial-page editor of the *Seattle Post-Intelligencer.*

Born August 13, 1957, Trahant studied at Pasadena (California) City College and Idaho State University. His career in journalism began as editor of the *Sho-Ban News,* the Shoshone and Bannock reservation newspaper, at Fort Hall, Idaho. Later Trahant edited *Navajo Times Today* and published *Navajo Nation Today,* when he lived with his wife's people in Window Rock, Arizona. Trahant entered mainstream journalism as a reporter at the *Arizona Republic,* in Phoenix. He was editor and publisher of the *Moscow-Pullman Daily News* in Idaho during 1997 and 1998. Trahant also worked as a columnist and executive editor at the *Salt Lake (City) Tribune* and as a columnist at the *Seattle Times.* Trahant resigned his job at the *Times* in 2000 during the Pacific Northwest Newspaper Guild's strike. "I wanted to keep my independence—I neither wanted to cross the picket line nor side with the union," Trahant said (McGann, 2003).

After holding several newspaper jobs, Trahant accepted a position as chief executive officer of the Robert C. Maynard Institute for Journalism Education, in Oakland, California. The institute focuses on training and promoting the careers of minority journalists. He also served on the board of trustees of the Freedom Forum, and has been president of the Native American Journalists Association (NAJA).

As editor of the *Post-Intelligencer*'s editorial pages, Trahant presided over the editorial board's meetings and manages editorial staff. His weekly Sunday column has been distributed nationally. Roger Oglesby, editor and publisher of the *Post-Intelligencer,* said that Trahant is "a good thinker, a talented writer and an experienced editor. He's also a good listener and pays attention to a wide variety of viewpoints" (McGann, 2003).

Trahant has authored a book, *Pictures of Our Nobler Selves* (1995), which describes the lives of Native Americans who work or have worked in mainstream journalism. He wrote the book while serving as a visiting professional scholar with the Freedom Forum First Amendment Center at Vanderbilt University. "The media has, for its own purposes, created a false image of the Native American. Too many of us have patterned ourselves after that image. It is time now that we project our own image and stop being what we never really were," Trahant has said. "Uncovering forgotten journalism history is the first purpose of this report. The second is to validate the notion that it is essential for American Indians and Alaskan Natives to work in the media, both tribal and mainstream" ("Pictures," n.d.).

The 52-page book begins with the invention of the Cherokee alphabet by Sequoyah, and its use in *The Cherokee Phoenix and Indian Advocate,* the first Native American newspaper, during the 1820s. Trahant then brings his history of Native American journalism to the present day, with personal stories such as Ora Eddleman Reed, a Cherokee and the first Native American talk show host in 1924, and Hattie Kauffman, the Nez Perce broadcaster who in 1989 became the first Native American news reporter on national television.

Trahant was a finalist for the 1989 Pulitzer Prize in national reporting while he worked at the *Arizona Republic* as co-author of a news series on federal government Indian policy. He was a Pulitzer Prize juror in 2004 and 2005. He won the best-columnist award from the Native American Journalists Association and the Society of Professional Journalists, and was co-winner of the Heywood Broun Award in 1987.

Trahant wrote a commissioned book, *The Whole Salmon,* published by Idaho's Sun Valley Center for the Arts. Trahant brought a personal perspective to his work on the Sun Valley Center's the Whole Salmon project because, as a boy, he fished in the Yankee Fork of the Salmon River with his family.

Trahant is married to LeNora Begay Trahant; they live on Bainbridge Island, near Seattle, with two boys, Marvin and Elias.

Further Reading

"Mark Trahant. Voices from the Past, Education for the Future: Fifth Annual Sequoyah Research Center Symposium. University of Arkansas at Little Rock: October 20–22, 2005." http://anpa.ualr.edu/symposia/2005_symposium/2005%20Speaker%20Biographies.htm#Trahant.

McGann, Chris. "P-I [*Seattle Post-Intelligencer*] Names Mark Trahant Editorial-page Editor; Pulitzer Finalist, Veteran Journalist Will Replace Retiring Joann Byrd." *Seattle Post-Intelligencer,* January 31, 2003. http://seattlepi.nwsource.com/local/106685_trahant31.shtml.

"Pictures of Our Nobler Selves." n.d. http://cherokeehistory.com/picture.html.

Trahant, Mark N. *Pictures of Our Nobler Selves: A History of Native American Contributions to News Media.* Nashville, TN: The Freedom Forum First Amendment Center, 1995.

TRUDELL, JOHN
BORN 1946 SANTEE SIOUX
POLITICAL ACTIVIST, POET, AND MUSICIAN

One of the founders and principal activists of the American Indian Movement (AIM), John Trudell by the early 21st century was well known nationally and internationally as a musician and a poet of uncommon political acuity. He was the subject of filmmaker Heather Rae's documentary film *John Trudell,* released in 2006. "He has one of the most engaging minds I have ever known," said Wilma Mankiller, former principal chief of the Oklahoma Cherokees (Trudell, 2008).

Trudell was born to a Santee Sioux father and Mexican Indian mother in Omaha, Nebraska, in 1946. Trudell's grandfather on his mother's side fought with Pancho Villa. Trudell spent much of his childhood on the Santee Sioux Reservation in northern Nebraska. He dropped out of high school shortly before he joined the U.S. Navy to escape oppressive surroundings. Trudell served two tours in or near Vietnam during the war, between 1965 and 1969. He met his first wife, Fenicia "Lou" Ordonez, while stationed in Long Beach, California.

By the late 1960s, Trudell became an early activist in AIM. He served as its national chairman between 1973 and 1979 and took part in the occupation of Alcatraz Island (1969–71), the Trail of Broken Treaties (1972), occupation of the Bureau of Indian Affairs Washington, D.C., headquarters in 1972, and confrontation at Wounded Knee (1973). Beginning in 1976, he coordinated AIM's work on behalf of AIM member Leonard Peltier. Between 1969 and 1979, the Federal Bureau of Investigation compiled a 17,000-page dossier on Trudell, finding him very intelligent and, therefore, very dangerous (Rae, 2006).

Trudell met his second wife, Tina, in 1971. She was an activist as well, well known for her high political profile regarding sovereignty issues on the Duck Lake Reservation in Nevada. In 1979, Tina, who was pregnant, was trapped and incinerated in a burning home with three children (ages one, three, and five) and Tina's mother. The Bureau of Indian Affairs issued a report asserting that the fire was caused by a faulty fireplace trap.

A private investigator hired by Trudell concluded that the trap had been plugged, making a fire from that source unlikely. Some witnesses said

Activist, poet, and performer John Trudell. (Christopher Felver/Corbis)

they saw a line of fire on the roof of the house that may have resulted from a firebomb. Speculation was widespread that the house had been set aflame in retribution for the Trudells' political activities. John said that any assumption that the fire was set solely to get back at him "minimizes who she [Tina] was" (Rae, 2006). The fire had occurred within hours after Trudell burned a U.S. flag on the steps of the FBI headquarters in Washington, D.C., to protest treatment of Peltier.

Six months after the fire, Trudell began to write poetry to cope with his grief—"a gift," he said, from Tina (Rae, 2006). He also became active in the antinuclear movement as well as other environmental issues after many Navajo uranium miners died of radiation-induced lung cancer. For indigenous peoples, he said, dying from uranium poisoning or alcoholism was just as effective a form of genocide as the use of bullets by an invading army.

Trudell is known as a trenchant critic of the established order. He is fond of telling people: "Don't trust anyone who isn't angry." "We cannot change the economic system until the people control the land," he said during Rae's film. "Civilization is not civilizing—it is brutalizing. Is it God's will to rape the land?" The words that lead Trudell's home page on the Internet are "I'm just a human being trying to make it in a world that is very rapidly losing its understanding of being human." Indian treaties, said Trudell, "are agreements between your ancestors and my ancestors [and] the supreme law of the land. If you do not obey the treaties, you have no spiritual connection to the land" (Rae, 2006).

Trudell continued to be active in AIM throughout his life and was one of the key organizers of a protest march that forced the cancellation of Denver's Columbus Day Parade in 1992, the 500th anniversary of Columbus' first voyage to the Americas.

Asked whether Native Americans should observe Columbus Day, he paused, then said that would be "like asking the American people to observe Osama bin Laden Day. Columbus was a terrorist to us" (Rae, 2006).

In 1982, Trudell began recording poetry with traditional Native music. In 1983, his debut album *Tribal Voice* was released on his Peace Company label. Trudell joined with Kiowa guitarist Jesse Ed Davis to record three albums during the 1980s: the first, *AKA Graffiti Man* (1986), was called the best album of that year by Bob Dylan. The music on *AKA Graffiti Man* mixes the spoken word, rock-and-roll, and Northern Plains musical traditions. Trudell's CD *Bone Days* (2002) was produced by actress Angelina Jolie on Daemon Records, at a time when he led a band called Bad Dogs. *Madness & The Moremes* (2007) encapsulated his music career. By 2007 he had produced about a dozen recordings and three books of poetry.

Trudell also has played notable roles in several motion pictures. He appeared in the documentary film *Incident at Oglala* (1992) and performed the role of Jimmy Looks Twice in the feature film *Thunderheart* (1992) Both films examine the incidents surrounding the trial of Peltier. He played a role in *Smoke Signals* (1998), which is based on a Sherman Alexie novel. In another role, Trudell played Coyote in Hallmark's made-for-television movie *Dreamkeeper* (2003).

Further Reading

Igliori, Paola. *Stickman: John Trudell*. New York: Inanout Press, 1994.

John Trudell Home Page. n.d. http://www.johntrudell.com/bio.html.

Rae, Heather, director. *Trudell*. (DVD) 2005.

Trudell, John. *This Ain't El Salvador*. West Chester, PA: Learning Alliance, 1996.

Trudell, John. *Lines from a Mined Mind: The Words of John Trudell*. Golden, CO: Fulcrum, 2008.

W

WARRIOR, CLYDE
1939–1968 PONCA
CIVIL-RIGHTS ACTIVIST

An important thinker, fiery orator, and activist in the Red Power movement, Clyde Merton Warrior blazed an intellectual trail through Indian Country in the 1960s before his sudden death of liver failure at the age of 28 brought on by acute alcoholism that he could not escape. He was, according to a friend, full of "thunder and lightning and tears" (Cobb, n.d.). Warrior has been compared with Malcolm X, as a powerful leader who died at a very young age.

Early Life

Warrior was born to Gloria Collins in Ponca City, Oklahoma, August 31, 1939, and grew up with Ponca traditions taught him by his grandparents Bill and Metha Collins. As a boy, he became known for his ability and agility to memorize and perform Ponca dances and music; by age 15, he was a well-known fancy dancer.

He attended the Chicago Conference in 1961, a workshop involving about 600 Native American leaders from across the United States, representing 67 tribes and nations that afterward was credited with incubating much of the activism that sparked the self-determination movement of the 1960s and 1970s. Attendees at the conference drew up a "Declaration of Indian Purpose" that they sent to President John F. Kennedy.

A year after the Chicago Conference, Warrior was elected as president of the Southwest Regional Indian Youth Council at Cameron Junior College, Lawton, Oklahoma. In 1962, he was named the group's outstanding student. Working at Cameron, the University of Oklahoma, and at Northeastern State College, Tahlequah, Oklahoma, in 1966, he earned a bachelor's degree in education.

Warrior was a prime motivator among young activists who were disappointed that older leaders were not moving quickly enough. He minced no words. "It was sickening to see American Indians get up and just tell obvious lies about how well the federal government was treating them, what fantastic and magnificent things the federal government was doing for us," he later recalled (Cobb, n.d.).

A Key Leader of the National Indian Youth Council

In August 1961, Warrior and several other young activists founded the National Indian Youth Council (NIYC) in Gallup, New Mexico, with the expressed purpose of attaining a better future for Native people. The NIYC's program formed a basis for decades of development of sovereignty, what years later came to be called "nation-building." He repeatedly asked Indian audiences: "How long will you tolerate this?"

Between 1962 and his death, Warrior was a key leader of NIYC. He worked with the Denver Commission on Human Relations, where he was co-editor of *Indian Voices,* the commission's journal. He advised the National Congress of American Indians and worked with the Rev. Martin Luther King, Jr.'s Poor People's Campaign, including the 1963 march on Washington during which King gave his "I Have a Dream" speech. Warrior also presented provocative speeches at the University of South Dakota and Oberlin College, among other colleges and universities. Warrior married Della Hopper, an Oto, in 1965. They had two daughters.

Warrior became known as a speaker who gave voice to a sense of anger that others shared but dared not express. A remembrance of him by the Ponca Nation outlined the sharp edge of his rhetoric:

> In essays such as "Don't Take 'No' for an Answer," "Which One Are You?," "Time for Indian Action," "How Should an Indian Act?," and "Poverty, Community, Power," he talked about taking pride in Indianness, demanded respect for traditions, and condemned the dominant society for dehumanizing and alienating tribal people. He threw his support behind the fish-ins in the Pacific Northwest, testified before Congress, cajoled the Commissioner of Indian Affairs, criticized established tribal leaders, and protested outside the White House. In word and deed and spirit, Clyde Warrior inspired the nationalist movement that would be known as Red Power. (Cobb, n.d.)

His Speeches Spared No One

Warrior's speeches spared no one, with their "vitriolic denunciations of the Bureau of Indian Affairs, middle-class American culture, and those Indians he variously labeled 'slobs,' 'jokers,' 'redskin white-nosers,' 'ultra-pseudo-Indians,' and 'Uncle Tomahawks'" (Cobb, 2003). He railed at a system that he called "a horrendous combination of colonialism, segregation, and discrimination" but never gave up hope that he and other activists could change it for the better (Cobb, 2003). He spoke of an imminent Indian rebellion that would make the Watts riots in Los Angeles look "like a Sunday School picnic" (Cobb, 2003).

Just as his career was reaching an early stage of maturity, Warrior died suddenly in Enid, Oklahoma, of cirrhosis of the liver in 1968. A friend, Mel Thom, a Walker River Paiute, said of him: "Our leader is gone, but the spirit of such a leader is never gone. We can still hear him teasing, laughing, cussing, singing, and talking as few men could. We will always hear him. His words made Indian people feel good. . . . In his short life he brought us a long way ahead in our struggle for human equality" (Cobb, n.d.).

Further Reading

Cobb, Daniel. "Clyde Merton Warrior (1939–1968)." Ponca Nation. n.d. http://www.ponca.com/warrior_memorial/warrior_memorial.html.

Cobb, Daniel M. "QUESTION: To What Extent Do Scholars Have a Responsibility to the Indigenous Communities They Study and How Can They Fulfill This Responsibility? Telling Stories." HNet: Humanities and Social Sciences On-line. April 16, 2003. http://h-net.msu.edu/cgi-bin/logbrowse.pl?trx=vx&list=H-AmIndian&month=0304&week=c&msg=HCsIvR1zFFV/%2BqdO3DWGLA&user=&pw=.

Cornell, Stephen E. *The Return of the Native: American Indian Political Resurgence*. New York: Oxford University Press, 1988.

Smith, Paul Chaat, and Robert Allen Warrior. *Like a Hurricane: The Indian Movement from Alcatraz to Wounded Knee*. New York: New Press, 1996.

Warrior, Clyde. 1964b. "On Current Indian Affairs." *Americans before Columbus* 2, no. 2 (May 1964): 2.

Warrior, Clyde. "Which One Are You? The Five Types of Young Indians." In *The New Indians,* edited by Stan Steiner. New York: Harper & Row, 1968.

Warrior, Clyde. "We Are Not Free." In *Red Power: The American Indians' Fight for Freedom*. 2nd ed., edited by Alvin M. Josephy, Jr., Joane Nagel, and Troy Johnson, 16–21. Lincoln: University of Nebraska Press, 1999.

Wilkinson, Charles F. *Blood Struggle: The Rise of Modern Indian Nations*. New York: W. W. Norton, 2005.

WATT-CLOUTIER, SHEILA
BORN 1953 INUIT
POLITICAL ACTIVIST AND ENVIRONMENTALIST

As international chair of the Inuit Circumpolar Conference (ICC) from 2002 to 2006, Sheila Watt-Cloutier brought Inuit struggles against persistent organic pollutants and global warming to the world. As president of the ICC in Canada and vice-president of the ICC before 2002, Watt-Cloutier was a key figure in negotiating the 2001 Stockholm Convention, which banned PCBs, dioxins, and other synthetic pollutants from lower latitudes that have been threatening the lives of

Canadian Inuit leader Sheila Watt-Cloutier accepts the 2005 Sophie environment prize in Oslo, Norway, on June 15, 2005, for drawing attention to the impact of climate change and pollution on the traditional lifestyles of the Arctic's indigenous people and others. (AP/Wide World Photos)

all living things in the Arctic, including her people. Forms of dioxin and PCBs had become so prevalent in the Arctic that they biomagnified up the food chain to a point where Inuit mothers could not breast-feed their babies without endangering their health.

Watt-Cloutier became well known around the world as an adroit diplomat and charismatic speaker. Sometimes, she brought diplomats to tears as she described the effects of polychlorinated biphenyls (POPs) and global warming on Inuit peoples. She also extended cooperation among Inuit around the Arctic, from Canada, to Greenland, Alaska, and Russia.

Formed in 1977, the ICC represents the common interests of roughly 155,000 Inuits in northern Canada, Greenland, Alaska, and Russia. As head of the ICC, Watt-Cloutier ranged the world on jets trying to protect her people, many of whom are only one generation off the land, from the effluvia of the industrialized world—to, as she told a world conference on climate change in Milan, Italy, in 2003, "bring a human face to these proceedings." She travels the world injecting "life," as she phrases it, into international negotiations with the delicacy of a diplomat and the verve of a social activist (Watt-Cloutier, 2003).

Watt-Cloutier's life illustrates how the Inuit struggle to retain some of their tradition as their icy climate is rapidly melting and negatively affected by pollution. She watches global warming manipulate the seasons from her home overlooking Frobisher Bay in Iqaluit (pronounced "Eehalooeet," meaning "Fishing Place"), capital of the semisovereign Canadian Inuit province of Nunavut ("Our Home"), on Baffin Island. Nunavut is four times the size of France with approximately 25,000 inhabitants, 85 percent of whom are Inuit.

Watt-Cloutier also has been active in promoting sustainable development, retention of traditional ecological knowledge, and other forms of education. In 2007, she was nominated for the Nobel Peace Prize for her ability to extend what were largely defined as environmental issues to threats to Inuit culture, health, and traditional way of life. She played a leading role in suing the United States for negligence regarding global warming in international legal tribunals, including the Organization of American States.

Early Life

Watt-Cloutier was born in Kuujjuaq, northern Quebec, December 2, 1953, daughter of Daisy Watt (1921–2002), who was a well-regarded Native elder, as well as a musician, interpreter, and healer. Charlie Watt, a brother of Sheila's, served in the Canadian federal Senate during the 1980s. After a youth of being raised traditionally, often traveling by dog sled, Watt-Cloutier was taken from her home to attend boarding schools from age 10 in Churchill, Manitoba, and Nova Scotia. She attended Montreal's McGill University during the mid-1970s, specializing in education, human development, and counseling. She also displayed her mother's gift for interpretation in Inuktitut at Ungava Hospital, the beginnings of a 15-year career in Inuit health care.

In 1992, Watt-Cloutier critiqued northern Quebec's educational system in a report, *Siatunirmut—The Pathway to Wisdom,* for the Nunavik Educational Task Force. She worked in land claims negotiations that led, in part, to the establishment of Nunavut as a semisovereign Inuit province of Canada. Her new career as an Inuit political leader and environmental advocate began during 1995 after she was elected to chair Canada's division of the ICC, to which she was re-elected in 1998. She also contributed to academic and ecological studies on the Arctic.

The Toll of POPs

The toxicological and climatic due bills for modern industry at the lower latitudes are being left on the Inuits' table in Nunavut. Native people whose diets consist largely of sea animals (whales, polar bears, fish, and seals) have been consuming a concentrated toxic chemical cocktail. Abnormally high levels of dioxins and other industrial chemicals are being detected in Inuit mothers' breast milk.

"As we put our babies to our breasts we are feeding them a noxious, toxic cocktail," said Watt-Cloutier. "When women have to think twice about breast-feeding their babies, surely that must be a wake-up call to the world" (Johansen, 2000, 27).

To a tourist with no interest in environmental toxicology, the Inuits' Arctic homeland may seem as pristine as ever during its long, snow-swept winters. Many Inuits still guide sleds onto the pack ice surrounding their Arctic-island homelands to hunt polar bears and seals. Such a scene may seem pristine, until one realizes that the polar bears' and seals' body fats are laced with dioxins and PCBs. Geographically, the Arctic could not be in a worse position for toxic pollution, as a ring of industry in Russia, Europe, and North America pours pollutants northward on prevailing winds. The Arctic ecosystems and Native peoples are particularly vulnerable because POPs biomagnify—that is, they increase in potency by several orders of magnitude—with each step up the food chain.

"Imagine for a moment," said Watt-Cloutier, "the shock of the Inuit as they discovered that what has nourished them for generations, physically and spiritually, is now poisoning them. Some Inuit now question whether they should eat locally gathered food; others ask whether it is safe to breast-feed their infants. What sort of public outcry and government action would there be if the same levels of POPs found among Inuit were found in women in Toronto, Montreal, or Vancouver as a result of eating poultry or beef?" (Watt-Cloutier and Fenge, 2000).

Persistent organic pollutants may cause cancer, birth defects, reproductive and immune-system problems, and neurological damage to both adults and children. They also are endocrine disrupters, provoking deformities in sex organs and failure of reproductive systems.

"At times," said Watt-Cloutier, "we feel like an endangered species. Our resilience and Inuit spirit and of course the wisdom of this great land that we work so hard to protect gives us back the energy to keep going" (Watt-Cloutier, 2001).

The Inuits Confront Climate Change

In addition to some of the planet's highest levels of toxicity, the Inuits have been forced to confront some of Earth's most rapid rises in temperatures. Climate change arrived swiftly and dramatically in the Arctic during the 1990s, including such surprises as warm summer days, winter freezing rain, thunderstorms at least once even in winter, and invasions of Inuit villages by heretofore unseen insects and birds. Yellow-jacket wasps have been sighted for the first time on northern Baffin Island.

The ICC developed a human-rights case against the United States (specifically the George W. Bush administration) because global warming has been threatening the Inuit way of life. The ICC has invited the Washington-based Inter-American Commission on Human Rights to visit the Arctic to witness the human effects of rapid warming. Introducing the legal action, Watt-Cloutier said: "We want to show that we are not powerless victims. These are drastic times for our people and require drastic measures" (Brown, 2003, 14). The Inuits say that by rejecting the Kyoto Protocol and refusing to cut carbon dioxide emissions in the United States, which make up 25 percent of the world total, the White House imperils their way of life (Brown, 2003). A hearing was held on the ICC petition in March of 2007. While the OAS provided a forum, it did not issue a ruling.

Addressing a U.S. Senate Commerce Committee hearing on global warming in 2004, Watt-Cloutier described the disorienting effect of rapid change on the Inuit: "The Earth is literally melting. If we can reverse the emissions of greenhouse gases in time to save the Arctic, then we can spare untold suffering." She continued: "Protect the Arctic and you will save the planet. Use us as your early-warning system. Use the Inuit story as a vehicle to reconnect us all so that we can understand the people and the planet are one" (Pegg, 2004). The Inuits' connection to their culture through hunting, which has continued for many centuries, may disappear by the time Watt-Cloutier's grandson is her age. Watt-Cloutier said, "My Arctic homeland is now the health barometer for the planet" (Pegg, 2004).

The Arctic climate is changing quickly. In February of 2006, Watt-Cloutier described a heretofore unheard-of event in Iqaluit in that month: rain, lightning, thunder, and mud. The temperature had risen to 6 to 8 degrees C, average for June, winds had reached 55 miles an hour, and the town was paralyzed in a sea of dirty slush. "Much of the snow has melted on the back of my house and all the roads are already slushy and messy. All planes coming up from the south were cancelled because the runways were icy from the rain," she wrote. "Unfortunately the predictions of the Arctic Climate Impact Assessment are unfolding before my very eyes" (Watt-Cloutier, 2006). Iqaluit hunters expressed concern for the caribou, which would go hungry once freezing temperatures returned and encased the lichen, their food source, in a crust of ice. Instead of waiting until spring, the usual hunting season, Inuits were taking caribou in early March, believing that they would be too skinny later to be useful as food.

"Snow Age" to "Space Age"

"We have," Watt-Cloutier remarked on one occasion, "gone from the 'snow age' to the 'space age' in one generation. I was born on the land in Nunavik, northern Quebec and we were still traveling by dog team when I was sent to school in southern Canada at the age of ten. Notwithstanding significant economic, and social changes Inuit remain connected with the land and in tune with its rhythms and cycles" (Watt-Cloutier, 2004). "Inuit live in two worlds—the traditional and the modern," she said. "To this day our hunting based culture remains viable and important. We depend on seals, whale, walrus and other marine mammals to sustain our nutritional, cultural and spiritual well being" (Watt-Cloutier, 2004).

By 2007, Watt-Cloutier had two grown children and a grandson. Displaying her grandmother's musical talents, Watt-Cloutier's daughter is a traditional Inuit throat-singer and dancer; her son is a pilot who became the youngest pilot hired by Inuit Air.

Further Reading

Brown, Paul. "Inuit Blame Bush for Impending Extinction." *Guardian,* December 13, 2003. http://www.smh.com.au/articles/2003/12/12/1071125653832.html.

Cone, Marla. "Dozens of Words for Snow, None for Pollution." *Mother Jones,* January–February 2004. http://www.hartford-hwp.com/archives/27b/059.html.

Cone, Marla. *Silent Snow: The Slow Poisoning of the Arctic.* New York: Grove Press, 2005.

Downie, David Leonard, and Terry Fenge, eds. *Northern Lights against POPs: Combatting Toxic Threats in the Arctic.* Montreal and Kingston: McGill-Queen's University Press, 2003.

Johansen, Bruce E. "Pristine No More: The Arctic, Where Mother's Milk Is Toxic." *The Progressive,* December 2000, 27–29.

Johansen, Bruce E. "Arctic Heat Wave." *The Progressive,* October 2001, 18–20.

Pegg, J. R. "The Earth Is Melting, Arctic Native Leader Warns." *Environmental News Service,* September 16, 2004. http://www.sustainablebusiness.com/index.cfm/go/news.display/id/4514.

Watt-Cloutier, Sheila. "Honouring Our Past, Creating Our Future: Education in Northern and Remote Communities." In *Aboriginal Education: Fulfilling the Promise,* edited by Lynne Davis, Louise Lahache, and Marlene Castellano, 14–128. Vancouver: University of British Columbia Press, 2000.

Watt-Cloutier, Sheila. Personal communication, March 28, 2001.

Watt-Cloutier, Sheila. "Speech Notes for Sheila Watt-Cloutier, Chair, Inuit Circumpolar Conference. Conference of Parties to the United Nations Framework Convention on Climate Change." Milan, Italy, December 10, 2003. http://www.inuitcircumpolar.com/index.php?ID=242&Lang=En.

Watt-Cloutier, Sheila. "Canada and Inuit: Addressing Global Environmental Challenges, Remarks by Sheila Watt-Cloutier, Chair, Inuit Circumpolar Conference at the Inaugural Environmental Protection Service Inuit Speaker Series." Ottawa, Ontario, January 16, 2004. http://www.inuitcircumpolar.com/index.php?ID=250&Lang=En.

Watt-Cloutier, Sheila. Personal communication, February 27, 2006.

Watt-Cloutier, Sheila, and Terry Fenge. "Poisoned by Progress: Will Next Week's Negotiations in Bonn Succeed in Banning the Chemicals That Inuit Are Eating?" Press Release, Inuit Circumpolar Conference, March 14, 2000. http://www.inuitcircumpolar.com/index.php?ID=250&Lang=En.

WELCH, JAMES
1940–2003 BLACKFEET/GROS VENTRE
NOVELIST AND POET

James Welch was one of the most prominent American Indian writers of the 20th century, an award-winning and internationally recognized novelist and poet. Welch wrote poetry in 1966 and published his first poem in 1967 before the Native American Renaissance was established as a movement. Welch's first book of poetry, *Riding the Earthboy 40* (1971), is one of the first poetry collections written by a Native American on indigenous subjects. In 1975, Welch won a Pacific Northwest Booksellers Award for a revised edition of his book of poems (McFarland, 2000). In 1974, Welch published his first novel, *Winter in the Blood,* which was called "an influential classic in the birth of contemporary native writing" (Caldwell, 1999, 85) and was later reprinted in an issue of *American Indian Quarterly* with several critical essays dedicated to it. Welch published four more novels: *The Death of Jim Looney* (1979), *Fools Crow* (1986), *The Indian Lawyer* (1990), *The Heartsong of Charging Elk* (2000); he also co-wrote a PBS documentary called *Last Stand at Little Bighorn* (1992); and published a nonfiction account of the battle at Little Bighorn called *Killing Custer: The Battle of Little Bighorn and the Fate of the Plains Indians* (1994), which tells the story of the famous battle through the perspective of Plains Indians. *Fools Crow* is widely recognized as Welch's best work and received far-reaching critical recognition including the *Los Angeles Times* Book Award, a Pacific Northwest Booksellers Award, and an American Book Award.

In addition to numerous awards and acclaim from North America, Welch was honored in Europe. France awarded Welch with a medal of the Chevalier de l'Ordre des Arts et des Lettres and full knighthood in 2000. Despite his literary successes, Welch often expressed his reluctance at being recognized as a Native

American spokesperson: "[I] would always say I was a writer who happened to be Indian, and who happened to write about Indians. I think ethnic and regional labels are insulting to writers and really put restrictions on them. People don't think your work is quite as universal" (Lee, 1994). Although Welch identified himself principally as a writer, he believed in the importance of debunking misconceptions about American Indians: "I do hope to point out . . . the differences in cultures, the clashes that can result from those differences and how a person or a group of tribal people have to struggle to maintain their individual and tribal identities in mainstream culture. Although I consider myself a storyteller first and foremost, I hope my books will help educate people who don't understand how or why Indian people feel lost in America" (Selden, 2003).

Growing Up on the Northern Plains

Welch was born in Browning, Montana, on November 18, 1940. As a young boy, he was schooled on the Blackfeet and Fort Belknap reservations. Welch remembered Browning as a great place to grow up though researchers have commented on the poverty in the area. Welch's parents were Catholic and Welch was raised in the Catholic faith, but as an adult identified himself as agnostic. "I do believe in the viability of spiritualism," he said (Lee, 1994).

Welch described his father, who was of Blackfeet heritage, as a Renaissance man: "He could weld . . . he ran a TB sanitarium up in Alaska, and he's worked as an administrator of hospitals. When he retired a couple of years ago he was ranching and farming" (McFarland, 2000, 1). Both of Welch's grandfathers were Irish. Welch's great-grandfather, Malcolm Clark, was an immigrant who married a Blackfeet woman. Malcolm was killed by Piegan Blackfeet warriors, an act that helped ignite the Marias River Massacre in 1870; 100 Indians were killed in the massacre. Welch's great-grandmother survived the attack and Welch drew on the incident and his great-grandmother's experiences to create *Fools Crow*.

Commenting on the massacre site, Welch said: "Here, during a smallpox winter, 173 people of the peace chief Heavy Runner's band, mostly women, children, and old ones (as the men were off hunting) were murdered by the United States Army. My great-grandmother was wounded but managed to escape, along with some other women and children. Now the site is forgotten, not even a marker to commemorate the Blackfeet dead" (Welch, 1995, xii). Welch's mother, Rosella O'Bryan, was a Gros Ventre who was raised on the Fort Belknap Reservation, home of the Gros Ventre and Assiniboine. She studied to be a secretary at the Haskell Institute in Kansas and then used her skills as a stenographer on reservations and in other Indian communities.

Welch's family moved to Minneapolis when he was a teenager. He graduated from Washburn High School in 1958, then briefly studied at the University of Minnesota before he returned to Montana. After taking a few classes at Northern Montana State University in Havre, Welch transferred and earned a BA from the University of Montana at Missoula in 1965. During this time, Welch also worked as a firefighter and an Upward Bound counselor. He began a master's of fine arts in the Writing Seminar at the University of Montana but never completed it.

In 1968, Welch married Lois Monk, a professor of comparative literature at the University of Montana. The two lived in a farmhouse outside of Missoula in Rattlesnake Creek. Welch died of a heart attack at the age of 62 in Missoula, on August 4, 2003, after a 10-month battle with lung cancer.

Representing Reservation Life

At the University of Montana, Welch met and was heavily influenced by poet Richard Hugo, who famously told Welch to write about what he knew. Welch talked about his Indian heritage and Hugo responded, "Go ahead, write about the reservation, the landscape, the people" (Moore, 1999). Until this point, Welch had been writing about "majestic mountains and wheeling gulls" (Wetzel, 2006, 44). Hugo became a mentor, an inspiration, and a friend to Welch. Early in his writing life, Welch was influenced by Euro-American writers, notably novelists Ernest Hemingway and John Steinbeck, and poets John Keats, William Shakespeare, and Italian writer Elio Vittorini. Welch said his early work often lacked Native American influences because very few American Indians were writing at the time.

Native American scholars and writers have praised Welch's writing, observing that it accurately represents reservation life. *Winter in the Blood* follows the struggles of its nameless protagonist who only finds a sense of self after uncovering the names and heritage of his ancestors. *The Death of Jim Looney* initially surprised critics with its dysfunctional, alcoholic, mixed-breed protagonist, Jim Looney, "who ponders his life and fate consciously" (Shanley, 2006, 9). One critic called it a "novel of emptiness or despair" but later, it became "increasingly admired by those who teach Native American literature" (McFarland, 2000, 4). *Fools Crow* follows a young Blackfeet Indian, White Man's Dog, as he and his tribe, the Lone Eaters, must decide to either assimilate to the growing presence of the white man ("Napikwans") or rebel against them.

Sylvester Yellow Calf, the protagonist of *The Indian Lawyer,* is a Stanford Law School graduate and a partner in a Helena law firm. Yellow Calf becomes personally involved with a prisoner through the Montana state parole board he serves on and eventually recommits to Indian people. The creation of his character may have been a result of criticism that Welch had not created "contemporary [Indian] role models in his books" (Lee, 1994). *The Heartsong of Charging Elk* describes Charging Elk's journey to France with Buffalo Bill's Wild West Show. Charging Elk is left behind in France after he falls ill and finds himself dreaming of the American plains and the Indian people he loved.

Welch's poetry and prose are considered by many as refreshingly unsentimental and honest, yet others, many of them non-Native readers, have called Welch's work depressing and bleak. In 2001 at the annual National Council of Teachers of English convention in Baltimore, Welch stated, "Happy characters are not interesting. Readers prefer characters with problems, problems that are unresolved or go unresolved. The psychological depth of such characters creates interest for the reader. . . . There are good Indians and bad Indians; there are good and bad white people" (Charles, 2004, 64). In response to questions about his representation of the Blackfeet in *Fools Crow,* Welch said, "That's really the idea I wanted to get across, the idea that historical Indians were human beings. They weren't clichés" (Moore, 1999).

Other critics have commented that Welch did not write with a "socioeconomic, political, or cultural agenda" and that this made his writing welcoming to a universal readership (McFarland, 2000, 11). Well-known Spokane/Coeur d'Alene American Indian writer Sherman Alexie, who calls *Riding the Earthboy 40* "one of my true holy bibles," said this of Welch's writing: "He gives us all a look at a tragic time in American history, a sharper examination of what those tragedies have taught us and what we have all failed to learn. Above all, Welch confirms and mourns the fact that the war between Indians and whites has never ended" (Caldwell, 1999, 86; Round, 2006, 82).

Welch remained characteristically modest throughout his career: "I'm just in my little house in Missoula, Montana, writing about Indians" (McFarland, 2000, 8). Yet Welch also acknowledged the importance of his work: "Indian writers might come from different eras, from different geographies, from different tribes, but we all have one thing in common: We are storytellers from a long way back. And we will be heard for generations to come" (Welch, 1997, 8).

Jody Lynn Keisner

Further Reading

Caldwell, E. K. *Dreaming the Dawn: Conversations with Native Artists and Activists.* Lincoln: University of Nebraska Press, 1999.

Charles, Jim. "'A World Full of Bones and Wind': Teaching Works by James Welch." *The English Journal* 93, no. 4 (March 2004): 64–69.

"James Welch, 1940–2003." *Native American Authors Project.* n.d. http://www.ipl.org/div/natam/bin/browse.pl/A7.

Lee, Don. "About James Welch: A Profile." *Ploughshares* (Spring 1994). http://www.pshares.org/issues/articlePrint.cfm?prmArticleID=3676.

Lupton, Mary Jane. "Interview with James Welch." [November 17, 2001]. *American Indian Quarterly* 29 (Winter/Spring 2005): 198–211.

McFarland, Ron. *Understanding James Welch.* Columbia: University of South Carolina Press, 2000.

Moore, Michael. "James Welch." The 100 Most Influential Montanans of the Century. *Missoulian Online.* 1999. http://www.missoulian.com/specials/100montanans/list/057.html.

Pearl, Nancy, and Jennifer Young. "Native Voices, Old and New." *Library Journal* 127, no. 14 (September 2002): 244.

Round, Phillip H. "There Is a Right Way." *Studies in American Indian Literatures* 18, no. 3 (2006): 82–89.

Selden, Ron. "Acclaimed Author James Welch Dies." *Indian Country Today,* August 17, 2003. http://www.indiancountry.com.

Shanley, Kathryn. "Circling Back, Closing In: Remembering James Welch." *Studies in American Indian Literatures* 18, no. 3 (2006): 3–13.

Welch, James. "Foreword." In *Sweet Medicine: Sites of Indian Massacres, Battlefields, and Treaties,* by Patricia Nelson Limerick. Albuquerque: University of New Mexico Press, 1995.

Welch, James. "James Welch's Introduction to Our Third Catalog of Native American Literature." 1997. *Ken Lopez-Bookseller.* http://www.lopezbooks.com/articles/welch.html.

Wetzel, William. "A Tribute to James Welch." *Studies in American Indian Literatures* 18, no. 3 (2006): 43–45.

West, W. Richard, Jr.
Born 1943 Southern Cheyenne and Arapaho
Lawyer and Founding Director of the National Museum of the American Indian

Attorney W. Richard West, Jr. worked in legal affairs for more than 15 years before he became the National Museum of the American Indian's founding director. Roger Kennedy, who was on the search committee that chose West for the job, said he admired West's "astonishing capacity . . . to maintain his balance between the buffeting and brevity of focus of the contemporary world and a steady commitment to enduring values derived from his own essential culture" ("Raising the Bar," 2003). "Rick West stands proudly in both cultures," said Kennedy. "He was the right person for the job" (Birnbaum, 2004).

Early Life

Born in San Bernardino, California, January 6, 1943, West was raised in Muskogee, Oklahoma, son of the renowned Walter Richard (Dick) West, Sr. (1912–96), a Southern Cheyenne painter and chairman of the art department at Bacone College from 1947 to 1970. West's mother was Maribelle McCrea West, of Scots ancestry, an accomplished classical pianist and a descendent of Baptist missionaries. The Wests and their two sons, Rick and Jim, the youngest, lived in a four-room log cabin on Bacone College's campus, a small school with a predominantly Native student body in Muskogee, Oklahoma.

A Navy veteran in World War II, the senior West not only illustrated books and painted murals in post offices (among many other works), but also shaped a generation of art students. He was a popular lecturer, art-show judge, and sign linguist who often appeared in public venues in his Cheyenne headdress and fringed leather. In 1954 he began a series of eight paintings, "Indian Christ." He also was a sculptor and the first American Indian fine arts master's degree alumnus of the University of Oklahoma.

Southern Cheyenne culture, including the Sun Dance, was a regular part of the family's life. The senior West told his children, "You are Cheyenne, and don't you ever forget that," leading his children to a "bona-fide rootedness" in Cheyenne culture that centered West's life. The senior Wests also hammered home the value of education. "We were pushed as fast as our little minds would run," West said ("Raising the Bar," 2003).

When Rick was 13, in 1956, the family traveled to New York City so that the two boys could dance in *Off to Adventure,* a television show. When they traveled, the family sometimes was denied food and lodging because they were not "white." They saw some signs that warned "No Indians or Dogs Allowed."

West took his father's advice regarding education to heart. In 1965, he graduated *magna cum laude* from California's University of Redlands, a member of Phi Beta Kappa. Three years later, he earned a master's degree in American history at Harvard University. Some of his mentors advised West to take a PhD and become a college professor, but he chose law school, believing that he could make more of a difference as a lawyer. West graduated from Stanford Law School in 1971. As a student there, he won the Hilmer Oelmann, Jr., Prize for excellence in legal writing, and helped edit the *Stanford Law Review.* West was the only American Indian enrolled at Stanford Law School in the late 1960s, and perhaps the second to enroll in the law school's history. The school was receptive to him, however. "It was even open to having Indian law taught there. In my third year, we succeeded in convincing Stanford to hire—as a professor on an adjunct basis—Monroe Price, a very distinguished [Indian law] professor from UCLA," West told the *Stanford Lawyer* (Birnbaum, 2004).

Legal Career

West's first full-time legal work involved cases in American Indian law with the law firm Fried, Frank, Harris, Shriver & Jacobson, one of the world's foremost Indian-law firms, with offices in Los Angeles, New York City, Washington, D.C., London, and Paris. West worked out of the Washington, D.C., office. He became a partner in 1979.

He defended Native land base, including cases that kept several thousand acres of Cheyenne River and Sioux Reservation in South Dakota from being lost. Working as a lobbyist, West during the early 1980s played an important role in enactment of the Tribal Governmental Tax Status Act, giving reservation governments the same powers of taxation as state governments.

In 1988, West left Fried, Frank, Harris, Shriver & Jacobson to become, briefly, co-founder of Gover, Stetson, Williams and West, P.C., a Native American–owned law office with its principal office in Albuquerque, New Mexico.

Service at the National Museum of the American Indian

In 1989, West became deeply involved in plans to establish the National Museum of the American Indian as part of the Smithsonian Institution. A year later, he was selected as the new museum's first director, while its main building on the

W. Richard West Jr., director of the National Museum of the American Indian and a citizen of the Cheyenne and Arapaho Tribes of Oklahoma, speaks before the U.S. Capitol during the grand opening of the Smithsonian's National Museum of the American Indian on the National Mall in Washington, D.C., in September 2004. (AFP/ Getty Images)

National Mall was still in its conceptual stages. He played a major role in raising money to build the museum from public and private sources and to superintend planning and construction. Congress required that at least one-third of the museum's construction expenses, more than $100 million, be raised from sources other than the federal government.

West had some lobbying on his own behalf to do in the director's position because he had never directed a museum. However, the job required more than a traditional director, and West had skills as a fund-raiser, construction supervisor, and lobbyist. Frankly, he said, the job also required an advocate for Native American people who could act as a bridge to the world of government bureaucracy.

An article on West in the *Stanford Lawyer* portrayed West's unparalleled joy on the job:

Very few people actually get the job of their dreams. Rick West of Washington, D.C., is one of those people—and it shows. He peppers his conversations with ecstatic phrases like "I love it" and "I'm thrilled!" Even his clothes are upbeat. He favors pastel-colored shirts and carefully tailored suits. In a town of bland bureaucrats and play-it-safe politicians, he stands out. "In a very singular way," said West with characteristic verve, "my job has pulled together the threads of my life." (Birnbaum, 2004, 18)

West saw the mission of the National Museum of the American Indian as "to offer a counterbalance to the distortions engendered by the painfully long exclusion of Indian people from the interpretation of their own history and culture" ("Raising the Bar," 2003). Under West's direction, the National Museum of the American Indian opened the George Gustav Heye Center in 1994; a Cultural Resources Center, in Suitland, Maryland, in 2000; and the main museum on the National Mall in 2004.

Approximately 25,000 Native people inundated the National Mall to celebrate the opening of the museum. The museum collections are drawn mainly from a private museum in New York City maintained by George Heye, a New York banker, whose efforts to acquire Native American art during the first half of the 20th century often have been characterized as ruthless.

West also advocated what he called the "Fourth Museum," which took the museum's work on the road across the entire Western Hemisphere, providing access to its programs and archives through traveling exhibits and Internet access. The director's job absorbed and tested West's considerable skills as fund-raiser, lawyer, historian, lobbyist, and advocate of Native American revival. As Republicans took over the presidency and both houses of government during the 1990s, West often had to fight for funding for the museum.

Late in his tenure at the museum, West was criticized in a series of *Washington Post* articles for spending on travel around the world and staging an expensive party celebrating his retirement, as the General Accounting Office scrutinized expenses at the Smithsonian. West said his expenses were within the scope of his office, but he did reimburse the Smithsonian $9,700. He retired from the directorship in 2007.

West also served on the Institute of American Indian Arts of Santa Fe's governing board and on the governing boards of Stanford University, the National Parks and Conservation Association, the Ford Foundation, the National Support Committee of the Native American Rights Fund, the American Indian Resources Institute, and the American Association of Museums. Perhaps West's most cherished public role was as a Peace Chief in the Southern Cheyennes' traditional government.

West married Mary Beth Braden, a Stanford graduate and an attorney and ambassador serving with the U.S. Department of State in Washington, D.C. They met in 1966 while he was enrolled at Harvard. She also was a professor of political science at the National Defense University. They have two grown children, Amy and Ben.

Further Reading

Birnbaum, Jeffrey H. "Blazing Trails: Rick West '71 Spent Years Championing Native American Legal Rights. Now He's in Charge of the Smithsonian's Newest Museum, the National Museum of the American Indian." *Stanford Lawyer,* Fall 2004, 18–21. http://www.law.stanford.edu/publications/stanford_lawyer/issues/70/blazingtrails.html.

Grimaldi, James V. "'Lavish' Spending Not Found Elsewhere at Smithsonian." *Washington Post,* October 30, 2008. http://voices.washingtonpost.com/washingtonpostinvestigations/2008/10/by_james_v_grimaldi_washington.html.

Klein, Julia. "Alumni: At the Interface." *Harvard Magazine,* April 11, 2003. http://www.abanet.org/publiced/rbwest.html.

Pogrebin, Robin. "Former Director to Pay Smithsonian." *New York Times,* October 29, 2008. http://www.nytimes.com/2008/10/30/arts/design/30arts-FORMERDIRECT_BRF.html.

"Raising the Bar: Pioneers in the Legal Profession: W. Richard West." American Bar Association. 2003. http://www.abanet.org/publiced/rbwest.html.

"W. Richard West." U.S. Department of the Interior. n.d. http://www.doi.gov/news/west.htm.

WESTERMAN, FLOYD RED CROW
1936–2007 SISSETON-WAHPETON SIOUX
MUSICIAN AND ACTIVIST

An influential Native singer and actor, Floyd Red Crow Westerman played important roles in the films *Dances with Wolves* (1990) and *Clearcut* (1992), as well as in two television series, *Northern Exposure* and *L.A. Law.* Before and during his career as an actor for mass audiences, Westerman was known in Native America as a folksinger and activist. His recordings included *Custer Died for Your Sins* (based on his close friend Vine Deloria, Jr.'s book of the same title), *Indian Country,* and *The Land Is Your Mother.*

Westerman was a participant and performer at the first annual Native American Music Awards (popularly known as "Nammys") in 1996, performing with Joanne Shenandoah in a tribute for Hall of Fame inductee, the late Buddy Red Bow. He was the recipient of the organization's Living Legend Award (2002). He received the Nammys' Best Country Recording for *A Tribute to Johnny Cash* in 2006. Cash was known throughout Indian Country for his support of Native-rights issues, evidenced as early as 1963 by release of an album, *Bitter Tears: Ballads of the American Indian,* with its sarcastic needling of George Armstrong Custer, its salute to treaty rights in "As Long as the Grass Shall Grow," and the haunting "Ballad of Ira Hayes."

Music was Westerman's first love. Born on the Sisseton-Wahpeton Dakota Sioux Reservation in South Dakota, he was sent to boarding school. He left home at a young age with an old guitar and a suitcase, traveling across the United States, playing country music standards, as well as his own songs. Many of these songs were drawn from Native-rights controversies based on battles for the land, Native identity and sovereignty, as well as protection of the environment. He graduated from Northern State College in South Dakota, then moved to Denver and played in piano bars.

Westerman's first recording contract, signed in 1969, produced his first album, *Custer Died for Your Sins.* In 1970, his second collection of recorded songs reflected the same themes. Westerman was very popular outside the United States, where he performed at least 60 times.

The American Indian Movement became a major activity for Westerman shortly after its formation in 1968. He also acted as a spokesman for the International Indian Treaty Council, traveling around the world and appearing before the United Nations to advocate improved social and economic conditions for indigenous peoples. In 1982, these themes and environmental issues were the main focus of his third collection of recorded songs, *The Land Is Your Mother.* During his musical career, Westerman played with well-known musicians, including Willie Nelson, Kris Kristofferson, Buffy Sainte-Marie, Joni Mitchell, Jackson Browne, Harry Belafonte (to protest nuclear power), and Sting (to protest destruction of rain forests).

Westerman's film and television appearances include the role of a shaman for Jim Morrison in Oliver Stone's *The Doors* and as the wise old sachem Ten Bears in *Dances with Wolves* (1990). His television roles have included playing Uncle Ray on *Walker, Texas Ranger,* One Who Waits on *Northern Exposure,* and several appearances as Albert Hosteen on the *X-Files.* He also played George Little Fox on *Dharma & Greg.*

He has received many other awards, including a Congressional Certificate of Special Recognition, the Award for Generosity from the Americans for Indian Opportunity, Cultural Ambassador by the International Treaty Council, a Lifetime Achievement Award from the City of Los Angeles, and the Integrity Award from the Multicultural Motion Picture Association.

Westerman passed on to the spirit world December 13, 2007, at Cedars Sinai Hospital in Los Angeles, following complications from leukemia. Mohawk journalist Doug George-Kanentiio remembered him this way: "Floyd . . . was not egotistical or full of rage. He went through the emotional and physical traumas of the notorious boarding school system yet whenever I met him he was given to laughter and ready for a good story. He was, in many ways, like his great friend Vine Deloria, aware of the absurdities of life but enjoying his time here. He was a strong presence on and off the stage and played a really hard guitar" (George-Kanentiio, 2007).

Further Reading

"Actor's Goal: Indian Rights." *New York Times* reprinted in *Omaha World-Herald,* December 30, 2007, 8-A.

"Floyd Red Crow Westerman Journeys On to the Spirit World." Native American Music Awards. December 13, 2007. www.nativeamericanmusicawards.com

George-Kanentiio, Doug. Personal communication, December 18, 2007.

WHITEBEAR, BERNIE
1937–2000 SIN AIKST, COLVILLE, LAKE INDIANS, NORTHERN SHOSHONE
COMMUNITY ACTIVIST

Bernie Whitebear, a long-time Native American community activist, was part of a unique pan-ethnic consensus in the Seattle area that produced strong support

American Indian activist, Bernie Whitebear, 1971. (Seattle Post-Intelligencer Collection, Museum of History & Industry, Seattle)

for fishing rights, as well as the Daybreak Star Center, one of the country's most notable urban Indian centers. Whitebear helped found Daybreak Star, then served as its long-term director.

Early Life

Whitebear was born Bernard Reyes in 1937 at the Colville Indian Agency in Nespelem, eastern Washington, as a Sin Aikst (Lake Indians). He graduated from Okanogan High School in 1955. In 1956, he spent a frustrating year at the University of Washington, then enlisted in the U.S. Army (101st Airborne Division and Green Berets) serving from 1957 to 1959. After his army enlistment, Whitebear bounced around short-term jobs in Tacoma. He fished on the Puyallup River and Commencement Bay with Puyallup activist Bob Satiacum, an activity that was then deemed illegal for Indians by the State of Washington's game and fishing officials, with copious harassment. During 1966, Whitebear moved to Seattle and worked for a time at the Boeing Company.

Whitebear's role as a community activist developed late in the 1960s when, in 1969, he became the first director of the Seattle Indian Health Board. Whitebear's vast sense of compassion led him to drive around Seattle seeking out Indians who needed help, an activity described by his brother, Lawney L. Reyes, in a book,

Bernie Whitebear: An Urban Indian's Quest for Justice (2006). The book has been seen as "a flattering vision of an extraordinary Sin Aikst man, a precious human being, someone worthy of enduring emulation and far-reaching respect" (Tyeeme-Clark, 2007, 147).

Whitebear was part of the "Gang of Four" pan-ethnic leadership in the Seattle area that united in a way that has been rare in American politics. A group of long-time friends played important roles in various ethnic groups—Whitebear, with Roberto Maestas, founder in 1972 and long-time director of El Centro de la Raza; Bob Santos, a Filipino and Asian American community leader; and Larry Gossett, who for many years has exercised an important political role in the black community, from student activist at the University of Washington to King County councilman.

Together, the Gang of Four lent support to each others' causes, such as Indian fishing rights, farm-worker rights, and a successful effort to rename (Rufus) King County after Martin Luther King, Jr. All four understood that ethnic identity and issues were interrelated. Maestas, for example, is partly Pueblo Indian, from New Mexico, and Whitebear was partially Latino.

Occupation of Fort Lawton

Shortly after the occupation of Alcatraz in the San Francisco Bay Area in 1969, similar circumstances gave birth to an occupation of land on the former World War II–era U.S. Army base in Seattle called Fort Lawton. Native people badly needed an urban center, and the same Indian-preference law that spurred the occupation at Alcatraz provoked an occupation in a wooded area not far from Seattle residential areas in the Queen Anne neighborhood.

While the occupation of Alcatraz did not produce any long-lasting results, the Fort Lawton action eventually produced the Daybreak Star Center, with a sweeping view of Puget Sound. Whitebear, a leader of the occupation as head of United Indians of All Tribes, became director of Daybreak Star and held the position for almost 30 years, until his death in 2000 from colon cancer.

Seattle's interethnic alliances gave the occupation of Fort Lawton extra support and a special "edge." The media came calling, too, when they sensed the irony of the Indians "attacking" an Army fort. The base was still active in 1970, even after plans to declare it surplus were being considered. In the spring of 1970, a half-mile-long caravan of cars lined up in blockade at the base's north and south entrances. Indians and their allies climbed fences, hauled in tipi poles, and prepared to stay awhile. Military police evicted them and they returned. The confrontation lasted seven years before a compromise was reached: the city of Seattle got most of the old fort for a park, but the United Indians of All Tribes received land on which to build the Daybreak Star Center, which was begun in 1975 and opened two years later.

Whitebear was remembered as a "soft-spoken person, given to working with people rather than confronting them. He was always ready with a bon mot, a joke, a tease, or a story. Some people called him a walking anecdote" (Chavers, 2007, 580).

Further Reading

Chavers, Dean. *Modern American Indian Leaders: Their Lives and Their Works.* 2 vols. Lewiston, NY: Edwin Mellen Press, 2007.

Reyes, Lawney L. *Bernie Whitebear: An Urban Indian's Quest for Justice.* Tucson: University of Arizona Press, 2006.

Tyeeme-Clark, D. Anthony. Review of *Bernie Whitebear: An Urban Indian's Quest for Justice,* by Lawney L. Reyes. *American Indian Culture & Research Journal* 31, no. 1 (2007): 145–48.

WILSON, RICHARD
1936–1990 OGLALA LAKOTA
POLITICAL LEADER

Richard Wilson was chairman of the Pine Ridge Indian Reservation Tribal Council during the 1973 Wounded Knee occupation in South Dakota, as well as during its violent aftermath. From the early 1970s until his defeat for the chairman's office by Al Trimble in 1976, Wilson outfitted a tribal police force that was often called the GOON (Guardians of the Oglala Nation) squad. It was financed with money from the federal government and cooperated with the Federal Bureau of Investigation (FBI). A book about Pine Ridge and the FBI described Wilson thusly: "He favored dark glasses and a habiliment of High Plains haute: two parts polyester, one part snakeskin. His hair was martially buzzed, his head was of medicine ball proportion, and the blood vessels of his cheeks suggested he was not afraid of a good tipple. His body was less brick than well-filled bag" (Hendricks, 2006, 47).

One result of the escalating conflict between Wilson and Oglala Lakota traditionalists allied with the American Indian Movement (AIM) was the 71-day occupation of Wounded Knee in 1973. The struggle between AIM and Wilson also took place in the realm of tribal electoral politics. When Wilson sought re-election in 1974, Russell Means, an Oglala who had helped found AIM, challenged him. In the primary Wilson trailed Means, 667 votes to 511 votes. Wilson won the final election over Means by fewer than 200 votes in balloting that the U.S. Commission on Civil Rights later found to be permeated with fraud. The Civil Rights Commission recommended a new election, which was not held; Wilson answered his detractors by stepping up the terror, examples of which were described in a chronology kept by the Wounded Knee Legal Defense-Offense Committee. One of the GOON's favorite weapons was the automobile; officially, such deaths could be reported as "traffic accidents."

Wilson had a formidable array of supporters on the reservation, many of whom criticized AIM for being urban-based and insensitive to reservation residents' needs. Mona Wilson, one of Wilson's daughters, who was 17 years of age in 1973, recalled that he cried in his mother's arms at the time during the deadly conflicts on the reservation. Speaking about the events two decades later, Wilson's wife,

Yvonne, and two daughters recalled him as a kind and compassionate father who had the interests of his people at heart. They said that Wilson supported AIM when it protested the 1972 murder of Raymond Yellow Thunder in the reservation border town of Gordon, Nebraska. Only later, as events culminated in the weeks-long siege of Wounded Knee, did Wilson and AIM leaders become deadly enemies.

Wilson was the first Oglala Lakota tribal chairperson to serve two consecutive terms. He became a self-employed plumber and owner of a gas station, and worked on other short-term projects after his defeat by Trimble for the tribal chairmanship in 1976. Wilson also held the traditional role of pipe carrier. He was known for feeding anyone who came to his door, and he had a major role in beginning a Lakota community college on the reservation, as well as a number of other tribal enterprises.

Wilson died of a heart attack in 1990, as he was preparing to run for a third term as tribal chairman.

Further Reading

Hendricks, Steve. *The Unquiet Grave: The FBI and the Struggle for the Soul of Indian Country.* New York: Thunder's Mouth Press, 2006.

Johansen, Bruce E., and Roberto F. Maestas. *Wasi'chu: The Continuing Indian Wars.* New York: Monthly Review Press, 1979.

LaMay, Konnie. "20 Years of Anguish." *Indian Country Today,* February 25, 1993, n.p.

Matthiessen, Peter. *In the Spirit of Crazy Horse.* New York: Viking, 1991.

U.S. Commission on Civil Rights. "Report of Investigation: Oglala Sioux Tribe, General Election, 1974." October, mimeographed. Washington, DC: Civil Rights Commission.

WOMACK, CRAIG S.
BORN 1962 CREEK, MVSKOKE/MUSKOGEE AND CHEROKEE
SCHOLAR AND NOVELIST

Craig S. Womack, one of the most important scholars of Native American literature who has tried to establish a Native American aesthetic movement, is also an important Native American novelist and scholar of gay/lesbian/bisexual/transgender studies. Womack has revolutionized the way Native Americans are viewed and perceive themselves within the artistic community. He also tries to give a voice to marginalized peoples within already-marginalized communities by addressing the concerns, both aesthetic and political, of individual tribes and homosexuals, at large and within the Native American community. Of his four book-length publications, his novel *Drowning in Fire* (2001) and his work of scholarship *Red on Red: Native American Literary Separatism* (1999) are considered touchstones of Native American literature.

According to the *American Indian Quarterly,* Womack's *Drowning in Fire* "looms like a spring thundercloud on the Plains. It arises on the horizon of a new Indian literature and new American studies as part of an emerging genre of texts that truly evokes the reciprocity between life and land and between past and future" (McCormick, 2002, 153–54). Womack's novel about homosexual Creeks growing up in eastern Oklahoma incorporates complex gender and racial politics. Womack sees land, Native American sovereignty, and homosexuality as related issues, not only for himself, but also for the Native American community at large and all Americans.

As an advocate for minority populations, Womack is driven by the requirements of documenting the Creek community, the homosexual community, and the Native American homosexual community. Recovery and historical contextualization of homosexual indigenous authors of the past is important to Womack. The life and works of homosexual Cherokee playwright Lynn Riggs have been a continued research interest of Womack's. Riggs was the author of the play *Green Grow the Lilacs,* the basis of the musical *Oklahoma,* who most likely is the most famous homosexual Native American author. Womack has felt compelled to bring Riggs's Native and homosexual identities to the forefront through his scholarship.

Early Life, Education, Scholarship, and Academic Career

Womack, who was born in 1962, is of Mvskoke (also known as Muskogee or Creek) and Cherokee heritage. He spent much of his childhood in the San Francisco Bay Area. Womack says that his family moved to California after World War II, before the Indian relocation policies in the 1950s, mostly as a precautionary measure. Womack is convinced that his family knew of the impending relocation effects. His maternal and paternal family moved together to California, and both of his grandfathers worked for Standard Oil in California as they had previously done in Oklahoma. While in California, they lived among an Okie community that had been in the area since the Depression era. They were working-class Californians who had strong family histories that went back to Oklahoma and Georgia.

Womack was a first-generation college student, receiving his BS from the University of Tennessee and his MA in English from South Dakota State University in 1991. He received his PhD from the University of Oklahoma in 1995.

Womack taught at the University of Nebraska at Omaha. He and his partner then moved to Canada, where he taught at the University of Lethbridge in Alberta. He taught 19th- and 20th-century Native American and gay and lesbian literature at the University of Oklahoma from 2002 until the fall of 2007. In 2008, he was teaching at Emory University in Atlanta. In the summer of 2008, he taught Native American and jazz literature at the Bread Loaf School of English Graduate Institute based out of Middlebury College, Vermont. Womack is also a member of Storytellers' National Caucus.

Writings

In addition to *Red on Red* and *Drowning in Fire,* Womack wrote *American Indian Literary Nationalism* (2006), with Jace Weaver and Robert Warrior. As of 2008, Womack's latest publications were *Reflections on Aesthetics* and (as co-author with Janice Acoose, Daniel Heath Justice, and Christopher B. Teuton) *Reasoning Together: The Native Critics Collective.* Womack won three awards sponsored by the Wordcraft Circle: Storyteller of the Year for "readings or performance" in 1997; Writer of the Year, Creative, for Prose and Critical Essays, in 2000 for *Red on Red;* and Writer of the Year, Creative, for Fiction, in 2003 for *Drowning in Fire.*

Red on Red is an extremely important work of criticism for academics because it asserts that Native American literature should be viewed only from the perspective of what is indigenous about a work. The *MultiCultural Review* has called *Red on Red* "a stunning model of how Indian scholars can explicate tribal-specific oral and written works with an understanding of the political ramifications for real Indian peoples" ("NCW," n.d.). *Red on Red* argues against the traditional view of Native American literature as a unifying homogeneous "genre" that draws a group of postcolonial literatures under the guise of one label. Womack's argument is that there is no one Native American literature, but rather multiple Native American interpretations.

The rise of indigenous literature in academic importance came about as two theoretical perspectives were receiving more attention in academic circles. The first, poststructuralism, is the rejection of the belief that nothing "new" is written because texts contain the same structure as previous works. Poststructuralists instead reject all "truths" or "facts," all literary structures, in favor of giving the power of a text to the reader not the writer. Postcolonialism is a theory that places importance on the literature written by individuals that were formerly colonized. However, in Womack's experience, poststructuralism and postcolonialism do not take into account the nature of Native American thought. He believes they should not be applied to literature written by indigenous populations. Womack holds that these populations are not influenced by structuralism and do not completely fall under the rubric of colonialism. As the experience of one Native American group cannot be completely understood through the worldview of another, each individual tribe should have its literature viewed independently. The remainder of Womack's book is a discussion of Creek literature and the traditions unique to it as a literary form.

Womack's political arguments have revolutionized understanding of texts written by Native authors. He takes the idea of indigenous sovereignty as promised to indigenous populations by the United States and explains that the U.S. government does not have the power to create sovereignty; indigenous peoples have that power. This belief parallels that of other Native American activists, such as the Haudenosaunee (Iroquois) Oren Lyons, who argues that political and cultural sovereignty is defined by its exercise, not by imposed outside power.

Red on Red has been both hailed and criticized within the Native American community. Nearly eight years after the book's publication, *Indian Country Today,* a newspaper owned by the Oneida Nation of New York, the largest Native American news organ in North America, called Womack's position "nationalist essentialism." The newspaper opined that Womack's assertion that only a Creek can understand Creek literature, and that only a Diné (Navajo) can understand Diné literature, undercuts any attempt at universalism, the predominant theoretical position used when reading Native American literature before the 1990s, that could come from Native American literature. The text has also been seen to ignore that fact that many Native American writers are of mixed blood. Such mixtures make a truly "Native" American literature nearly impossible to define, document, or critique (Lincoln, 2007).

Drowning in Fire

Womack's novel *Drowning in Fire* is a thinly veiled tale of a homosexual Muskogee Creek growing up in rural Oklahoma from the late 1960s to the early 1980s. The title character, Josh Henneha, journeys through and within history, both personal, tribal, and sexual to come to an understanding of his many identities. In its brutal perspective on reality, the reader confronts the fact that a gay Indian is still an Indian in the gay community and still gay in the Indian community.

Drowning in Fire incorporates not only the life of "modern Indians," it also provides context into Creek oral tradition and the tribe's traditional ways of looking at sex roles. Compared with the dominant culture mores that Josh is being indoctrinated with in the majority community, the traditional Creek views give him latitude to understand his sexuality, not condemn it. Womack not only questions the way that the Creek have been forced to change their historic perceptions of homosexuality in order to assimilate with the majority culture, but through the character of Josh's great-aunt, Lucy, he tries to rectify the way that the Creek traditions were more accepting of a greater role for woman as well.

Jason R. Gallagher

Further Reading

Acoose, J., L. Brooks, T. Foster, L. Howe, D. H. Justice, and C. S. Womack. *Reasoning Together: The Native Critics Collective*. Norman: University of Oklahoma Press, 2008.

Baker, A. K. "'For 500 Years, Others Spoke for Us': Reprint of an Interview with Native American Author Craig Womack." BC: Blogcritics Magazine. September 21, 2005. http://blogcritics.org/archives/2005/09/21/121220.php.

Bergans, J. "'Queer Symposium' Addresses Native Identity." *The Johns Hopkins News-Letter,* September 17, 2004. http://media.www.jhunewsletter.com/media/storage/paper932/news/2004/09/17/News/queer.Symposium.Addresses.Native.Identity-2244772.shtml.

"Craig Womack." The University of Oklahoma Department of English. n.d. http://www.ou.edu/cas/english/people/faculty/facultypages/womack.htm.

Gozen, J. "Beautifully, Wonderfully Red: Julie Gozen Talks with Native American Author Craig Womack." *Lambda Book Review,* March 1, 2004. http://goliath.ecnext.com/coms2/gi_0199-1528170/Beautifully-wonderfully-red-Julie-Gozen.html#abstract.

Lincoln, K. "Lincoln: Red Stick Lit Crit." *Indian County Today,* April 5, 2007. http://www.indiancountry.com/content.cfm?id=1096414815.

McCormick, P. J. "Drowning in Fire." *American Indian Quarterly* 26, no. 1 (Winter 2002): 153–54.

"Native American Authors: Craig S. Womack." The Internet Public Library. http://www.ipl.org/div/natam/bin/browse.pl/A453.

"NCW (Nebraska Center for Writers)—Craig Womack." Creighton University (Omaha). n.d. http://mockingbird.creighton.edu/ncw/womack.htm.

Schneider, B. "Oklahobo: Following Craig Womack's American Indian and Queer Studies." *South Atlantic Quarterly* 106, no. 3 (Summer 2007): 599–613.

Weaver, J., C. S. Womack, R. Warrior, O. J. Simon, and L. Brooks. *American Indian Literary Nationalism.* Albuquerque: University of New Mexico Press, 2006.

Womack, C. S. "Howling at the Moon: The Queer but True Story of My Life as a Hank Williams Song." In *As We Are Now: Mixedblood Essays on Race and Identity,* edited by William S. Penn, 28–49. Berkeley: University of California Press.

Womack, C. S. *Red on Red: Native American Literary Separatism.* Minneapolis: University of Minnesota Press, 1999.

Womack, C. S. *Drowning in Fire.* Tucson: University of Arizona Press, 2001.

Womack, C. S. Review of *The Cherokee Night and Other Plays,* by Lynn Riggs and Jace Weaver. *Studies in American Indian Literatures* 17, no. 1 (Spring 2005): 114–21.

Womack, C. S. "Baptists and Witches: Multiple Jurisdictions in a Muskogee Creek Story." *Southern Spaces.* December 6, 2006. http://www.southernspaces.org/contents/2007/womack/1a.htm.

Womack, C. S. "Aestheticizing a Political Debate: Can the Creek Confederacy Be Sung Back Together?" *Southern Spaces.* [A video lecture]. April 13, 2007. http://www.southernspaces.org/contents/2007/womack/2a.htm.

YELLOWHORSE, MOSE
1898–1964 PAWNEE
MAJOR LEAGUE BASEBALL PITCHER

Mose (Moses) YellowHorse, a Pawnee, probably was the first full-blooded Native American to play major league baseball. YellowHorse, who like many other Native baseball players, was called "Chief," also became known for beaning Ty Cobb with a pitch between the eyes that knocked him out after Cobb, arguably the most famous baseball player of his time, unleashed a stream of racial slurs at YellowHorse during an exhibition game. Inhibited by acute alcoholism, YellowHorse played two years in the major leagues. He eventually stopped drinking completely and became an esteemed elder among the Pawnees.

Mose's parents, Clara and Thomas YellowHorse, were removed from Nebraska to Oklahoma as children during 1875. Thomas walked 400 miles from Nebraska to Oklahoma. Within 15 years, the Pawnees' population, estimated at 1,440 in 1879, had dropped

Mose YellowHorse, Native American baseball player, 1920. (Library of Congress)

295

by half, due mainly to hunger and disease. Thomas and Clara married in Oklahoma Territory.

Mose J. YellowHorse was born on January 28, 1898, near the town of Pawnee, on a family farm, in the Skidi (Wolf) Band. His birth name was "Moses," which became "Mose" in popular usage. As a young man, YellowHorse's right arm was strong enough to propel rocks that killed small game, including rabbits and crows, from a considerable distance for the family table. Powerfully built at 5-foot-10, about 180 pounds, YellowHorse was known for his sense of humor from an early age. As a youth, YellowHorse performed with Pawnee Bill's Wild West Show, assembled by Major Gordon W. Lillie, who employed hundreds of Indians from across North America. According to YellowHorse's biographer, "One writer described YellowHorse rather insensitively as being 'as dark as the previous night's lunar eclipse.' Mose YellowHorse 'possessed an intensity in his eyes that was mesmerizing'" (Fuller, 2002, 31).

YellowHorse first pitched at Chilocco Indian School in Oklahoma. He was something of a sensation from the start, posting a record of 17 wins and no losses at the school in 1917. His professional baseball career started with the Arkansas Travelers of the Southern Association in 1920. YellowHorse went 21–7 as the team won its first league championship. Kid Elberfeld, YellowHorse's manager at Arkansas, said that his fastball rivaled that of the famed Washington Senators' pitcher Walter Johnson, the best in the major leagues at the time. As a player, Elberfeld had faced Johnson's fastball as a batter.

Reaching the majors in 1921 as relief pitcher, YellowHorse posted an 8–4 won-loss record and a 3.93 earned-run average with the Pittsburgh Pirates during 1921 and 1922 before an arm injury required surgery.

YellowHorse faced Ty Cobb September 26, 1922, in an exhibition game in Detroit between his National League Pirates and the American League Detroit Tigers. Cobb, crowding the plate as usual, hurled racist expletives in an attempt to unnerve YellowHorse. Instead of losing his nerve, YellowHorse shook off four pitches. The fifth was a fastball aimed directly at Cobb's forehead.

Norman Rice, a Pawnee who related the story as YellowHorse had told it to him, said that "Cobb was up there yelling all kinds of Indian prejudice, real mean slurs at Mose, just making him mad . . . [and] Mose knocked him cold. . . . They carried Ty Cobb off the field" (Fuller, 2002, 102–3). The beaning provoked a brawl involving both teams. In a biography of YellowHorse, three versions of the beaning are given. None of the accounts included the specific slurs that provoked the famous fastball.

At Pawnee, and across Indian Country, Native American people cheered "a bean for the Georgia Peach" (Cobb's nickname). A poem contained the line "All the smart ass in the world won't protect Cobb's face from Pawnee intentions. . . . When you mess with the bull, you get the horn" (Fuller, 2002, 105–6). Long after his baseball career ended, Native people celebrated YellowHorse as a warrior who had "counted coup" on Cobb.

Other injuries and YellowHorse's penchant for drinking and after-hours partying limited his effectiveness as a pitcher during the 1922 season, even as fans chanted "Put in YellowHorse!" Groundskeepers at the Pirates' ballpark sometimes slipped YellowHorse jiggers of whiskey as he pitched. During 1923, he was sent to the minors. Injuries and drinking continued to impede his performance with Sacramento of the Pacific Coast League. Even so, YellowHorse won 22 games that year. His professional baseball career ended May 1, 1926, in his last pitching assignment for a minor-league team in Omaha. After 1926, YellowHorse played semipro baseball, "becoming legendary for his ambidextrous and underhanded deliveries" (Horowitz, 2002, 78).

From 1927 to 1945, YellowHorse, still drinking heavily, held a series of odd jobs. In 1945, however, he suddenly stopped drinking and soon found a steady job with the Oklahoma State Highway Department. He was welcomed home in Pawnee. He coached youth baseball as well. He "was feted in high style by the fans, sports magnates, and civic leaders of the cities in which he once was lionized as a great pitcher and gregarious personality" (Horowitz, 2002, 79).

YellowHorse died of a heart attack April 10, 1964, in Pawnee, aged 66. His burial plot and headstone was provided by the people of Pawnee because he had no living family. YellowHorse never married and had no children.

Further Reading

Berger, Ralph. "Chief Yellow Horse." Baseball Biography Project. n.d. http://bioproj.sabr.org/bioproj.cfm?a=v&v=l&pid=15620&bid=729.

Fuller, Todd. *60 Feet 6 Inches and Other Distances from Home: The (Baseball) Life of Mose YellowHorse.* Duluth, MN: Holy Cow! Press, 2002.

Horowitz, Mikhail. "Wholly Mose." Review of *60 Feet 6 Inches and Other Distances from Home: The (Baseball) Life of Mose YellowHorse,* by Todd Fuller. *Elysian Fields Quarterly: The Baseball Review* 19, no. 4 (Fall 2002): 77–80.

Mallozzi, Vincent M. "The American Indians of America's Pastime." *New York Times,* June 8, 2008. http://www.nytimes.com/2008/06/08/sports/baseball/08cheer.html.

Selected Bibliography

Acoose, J., L. Brooks, T. Foster, L. Howe, D.H. Justice, and C.S. Womack. *Reasoning Together: The Native Critics Collective*. Norman: University of Oklahoma Press, 2008.

Akwesasne Notes, ed. *A Basic Call to Consciousness*. [1978]. Rooseveltown, NY: *Akwesasne Notes,* 1986.

Allen, Paula Gunn. *The Sacred Hoop: Recovering the Feminine in American Indian Traditions*. Boston: Beacon Press, 1986.

American Friends Service Committee. *Uncommon Controversy: Fishing Rights of the Muckleshoot, Puyallup, and Nisqually Indians*. Seattle: University of Washington Press, 1970.

Armstrong, Virginia Irving. *I Have Spoken: American History through the Voices of the Indians*. Chicago: Swallow Press, 1971.

Austin, Alberta. *Ne'Ho Niyo' De:No': That's What It Was Like*. Lackawanna, NY: Rebco Enterprises, 1986.

Ballentine, Betty, and Ian Ballentine. *The Native Americans Today*. Atlanta: Turner, 1993.

Banks, Dennis, and Richard Erdoes. *Ojibwa Warrior: Dennis Banks and the Rise of the American Indian Movement*. Norman: University of Oklahoma Press, 2004.

Banning, Evelyn L. *Helen Hunt Jackson*. New York: Vanguard Press, 1973.

Barreiro, Jose, and Tom Johnson, eds. *America Is Indian Country: The Best of Indian Country Today*. Golden, CO: Fulcrum, 2005.

Barrows, William. *The Indian's Side of the Indian Question*. Boston: D. Lothrop Co., 1887.

Barsh, Russel L. *The Washington Fishing Rights Controversy: An Economic Critique*. Seattle: University of Washington School of Business Administration, 1977.

Barsh, Russel, and James Henderson. *The Road: Indian Tribes and Political Liberty*. Berkeley: University of California Press, 1980.

Beidler, Peter G, and Gay Barton. *A Reader's Guide to the Novels of Louise Erdrich*. Columbia: University of Missouri Press, 1999.

Benedict, Jeff. *Without Reservation: The Making of America's Most Powerful Indian Tribe and Foxwoods, the World's Largest Casino*. New York: HarperCollins, 2000.

Bland, Celia. *Peter MacDonald: Former Chairman of the Navajo Nation*. New York: Chelsea House, 1995.

Brand, Johanna. *The Life and Death of Anna Mae Aquash*. Toronto: Lorimer, 1978.

Brody, J.J. *Indian Painters and White Patrons*. Albuquerque: University of New Mexico Press, 1971.

Brown, Bruce. *Mountain in the Clouds*. New York: Simon & Schuster, 1982.

Bruchac, Joseph. *Survival This Way: Interviews with American Indian Poets*. Tucson: Sun Tracks and the University of Arizona Press, 1987.

Caldwell, E.K. *Dreaming the Dawn: Conversations with Native Artists and Activists*. Lincoln: University of Nebraska Press, 1999.

Calloway, Colin, ed. *Our Hearts Fell to the Ground: Plains Indian Views of How the West Was Lost*. Boston: Bedford Books/St. Martin's Press, 1996.

Carr, Lucien. *The Social and Political Position of Women among the Huron-Iroquois Tribes*. Salem, MA: Salem Press, 1884.

Cassirer, Ernest. *An Essay on Man*. New Haven, CT: Yale University Press, 1944.

Champagne, Duane, ed. *Native America: Portrait of the Peoples*. Canton, MI: Visible Ink Press, 1994.

Chavers, Dean. *Modern American Indian Leaders: Their Lives and Their Works*. 2 vols. Lewiston, NY: Edwin Mellen Press, 2007.

Chavkin, Allan, ed. *The Chippewa Landscape of Louise Erdrich*. Tuscaloosa: University Alabama Press, 1999.

Churchill, E. Richard, and Linda Churchill. *45 Profiles in Modern Music*. Portland, ME: J. Weston Walch, 1996.

Churchill, Ward. *From a Native Son: Selected Essays in Indigenism, 1985–1995*. Boston: South End Press, 1996.

Churchill, Ward, and Jim Vander Wall. *Agents of Repression: The FBI's Secret War against the Black Panther Party and the American Indian Movement*. Boston: South End Press, 1990.

Cobb, Daniel M., and Loretta Fowler, eds. *Beyond Red Power: American Indian Politics and Activism since 1900*. Santa Fe, NM: School for Advanced Research, 2007.

Cohen, Felix. *The Legal Conscience: Selected Papers of Felix S. Cohen*. Edited by Lucy Kramer Cohen. New Haven, CT: Yale University Press, 1960.

Colden, Cadwallader. *History of the Five Nations*. New York: New Amsterdam Book Company, 1902.

Collier, John. 1963. *From Every Zenith*. Denver, CO: Sage Books, 1963.

Coltelli, Laura. *Winged Words: American Indian Writers Speak*. Lincoln: University of Nebraska Press, 1990.

Commager, Henry Steele. *Documents of American History*. 7th ed. New York: Appleton, Century, Crofts, 1963.

Cornell, Stephen E. *The Return of the Native: American Indian Political Resurgence*. New York: Oxford University Press, 1988.

Costo, Rupert. *Redmen of the Golden West*. San Francisco: American Indian Historical Society, 1970.

Costo, Rupert. *Textbooks and the American Indian*. San Francisco: American Indian Historical Society, 1970.

Costo, Rupert, and Jeanette Henry. *Indian Treaties: Two Centuries of Dishonor*. San Francisco: American Indian Historical Society, 1981.

Costo, Rupert, and Jeanette Henry. *A Thousand Years of American Indian Storytelling*. San Francisco: American Indian Historical Society, 1981.

Costo, Rupert, and Jeanette Henry. *The Missions of California: A Legacy of Genocide*. San Francisco: American Indian Historical Society, 1987.

Costo, Rupert, and Jeanette Henry. *Natives of the Golden State: The California Indians*. San Francisco: American Indian Historical Society, 1995.

Covey, Cyclone. *The Gentle Radical: A Biography of Roger Williams*. New York: Mac-Millan, 1966.

Croy, Homer. *Our Will Rogers*. New York: Duell, Sloan, and Pearce, 1953.

Cullum, Linda. *Contemporary American Ethnic Poets: Lives, Works, Sources*. Westport, CT: Greenwood Press, 2004.

Dando-Collins, Stephen. *Standing Bear Is a Person: The True Story of a Native American's Quest for Justice*. New York: Da Capo Press, 2004.

Davis, Lynne, Louise Lahache, and Marlene Castellano, eds. *Aboriginal Education: Fulfilling the Promise*. Vancouver: University of British Columbia Press, 2000.

Davis, Mary B., ed. *Native America in the Twentieth Century: An Encyclopedia*. New York: Garland, 1996.

Day, Donald. *The Autobiography of Will Rogers*. Boston: Houghton Mifflin, 1962.

Deloria, Vine, Jr. *Custer Died for Your Sins*. Norman: University of Oklahoma Press, 1969.

Deloria, Vine, Jr. *We Talk, You Listen: New Tribes, New Turf*. New York: Macmillan, 1970.

Deloria, Vine, Jr. *The Metaphysics of Modern Existence*. San Francisco: Harper & Row, 1979.

Deloria, Vine, Jr. *Behind the Trail of Broken Treaties: An Indian Declaration of Independence*. [1974]. Austin: University of Texas Press, 1985.

Deloria, Vine, Jr. *God Is Red: A Native View of Religion*. 2nd ed. Golden, CO: North American Press/Fulcrum, 1992.

Deloria, Vine, Jr. *Red Earth, White Lies: Native Americans and the Myth of Scientific Fact*. New York: Scribner, 1995.

Downie, David Leonard, and Terry Fenge, eds. *Northern Lights against POPs: Combatting Toxic Threats in the Arctic*. Montreal and Kingston: McGill-Queen's University Press, 2003.

Dubin, Margaret, ed. *The Dirt Is Red Here: Art and Poetry from Native California*. Berkeley, CA: Heyday Books, 2002.

Eisler, Kim Isaac. *Revenge of the Pequots: How a Small Native American Tribe Created the World's Most Profitable Casino*. New York: Simon & Schuster, 2001.

Erasmus, Georges. *Dene Rights*. Ottawa: Privately published, 1976.

Erdrich, Heid, and Laura Tohe, eds. *Sister Nations: Native American Women Writers on Community*. St. Paul: Minnesota Historical Society, 2002.

Erdrich, Louise. *The Antelope Wife*. New York: HarperCollins, 1998.

Ferris, Jeri. *Native American Doctor: The Story of Susan Laflesche Picotte*. Minneapolis, MN: Carolrhoda Books, 1991.

Fikes, Jay C., and Walter E. Echo-Hawk. *Reuben Snake: Your Humble Serpent*. Santa Fe, NM: Clear Light, 1996.

Foner, Eric, and John A. Garraty, eds. *The Reader's Companion to American History*. Boston: Houghton-Mifflin, 1991.

Fuller, Todd. *60 Feet 6 Inches and Other Distances from Home: The (Baseball) Life of Mose YellowHorse*. Duluth, MN: Holy Cow! Press, 2002.

Gage, Matilda Joslyn. *Woman, Church and State*. [1893]. Watertown, MA: Persephone Press, 1980.

George-Kanentiio, Douglas M. *Iroquois on Fire: A Voice from the Mohawk Nation*. Westport, CT: Praeger, 2006.

Giago, Tim. *The Aboriginal Sin: Reflections on the Holy Rosary Indian Mission School.* San Francisco: Indian Historian Press, 1978.

Giago, Tim. *Notes from Indian Country.* Pierre, SD: Keith Cochran, 1984.

Giago, Tim. *The American Indian and the Media.* Minneapolis, MN: National Conference of Christians and Jews, 1991.

Gorman, R. C. *The Radiance of My People.* Houston, TX: Santa Fe Arts Gallery, 1992.

Gorman, R. C., and Virginia Dooley. *Nudes and Food: R. C. Gorman Goes Gourmet.* Flagstaff, AZ: Northland Press, 1981.

Gorman, R. C., and Virginia Dooley. *R. C. Gorman's Nudes & Foods in Good Taste.* Santa Fe, NM: Clear Light, 1994.

Grassian, Daniel. *Understanding Sherman Alexie.* Columbia: University of South Carolina Press, 2005.

Grinde, Donald A., Jr., and Bruce E. Johansen. *Ecocide of Native America: Environmental Destruction of Indian Lands and Peoples.* Santa Fe, NM: Clear Light, 1995.

Hamilton, Charles. *Cry of the Thunderbird.* Norman: University of Oklahoma Press, 1972.

Harjo, Joy, and Gloria Bird, eds. *Reinventing the Enemy's Language: Contemporary Native Women's Writing of North America.* New York: W. W. Norton, 1997.

Hauptman, Laurence M. *The Iroquois Struggle for Survival: World War II to Red Power.* Syracuse, NY: Syracuse University Press, 1986.

Hayes, Robert G. *A Race at Bay:* New York Times *Editorials on the "Indian Problem."* Carbondale: Southern Illinois University Press, 1997.

Hendricks, Steve. *The Unquiet Grave: The FBI and the Struggle for the Soul of Indian Country.* New York: Thunder's Mouth Press, 2006.

Henry, Christopher, and W. David Baird. *Ben Nighthorse Campbell: Cheyenne Chief and U.S. Senator.* New York: Chelsea House, 1994.

Hirschfelder, Arlene, and Martha Kreipe de Montano. *The Native American Almanac.* New York: Prentice-Hall, 1993.

Hornung, Rick. *One Nation under the Gun: Inside the Mohawk Civil War.* New York: Pantheon, 1991.

Hughes, J. Donald. *American Indian Ecology.* El Paso: University of Texas Press, 1983.

Igliori, Paola. *Stickman: John Trudell.* New York: Inanout Press, 1994.

"Inventing 'the Indian':" The West as America: Reinterpreting Images of the Frontier, 1820–1920. Washington, DC: Smithsonian Institution, 1991.

Iverson, Peter. *Carlos Montezuma and the Changing World of American Indians.* [1982]. Albuquerque: University of New Mexico Press, 2001.

Jackson, Helen Hunt. *A Century of Dishonor: A Sketch of the United States Government's Dealings with Some of the Indian Tribes.* [Boston: Roberts Bros., 1888]. St. Clair Shores, MI: Scholarly Press, 1972.

Jacobs, Connie A. *The Novels of Louise Erdrich.* New York: Peter Lang, 2001.

Janda, Sarah Eppler. *Beloved Women: The Political Lives of LaDonna Harris and Wilma Mankiller.* DeKalb: Northern Illinois University Press, 2008.

Jemison, Peter, and Anna M. Schein, eds. *The Treaty of Canandaigua 1794: 200 Years of Treaty Relations between the Iroquois Confederacy and the United States.* Santa Fe, NM: Clear Light, 2000.

Jennings, Nadine Nelson. "In the Spirit of the Kaswentha: Cultural Literacy in Akwesasne Mohawk Culture." PhD diss., Indiana University of Pennsylvania, 1998.

Jensen, Richard E., Eli Paul, and John E. Carter. *Eyewitness at Wounded Knee.* Lincoln: University of Nebraska Press, 1991.

Johansen, Bruce E. *Life and Death in Mohawk Country.* Golden, CO: North American Press, 1993.

Johansen, Bruce E. *Native Peoples of North America.* Westport, CT: Praeger, 2005.

Johansen, Bruce E. *Silenced! Academic Freedom, Scientific Inquiry, and the First Amendment under Siege in America.* Westport, CT: Praeger, 2007.

Johansen, Bruce E., and Roberto F. Maestas. *Wasi'chu: The Continuing Indian Wars.* New York: Monthly Review Press, 1979.

Josephy, Alvin, Jr. *The Patriot Chiefs.* New York: Viking, 1961.

Josephy, Jr., Alvin M., Joane Nagel, and Troy Johnson, eds. *Red Power: The American Indians' Fight for Freedom.* 2nd ed. Lincoln: University of Nebraska Press, 1999.

Kashatus, William C. *Money Pitcher: Chief Bender and the Tragedy of Indian Assimilation.* University Park: Pennsylvania State University Press, 2006.

Katanski, Amelia V. *Learning to Write "Indian": The Boarding School Experience and American Indian Literature.* Norman: University of Oklahoma Press, 2005.

Kawagley, Angayuqaq Oscar. *A Yupiaq Worldview: A Pathway to Ecology and Spirit.* 2nd ed. Long Grove, IL: Waveland Press, 1995.

LaDuke, Winona. *All Our Relations: Native Struggles for Land and Life.* Cambridge, MA: South End Press/Minneapolis, MN: Honor the Earth, 1999.

LaDuke, Winona. *Last Standing Woman (History and Heritage).* Stillwater, MN: Voyageur Press, 1999.

LaDuke, Winona. *The Winona LaDuke Reader: A Collection of Essential Writings.* Stillwater, MN: Voyageur Press, 2002.

LaDuke, Winona. *Recovering the Sacred: The Power of Naming and Claiming.* Cambridge, MA: South End Press, 2005.

Lupton, Mary Jane. *James Welch: A Critical Companion.* Westport, CT: Greenwood Press, 2004.

Lyons, Oren, John Mohawk, Vine Deloria, Jr., Laurence Hauptman, Howard Berman, Donald A. Grinde, Jr., Curtis Berkey, and Robert Venables. *Exiled in the Land of the Free: Democracy, Indian Nations, and the Constitution.* Santa Fe, NM: Clear Light, 1992.

MacDonald, Peter. *The Last Warrior: Peter MacDonald and the Navajo.* London: Orion Books, 1993.

Mails, Thomas E. *Fools Crow.* Lincoln: University of Nebraska Press, 1990.

Mankiller, Wilma. *Every Day Is a Good Day: Reflections of Contemporary Indigenous Women.* Golden, CO: Fulcrum, 2004.

Mankiller, Wilma, and Michael Wallis. *Mankiller: A Chief and Her People.* New York: St. Martin's Press, 1993.

Mann, Barbara Alice. *Iroquois Women: The Gantowisas.* New York: Peter Lang, 2000.

Mann, Barbara Alice. *George Washington's War on Native America.* Westport, CT: Praeger, 2005.

Mann, Barbara Alice. *Daughters of Mother Earth: The Wisdom of Native American Women.* Westport, CT: Praeger, 2006.

Massey, Rosemary, et al. *Footprints in Blood: Standing Bear's Struggle for Freedom and Human Dignity.* Omaha, NE: American Indian Center of Omaha, 1979.

McFarland, Ron. *Understanding James Welch.* Columbia: University of South Carolina Press, 2000.

McNickle, D'Arcy. *They Came Here First: The Epic of the American Indian.* Philadelphia, PA: J. B. Lippincott, 1949.

Means, Russell. *Where White Men Fear to Tread.* New York: St. Martin's Griffin, 1995.

Mohawk, John C. *Utopian Legacies: A History of Conquest and Oppression in the Western World*. Santa Fe, NM: Clear Light, 2000.

Monthan, Doris. *R. C. Gorman—A Retrospective*. Flagstaff, AZ: Northland Press, 1990.

Mooney, James. *The Ghost Dance Religion and the Sioux Outbreak of 1890*. Lincoln: University of Nebraska Press, 1991.

Moquin, Wayne. *Great Documents in American Indian History*. New York: Praeger, 1973.

Morgan, William. *Aboriginal Voices: Amerindian, Inuit, and Sami Theatre*. Baltimore, MD: Johns Hopkins University Press, 1992.

Moses, L. G., and Raymond Wilson, eds. *Indian Lives: Essays on Nineteenth- and Twentieth-century Native American Leaders*. Norman: University of Oklahoma Press, 1985.

Nabokov, Peter. *Native American Testimony*. New York: Viking, 1991.

Nottage, James H., ed. *Diversity and Dialogue*. Seattle: University of Washington Press, 2008.

Oakes, Elizabeth H. *American Writers*. New York: Facts On File, 2004.

Ortiz, Simon J. *Woven Stone*. Tucson: University of Arizona Press, 1992.

Ortiz, Simon J. *Speaking for the Generations*. Tucson: University of Arizona Press, 1998.

Parker, Arthur. *The Code of Handsome Lake, the Seneca Prophet*. New York State Museum Bulletin No. 163. Albany, 1913.

Parker, Arthur. *Parker on the Iroquois*. Edited by William N. Fenton. Syracuse, NY: Syracuse University Press, 1968.

Parks, Stephen. *R. C. Gorman, A Portrait*. Boston: Little, Brown, 1983.

Payne, William, and Jake Lyons, eds. *Folks Say of Will Rogers: A Memorial Anecdotage*. New York: G. P. Putnam's Sons, 1936.

Penn, William S., ed. *As We Are Now: Mixedblood Essays on Race and Identity*. Berkeley: University of California Press, 1997.

Philip, Kenneth R. *John Collier's Crusade for Indian Reform: 1920–1954*. Tucson: University of Arizona Press, 1977.

Reilly, Hugh. "Treatment of Native Americans by the Frontier Press: An Omaha, Nebraska Study, 1868–1891." Master's thesis, University of Nebraska at Omaha, 1997.

Reyes, Lawney L. *Bernie Whitebear: An Urban Indian's Quest for Justice*. Tucson: University of Arizona Press, 2006.

Richardson, Boyce. *Drumbeat: Anger and Renewal in Indian Country*. Toronto: Summerhill Press/Assembly of First Nations, 1990.

Ritter, Lawrence, and Donald Honig. *The 100 Greatest Baseball Players of All Time*. [1981]. New York: Random House, 1988.

Rogers, Betty. *Will Rogers*. Norman: University of Oklahoma Press, 1941.

Rogers, Will. *The Writings of Will Rogers*. 21 vols. Stillwater: Oklahoma State University Press, 1973–83.

Rosenstiel, Annette. *Red & White: Indian Views of the White Man, 1492–1992*. New York: Universe Books, 1993.

Russo, Kurt, ed. *Our People, Our Land: Reflections on Common Ground*. Bellingham, WA: Lummi Tribe and Kluckhohn Center, 1992.

Salisbury, Luke. *The Cleveland Indian: The Legend of King Saturday*. Mill Creek, WA: Black Heron Press, 1992.

Schmitt, Martin F., and Dee Brown. *Fighting Indians of the West*. New York: Charles Scribner's Sons, 1948.

Scott, Steven D. *The Gamefulness of American Postmodernism: John Barth and Louise Erdrich*. New York: Peter Lang, 2000.

Simpson, Jeffrey. *Faultlines: Struggling for a Canadian Vision.* Toronto: Harper and Collins, 1993.

Smith, Paul Chaat. *Everything You Know about Indians Is Wrong.* Minneapolis: University of Minnesota Press, 2009.

Smith, Paul Chaat, and Robert Allen Warrior. *Like a Hurricane: The Indian Movement from Alcatraz to Wounded Knee.* New York: New Press, 1996.

Spack, Ruth. *America's Second Tongue: American Indian Education and the Ownership of English, 1860–1900.* Lincoln: University of Nebraska Press, 2002.

Speroff, Leon. *Carlos Montezuma, M.D.: A Yavapai American Hero.* Portland, OR: Arnica, 2003.

Stone, Jana, ed. *Every Part of This Earth Is Sacred: Native American Voices in Praise of Nature.* San Francisco: HarperCollins, 1993.

Stookey, Lorena L. *Louise Erdrich. A Critical Companion.* Westport, CT: Greenwood Press, 1999.

Studie, Wesley. *The Adventures of Billy Bean.* Cherokee Bilingual/Cross Cultural Education Center, 1982.

Studie, Wesley. *More Adventures of Billy Bean (also known as The Further Adventures of Billy Bean).* Cherokee Bilingual/Cross Cultural Education Center, 1983.

Swift, Tom. *Chief Bender's Burden: The Silent Struggle of a Baseball Star.* Lincoln: University of Nebraska Press, 2008.

Tebbel, John W. *The Compact History of the Indian Wars.* New York: Hawthorn Books, 1966.

Tibbles, Thomas Henry. *The Ponca Chiefs: An Account of the Trial of Standing Bear.* [1880]. Lincoln: University of Nebraska Press, 1972.

Tohe, Laura. *No Parole Today: Poetry and Stories.* Albuquerque, NM: West End Press, 1999.

Tohe, Laura. *Tséyi': Deep in the Rock, Reflections on Canyon de Chelly,* with Stephen E. Strom (photographer). Tucson: University of Arizona Press, 2005.

Tong, Benson. *Susan La Flesche Picotte, M.D.: Omaha Indian Leader and Reformer.* Norman: University of Oklahoma Press, 1999.

Trafzer, Clifford E., ed. *Blue Dawn, Red Earth: New Native American Storytellers.* New York: Anchor Books, 1996.

Trahant, Mark N. *Pictures of Our Nobler Selves: A History of Native American Contributions to News Media.* Nashville, TN: Freedom Forum, 1995.

Trudell, John. *This Ain't El Salvador.* West Chester, PA: Learning Alliance, 1996.

Trudell, John. *Lines from a Mined Mind: The Words of John Trudell.* Golden, CO: Fulcrum, 2008.

Unrau, William E. *Mixed Bloods and Tribal Dissolution: Charles Curtis and the Quest for Indian Identity.* Lawrence: University Press of Kansas, 1989.

Wagner, Sally Roesch. *The Untold Story of the Iroquois Influence on Early Feminists.* Aberdeen, SD: Sky Carrier Press, 1996.

Waters, Frank. *Brave Are My People.* Santa Fe, NM: Clear Light, 1992.

Weaver, J., C. S. Womack, R. Warrior, O. J. Simon, and L. Brooks. *American Indian Literary Nationalism.* Albuquerque: University of New Mexico Press, 2006.

Weeks, Philip. *Farewell, My Nation: The American Indian and the United States, 1820–1890.* Arlington Heights, IL: Harlan Davidson, 1990.

Wertheim, Arthur, ed. *Will Rogers at the Ziegfeld Follies.* Norman: University of Oklahoma Press, 1992.

Wheeler, Robert W. *Jim Thorpe: The World's Greatest Athlete.* Norman: University of Oklahoma Press, 1981.

Wiget, Andrew, ed. *Handbook of Native American Literature*. New York: Garland, 1996.

Wilkerson, J. L. *A Doctor to Her People: Dr. Susan LaFlesche Picotte*. Kansas City, MO: Acorn Books, 1999.

Wilkinson, Charles F. *American Indians, Time, and the Law: Native Societies in a Modern Constitutional Democracy*. New Haven, CT: Yale University Press, 1987.

Wilkinson, Charles F. *Blood Struggle: The Rise of Modern Indian Nations*. New York: W. W. Norton, 2005.

Wilkinson, Charles F., and Hank Adams. *Messages from Frank's Landing: A Story of Salmon, Treaties, and the Indian Way*. Seattle: University of Washington Press, 2000.

Wilson, Dorothy Clarke. *Bright Eyes: The Story of Suzette LaFlesche*. New York: McGraw-Hill, 1974.

Wilson, Edmund. *Apologies to the Iroquois*. New York: Farrar, Straus & Cudahy, 1960.

Witt, Shirley Hill, and Stan Steiner, eds. *The Way: An Anthology of American Indian Literature*. New York: Vintage, 1972.

Womack, C. S. *Red on Red: Native American Literary Separatism*. Minneapolis: University of Minnesota Press, 1999.

Womack, C. S. *Drowning in Fire*. Tucson: University of Arizona Press, 2001.

Yagoda, Ben. *Will Rogers: A Biography*. New York: Alfred A. Knopf, 1993.

About the Author
and Contributors

Bruce E. Johansen is Professor of Communication and Native American Studies at the University of Nebraska at Omaha. He is a prolific author on Native American and environmental topics. He co-edited the *Encyclopedia of American Indian History* (ABC-CLIO, 2007) and authored *Shapers of the Great Debate on Native Americans—Land, Spirit, and Power* (2000), *Indigenous Peoples and Environmental Issues: An Encyclopedia* (Greenwood, 2003), *The Native Peoples of North America* (Praeger, 2005), and the *Praeger Handbook of Contemporary Native American Issues* (2007), among other titles.

Jason R. Gallagher is a graduate student in English at the University of Nebraska at Omaha.

Jody Lynn Keisner is a graduate student in English at the University of Nebraska at Omaha.

Barbara Alice Mann is Instructor of English, University of Toledo, Ohio.

Barbara K. Robins is Associate Professor of English, University of Nebraska at Omaha.

Natalie Russell is a graduate student in English at the University of Nebraska at Omaha.

Vera Martina Saarentaus is a graduate student in English at the University of Nebraska at Omaha.

Milica Vukovljak is a graduate student in English at the University of Nebraska at Omaha.

Sally Roesch Wagner is director of the Matilda Joslyn Gage Foundation.

Index